Conflict and Cooperation

To my muse, Kay

Conflict and Cooperation

Institutional and Behavioral Economics

A. Allan Schmid

Blackwell Publishing

350 Main Street, Malden, MA 02148-5020, USA
108 Cowley Road, Oxford OX4 1JF, UK
550 Swanston Street, Carlton, Victoria 3053, Australia

First published 2004 by Blackwell Publishing Ltd

Library of Congress Cataloging-in-Publication Data

Schmid, A. Allan (Alfred Allan), 1935–
    Conflict and cooperation : institutional and behavioral economics /
A. Allan Schmid.
        p.   cm.
Includes bibliographical references and index.
    ISBN 1-4051-1355-3 (hardcover : alk. paper) – ISBN 1-4051-1356-1
(pbk. : alk. paper)
1. Institutional economics.   2. Economics–Psychological aspects.   3. Social
conflict.   4. Cooperation.   5. Economics–Moral and ethical aspects.   I. Title:
Institutional and behavioral economics.   II. Title: Behavioral economics.
III. Title.

    HB99.5.S36 2004
    330–dc22

                                                                2003018398

A catalogue record for this title is available from the British Library.

Set in 10/12½ Galliard
by Graphicraft Limited, Hong Kong
Printed and bound in the United Kingdom
by MPG Books, Bodmin, Cornwall

For further information on
Blackwell Publishing, visit our website:
http://www.blackwellpublishing.com

Contents

Foreword
by Warren J. Samuels

The mainstream of neoclassical economics has been successful for a number of reasons. One reason is that it has strenuously pursued a division of labor, assigning itself two courses of action. It has, first, projected a pure a-institutional abstract conceptual model of the economy. It has, second, followed a research protocol that seeks unique determinate optimal equilibrium solutions to problems. In pursuit of both it has assumed one or another version of rational behavior and of competition.

Such a program has great strengths but also serious limitations. For one thing, it does not apply directly to the real world of actual economies. The pure a-institutional abstract conceptual model of the economy helps tell us much about the operation of the pure abstract price mechanism. But actual markets are a function of the institutions that form and operate through them; the price mechanism operates only within and through these institutionalized markets. The research protocol seeking unique determinate optimal equilibrium solutions can only be successful by eliminating all variables and considerations that interfere with reaching its goal, variables and considerations that operate in actual economies. In particular, the common assumptions of rational behavior and competition tend in practice to exclude consideration of factors and forces that not only operate in but tend to dominate actual economies.

The two domains, therefore, that neoclassical economists, in pursuit of their own slices of the division of labor, tend to exclude are institutions and behavior. But this is not strictly true, depending upon one's definition of who is and who is not a neoclassical economist.

Consider, for example, the two-pronged work of Ronald Coase. In his theory of the firm, the scope and structure of markets are a function of decisions by firms as to their own domain. Markets are not given; they are socially constructed and have allocative consequences. In his theory of social cost, different structures of legal rights engender, among other things, different structures of transaction costs. Rights assignments, and their respective markets, are not allocatively neutral; they are socially constructed and have allocative consequences. As Coase himself puts the patter, in two words, institutions matter. In actual economies, institutions, not pure markets, govern the allocation of resources. Oddly enough, that has been a major theme of the institutional economics of Thorstein Veblen, John R. Commons, and Clarence E. Ayres. As for Coase, his work is as revolutionary in prospect, if not in intent, as that of any other twentieth-century economist. It introduces degrees of institutional importance and of problematicity quite at odds with conventional neoclassicism. However, it is not only possible but also true both that some economists consider his work eminently neoclassical in spirit and that some other economists consider his work as at least a significant departure from neoclassicism. No doubt that Coase, being human, seeks both the praise of the hegemonic school of economics but also the identity of a major differentiated product.

Coase is not alone in this gray area delimiting who is and who is not a neoclassical economist, of what is and what is not neoclassicism. He is joined, in his work on institutions, by economists such as Douglass North and Olliver Williamson. And their ambiguous position is replicated by a host of economists trying to make sense of the actual behavioral psychology of actual economic actors in actual economies, including such authors as Jon Elster, Robert H. Frank, D. Kahneman, Tibor Scitovsky, Amartya Sen, Vernon Smith, Richard Thaler, and A. Tversky. In each of these cases, some of their work is clearly a departure from the core belief system of neoclassicism and some is not; altogether it is unclear whether and, if so, in what ways neoclassicism is itself changing.

Allan Schmid, the author of this book, is self-consciously an institutional economist. He is that type of institutionalist who does not envision a necessary, insurmountable divide between being an institutionalist and being a neoclassicist, or between doing institutionalist and doing neoclassical economics. Thus, he welcomed the awarding of the Nobel Prize in Economic Science in 2001 to George A. Akerlof, A. Michael Spence, and Joseph E. Stiglitz for their work on asymmetric information. Schmid considers their work to be important contributions to our knowledge of the operation and formation of institutions and thereby also to our understanding of economic behavior.

The division of labor pursued, therefore, in this book is the analysis of those two domains more or less officially left by neoclassicism to others, including some putative neoclassicists: institutions and behavior. Schmid believes both that these two domains are important parts of economics and that sufficient work – by neoclassicists, institutionalists, and others – has been done to warrant his attempt at systematization. It may well be the case that, just as the time was once or twice ripe for the systematizing stabilization of price theory, the time is now ripe for a similar development of our knowledge of institutions and behavior. Schmid would insist, however, that stabilization need not and indeed should not mean reification and preclusion of revision and extension.

Schmid's approach to his twin subject matter is along the following lines.

He believes it important to distinguish between questions of impact and change: what is the impact of institutions and behavior, and how is it manifested; and what generates change of institutions and behavior, and how? In other words, institutions and behavior are both independent and dependent variables – or, as he puts it, from individual experience to institutions and back again. Throughout this book Schmid attempts to present what we know about the impacts and change of institutions and behavior and their interaction.

He believes that the psychology of economic behavior has been shown to consist of a number of topics and to involve, even at this early stage, of a number of reasonably concrete findings.

He believes that there is no given, transcendent economic system with respect to which particular institutions are only so many epiphenomena. Actual economic systems and institutions are what they are because of their particular social construction. For example, it is one thing, and in many respects not very much, to speak of the institution of private property; it is another thing, and in many respects very important, to speak of the particular elements of the institution of private property; and it is still another thing, and it too in many respects very important, to speak of changing the particular elements of the institution of private property, i.e., the change of the law of property.

He believes that if one is to understand the roles of institutions and the nature of economic behavior, one has to appreciate, indeed know well, the sources of human interdependence. To posit the autonomous individual is to foreclose consideration of the system and structure of human interdependence with respect to which institutions and behavior exist and operate.

Schmid is aware that our knowledge of economic institutions and behavior is a function of the research methods – the analytical tools and operations – used by the economic analyst. The picture of institutions and behavior that emerges is a function both of people's actual behavior and their institutions and of the techniques of analysis used in studying them.

Schmid considers several subsidiary substantive domains as particularly important for the study of behavior and institutions. These include, in addition to markets in general, money and banking, capitalism per se, technology, the institutions of the labor market, and government.

This book is, accordingly, not for those who want simple answers to simplistic questions, who are comfortable only with determinacy and closure, and who see economics as properly driven by some ideology. This book will be welcomed by all those who are comfortable with the openness and radical indeterminacy of actual economies, and who seek to understand the manifold complexity of and interactions between behavior and institutions. No one book can cover everything imaginably pertinent to its author's chosen topic. Schmid's book, nonetheless, identifies and explores what is known about many aspects of his chosen topic.

Preface

I don't have a slogan or neat metaphor to describe the economy of today and predict the one of tomorrow or offer a new strategic variable to insure economic development. I am moved to object to many of the concepts that we use as lenses to see the world. Sure I am for efficiency, but whose? For freedom, but whose? For cost minimization, but whose?

I have chosen the subtitle "Institutional and Behavioral Economics," rather than some piece of it such as transaction cost economics, property rights economics, public choice economics, law and economics, socio-economics, etc. because I think we can use a bit of integration and a little less product differentiation. The performance of an economy is the result of many variables that are sometimes substitutes, but often complements. My students complain because we identify so many different causes of human interdependence and therefore many different formal and informal institutions that sort it out. I do want to provide in one place the best of institutional economics that I believe is the cutting edge of economics as suggested by those institutionally oriented economists who have won the Nobel Prize – Akerlof, Allais, Arrow, Buchanan, Coase, Hayek, Kahneman, Kuznets, Myrdal, North, Sen, Simon, Stiglitz, and others – in such a way that their cumulative contributions to an institutional and behavioral economic theory can be better understood.

My students probably would say my favorite question is "Where's the blood?" Who gains and who loses with alternative institutions? I understand the angst that drives scholars and citizens to demand aggregate welfare measures by which to scientifically judge the desirability of alternative institutions. But, I am not moved to supply their psychic balm. I am moved to try to improve their analytic ability to see the institutions that affect who gets what and what gets defined as progress. That is hard work, which defies neat metaphors and slogans.

A word about what this book is not. It is not a critique of the market (or any particular policy); rather it notes that there are many alternative market rules. It is not an argument for planning; rather it argues that any contemporary economy is planned in the sense that market rules (property rights) are necessarily chosen by governments and any private governance takes place within these rules. It is not an argument that distribution is more important than efficiency; rather efficiency is not a single thing and the choice is what to be efficient about. It is not obsessed with power issues; rather it argues that power is inevitable, ordinary, and ubiquitous. It is not an argument for a particular moral position, though it insists that moral choices are necessarily involved when policies are chosen in an interdependent world of people with different preferences. While I believe that the quality of public debate would be improved by these distinctions, this is not the main point of the book. Rather it is to provide a set of tools (concepts, variables, relationships) that will help improve our ability to better predict the substantive consequences of alternative institutions – in short a theory to guide empirical inquiry.

Many, many thanks to my long-time friends and colleagues Warren Samuels and James Shaffer for their intellectual stimulation. Thanks to Laura McCann who gave me painstaking feedback on the entire manuscript. And thanks to Larry Busch, Dan Bromley, Liu Can, Lynne Dallas, Gianluigi Galeotti, Ian Hodge, James Oehmke, Lindon Robison, and Randall Wray for critical review of portions of the book. Thanks to the librarians of my University, and the London School of Economics and the University of Cambridge where I spent a sabbatical leave in 1998. And finally, thanks to the students in my seminar in Institutional and Behavioral Economics at Michigan State University over the years for aiding in the evolution of these ideas. They continue to supply me with applications and inspiration.

I want to thank my editor, Seth Ditchik, and my desk editor, Paul Stringer, for their careful and creative contributions.

A.A.S.
East Lansing

Chapter 1
Introduction

1.1 Institutional Analysis

Institutions are human relationships that structure opportunities via constraints and enablement. A constraint on one person is opportunity for another. Institutions enable individuals to do what they cannot do alone. They structure incentives used in calculating individual advantage. They also affect beliefs and preferences and provide cues to uncalculated action. They provide order and predictability to human interaction. The mental images created by law and custom coordinate human action to one purpose or another and determine whose interests count and the very meaning of economic and social development. This book is written to better understand the connection between alternative institutions and the performance of the economy. Such understanding will require empirical investigation into learning, bounded rationality, and evolution rather than assumptions of stable preferences, rationality, and equilibrium.

To design institutions that can achieve a particular economic performance, it is useful to understand the sources of human interdependence. Different kinds of goods and services create different kinds of interdependencies, and thus it takes different institutions to control and direct them. Institutions define the opportunity sets of interdependent transacting parties. When one party's choices affect another party, Alpha's opportunity is Beta's constraint and vice versa. There are opportunities for cooperation and conflict.

Some economic institutions are formal such as laws, administrative regulations, and court decisions, while others are informal such as ideology, custom, and standard operating procedures. Some are public and some private. A corporation makes rules for its employees and structures itself *vis-à-vis* other corporations. Again, some of this is formal and some informal, often referred to as business culture.

Analysts are called upon to determine which current institutions contribute to current performance that someone regards as a problem, and to suggest institutional changes to policy-makers and citizens that can achieve a particular performance. Analysts may also be asked to suggest political institutions within which economic institutions change. But the formal constitutional rules for making economic rules are only part of the picture. Just as there are ideologies and customs that complement formal economic institutions, there are informal rules that complement the formal rules for making rules. The evolution of institutions then is a function of both formal and informal processes.

The scope of this book is immodest. It would include conceptualization of the substantive impact of alternative economic institutions, including those that are formal and informal as well as those made by public and private bodies. In addition, it would conceptualize the impact of alternative rules for making rules, both formal constitutions and informal custom. The structured process of making rules is integral to understanding of institutional change over time. There is no intent, however, to provide a general theory containing features assumed to be common to all economies over time and space. The theory provides no deterministic conclusions deduced from assumptions. Rather it guides the collection of observations in their historical and spatial context.

To support this analysis, it will be necessary to build a solid foundation in cognitive science. The study of institutions is often framed in terms of the structure of incentives. But the human response to the external structure of incentives (payoffs) is itself structured by the learned internal preferences and patterns of cognition. Institutions shape preferences as well as the external payoffs to different choices.

Theory is needed to better learn from our experiences the connection between alternative institutions and performance. The institutional and behavioral theory of this book is open to changing preferences, non-rational and non-instrumental choice, and evolution.[1] This book intends to form a new synthesis and assembly of ideas from many writers who do not necessarily consider themselves institutionalists. It is time for institutional economics to emerge from its critical role. The problem of institutional economics is not that it has no theory, but that it has too many theories that are not well integrated.

One purpose of institutional analysis is to inform institutional choice, though all institutions are not the product of explicit choice. People are continuously choosing among institutional alternatives at several levels. One choice is at the constitutional and political level. A second is at the level of everyday working rules of individuals and organizations. A third is within organizations. The actors need information on the consequences (impact) of these alternatives so they can chose the ones that serve their purposes. The objective of institutional theory is to make these choices less blind. As Buchanan (1996: 35) puts it, "the political economist is allowed to treat the set of structural parameters (the laws or constitution) as variables and to apply the principles of the science in generating predictions about the working properties of alternative sets of constraints." This requires an understanding of how our political economy works and the nexus of constraint and enablement.

The institutional economics of this book starts with the observation that people are interdependent. Their welfare is affected by the acts of others. They have different interests and experience, and thus the possibility of conflict. Coordination of activity makes a difference in economic output and thus the interest in co-operation. Institutions provide order and predictability to human transactions. The observation of the context of conflict suggests that measures of performance outcomes must be disaggregated and substantive, not presumptively aggregated. Interdependence is related to the inherent characteristics of goods, such as incompatible use, degree of exclusion cost, cost of another user, economies of scale, transaction costs, etc.

We can ask about the impact of alternative institutions as well as the process of change and evolution. The consequences of today's institutions are part of the process of evolving tomorrow's. Our purpose is always to inform choice of the various participants recognizing that not all can and want to use the knowledge. The purpose is not to predict the future; not what will happen next; not whether rule A or B will be chosen next year, but rather if rule A were chosen, will it serve group X's interests? Prediction is limited. Still, analysis can be useful if it tells people which rights facilitate their interests even if it can't predict the exact point at which their interests will be achieved as events evolve.

Consider the kinds of questions at the *constitutional level*. What consequences ensue and thus whose interests are served with parliamentary vs. non-parliamentary forms of government? An elected judge vs. appointed? Unanimity rules vs. majority rule? Subject matter vs. functional legislative committees? Federal vs. unitary systems? Unlimited campaign contributions vs. limited? Etc. Who gets what everyday-level institution from the legislature or court under these alternatives? If constitutional rule A were chosen, will it serve group X's interests via favorable everyday rules emerging from power play among contending interests? Questions such as whether the German economic institutions will become more like those of the US are interesting, but not the ones posed here. The question is rather how the rules for changing rules affect how everyday rules might be changed. Bromley (1989: 49) refers to everyday rules as governing "commodity transactions." Informal habits and ideology are expected to play a role in constitutional change as well as feedback from the performance of existing everyday-level institutions. These questions are addressed in chapter 12, "Political Institutions."

Consider the kinds of questions at the *everyday level* as opportunities are apportioned to individuals and groups by alternative formal property rights in the context of given habits/customs and given technology. For example, what consequences and thus whose interests count with land use zoning vs. tort liability? Publicly owned electric utilities vs. private? Marginal cost pricing vs. average cost pricing rules? Prohibition vs. right of labor to bargain collectively? Public finance of schools vs. private for fee education? Public vs. private charity? Etc. Who gets what goods and services under these alternatives? These questions are explored in chapter 6, "Sources of Human Interdependence" and chapter 8, "Markets."

Formal institutions cannot be chosen with intelligence unless it is understood how everyday rule A vs. B, (1) interacts with the existing informal habits and (2) changes these habits over time and vice versa. Prevailing customs are not explicitly chosen, but nevertheless change and thus modify, amplify, and limit chosen formal institutions; thus the interest in informal institutional change. Informal customary habits may wholly control an area of interdependence. For example, non-governmental informal rights control the use of some common pool resources such as fisheries (Ostrom 1990: ch. 3).

Consider the kinds of questions at the *organizational level* as the participants choose their internal rules for relating to each other within the organization and how they wish to relate to other organizations. What is the consequence of continuously bargained contracts vs. agreements to participate in hierarchical administrative frameworks? Multi-division firms vs. functional divisions? Putting out contracts vs. internal production? Individual vs. team production? How are the above choices conditioned by the system of everyday property rights noted above: for example, how do rules of corporate liability shape the internal organization of firms? These issues are discussed in chapter 8, "Markets."

Why do institutional *change analysis*? Not to do grand predictions of historical inevitability *à la* Marx. Not to find out what is natural and therefore better left alone. One reason is to better inform the choice of constitutional alternatives and to better inform any particular group on how to better use existing political institutions to their advantage. We want to learn how past formal and informal changes shape the field of choice today. On the cognitive level we have the art of the "spin doctors" who try to influence widely held public images of particular candidates and policies. Part of this can be described as trying to affect preferences. Not all institutional change is by explicit choice, but there is an interaction between habit and choice of formal institutions. The choice of formal institutions affects the evolution of habits and informal institutions, and vice versa. Even if the learning and modification of informal institutions are unconscious, knowledge of and experience with institutions is an input to the process.

Why do institutional *impact analysis*? Not to label one institution or property right as producing more total welfare than another. Rather it is to provide information to citizens so that they will know which institutions serve their particular interests; in other words, to better inform their support of alternative formal institutions and to work out their accommodation with others with different interests (Bromley 1997).

1.2 Outline of This Work

The components of an institutional and behavioral economics theory will be outlined in the next chapter. Chapters 3 and 4 lay a foundation for the analysis rooted in cognitive science. Bounded rationality and the limited information capacity of the human brain are fundamental. Chapter 5 distinguishes institutions and organizations and conceptualizes the human relationships guiding the physical system of production. It includes ways to conceive of the role of the state as well as performance criteria for judging alternative institutions. An argument is made for the necessity for moral judgment as to whose interests are to count. The core of the analytic system is the situation, structure and performance framework that is developed in chapter 6. Various inherent features of goods provide the situation of interdependence that institutions sort out and give direction.

Since this work is intended to provide a basis for empirical observation of the substantive performance of alternative institutions, chapter 7 is devoted to the strengths and weaknesses of various methods for establishing the connection. Methods include experiments, case studies, econometrics, and simulation. The balance of the book illustrates the application of the theory and methods with many references to the empirical literature. Chapter 8 focuses on markets, and makes the point that there are many alternative market rules. Macroeconomic institutions are featured in chapter 9. The rules contained in the banking and credit system are property rights as much as any rule of liability or corporate law. Technology has always been a topic of special interest to institutional economists. Chapter 10 notes that technological change both drives institutional change and is itself the product of institutions.

Labor institutions are the special interest of chapter 11 because labor is not an ordinary commodity. Humans are both a means of production and a product of the economy. It is an input with a head such that its treatment affects its marginal product. Chapter 12 on political institutions examines the impact of the rules for making the everyday rules of the economy. There are as many different democratic rules as there are different market rules. Details matter again. Chapter 13 applies the theory to understand institutional change and evolution. Finally, the last chapter reviews in schematic form the common elements of theory that organize observations on both formal and informal institutions and both impact and change analysis.

NOTE

1. Cf. Eggertsson (1990: 10) who places stable preferences, rational choice, and equilibria into axiomatic assumptions.

Chapter 2
Institutional and Behavioral Economics Theory

Institutional economics is not merely defined by its subject matter: institutions are a concern of all economic policy analysis. Rather it is a matter of choice of variables, hypothesized relationships, and questions asked about these institutions. Is there a common theoretical framework whose key variables and relationships help illuminate the above questions and inform choice? The key starting place is to find a suitable unit of observation.

2.1 Transactions as the Unit of Observation

What shall be the most basic unit of observation for an institutional and behavioral economics that is applicable at the constitutional, everyday, and within-firm levels and include both formal and informal relationships? Shall it be the individual, a group, a network, an institution, or a transaction process between individuals? To answer the question it is important to understand institutions connecting individuals and other elements.

Institutions are sets (networks) of ordered relationships (connections) among people that define their rights, their exposure to the rights of others, their privileges, and their responsibilities. A set at one level is embedded in a set at a higher level to make up a complex system. To say that one system is embedded in another is not to say that higher levels determine lower levels. Different levels are interdependent and mutually defined. This is a source of emergence where the whole can be greater than the sum of the parts. For example, the relationships among members of a firm are embedded in relationships among firms in an industry that in turn make up the economy. The rules made by the firm are conditioned by everyday general rules, which in turn are influenced by the political rules for making everyday rules. All co-evolve.

Institutions structure the flow of feedback (reinforcers) from others to the actor. While these relationships are relatively enduring and widely shared, they evolve. They are not given by nature, such as the law of gravity. "These dimensions do not exist *a priori*, but are created in the processes of economic coordination. By looking forward into the future, economic agents thereby create that future" (Potts 2000).

Social systems are thus open systems in which human perception and imagination play an important role.

Commons said, "An institution is collective action in control, liberation, and expansion of individual action" (Commons 1950: 21). The definition of Veblen at first appears different: "a way of thought or action of some prevalence and permanence, which is embedded in the habits of a group or the customs of a people" (Veblen 1919: 239). "Institutions play an essential role in providing a cognitive framework for interpreting sense data . . ." (Hodgson 1998: 171). A formal property right that says person A may farm a piece of land and B must keep off is an ordered relationship among people that defines opportunities and exposures. Is it also a habit? It might be. A full understanding of institutions must include informal, tacit, and internalized rights as well as those formal relationships legislated and sanctioned by the state. North (1994) includes both informal and formal institutions in his definition: "the formal rules (constitutions, statute and common law, regulations, etc.), the informal constraints (norms of behavior, conventions, and internally imposed rules of conduct), and the enforcement characteristics of each." Institutions are more than the rules of the game providing constraints. They are also enablement to do what the individual cannot do alone. They also affect beliefs and preferences, and provide cues to uncalculated action.

The transaction as the unit of observation has deep implications as it departs from the usual substantialist view. "The very terms or units involved in a transaction derive their meaning, significance, and identity from the (changing) functional roles they play within that transaction" (Emirbayer 1997: 287). Things or elements "are not assumed as independent existences present anterior to any relation, but . . . gain their whole being . . . first in and with the relations which are predicated on them" (Cassirer 1953: 36). A property right is not something a person has independent of the relationship of that person to others.

Language is the carrier of formal rights. Sharing a language facilitates the understanding of relative opportunities. The meaning we attach to words is vital. Words do not speak for themselves, so they get translated into action via cognition. The behavior of an owner and non-owner can't be understood fully from a written statement of a property right. Not all opportunities are seized. And, not all nominal opportunities are backed up by the state and neighbors. We need to know what self-limits people place on themselves and this is a matter of cognition and meaning. If the interdependent parties have not learned a whole set of ideas which go along with the notion of individual private property rights, the job of the state or neighbors in insuring the opportunity of an owner will be very much greater, if not impossible.

Informal rights include such things as habits of tipping, honoring of queues, access by seniority, and basic ideas of honesty and fair dealing. Analysts infer their presence by observing widespread regularities in behavior. A cognitive process connects the stimulus of the environment to action. Elements are necessarily selectively connected, rather than everything being connected to everything. Some widely shared habits get codified into formal law and some are rejected and reversed by formal law. Some are reproduced and live on and some change or die in an evolutionary process.

Custom may be distinguished from routines and conventions such as driving on the right that are learned to have instrumental advantage. Schlicht (1998: 2) emphasizes "the motivational force that arises from the individual's striving for coherence and justification. Custom is portrayed as emerging from the individual's desire to align behavior, conviction, and emotion tightly with one another. Individuals have a preference for patterned behaviour, for acting according to their convictions, and for forming their convictions in accordance with what they are experiencing." Violation of someone's customary property right brings forth an emotional response not forthcoming from a violation of a mere routine. Individuals stick to certain customs even if costly because of their emotional commitment and self-identity.

There is a large domain of habit and routine that has little to do with rights sorting our competing interests. I am in the habit of brushing my teeth in the morning or having coffee for breakfast. That affects the economic interests of toothpaste manufacturers and coffee growers, but is not what most would regard as a matter of contention. On the other hand, some people are in the habit of seeing private debt as equivalent to public debt. They thus want a balanced budget amendment. This meaning and cognitive framework certainly do affect economic interests. It favors those who wish to minimize government spending. Similarly, if we have learned that holders of great wealth deserve and have earned it, their riches are more secure than if the vast poor regard it as unearned. So these habits of thought certainly are a part of the real opportunity set structure. They also lie behind which available opportunity is actually pursued.

2.1.1 Individuals and institutions

How shall we conceptualize the relationship of individuals to institutions? The question might be usefully rephrased as how to conceptualize the relationship of one individual to other individuals. Individuals shape institutions and institutions shape individuals (Hodgson 1999b). Neither the individual nor institutions have ontological superiority. They are separable, but interdependent and evolving. The individual grows up in a social setting and is continuously interacting with others. Parts of the body such as the liver, lungs, and heart are in some sense separate entities, but they cannot be fully understood apart from the total system of the body of which they are a part. One can say that only individuals make decisions, but those decisions are part of a system of decisions which constitute the environment of any individual. We can say that institutions reinforce individual behavior if we mean that the behavior of individuals A and B reinforce the behavior of individual C. When C acts, there is feedback from the environment including the acts of A and B. This can reinforce C such that there is a higher probability that C will repeat the action in a similar circumstance. There is nothing reified in the term institutions if we mean it to be the aggregate of individuals A and B who act in a certain way with respect to individual C in a certain situation. Institutions, while contained in the minds of individuals, are real environmental entities that exist outside of any one mind. Put in cognitive terms, the meaning that C attaches to an event is influenced by the meaning that A and B attach and their behavior. The behavior of others is a feedback to a person's behavior and reinforces that behavior or extinguishes it. An institution is not something apart from individuals, but rather the system of individuals. This is important to avoid the conception of individual vs. government when the issue is really individual A vs. individual B. The components of a system of interactions may be referred to as transactions that become the units of observation for an institutional economics. It may involve a series of transactions over time and at different levels.

Individual → other individuals → individual →

The acts of individual A are part of the environment of others, and the acts of others are part of the environment of individual A.

Individual → institutions → individual →

Individuals create institutions, and these institutions shape individual action. And, then action may again modify either formal or informal institutions.

These circular chains are equivalent if by institutions we mean the structured, ordered, mutually expected behaviors of interacting individuals. The language of the former appears less reified and less threatening to those who learned the conception of methodological individualism. It keeps the idea of individual choices while making them part of a social system. The individuals are who they are because of their interactions, and their opportunities are shaped by what others do.

The structured behaviors of self and others have a certain stability because they require new thresholds of shared, collective behavior before the system's functioning changes. An institution contains an idea of critical mass. So even if one person wakes up in the morning with a different idea for behavior, unless a certain threshold of others join in that conception, the individual has little opportunity to accomplish a different result. Still, systemic change does occur. An important element in stability is the fact that much learning is unconscious. It is impossible to organize people to make a change in behavior when that behavior seems a part of the natural order and is not seen as a choice.

If you lived at a time when the divine right of kings was prevalent, few thought of any other alternative. Still, ideas evolve in the human imagination and creativity, and the American, French, and Russian revolutions did occur. And the fact that they did raised a consciousness in other countries as to what was a variable and subject to conscious choice. The kings had their laws and police, but the relative opportunities created thereby were embedded in habits of thought about what was seen as natural, proper, and legitimate. To understand the behaviors of lords and villeins, one needs to understand the mutual expectations behind their transactions – the expectations of lords, sheriffs, clergy, and neighbors.

Rights (relative opportunities) are not some objects out there. They are in our heads as perceptions of what we may or must do in certain situations and what we can expect others to do. They are subjective, but condition behavior that is part of a shared system of behaviors, and thus there is a real environment that feeds back to these cognitions.

Let's try this conception out on a major evolution of rights, namely that from tangible to intangible property. This has been documented by Commons (1924). In Roman law, rights in tangible property were well understood. It was clear that to own land was to be free of physical trespass. If you could keep the neighbor's cows from eating your corn, its value was preserved. But as self-subsistence and payment of taxes to Caesar's agents evolved to market exchange, use value was supplemented by exchange value. And exchange value could be affected by more than physical trespass. Still, legal reasoning was dominated by concepts of physical, tangible property. Commons identified a major turning point in legal thinking in the Louisiana slaughterhouse case (16 Wall. 36, 1872). The court realized that a monopoly of slaughterhouses could affect the value of a farmer's livestock and a butcher's assets as much as rustlers and other physical thieves. This case is explored in detail in chapter 13 on institutional change.

Commons described this evolution in the character of transactions in terms of observable rights, exposures, freedoms, and obligations. Veblen might have described it in terms of habits and routines. These habits of thought can be inferred, but not always directly observable. We can't know fully what was in the minds of the litigants or the judge. The result, however, was a change in the meaning of property to more than physical protection. Performance was only partly predictable. This interactive process of informal and formal change was surely the result of many changes in the culture and environment other than livestock technology. While the Supreme Court decision was a conscious collective choice, it was preceded by lots of informal, learned, internalized changes in cognition. For some, the regulation is now not something explicit but part of the natural order of "just the way things are." Businesses and consumers have now developed routinized habits without calculating whether they are following the law or not. The formal law feeds back on the informal ways of thinking.

A full understanding of institutional change must account for rather global changes in cognition and ideas that are broader than any specific industry such as meat noted above. But at the same time it must account for the conflicting interests and their ability to use government. Who has access to the Supreme Court and the legislature? How do constitutional and other rules for making rules affect the outcomes of these interest group struggles? A theory of institutional change without an analysis of politics is as incomplete as it would be if it ignored the evolution of ideology and images.

The transaction is a useful basic unit of observation. The term captures the idea of interaction for whatever result whether as part of the socialization process or day-to-day commerce, or constitution building. Today's transactions are structured by past and expected interactions. The transaction can be used to conceptualize the formation of habits and ideologies, explicit collective actions such as law making, and the day-to-day commerce under given rules. Whether people are taking advantage of rightful opportunities, making gifts, exchanges, tributes, bribes, collecting rents, paying taxes, voting, or making laws, reinforcing habits and changing the mind-set and cognition of their fellows, they are involved in a complex system of transactions. An institutional analysis requires a basic unit adaptable to all of these kinds of transactions.

Let's review what has already been said explicitly in these terms. Consider first matters of institutional/structural change. At one level, firms and consumers are making choices within their opportunity sets. Transacting, interacting parties are affecting each other's substantive world-view. This is involved in seeing individuals as both affected by physical trespass and by market power. At another level, there is a transaction involved in bringing suit in the Supreme Court with its rules of evidence, procedure, jurisdiction, etc. In the slaughterhouse case, the court was approving a legislative decision which was in turn a product of its rules of voting, boundaries, campaign contributions, etc. Out of this grows a particular set of rules regulating slaughterhouses in their transactions with consumers and farmers that structure their day-to-day opportunities relative to the slaughterhouse owners. It defines what it means to be an owner. It defines what effects (pecuniary or techno-logical) are to be registered as costs and thus the prices that emerge from exchange. The informal structure of belief influences formal property rights, which together structure day-to-day transactions, and puts certain people in the position of making an exchange, gift or whatever. Some of these structures as rights work informally, routinely, and unconsciously while some are part of calculations of advantage by the parties as they compete to use government to get the everyday formal institutions that they want.

If institutions are both formal rights and informal habits, and include things ranging from money, language, contract laws and constitutional rules, then we need a unit of analysis that can accommodate them all. That concept is the transaction. It is a cognitive understanding among people and should not be confused with the resulting physical movement of goods. This contrast is developed in chapter 5, "Institutions and Organizations."

2.2 Levels of Analysis and Questions Asked

The essential categories of institutions have now been sketched. These include three levels: the constitutional, everyday, and within-firms; two degrees of formality: the formal legislated institutions and the informal cultural institutions; and two broad questions: impact and change analysis. An adequate general theory must handle all of these. First, understanding the impact of a given institution may be distinguished from understanding institutional change.

2.2.1 Impact analysis

The first level of impact analysis attempts to explain how alternative formal and informal everyday institutions affect commodity transactions and substantive eco-nomic outcomes of wealth, and its distribution; and for this purpose formal institutions are treated as alternative variables to be chosen. Here, informal habits, organizations, and preferences are treated as given and human interaction is shaped by the formal institutions. For example, for a short-run analysis of a Prisoner's Dilemma situation, the habits relevant for cooperation are given.

The second analytical level of impact analysis attempts to explain how alternative internal structures of economic organizations and contractual arrangements affect performance. In each case the institutional framework of the first level defines and limits the set of practical forms of economic organization available to economic actors. One focus is on transaction costs (measurement and enforcement) implied by the types of commodities exchanged and the nature of exchange (Eggertsson 1990: 10). Another focus is on creativity and knowledge as organization members imagine the future (Hodgson 1999b: ch. 11). In some cases, the impact of an everyday institution cannot be traced unless its effect on the internal structure of firms is understood.

If one of the institutional structures being compared is currently in place, then contrasting its performance with that expected with a different structure is an analysis of the probable consequences of change. This says nothing about how to put the alternative in place. Comparing the consequences of a hypothetical change is not what is meant by change analysis as outlined below.

2.2.2 Change analysis

The understanding of institutional change requires an evolutionary model. Individuals are born into an institutional world that shapes their thinking, and their thinking shapes the institutional world. "Neither individual nor institutional factors have complete explanatory primacy" (Hodgson 1998: 184). Change analysis is essentially about the learning process combined with the existing rules for making rules. It must explain change in informal institutions and culture as well as formal institutions created by legislatures and courts.

"For the analysis of institutional change, the short run framework . . . no longer applies" (Eggertsson 1990: 11). This requires a model with feedback and can be illustrated with a circle of variables. Technology, population, resources, and imagination are relevant for institutional change. Technology affects institutions, and the latter affect the path of technology, the subject of chapter 10. To understand the changes in informal rules, it is necessary to understand the learning process of belief and ideology: habit formation, seeing institutions as variables, possibilities.

To understand change in formal institutions, it is first of all necessary to understand the informal cognitive processes that feed demand for change into the formal legislative and judicial channels. Next it is necessary to understand how alternative constitutional and political rules affect whose demands for change count (a power issue). The latter inquiry is a kind of impact analysis of alternative constitutional and political rules. Again, the task is not a prediction of the future but rather to create information which parties can use as they participate to shape the future.

2.2.3 Situation, structure, and performance (SSP)

To construct a theory for institutional analysis it is necessary to specify the dependent variable of interest and the broad categories of independent variables. For impact analysis, institutional alternatives are an independent variable. The dependent variable is some measure of substantive performance – who gets what. The set of independent variables with which institutional variables interact contains those aspects of the environment (character of goods) that create human interdependence. This will be termed the "*Situation.*" The "*Structure*" of institutional variables then sort out and order the interdependence and influence the outcome or "*Performance.*" The SSP variables and process links will be explained in the next section. (In what follows the term "function" should be read as "facilitates" since institutional economics models processes which involve imagination and are seldom or never fully deterministic.)

IMPACT ANALYSIS

In impact analysis, the technology/situation is given and we ask how different institutions affect the outcome of the interdependence that the technology creates in the context of different interests of different people. The institutions may be *formal* or *informal* or usually a mixture.

Stated in functional form,

> Performance = function of institution X, or institution Y, holding technology (situation) constant.

In diagrammatic form, we have

> Situation → institutional structure → performance

The linkage between situation, structure, and performance is a function of cognition and behavioral regularities of people experiencing the situation and their structured opportunity set.

CHANGE ANALYSIS

In change analysis, institutions become the dependent variable. In chapter 13, we ask how changes in technology, demographics, etc. alter the performance of existing institutions and how these changes are perceived and possibilities imagined by conflicting groups.

If everyday institution X above is chosen in time 1, and then the situation may change in time 2, the performance changes; and this in turn may lead to informal and formal institutional change in time 3 depending on perception and power.

Change in formal institutions: Formal institutions change in part when everyday performance changes interrupt routines or depart from the performance desired by some group with the power to change the institutions, given the constitution in place at the time. Change may result from either (or both) a change in the rules for making rules or the environmental situation.

Stated in functional form,

> Change in everyday formal institutions = function of rules for making rules, change in the situation.

Change in informal institutions: Informal institutions form out of largely unconscious learning.

Stated in functional form,

> Change in everyday informal institutions = function of changes in widely shared learning, functionality, power, and the situation.

In diagrammatic form for both formal and informal institutions,

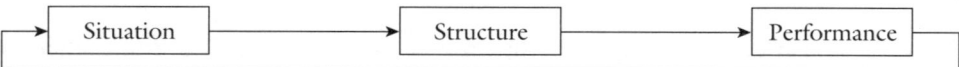

the new institution's performance may feed back and change the situation including the thought processes of the actors as well as technology causing continuous evolution.

If the physical situation does not change, then the only source of institutional change is ideology (preferences?) and cognition. However, technology and ideology may also interact as technology gives a different world-view. Technology can act as a metaphor and affect institutions apparently unrelated – for example the change may be in astronomy, computers, or biology and have effects on thinking in economics as applied to markets, etc. (Mirowski 2002).

Socialized, transacting individuals are subconsciously doing what the analyst is trying to do – make sense out of institutional impact, plus creating themselves. They cannot be conscious of all the situation variables that the analyst may find explicitly useful, but these same interdependence creating characteristics of goods are out there. People will necessarily find some simplifying conception that will be the basis for their sharing informal institutions and working toward altering formal institutions.

Change in rules for making everyday rules: This may be referred to as change at the constitutional level although it includes more broadly all political rules. While the constitution is itself a function of rules for making constitutions, all of this ultimately rests on fundamental ideology carried largely in people's heads that evolves as a result of functionality, power, and isomorphic and learning processes.

In functional form,

> Change in rules for making rules = function of changes in widely shared learning, functionality, power, and the situation.

2.2.4 Complementary theoretical frameworks: economizing and power

The range of questions asked here can be contrasted to those asked in neoclassical economics and the "new institutional economics." Oliver Williamson (2002) typifies the neoclassical approach as a theory of *choice* by consumers and firms in contrast to his new institutional economics as a theory of *contract*. The former conceives of the firm as production function. Resource inputs are combined as a function of relative prices and marginal products. How the resources are obtained is subsumed by reference to spontaneous competitive markets. Williamson shifts the focus to the organization of economic activity (the choice of alternative modes of private governance) within which to embed transactions (including contracts between employers and employees) given the broad collective rules of the game. Surely, there is a difference between choice of resource combinations and choice of governance structures, but the fundamental lens is still economizing (subject to the rules of the game and making provision for strategic behavior if the requisite conditions for pre-existing market power are satisfied). These given rules of the game determine who has what to economize. Whether the choice is of production functions or private governance, the model is one of calculation, albeit with limited information (necessarily incomplete contracts).

Williamson's main alternative structures are markets, hybrids, firms (hierarchies), and bureaus. This is a very limited set compared to the range of institutions considered in this book. What is here called the "situation," Williamson refers to as "attributes" of transactions. He refers primarily to asset specificity and non-verifiability of contract performance. Many other sources of human interdependence will be described here.

Because of the economizing framework of the new institutional economics, performance is described in terms of efficiency. Institutions are compared by the degree to which alternative private modes of governance are aligned (fit) the inherent attributes of transactions ("logic of efficient alignment"). Predictions then take the form of what governance structures will be used to organize transactions with different attributes. The "old institutional economics" and that of this book is primarily concerned with the alternative fundamental rules of the game that are the given starting place for Williamson. These institutions are antecedent to the private governance choices. Alternative rules of the game determine the context of efficiency. Power issues precede economizing. Therefore, in this book, prediction takes the form of whose interests count if one institution or another were put in place. Better knowledge of this sort may affect the power play involved in creating both the fundamental rules of the game and private governance (and the feedback between them).

Neoclassical theory suggests nothing is between the sovereign (undifferentiated) consumer and producers of goods and services; just a mythical, magical mechanism serving as auctioneer. This a-institutional view ignores the numerous institutions that influence whose preferences count. There is much more to it than budget constraints and physical production functions. "Economizing is not the whole of economics" (Reisman 2002: 252).

The broad conception outlined above will now be detailed below and illustrated throughout the book.

2.3 Theory: Variables and Processes

A theory is composed of variables and relationships among the variables (processes).[1] It identifies categories of variables whose presence and magnitude are expected to influence some measure of performance. Further, theory suggests how these variables are related to each other in some kind of process. In formal models, we say dependent variable X is a function of variables Y and Z. In informal models we describe the process by which X is expected to vary with changes in Y and Z. To be manageable, a theory must be abstract and selective. Its power depends on the selection. Institutionalists find that while theory is necessarily "unreal" in detail, it works best if not counterfactual. Application of institutional theory begins with observation of the selected variables, not assumptions about their character and magnitude. For example, the character of rationality is to be observed in the context, not assumed.

A theory need not be deterministic in the sense that a change in Y interacts with Z to produce some subsequent state of equilibrium where X remains unchanged until further changes in Y. Institutional theory includes phenomena with no equilibrium such that any change in Y sets in motion feedback on Y itself (or Z) as well as directly on the dependent variable. These non-equilibrating processes are often described as evolution. The evolving system may have periods of stability punctuated with change. A theory can be useful if it specifies independent variables that facilitate change in a dependent variable even if it does not fully determine the dependent variable.

2.3.1 Variables

What then are the major categories of variables in an institutional theory? The categories of situation, structure, and performance (SSP) along with behavioral, signal, technology, and time variables will be outlined here and then linked in section 2.3.2 below. A full discussion is in chapter 6, "Sources of Human Interdependence."

Situation refers to the inherent characteristics of goods and environments that affect human interdependence that must be sorted out by institutions giving order to human transactions?[2] Each physical situation subsystem is governed by an institutional structure subsystem. Situation includes the degree of incompatibility (scarcity), exclusion cost, economies of scale, effect of another user on cost, information costs, etc. These are aspects of a given technology which, for impact analysis, are taken as a given, even if in the longer run they may change. For example, broadcast TV is a high exclusion cost good (see below). But technology has now given us low exclusion cost cable and satellite transmission that can be scrambled. The impact of a particular institution is thus altered.

Incompatibility in use means that the opportunity of one person is limited by the opportunity of others. In other words, there is scarcity. Institutions will determine the starting place distribution of opportunities. Subsequent to the starting place the opportunity holder may also be given the right to use, trade, give away, etc.

Exclusion cost affects whether the nominal holder of an opportunity will be able to actually exercise it or whether it will also be accessible in fact by others. This characteristic interacts with institutions such as private property rights and trade and influences whether the goods will be produced and who pays for them.

Economies of scale and the effect of another user on cost create an interdependence that differs from that of constant or rising cost. It is sorted out by pricing rules.

Information cost creates a context affecting human interaction. It may make it difficult for an actor to judge the quality of a good or predict a future state of the world. Institutions affect the outcome of this interdependence including who shares in the cost of inevitable mistakes. Individuals learn rules of thumb that they apply to certain patterns of experience.

Ubiquitous interdependencies mean that many institutional details matter. Actual markets are as diverse as there are different combinations of rules governing these interdependencies. But, each source of interdependence has only a limited number and kind of institutional structures that control it. SSP theory suggests a few limiting structural factors relevant to a particular problem context. Any theory is a rationale for why some connections among actors matter while others are necessarily ignored in the name of practicality and bounded rationality.

Structure refers to the institutional alternatives that people can choose to order the interdependencies created by the situation of various technologies. The actual "choice" may be informal and unconscious as well as formal. Structure is subject to human choice, but when informal structures change only slowly, they are often given in the short-run impact analysis of formal institutional alternatives. The theory can be used to produce knowledge to better inform the choice of institutions so that different people with different interests can work to achieve the institution that provides the performance that they want. However, analysts should not overestimate their ability to predict impact. There are inescapable uncertainties and surprises. One of the important impacts of institutions is how they affect how the costs and benefits of inevitable surprises are shared.

Structure describes the relationships between people that define their relative opportunity sets. These shared, systemic structures exist in people's heads and constitute their expectations of where they may act and how they may expect others to act in predictable ways. As described above, these may be recorded in formal laws or exist only in habits of the mind. There is a structure to everyday business transactions as well as structure for changing these rules. The latter include constitutions and political rules. People may be very aware of some of this structure and other parts are working unconsciously.

An institution is more than that which affects the payoffs as seen by a rationally calculating actor. Institutions also shape preferences, the perception of relevant alternative courses of action, keep some possible alternative choices off a person's agenda, and frame the decision so that one or another standard operating procedure applies.

People may be arranged hierarchically with one person in a transaction being superior to another and entitled to issue orders within some bounds. This may be referred to as an *administrative transaction*. While there is a superior and an inferior, the relationship may have been entered into voluntarily as when a worker agrees to follow the orders of the foreman within a specified range of activity or when a citizen agrees to follow laws approved by majority voting.

People may also be arranged as legal equals and negotiate an exchange of whatever opportunities they may have been given. This may be referred to as a *bargained transaction*. While the parties are legal equals, they may not be equal in terms of wealth and bargaining power. Bargained (negotiated) transactions are not synonymous with the market. Many markets are based on posted prices and involve no explicit bargaining. And many administrative and hierarchical organizations nevertheless have considerable negotiations among the parties.

Prior to bargaining or administration are rule-making transactions whose product is the rights/opportunities of the parties. There are rule-making transactions which establish who is superior in administration. There are rule-making transactions that are antecedent to bargaining that establishes who is buyer and who seller of a particular interdependent opportunity. I will not make an offer to buy something that I consider already mine. The rules for making the rules of everyday bargaining and administration may be formal legislative and judicial processes shaped by constitutional and political rules[3] or informal cultural processes.

Customary transactions are the third major way people may be related to each other. Surveys indicate that about half of all work takes place outside the labor market (Folbre and Nelson 2000: 66). The motivation for such transactions is learned, internalized, and informal. A person occupying a certain status, role, or position expects and is expected to act toward other positions in a learned habitual manner. When these are widely held, they are often called social norms. There is little calculation, one just does the right thing. For example, in the household sector, a parent provides for children and adult children care for elderly parents. A richer person provides emergency help for a poor friend. People give blood to those who need it. An employee identifies with the goals of the organization even if opportunistic behavior is possible. People contribute to the production of goods even if free-ridership is possible. When these norms are violated, the person's conscience produces guilt. It may also produce disapproval and social pressure from others. Custom often results in one-way flow of goods – a transfer or grant rather than two-way exchange (Boulding 1973; Schmid 1973). Status may or may not also carry an emotional element.

The grant is non-calculated. It may reside in the sympathy and caring (social capital) one person has for others. Or, a person may act according to a norm without any necessary sympathy. One may make a transfer to another because that person's welfare is part of the giver's welfare even if there is no general social norm to make the grant. In the case of a status-rooted transaction, the material transfer carries no necessary emotional overtones. The giver regards it as obligatory and so does the recipient. But, in the case of the grant rooted in caring, the material carries with it a socio-emotional good. The material symbolizes the care and regard that the giver has for the receiver, and the receiver may reciprocate that regard. Emotion in the giver creates an emotion in the recipient with possible feedback again. Norm following and sympathy are in practice bound together and reinforce each other.

The not-for-profit sector has a different motivation than the usual business firm. It is common in hospitals, universities, foundations, and various community service organizations, some faith-based. Non-governmental organizations (NGOs) are common in developing countries funded by governments and private groups. The final product may be given free as a grant or sold, but the managers are motivated by a cause and not profit. The managers are usually paid, but volunteer labor is attracted to the cause.

Threat transactions complete the major ways that people interrelate. People exchange threats of bads (not exchange of goods) and there is no forbearance. Physical capacity is everything. Parties treat each other as objects. The prevalence of local wars today is testimony that there is no guarantee that people can create property rights. The delivery of the threat often leaves both parties materially worse off.

Administrative, bargained, and customary transactions, both formal and informal, and for both everyday economic and political functions, are interlinked in an evolutionary, ever changing, non-equilibrating meta-process. Opportunities in one context can be used to alter opportunities in another.

The boundary of each type of transaction determines who participates. Institutions are often bounded by nation states, but increasingly there are international boundaries to rule-making jurisdiction. Organizations also represent boundaries. We speak of "members" who participate. In the business world, the boundary of the firm and its internal organization are major institutional decisions. Other examples are religious denominations, trade associations, citizen associations and clubs, a university, etc. Boundary is a concept that cuts across all kinds of public and private organizations. Rules may form within one boundary and be useful within that boundary, but dysfunctional for people outside. We speak of "honor among thieves," for example.

Sanctions are an important component of structure. Broadly this is the feedback from the environment that increases the probability of behavior being repeated in the same situation. The sanctions may range from a fine imposed by a judge to social pressure and ostracism imposed by one's reference group.

Models or beliefs of how the world works is another component of structure. When these models are shared widely they affect the general way that institutions affect performance and perceptions of their legitimacy.

Comparison of institutional alternatives at a high level of abstraction such as administration, bargained, and customary can be useful, but in many cases detail matters a great deal. Structure can be further delineated into position, boundary, authority, aggregation, scope, information, and payoff rules (Ostrom, Gardner, and Walker 1994: 41–2).

Performance refers to who gets what. Since we began with the observation that people have different interests that may conflict, no aggregate measures of total welfare are possible. Performance consequences of alternative institutions must be disaggregated and in substantive terms of who gets what goods. The performance measures should answer the question of whose interests count with institution A compared with institution B. All performance measures have a stakeholder or interest group subscript reflecting the parties to a transaction whether formal or informal, bargaining, administrative or political rule making. The concept of substantive performance is developed throughout this book, especially sections 5.5.2 and 12.5.

As for *behavioral regularities*, there is no simple mechanical connection between institutional structure, situation, and performance. Even the computer is not an apt metaphor (Mirowski 2002). The linkage is a mental one of cognition and formation of images and meanings. Institutions structure opportunities, but these have to be perceived and acted upon. There is a difference between a theory of objective advantage and a theory of behavior. Institutional economics is firmly rooted in the behavioral sciences and its theory is built on our best understanding of how the human brain works. It is built on an understanding of behavioral regularities of a population, not a particular individual.

Among the behavioral regularities to be explored in chapter 3 is a heavier weighting of losses than gains and various judgmental heuristics (Frank 1997: ch. 8). People often continue to do in the future what worked in the past. People learn to respond to cues as a function of the flow of reinforcers.

Perhaps the most salient fact of the human mind is captured in Herbert Simon's concept of bounded rationality. The human brain has limited information processing capacity. It can make detailed calculations prior to action only in limited areas and the rest must be governed by habit, rules of thumb and, standard operating procedures. To understand the impact of alternative institutions, it is necessary to gather data reflecting the actual decision heuristics that people use. A simple assumption that more is preferred to less will not do because the units of more are a matter of perception and shaped by institutions.

Observation suggests that preferences vary among individuals (and among groups) and change over time. The very concept of preference is problematic in that much learning involves evolving patterns of the environment that are sensed and behavior fitted unconsciously. We are quite capable of holding conflicting and ambiguous ideals and finding that what we thought we wanted did not actually bring satisfaction. Cyert (1988) uses the term "committee of goals" rather than preferences.

A view of behavioral regularities from behavioral science can be used in both impact and change analysis. Counterfactual assumptions work on an "as if " basis only in limited instances.

Signals. Because the connection between institutional structure and performance outcomes is not mechanical, the content of the communication among transacting parties is an important variable. The things that are observed by people are always selected and interpreted in an institutional context. These include prices, quantities, qualities, approval, orders, condemnation, fines, sanctions, what others are doing, etc.

Technology. Physical characteristics of goods affect human interdependence and have already been discussed above as situational variables. When technology changes it changes the outcome of human interdependence under existing institutions and thus may occasion demands for new institutions by some and protection of old advantages by others. Also, we are what we do to a major extent as Marx among others has observed. Technology affects the way we think about the world and our place in it (ideology). Attention to technology is a hallmark of institutional economics and the focus of chapter 10.

Time: Time subscripts on all of the above variables are vital. Time is important because of human learning. Time is important in many production and adjustment processes. The past constrains and shapes (not determines) the future. History matters. Path dependence is a phenomenon to be investigated.

2.3.2 Processes (aspects of linked transactions)

A theory must identify variables, as was done above, and also specify the connections and functional relationship among them. What are the underlying processes that give direction to the interaction of the variables to produce performance? For many questions of institutional choice, the actors will be informed by an understanding of direction and existence. Are the variables negatively or positively correlated and which are substitutes and which complements? The key linkages and processes are: (1) situation, structure, and performance; (2) changes with feedback. Both processes are applicable at the level of everyday business transactions, rules for making rules, and within-firm organization. And both processes are applicable to impact and change analysis. It is the feedback loop that links impact and change analysis. Within these major processes there are sub-processes and subject matter applications.

SITUATION, STRUCTURE, AND PERFORMANCE LINKAGES

As mentioned above, human interdependence is partly determined by the physical characteristics of goods and services. The potential interdependence is ordered by institutional structure to influence performance within the context of the way the human mind works. Two specific examples illustrate how the theory is constructed.

Goods such as environmental air quality are high exclusion cost goods (situation variable). This creates an interdependence such that contributions to inputs to produce improved environmental quality are required from many in the airshed, but there is an opportunity to free ride on the efforts of others. To predict the likely substantive performance of whether the good will be produced and who will pay for it, it is necessary to understand the process linking institutions to situation, namely human mental processes. Theory suggests that human cognition is critical to contrast the performance of market and administrative transactions. It is necessary to observe whether this situation triggers calculation or if it is covered by some rule of thumb. Assumptions of opportunism will not do because that is the behavior in question. Theory tells the analyst where to look for relevant variables and the expected relationship (connection) among them. In this case, the theory suggests that mental framing and the past history of cooperation matters. The possibility for signals of approval and other reinforcements are relevant.

The same general theory can be used to understand the impact of alternative forms of organization of firms. The dependent variable is whose interests are facilitated by the boundaries of the decision unit and what sub-objectives emerge from the negotiations within or between units. The independent variables include situation variables (the degree of uncertainty, the specificity of assets, etc.) and institutional structures that affect individual opportunism and participation. The most general structures are market or hierarchy, but the detail of the hierarchy matters: for example, whether the firm is organized functionally or by product or region to name only a few dimensions. Also the market is not a single thing, but may be composed of many alternative market rules.

The performance objective is not assumed, but rather is seen as a function of individual learning, rules of thumb, and the internal structure of human relationships in an organization that affect information flows and signals by which the players are made selectively aware of and create the organization's production and demand functions. The signals that an individual responds to are many. Signal variables include: prices, quantities, inventories, sanctions, regard, media, and many other aspects of others' behavior.

Alternatively, the choice of market or administrative (hierarchical) transactions can be made the dependent variable and the degree of uncertainty and asset specificity the independent variables. Assuming an efficiency objective, Williamson (1985) uses the degree of asset specificity to predict the dominant institutional structure of an industry. The approach of this book is rather to predict the substantive performance of the extant or proposed institutional structure.

With the above theoretical framework a variety of sub-processes (systems) can be identified and subject matter applications can be made as follows.

Cost, a function of rights: Opportunity cost is a central concept in economics. The institutional perspective observes that cost is always selective, never a matter simply of technology. Lots of things are physically forgone when a given good is produced, but only a selection is taken into account by producers as a function of property rights (Samuels and Schmid 1997). Processes can be nested. For example, the choice of input combinations by a firm is a function of cost and cognition thereof. The theory emphasizes that cost involves expectations and perceptions. But what social relationship produces feedback that reminds an actor that an action has cost? Cost is a function of rights. It is rights that determine whose interests are a cost to others. It is these rights that make it possible for one person's interests to become a cost to another. Given human interdependence and conflicting interests, there necessarily are winners and losers. To have a right is to have the opportunity to require others to pay you to give it up. Samuels speaks of the "inevitability of non-compensated losses."

The interdependence of parties depends on knowledge of the physics and biology. For example, ornamental cedar trees may harbor a pest detrimental to apples, but this is irrelevant until there is scientific knowledge of it. This knowledge is socially conditioned. Law and technology call attention to a physical connection that was previously ignored. Once the physical connections are selected, the value of securing or avoiding the effect is also socially conditioned. Preferences are learned. For example, a consumer product agency in formulating grades and standards may create a demand for differentiated products that some consumers did not previously have. If A's interests are made a cost to B by A's rights, then anything that affects A's valuation of that interest changes the cost to B.

Power: The relationship between A's opportunity and B's exposure and obligation define their relative power. When preferences differ and there is scarcity of opportunity (preferences conflict), it is the institutional structure established in rule-making transactions that sorts it out. The everyday rules make one party or the other the holder of the opportunity and thus able to be a seller in a bargained transaction. Market power or the ability to affect price in exchange is only one dimension of power. More fundamental is whether you are a buyer or a seller. The poor are those who have little to use or sell and thus their consent need not be sought via purchase or other persuasion. It was Marie Antoinette who remarked that the poor and rich are equal in their right to sleep under the bridges. But the point of power is that the rich have other options and command over other resources that they can deny those with little to offer in exchange. Economic power is an input into political power to alter rights and vice versa. Power is not a separate process, but a way to describe how rights influence costs.

Power and freedom mean nothing apart from a set of human relationships. Stinchcombe (1995: 126) following Commons says, "A liberty creates an exposure of others to the different consequences of different choices by the free person. . . . The definition, then, is a sum of practically available liberties including in particular the social capacity to get others to suffer the consequences of [one's] practical . . . freedom . . . to decide." This parallels the legal reciprocals of Hohfeld (1913).

Change with feedback: There are many processes where a change in one variable feeds back on the magnitude of another variable (or a change in one system feeds back on another sub- or higher system). A coefficient may be influenced by the place of its variable in a system of variables. Some authors refer to this as a "part–whole relationship" where the significance of a part depends on the evolving character of the whole (Ramstad 1986). This is particularly important in the long term. In formal models this is referred to as overdetermination. The dependent variable may become independent and vice versa. Examples of change with feedback include cumulative causation, non-marginal change, reaction functions, learning, and evolution.

Circular and cumulative causation: An initial change in an independent variable may change the relationship between it and the dependent variable. This circularity is cumulative if the change in the dependent variable in turn causes a change in the formerly independent variable in the same direction as the initial movement. Thus, a small initial change can become magnified. With feedback, a system evolves rather than settling to an equilibrium. A cumulative effect is achieved if the feedback reinforces and amplifies the original change. This process captures the essence of a large number of phenomena ranging from racial discrimination (Myrdal 1944), increasing returns in the context of economic development (Young 1928) and the relationship of scale and labor productivity (Kaldor 1972), to institutional change and path dependence (North 1990).

Consider again the earlier example of interdependence with respect to air quality. The SSP process hypothesizes that contributions to provision of the good are a function of the degree of exclusion cost and the formal institutions of market or administrative transactions plus learned habits of cooperation. The experience of cooperation at time 1 feeds back on habits in time 2. If the effect is cumulative, the result may be a path of increasing or decreasing cooperation through time.

Non-marginal change: Institutional economics is not concerned with changes at the margin, but rather instances where the change in a variable is large enough to feedback on other variables. Income effects are an example. A change in ownership of opportunities may cause a change in the marginal utility of money and thus shift demand curves for various products. This may cause a difference between bid and reservation prices. Many investment decisions change the basics of the firm and are not marginal.

Reaction functions: The outcome of transactions depends on the degree of arousal of one party to send a signal to another party, and on the reaction of the other party to the first mover. This is a key process in situations that have characteristics of Prisoner's Dilemma games. It is central to understanding pricing in oligopoly and monopoly, labor–management negotiations, customer–producer interaction, etc. Reaction functions are a matter of cognition and, while not mechanistic, are predictable to some degree.

Learning: Humans act, and feedback from the environment affects the next action in a never-ending loop. Some of that feedback reinforces the previous action and some extinguishes it. We follow others and also try new things. The resulting environment feeds back. Some is unconscious reinforcement and some conscious evaluation. The implicit or explicit valuations of the results change over time and differ among individuals with the same experience. We develop ideologies to make sense out of otherwise unmanageable complexity. We act upon recognition of a pattern previously experienced with what appear to be acceptable results. This means that variables describing standard operating procedures (SOPs) and rules of thumb are important to theory specification (Schwartz 1998). Just one example is noted here. One of the most remarked observations in economics is the downward sloping demand curve that depicts a greater quantity being purchased at lower prices. If there were no learning associated with the experience of a higher price, when the price returned to its previous base point, the quantity purchased would be expected to be the same. Frequently, however, one observes that when the price returns to its pervious level, the quantity purchased may not return to the previous level. Learning has taken place. There is an evolution rather than an equilibrium. People may not be the same after consuming more of a substitute good. They develop new habits with an inertia of their own.

Many of the signal variables identified above in situation, structure, and performance processes are equally applicable in feedback processes. Prices, quantities, inventories, sanctions, regard, and other's behavior act as reinforcers and constitute patterns to which learned behaviors are fitted.

Evolution and co-evolution: Individuals change and evolve, institutions evolve, and technology evolves. Change in any component sets other components in motion. Some part may change and produce no change in other components for a long time causing large changes in performance whose source may not be identified, or those suffering may not be able to change it. See Hodgson (1993), Samuels, Schmid, and Shaffer (1994), Norgaard (1994), and chapter 13, "Institutional Change Analysis."

Multiple equilibria: If the concept of equilibrium is useful at all, it must include processes that are capable of producing multiple equilibria: see Arrow (1986: S395).

2.4 Some Implications of the Variables and Processes: Systems Views

There are processes within processes. The elements of variables and processes above can be built into systems of differing scope. An analogy is provided by a series of nested equations: at the macro level, $x = f\,y$; at the market sector level, $y = f\,z$; at the within-firm level, $z = f\,B$; and a feedback loop, $B = f\,x$ wherein a dependent variable at one point in time becomes independent at another. Thus, a theory of the state differs in scope and aggregation from a theory of the firm.

2.4.1 Continuity and change

The continuity vs. change of institutions is one of the tensions in the rights creation and maintenance process (Samuels 1992b: 24–8; Potts 2000: 107). Continuity (stability) is often regarded as a prerequisite to economic development (North 1990). People do not invest without some assurance that the returns will not be confiscated. Still, capitalism has been cogently described as a process of "creative destruction" (Schumpeter 1950). Economic development would be quite slowed and different if every innovator had to get everyone's permission so that no one would suffer a loss from introduction of a new product. It is hypothesized that development is shaped by institutions that selectively make some innovator the new owner and seller of an opportunity rather than it being a cost.

2.4.2 Collective action

Individuals may act with little or no conscious coordination with others. This is the vaunted and much celebrated accomplishment of markets. The popular metaphor of Smith argued that the butcher and baker need not care or be concerned with others, but would nevertheless be coordinated to an optimal extent by market prices. This of course ignores the question of what rights each has to trade and the rules for trade. It raises no question about how performance might be altered by alternative institutions where conscious collective action changes opportunity sets. It raises no question of how informal cultural change affects ideologies and values. A major research question to be understood (rather than assumed) by institutional economists involves the consequences of collective and group action whether formally public and governmental or private in the context of firms and other organizations. It is hypothesized that in particular situations, individuals sharing a performance preference cannot get what they want acting as isolated individuals at the margin within existing opportunity sets. It is a tragedy when individuals make their most advantageous choice and wind up where they do not want to be because of the emergent aggregate effect of others doing the same thing. This is not the tragedy of the commons but the tragedy of isolated individualism. This is not individual interest vs. the collective, but a failure of like-minded individuals.

2.4.3 Theory of the state (legal–economic nexus)

The situational variables suggest the sources of human interdependence that must be given order by the institutional structure. If people are interdependent, there is an institution that gives order to it, or there is war and chaos. The state with its rules for making rules is the formal process by which this order is created. Cultural

evolution is the informal process. Informal institutions arise and give order to interdependencies. In primitive societies, informal rules are reinforced by social pressure,
threat of supernatural penalty, and force by strong-arm chiefs. As interdependence
increased and widened geographically, informal institutions alone could not provide
order. More formal institutions were created that ultimately were sanctioned by an
organization that tried to maintain a monopoly on physical force as a sanction.

A theory of the state combines theories of the impact of alternative constitutional
rules and theories of institutional change. The state and the economy evolve together
constituting a nexus (Samuels 1989). The state is a name for some of the necessarily
collective processes that define formal rightful opportunities that are antecedent to
the market (Schmid 1999b). Or, as Callon (1998: 41) puts it, "the state constitutes,
rather than intervenes, in the economy." There are also informal rights and those
formulated within organizations. Without some threshold of legitimacy for rights
there is no order to either administrative or bargaining transactions, only might.
Nevertheless, power and opportunity in access to the state are used to obtain power
and opportunity in the everyday economy, and vice versa as noted above. There is a
power play between those who find the informal rules to their liking and those who
wish to use the state to override them. The formal rules are also affecting the
evolution of informal habits. The processes are expected to be heavily path dependent with dependent variables becoming independent over time. A theory of the state
is further developed in section 5.4 and chapter 12.

2.4.4 Economizing, power, and knowledge

Institutional economics embraces three levels of analysis: economizing, power, and
knowledge. *Economizing* asks which institution is more efficient, but begs the question
of whose interests count. *Power* analysis asks whose preferences count in economizing.
Who has what to trade? Which institution is efficient to whose purposes? *Knowledge*
analysis asks how preferences and purposes are formed and how technology and
institutions change. These themes will be developed in subsequent chapters.

2.4.5 The place of institutional economics in policy analysis

Institutional economics is a complement to the theory of the firm and to policy
analysis in general. There is more to policy analysis than the impact of alternative
rights or adding behavioral science. Institutional economics focuses on the link
between institutional alternatives and human behavior while production theory
focuses on the link between that behavior and the output of goods and services.
In chapter 5 it will be suggested that institutions are not part of the physical
production function, but rather affect the presence and combination of inputs in
that function. For example, consider a policy analysis of speed limits as a promoter
of highway safety. The institutional question is the impact of a law limiting speed
with police sanctions on speed actually driven. The production function question is
the physics of speed and accidents and injuries. The institutional question is how

people will respond to the possibility of fines, how they are administered, the court and penal system, etc. A total policy analysis requires both institutional analysis and the physical production function (Schmid 1972).

Another example is an analysis of tariff policy, a right to access buyers. Neoclassical economics and the theory of comparative advantage are useful in examining the potential gains from trade and how the location of production might change with a reduction of tariffs. Institutional analysis would add how traders evade border controls, pay off inspectors (and their reaction functions), and the time managers spend on altering production vs. trying to get the law changed. A total policy analysis requires both institutional analysis and the standard theory of the firm and markets.

2.4.6 Conceptual pluralism

Institutional economists have debated whether their objective is one grand unified theory of economics or greater pluralism (Dow 2000; Garnett 2002). This author has not come to a firm conclusion. Sometimes I am of the mind that if we selected the best from various authors across the spectrum of economists, a more powerful core theory would emerge (Schmid 2001). At the same time, no one grand theory has a lock on the truth (Samuels 1997). Different perspectives produce different insights. The SSP framework can facilitate trade in conceptual ideas by comparing various authors who address the same source of interdependence with different terms. The structure of any particular economy at a point in history is the working out of all the interdependencies extant. Study of different subsystems involving different aggregations of structures controlling different interdependencies produces different insights. Some may combine different subsystems of structure to define capitalism, socialism, the welfare state, etc. and compare their aggregate performance. Others may focus on various subsectors and commodities or a particular performance category such as employment or income distribution. Hopefully, SSP is a useful foundation for studying systems of different scope.

NOTES

1. Some say institutionalists have no theory. However, they may only be saying that it does not look like neoclassical theory. The constructivist view of Yonay (1998: 19) reminds us that in the competition among theories and what counts as theory, "'success,' 'neatness,' and 'usefulness' are not given by Nature but constructed in a process of negotiation and conflict."
2. Among analysts who explicitly make the nature of the good central to predicting the performance of alternative institutions is Ostrom. (See Ostrom et al. (2002: ch. 2 and p. 241) and Ostrom, Gardner, and Walker (1994: ch. 2).) Ostrom refers to the combination of physical/material conditions, attributes of community and actors, and rules-in-use as the "action arena."
3. The analysis of rules for making rules is sometimes referred to as constitutional economics (Buchanan 1991).

Chapter 3
Behavioral Economics

Institutional economics is built on a foundation of behavioral science. A working model of variables and processes describing the way the brain works is essential to underpin institutional impact and change analysis. Four aspects of the human brain[1] are highlighted below that are important for economics. The first is bounded rationality that notes the limited information processing capacity of the brain and its modularity. Second, the brain is an evaluative process, emotive and feeling. Third, there are several behavioral regularities that affect the performance of institutions. Fourth, the brain is open-ended and humans learn. And finally, all this takes place in a social system of human transactions.

3.1 Bounded Rationality

Two features of the brain provide foundations for behavior and decision-making. One is its *limited information processing capacity*. Humans are purposeful but bounded. They are generally not irrational or random in behavior. They are procedurally rational and use whatever reasoning power is available, but know that they cannot be substantively rational in the sense of considering everything (Simon 1982).

The second is its *modularity* – different brain components have some ability to affect behavior independently of other modules. In other words, the brain is not unitary and necessarily internally consistent (Carter 1998). Some behaviors are domain specific, not universal in applicability.

In situations of fundamental uncertainty, no amount of information processing will solve the problem. One cannot speak of biased decisions since the reference point is not given. The problem is one of adaptation and learning, not optimization from given ingredients. Bounded rationality involves some innate and evolving search, stopping and decision rules that provide for order and survival. Bounded rationality is not an inferior form of rationality (Gigerenzer and Selten 2001: 6).

3.1.1 Limited information processing capacity

The human brain is impressive in its scope and capacity, but nevertheless limited in its capacity to process information. The capacity of the brain is the ultimate limited resource in behavior. To make the point, consider the more than 30,000 items in the modern supermarket. Even if consumers had access to a book describing the features of these items, they would not have time to consult it before starving to death. There is no way to rank these items in terms of their relative value in serving the consumer's interests if it is indeed possible to conceive of a complex list of interests and the connections between the products and the interests. The same problem exists for producers of complex products and services. Even if information were available on all production functions and demand functions now and in the future, the brain could not keep track of it. The same is true of public affairs. There is no way for citizens to be informed on all of the issues before a legislature.

There is no extensive pre-existing structure of values attached to goods and actions. As Kahneman (1999: 22) puts it, "people evidently compute an answer to the subjective happiness question on the fly, instead of retrieving a prepared answer from memory." They are formed in the particular case and are description, context, and procedure dependent.[2]

How then do we cope? In a word, we necessarily simplify. We make mental accounts, organize choices lexicographically, engage in selective perception, and develop habits and standard operating procedures that are keyed to perceived environmental patterns, and identify sub-goals.

Mental accounts: Consumers may have allocated their income to a limited number of accounts (Thaler 1985). Choices of goods are then made within these accounts without further re-examination across accounts. This saves scarce mental resources. For example, a person may have a leisure time budget and various items are compared and traded off within the budget but not against all possible ways the person might spend their money.

Lexicographic choice: Products have many features, and thus ranking them fully would require each feature to be weighted and summed. It saves brain power if the most important features are arranged in order and then alternative products compared with respect to that feature (Earl 1983: 87–8). If both products are equal with respect to that feature, the consumer goes to the next ranked feature. But if one good is superior, the comparison may stop and the good is purchased. This can happen even if the sum of the value of the lower ranked features could in principle be larger for the rejected good. Price is just one feature of a good and frequently not the highest ranked. A hierarchy of preferences is more consistent with the brain's ability to process information than achieving the commensurability of all wants in all dimensions (Georgescu-Roegen 1968).

Habits and standard operating procedures: One answer to complexity is to do what you did before in a similar case. This can be open ended because what is considered a similar case is a matter of perception that is influenced by description, context, and procedure, all of which may not actually be objectively relevant. (This is discussed in section 3 below.) To understand behavior, this phenomenon leads Herbert Simon to collect data on what standard operating procedures firm managers actually use. How habits are learned is explored below in section 5.

Is it possible to formulate an economic theory based on less than fully rational utility maximization? (Can the concept of utility be dispensed with altogether?) Can a behavioral economics theory explain certain market phenomena such as market clearing given budget constraints? Arrow suggests that "habit formation can be made into a theory; for a given price–income change, choose the bundle that satisfies the budget constraint and that requires the least change . . . from the previous consumption bundle" (Arrow 1986: S386). Such a standard operating procedure is consistent with bounded rationality. The budget constraint has a chosen time dimension. When prices change, a person must eventually alter the consumption bundle, but the old daily bundle may not alter until the end of the month (as opposed to a continuous alteration in accordance with prior preferences).

Sub-goal identification: Where the linkages between a particular action and ultimate desired outcome are not clear, a person may identify a sub-goal. Simon (1979: 500) observes, "When goals of an organization cannot be connected operationally with actions (when the production function can't be formulated in concrete terms), then decisions will be judged against subordinate goals that can be so connected. There is no unique determination of these subordinate goals. Their formulation will depend on the knowledge, experience, and organizational environment of the decision-makers. In the face of this ambiguity, the formulation can also be influenced in subtle, and not so subtle, ways by his self-interest and power drives." The procedure is one of "problem representation" which is a key concept in cognitive psychology. People organize a mass of information into a problem formulation that can be solved. The available procedures include: (1) satisfice, (2) replace abstract global goals with tangible sub-goals whose achievement can be measured and observed, and (3) divide the decision among many specialists, coordinating their work by means of a structure of communications and authority relations (501).

Cognitive limits cause people to form sub-goals that can be measured in the situation that explains the role of stylized measures of profits, market share, etc. "Even if these measurements are only rough approximations of the things they are supposed to be measuring, they are likely to replace the 'real' unmeasured concepts in the decision process" (Simon 1991: 37).

Selective perception: Humans are both necessarily and opportunistically selective in their perception. Noise must be eliminated. We cannot see everything. And, we often screen out information that is available if it does not fit our preconceptions or would challenge our identity and interests. "Our knowledge, as well as our ignorance, at any time and on every issue, tends to be opportunistically conditioned, and thus brought to deviate from the truth" (Myrdal 1975: 413). Our view of the world is influenced by the way we earn our living (as Marx observed). We can easily reject evidence that does not support our position. Dearborn and Simon (1958) describe the tendency of managers to regard the biggest problem of the corporation as lying within their own special department and function. Simon (1991: 37) further observes that organizational identification shifts when a person's position shifts because "a shift in organizational position exposes the employees to new 'facts' and phenomena, to a new network of communications, and to new goals. . . . Behavior is very much a function of position."

If people are reminded of a discrepancy between announced objectives and their current behavior, there is cognitive dissonance. The pain of this discrepancy is often reduced by selectively rejecting the information or reducing the value of the objective, rather than changing the behavior.

It is not enough to know an agent's "objective" situation. Rather one must gain insight into the agent's perception and experience. "Economic decision is seen as the result of symbol processing, rather than as mere choice among alternatives" (Rizzello 1999: 63).

Satisficing: All of the above behaviors are a kind of "satisficing," a term created by Herbert Simon. The term is perhaps unfortunate because of its several connotations. One meaning is "to denote problem solving and decision making that sets an aspiration level, searches until an alternative is found that is satisfactory by the aspiration level criterion, and selects that alternative" (Simon 1972: 168). It might be the lazy person's level of effort meaning "good enough." Another meaning is a kind of calculation in which the person considers the cost and benefits of more information and search. Simon explicitly rejects this meaning since the whole point of bounded rationality is limits to calculation. It is not helpful to require people to calculate yet another tradeoff involving the possible returns to a margin of further search. Without making an explicit reference to aspirations, a behavior is often seen as fitting an environment. When the fit is made (and it may be unconscious), we are at peace and searching stops. (See section 3.5.1 below.) Simon points out that some "essential processes are subconscious and not open to direct observation or even self-observation" (Simon 1992: 105). Emotion also can stop searching.

Maximization: Calculated maximization over some range of data is just another standard operating procedure. We do it when we think the situation calls for it. The only point with respect to bounded rationality is that we can't do it for all behaviors and decisions. This is consistent with the fact that persons trained in maximization techniques often fail to use them when not reminded that the problem calls for it. Much of the time they necessarily use the same heuristics as people who are ignorant of applicable maximization techniques.

Calculated maximization for all products interacting with changing prices is essential to the standard consumption theory of constrained maximization. It is further assumed that preferences are consistent or transitive. If the consumer prefers basket A to basket B and basket B to C, then the consumer will prefer A to C. Finally, everything is commensurate and more is preferred to less. People know what they like and act accordingly. With this simple representation of the way people think, rational choice theory can be used to deduce consumer choice and analyze the welfare effects of public policy. For example, the efforts of sales persons to change the order or context of choice could not affect choice. The effort of government to increase savings by requiring investments in pension plans would be unsuccessful because people would just substitute one form of saving for another. However, people in business and public policy act as if they do not believe that the above conception of "supra-rationality" describes the way people think. There is considerable evidence that contradicts supra-rationality (Sippel 1997).

Some behavioral regularities cause behavior to deviate from maximization where the optimum is known to the analyst and knowable to the subject. But, with fundamental uncertainty and complexity, maximization has no meaning. Nevertheless, people have innate and learned heuristics that work. Mental accounts, lexicographic choice, standard operating procedures, sub-goals that may be incommensurate with each other, and satisficing are not second best processes, but describe human capacities without which we would be dead. They constitute our adaptive toolbox.

3.1.2 The modular brain, multiple self, and bounded self-control

Different parts of the brain can take in information from the environment and issue "orders" for action without the participation of other parts. Our brains are not completely integrated and hierarchical. This is probably a good thing since if we had to carefully evaluate each action, we would never get out of bed. This feature is our strength and weakness. We can act and then regret it. On the one hand we want to diet and on the other we pig out. The planner brain may castigate the action brain, but it is not always in charge. We often speak of being of two minds. The conception of the modular brain is consistent with observed non-transitivity in choices, which will be described in another section below.

One economic application is to people's discounting of future values. Rabin suggests that, "Researchers have shown that a (relatively) simple multiple-self model of time-inconsistent discounting tractably modifies our familiar exponential model to yield a model that is manifestly more realistic behaviorally and surely has important economic consequences" (Rabin 1998: 33).

Elster (1984) uses the story of Ulysses tying himself to the mast to avoid the temptation of the ship-wrecking sirens. Which is the real person? Is it the person who would like what the sirens promise or is it the person who fears the rocks? The fact is that we are multiple selves. This has important institutional implications. Institutions serve the function of putting the planner self in charge by tying our hands to the mast by building up a set of expectations and reinforcements which prevent us from considering some alternatives. It is made operational by internalized learned habits and reinforced by the shared expectations of others.

Experiments with people whose brain hemispheres have been surgically severed suggest that the planner brain will provide reasons for action even when it could not have been in charge (Gazzaniga 1985). An image (chicken claw) is flashed to the right of a dot on a screen and is registered in the left hemisphere of the brain that controls the right hand. If the patient is given a series of cards with different subjects pictured, the patient chooses the head of a chicken. So far, so good. Next a snow scene is flashed to the left of the dot and is registered in the right hemisphere. The patient then uses his left hand to point to a card showing a snow shovel. But in this case of severed hemispheres, the verbal left hemisphere has only seen the claw, but is faced with verbalizing why the left hand choose the shovel card. The patient responds with a creative rationalization, "The chicken claw goes with the chicken and you need a shovel to clean out the chicken shed" (72).

Humans seem to like to have reasons for what they do even if the reasons were not actually involved. Perhaps this is why the neoclassical story is so popular. "The normal human is compelled to interpret real behaviors and to construct a theory as to why they have occurred" (Gazzaniga 1985: 74). And, once we have conscious reasons, we are much more likely to be overconfident in predictions of our behavior. An experiment found that people who wrote down the reasons for their predictions were less accurate than the control group in predicting their actions (Wilson and LaFleur 1995).

Parts of the normal brain are connected, but not necessarily hierarchically or in such a way to avoid inconsistency. "The normal person does not possess a unitary conscious mechanism in which the conscious system is privy to the sources of all his or her actions" (Gazzaniga 1985: 74). The brain is composed of functionally specific circuits rather than only being a general cognitive machine whose reasoning is context-independent (Cosmides and Tooby 1994b: 64). Domain-specific circuits need not solve the combinatorial explosion of complexity, but can "fill in the blanks when perceptual evidence is lacking or difficult to obtain" (57). Matching the 30,000 items and prices in a grocery store to a preference map is an example of combinatorial explosion.

We are generally poor at solving general logic problems, but when they are reformulated in terms of social interactions, the same problem is more easily solved. The effect of context will be explored further below.

What are the possible manifestations of the modularity of the human brain and the evidence of the multiple self? This aspect of the brain is consistent with preference reversals and intransitivity among alternatives. It fits with the inconsistent behavior that is often observed.

Which is our true self? The one that is concerned about our weight and wants to diet or the one that just had a second helping of ice cream? Is it the one that wants to have money to buy gifts at Christmas time or the one who spends all income for instant gratification? Both are present, but it is institutions that can affect which self wins. For example, the University of Western Australia regularly gives extra money to employees just before Christmas. Many people join Christmas Savings Clubs where they put in monthly savings that earn little or no interest but the funds are difficult to withdraw. How do we explain this apparent irrational loss of opportunity? If people want money for Christmas why don't they just save it in a regular savings account? The Christmas Club is similar to Ulysses tying his hands to the mast. The planner brain defeats the action brain. If lots of other people are doing the same thing and congratulating the saver, the behavior is reinforced. Common knowledge of others' behavior makes a difference (Chwe 2001). This is what institutions do.

Many US states have laws that permit cancellation of a consumer purchase contract within X days. If we were of one mind and had perfect information, this institution would have little impact.

The multiple self creates problems for public policy and collective choice. There are many instances of people who, acting alone as individuals, do one thing and yet vote for another thing in collective choice. Often evidence of the former is used to argue that big government is out of hand and defeating individual liberty. But it can also be seen as the individual's planner brain defeating the individual's action brain.

3.1.3 Evolutionary psychology

Economics must be built on a firm foundation of behavioral science – how the brain works (Cory 1999). The brain is a physical thing of neural circuits, electrical charges and chemicals. Thinking is a product of the chemicals present and creates new ones. (Franklin 1987) insists that mind and matter are the same thing. Knowing something about the evolution of the brain gives insight into how it works. Cosmides and Tooby (1997) sum up the findings of research in evolutionary psychology saying "all normal human minds reliably develop a standard collection of reasoning and regulatory circuits that are functionally specialized and, frequently, domain-specific. These circuits organize the way we interpret our experiences, inject certain recurrent concepts and motivations into our mental life, and provide universal frames of meaning that allow us to understand the actions and intentions of others. Beneath the level of surface variability, all humans share certain views and assumptions about the nature of the world and human action by virtue of these human universal reasoning circuits." Paraphrasing Cosmides and Tooby (1997), these principles emerge which are consistent with the limited information processing capacity and modular brain conceptions:

1. The brain is a physical system and its circuits are designed to generate behavior that is appropriate to environmental circumstances.
2. Our neural circuits were designed by natural selection to solve problems that our ancestors faced during our evolutionary history.
3. Consciousness is just the tip of the iceberg.
4. Different neural circuits are specialized for solving different adaptive problems.
5. Our modern skulls house a Stone Age mind.

The human brain is more than a logic machine. It may be described as capable of recognizing patterns to which some appropriate action is attached. It can leap to conclusions and action without anything that we would ordinarily call thought. We would have been eaten by the lions long ago if we had to calculate the probability that a shadow in the bush was dangerous. Such intuitive skill is valuable in evolution so it is hard to label it as irrational, even though it can get us into trouble, at which point it gets labeled as emotional and rash. Once these patterns get embedded, they may resist change. They seem more rooted in past neural connections and chemicals than in any forward calculation of costs and benefits.

3.2 Emotions and Evaluation

People's minds react to things and other people. "The brain continuously constructs an affective or hedonic commentary on the current state of affairs . . ." (Kahneman 1999: 7). This commentary need not be conscious (Zajonc 1997). Things and people bring pleasure or pain and we seek or avoid them. These hedonic reactions are usefully thought of along a good/bad dimension. Economists speak of utility as the starting point for calculated rationality, bounded or full. But, pleasure–pain is itself not calculated in any means–ends relationship, but is the material of calculation or direct action. To say that emotions have an element of unconsciousness is not to say that they are independent of experience (Nussbaum 2001).

Elster (1998) provides a list of emotions: anger, hatred, guilt, shame, pride, liking, regret, joy, grief, envy, malice, indignation, jealousy, contempt, disgust, fear, and love. At first glance these things (except for liking) seem of a different order than the utility derived from goods and services for which economists construct demand curves with prices and quantities. But, an institutional economics must integrate them.

Consider the experimental experience with ultimatum games (Roth 1995); (Camerer and Thaler 1995). A "Proposer" is given a sum of money and makes a proposal to split the money with the "Respondent." If it is accepted, the money is split accordingly. If it is rejected, neither party gets anything. Experimental results show that offers of less that 20 percent to the Respondent are frequently rejected. If a single metric were involved and more is always preferred to less, any proposal however small would be accepted. Money, pride, disgust or whatever are all given a hedonic valence, but not necessarily commensurable. It is not useful to call one of these an economic variable and exclude the others or to call the value valence of money a matter of rational thought and the valence of pride or fairness as an emotion. All are emotions and many are hard-wired.[3] This is not to say that learning is absent or that there is no feedback from the environment.

The modal offer of Proposers is between 40 and 50 percent. Does this reflect a preference for fairness? This would imply that all values are commensurate. But, some values are irreducible, context dependent, and incommensurable (Huigens 2001). The fact that behavior involves a consequential tradeoff (for example, money vs. pride or fairness) does not prove that these values were commensurate and the basis for the behavior. The various consequences were nominally "priced," but these prices may have had nothing to do with the behavior and may not reveal preferences. The behavior may have been cued by such contingencies as availability and anchoring (see below) or the result of habits and norms. Things can be compared without being commensurable. The comparison may be rational, considered, and influenced by experience without being ultimately commensurable. The frequent observation that similar situations with respect to prices and incomes produce different behaviors may not have anything to do with preferences, current or past, but rather with differences in cues, contingencies, and context. Understanding these differences for a population may be more predictive than assuming behavior will be the same over time if prices and incomes are the same. Revealed preference (commensurabilty) must be an empirical matter and not an axiom.

"Well-being and experienced quality of life are emotional notions . . ." (Frijda 1999: 190). Cognitive scientists distinguish sheer liking, as in "I like this odor," from desire and a disposition for action, but this is a continuum rather than either/or. Emotions are feeling states of positive or negative valence, but not necessarily commensurable along a single metric. One dimension is autonomic arousal; such things as increased heart rate, sweating, or blushing. This may be related to responses to events and things that define the identity and self-image of a person. "Emotions are elicited primarily by events or contingencies considered relevant to the actual or expected achievement of or harm to major goals, motives, and values" (Frijda 1999: 192). Nussbaum (2001: 19) argues that emotions "involve judgments about important things, judgments in which, appraising an external object as salient for our own well-being, we acknowledge our own neediness and incompleteness before parts of the world that we do not fully control." When these goals, motives and values are interrupted, there can be emotional upheavals. Strong emotions take precedence over habitual behavior, call our attention to phenomena, and may be the context for rethinking behavior or non-deliberative reaction. Strong emotions may or not be mediated by conscious deliberation. "Consciousness is not an essential mediator of human behavior because behavior can occur in elaborate, lawful, and predictable patterns without consciousness" (Baumeister and Sommer 1997). "People's introspection about the causes of their own behavior lead them to under-appreciate the influence of visceral factors and to exaggerate the importance of higher-level cognitive processes" (Loewenstein 2000). Feelings can trigger behavior without any conscious calculation such as that implied by standard consumer theory.

Whether one calls solving the question of response to a dictator game, or of what to have for dinner, or of which car or house to buy, or what job to take as having emotional content, they all have economic content and stem from the mind's feelings of right–wrong, good–bad, pleasure–pain about things and people. Whether tangible, intangible, or human relationships, all sensations get converted to feelings stored as chemicals and electric charges (Carter 1998); (Franklin 1987).

Emotions are triggered by beliefs (Elster 1998). They provide a meaning and sense of direction to life. Social learning and norms influence the generation of valuations and behavioral responses to them (Knight and North 1997). "We do not perceive our sense data raw; they are mediated through a highly learned process of interpretation and acceptance" (Boulding 1961: 14).

Can we speak only of the quality of means and not ends? Sen (1977) asks if we have become "Rational Fools." Without valuation, there is nothing to be rational about. Feelings of pleasure–pain and good–bad (preferences) are a product of the brain as is the limited ability to logically relate costs and preferences. Calculation is just one of the brain processes that is cued by making meaning of the environment (sensing patterns), just as any other action and behavior. Feeling and calculation are a nexus wherein each defines the other. Elster (1998) suggests a dual role of emotion. It can replace calculation and it can alter the values used in the calculation. If the previous values are seen to be the result of feeling (evaluation), then we have emotion 1 changing emotion 2 in an interacting evolution and learning.

Anger may cause cessation of calculation of benefits and costs (stopping search rule) as when a person pursues a court action against a wrong-doer even when the cost of proceeding exceeds the benefits of recovering damages. This sanctioning of norm violation may be an innate predisposition. This can be seen as a departure from normal logical behavior. But, logical behavior is with reference to some set of values that are also the product of feeling, an emotion. Again, logic (rationality) and emotion (feeling and evaluation) constitute a nexus. It makes no sense to speak of balancing emotion and rationality when rationality is about implementing emotions.

If preferences are learned and changing, it makes the testing of maximization intractable. Is a person acting irrationally or just from a changed set of preferences or contingencies? How can an economy be judged if resources can both be used for production to meet prior preferences or to alter those preferences? Rather than assume narrow self-interest, the supply of caring can be investigated, etc. The pragmatist believes that preferences are not fully formed until the act of investigating choice, making behavior contingent and contextual. The study of means may affect and create values. Pragmatic decision-making where the end is formed in the process of deciding is incompatible with theory that presumes value is fixed in advance and the only task is to calculate maximum utility.

Supra-rational theory cannot explain the presence of cooperation commonly observed in one-shot Prisoner's Dilemma situations (Field 2001). There are situations of interdependence investigated by game theorists where individual greed and the calculated gains from specialization and trade might drive the parties to Pareto-better equilibrium. But the one-shot Prisoner's Dilemma is not one of them. The dominant choice from each one trying to maximize acting alone results in an inferior outcome. Only if the commitment problem can be solved can the best payoff be achieved. Fortunately, learning to do the right thing is possible and often displayed, but is often lacking as well. The abandonment of isolated maximization might be labeled as an expression of passion. If so, it is a passion with a reason even if the participants are unaware of its utility (Frank 1988). There is also evidence of a predisposition toward some cooperation in situations similar to the one-shot Prisoner's Dilemma that is consistent with evolution at the population level (Field 2001).[4] The latter makes it possible for genetic traits to survive even if not favorable to the individual. Learning may complement genetic tendencies and account for differences in cooperation in different instances.

Policy prescriptions are influenced by conceptions of what is possible to expect of reason. Economists are deservedly proud of their advice that price will solve problems of excess demand as consumers maximize utility by shifting to substitutes. But perhaps this contributes to over confidence with respect to advising increased penalties for such problems as drugs, teen-age sex, and crime. Spending more on prisons has provided questionable deterrence. Where these penalties are not implementable, maximizing conceptions leave us empty handed. Most of us do the right thing because our pattern recognition cues the action and no alternative is on our thought agenda. Law sometimes can provide an imitable standard of behavior even when monitoring costs prevent sanctions. As in the case of the Prisoner's Dilemma, we can learn what is right even when no contracts can be prearranged or direct incentives provided.

Some theories built on substantive supra-rationality de-emphasize the role of institutions. Much of the theory of "rational expectations" suggests the futility of public policy as individuals see through the frame and intent of policy and thereby offset it. Cognitive theories however, emphasize the role of collective learning. Beginning with language and symbols we alter the consequences of inescapable uncertainties of nature and competition with shared institutions. Rational expectation theorists find that the stability of the economy is rooted in immutable individual preferences and decision rules of maximization. Others find it in collective action, institutions, and habits, some conscious and some unconscious. These latter constitute a macro-institutional foundation to individual choice and microeconomics.

3.3 Behavioral Regularities: Characteristics of the Agent

There are many behavioral regularities that are consistent with bounded rationality and the limited information processing capacity of the brain. Others are related to the modularity of the brain. The origin and bases for still others is less clear. By "regularities" it is suggested that these characteristics are generally true of a population in most instances. It does not imply that everyone exhibits them all the time.

3.3.1 The power of particulars and defaults

We generally ignore base-rates and category statistics when estimating the frequency of category. For example, new entrepreneurs consistently overestimate their chances for success. In spite of the fact that the majority of new businesses fail, four fifths of a sample of new entrepreneurs believed that their chance of success was greater than 70 percent and a third thought their success was certain. (Is this related to our inability to get all the facts, or just a general overconfidence in our exceptional ability?) As a general rule, we know that estimates of the cost of original projects are greatly underestimated. For example, the Sidney opera house was estimated to cost 7 million but actually cost 102 million. We tend to focus on the particulars that are anchored in our own plans. Kahneman calls this the "inside view" as opposed to the outside view where the case is a member of a category that has a baseline statistic that one could use as a starting point. Instead, the inside view seems more natural and we prefer to use our own plans and desires as a starting point.

Generally people are insensitive to prior probability of outcomes, to sample size, to predictability, and have misconceptions of chance, of validity, and regression to the mean (Tversky and Kahneman 1982b). For example, even professors often fail to interpret regression to the mean over a series of student exams.

3.3.2 Availability

We tend to evaluate categories by salient examples that are often based on a recent experience that comes quickly to mind. This may be a clever slogan which a politician or advertisement offers us. "A pervasive fact about human judgment is that people disproportionately weight salient, memorable, or vivid evidence even when they have better sources of information" (Rabin 1998: 30). Kahneman refers to this as the "availability heuristic." These behaviors are consistent with bounded rationality and save scarce mental capacity. For example, people tend to estimate the probability of a flood level by the most recent example they have experienced. We seem quite content to give small samples great confidence. People tend to believe in the "law of small numbers" rather than the "law of large numbers." People understate the resemblance of large samples to the universe from which they were drawn (Tversky and Kahneman 1982a).

3.3.3 Anchoring

A common heuristic for estimation is to make a preliminary estimate (the anchor) and adjust it using other information considered relevant. Even if an initially conceived or given value is arbitrary, it has an effect on subsequent estimates. (For a survey of the literature see Camerer 1995.) When we extend our experience over time we generally make faulty estimates. For example, when construction workers estimate the probability of injury in one year they report 34 percent. When the time is extended to four years, the estimated rate was only 43 percent. When taxpayers are asked of the probability of a tax audit in two years time, they reported 28 percent. When the time was extended to eight years, the estimate was only slightly larger at 35 percent (Fetherstonhaugh 1997). Proportionate adjustments seem quite easy in isolation, but in the daily press of time we do not make these adjustments well.

Faulty extensions create problems in surveys of demand (contingent valuation) for high exclusion cost goods. For example, the value of 57 wilderness areas was only 34 percent higher than for one (McFadden and Leonard 1993). The value of saving 12 lives was only 20 percent higher than four (Jones-Lee and Loomis 1995). It is possible that this reflects a rapidly diminishing marginal utility for the extra quantity, but this does not seem to fit our experience. It saves brainpower to make only a small adjustment from our base estimate.

Limited brain capacity means that we cannot make all possible comparisons. The value of a product is evaluated on its own relative to some limited set of alternatives that are evoked in the context and framed by the environment of the particular case. So if people are asked their willingness to pay for product X and then for product Y, the relative values may be of a different order than if the two products were put up together for choice. Explicit comparisons can yield preference reversals. For example, people in Chicago were asked what they would pay for improvement of air quality in the Grand Canyon. Then another sample from the same population was asked what they would pay for air quality improvement in Chicago at the same time that they were asked what they would pay for improvement in the Grand Canyon. The valuations for the Grand Canyon alone were significantly higher than when people were asked to make an explicit comparison (Hoehn and Randall 1989). If our brain could attach values to every conceivable product and hold these values in memory, then all comparisons have already been made and reminders of particular tradeoffs would not have any effect. No general preference order exists. Institutions are one source of anchors and reference points.

Institutions can affect which behavior is seen as the reference point by the designation of the default option. For example, two levels of rights to sue for auto accidents are available in insurance policies in New Jersey and Pennsylvania. The lower level of course is cheaper to buy. Limited rights to sue is the default option in

New Jersey and if you want more coverage, you must ask for it. The reverse is the case in Pennsylvania. Seventy percent of New Jersey insurance buyers choose limited rights, while only 16 percent do so in Pennsylvania where they had to make an effort to get the lower rights and lower cost (V. Johnson 1993). The frame provided by the default made a difference. It is hard to imagine that drivers in the two states have such fundamentally different preferences. It is also hard to imagine that the opportunity cost of the effort to ask for the lower cost insurance explains the difference. It is not that we calculated that we had a better use for our time, but rather that the default is such a powerful anchor that no calculation is made at all. Such is the stuff of fortunes. Insurance companies made an extra 200 million dollars in revenue because of the Pennsylvania institution. (For another example, see Bernatzi and Thaler 1995.)

Which insurance option reflects the true demand of insurance buyers? The question is misleading. Both demands are real, just different. Demand for alternatives is necessarily influenced by context since the brain cannot compare everything. The only choice is which context.

Both formal and informal institutions provide context. We learn the salience of a context growing up in a culture. Schelling (1978) provides the example of many people who become separated in New York City will go to Grand Central Station to rejoin their friends or family. It comes easily to mind because of myth, story, and film. A French couple separated in New York might not have a salient point. These reference points may be terribly inefficient in the sense that in this case the parties may discover their separation when at a great distance from Grand Central, but it is much better than wandering about at random.

3.3.4 Experience over time: evaluation by representative moments

The only experience that can inform today's choices is what can be remembered. But, "Judgment tasks that require integration of perceptual experience over time are difficult" (Kahneman 1999, 15). The summary representation of experience over time leading to continuation, cessation, or indifference toward an activity is a normative construction subject to limited information processing capacity. We are not able to apply weights to all the moments and sum them. Rather, we seem to select representative moments. Representation of experience over time is heavily influenced by peak and end valuation. Duration is relatively neglected (19). For example, in an experiment, people place their hand in mild cold. One episode was short – 60 seconds at 14 degrees C. The second was long at 60 seconds at the same 14 degrees plus 30 seconds at a slightly warmer 15 degrees. When asked which they would rather repeat, two-thirds preferred the long experience (Kahneman et al. 1993). We seem to distort peak memory.

Are different parts of the brain involved in memory, current experience, and calculating the future and are they imperfectly related? If so, which one is in charge? Can institutions affect the result? This is something that consumers can watch for and sellers take advantage of. Perhaps the idea is captured by the show business advice to leave them laughing and they will forget all the mediocre jokes in between.

Business and politicians can take advantage of the fact that "satisfaction judgments typically refer to a broad domain of life rather than to a single experience, and the anchor of a satisfaction scale is a standard of acceptability or aspiration level, not an adaptation level" (Kahneman 1999: 21). "Reports of subjective happiness are highly susceptible to manipulations that attract attention to particular domains of life" (21–2).

3.3.5 Predicting pleasure–pain

How good are we at predicting our pleasure? How many times have you achieved some good and found that it did not satisfy (not because of faulty construction, but because it was not as exciting as you supposed)? We tend to underestimate our learning and adaptive capacities and thus our future mental state. Kahneman observes what he calls a "focusing illusion." Whenever you focus on an aspect of life, you exaggerate its importance (Kahneman 1999: 16). For example, when people are asked to estimate what percentage of the time a paraplegic is in a good mood, people who do not know a paraplegic give much lower estimates than those familiar with a paraplegic (Brickman, Coates, and Janoff-Bulman 1978). We tend to focus on distinctive aspects of a good and fail to predict how we might allocate our attention over time. This has implications for contingent valuation surveys which call attention to a particular good.

This is involved in a phenomenon observed in chapter 2, namely the non-reversibility of demand curves. When we experience a substitute for a good replaced when its price rose, we are not the same person anymore. We are now focused on the replacement good and have only a remembered utility of the old good.

Most who play the lottery expect that winning would make them deliriously happy. But, the reported satisfaction of lottery winners suggests that people are not good at predicting pleasure. Lottery winners were not significantly happier than a control group (Brickman, Coates, and Janoff-Bulman 1978). People in all states of the US believe that people in California are happier. But psychological tests do not support it. We can become habituated to a wide range of situations. It is departure from our new reference level that has the greatest effect on satisfaction. (The neo-classical model of fixed indifference curves of utility yields the deductive conclusion that utility must increase if the budget constraint is reduced. Since it is a deduction, no empirical evidence can challenge the conclusion. Yet, as noted above, when people are asked, they do not necessarily report increased satisfaction. The logic is sound, but the model premises are wrong.)

The endowment effect documented by Loewenstein and Adler (1995) is another example of behavior changing with experience. Once a good is experienced, its value changes and willingness to pay differs from willingness to accept. Losses of some goods can't be offset by gains in other goods of equal dollar value (Knetsch 1989; Thaler 1980). It is also an example of a framing effect and social capital and loss aversion. It is often claimed that dollars give us unique measures of the value of market goods as compared to the soft indicators of the value of non-marketed goods. This claim may be misplaced as both are contextual and contingent.

The endowment effect and loss aversion (avoidance of regret) are often interpreted as bounded rationality phenomena. But Huigens (2001: 554) argues, "because values arise from diverse and discrete practical contexts, they often are intransitive."

Knowing what goods increase our utility or satisfaction is problematic (Mantzavinos 2001: 197–203). In the face of uncertainty, consumers develop routines. Consumption is a "matter of learning about, choosing among, and creating routines" (Langlois and Cosgel 1998). Consumers selectively perceive of consumption opportunities, classify them, and apply a routine behavior that was worked out in the past – produced a satisficing result. If the environment is perceived as new, the consumer must experiment until a new routine emerges. This process is social to a large extent as people imitate others. Product innovators are trying to guess how their product might fit into present consumer routines or might stimulate a new one.

3.3.6 Time-variant preferences

"Casual observation, introspection, and psychological research all suggest that the assumption of time-consistency is importantly wrong. Our short term tendency to pursue immediate gratification is inconsistent with our long term preferences" (Rabin 1998: 38). This can't be represented by discounting exponentially over time.

There are lots of cases where a good will be sought if available, but our longer term experience and meta-preference may be to remove the good from our temptation by collective choice (prohibition of sales). One self violates the freedom of the other self. The fact that some people have different meta-preferences further makes it look like a violation of freedom when the majority use collective choice.

Simple assumptions are not useful. Where and what people maximize and where and why they use other behaviors are empirical questions. The constancy of preferences is also an empirical issue. And the facts are hypothesized to be heavily dependent on institutions. Institutions are particularly relevant for meta-preferences – our preferences for preferences. It is here that we can think about what adaptations to our environment we want to make and which of our possible selves we want to win.

3.3.7 When a dollar is not a dollar

It would be very convenient for analysis if money tracked satisfaction (psychological states) and if money values were easily netted and summed in psychological terms. Alas, this is often not the case. "Overwhelming evidence shows that humans are often more sensitive to how their current situation differs from some reference level than to the absolute characteristics of the situation" (Rabin 1998, citing Helson 1964).

Gains and losses. The value function is not symmetrical over gains and losses (Kahneman and Tversky 1979). A dollar of loss is psychologically greater than a dollar gain. What is perceived as a loss is contextually influenced (subject to internal or external manipulation). An asymmetrical value function is consistent with observed differences between willingness to sell and willingness to buy. A person who has a good in hand often would require more compensation to part with it than they would be willing to pay for it if not already in hand, even if the wealth effect is marginal.

Regrets of omission and commission: There is an asymmetry between action and inaction even if the dollar consequences are the same. This is illustrated in the following experiment. Mr. Paul owned shares in company A. During the past year he considered switching to stock in company B, but he decided against it. He now finds that he would have been better off by $20,000 if he had switched. In contrast, Mr. George owned shares in company B. During the past year he switched to stock in company A. He now finds he would have been better off by $20,000 if he had kept the stock of company B. People are asked whether Mr. Paul or Mr. George would be the most upset. More choose Mr. George even though the lost opportunity for both is equal (Kahneman and Tversky 1982). The apparent default is inaction and we can live with it better than acting and making a mistake. Default choices reduce regret. Defaults are culturally learned or formally structured by legal institutions. In a community of gamblers, aggressive action might be the default. Rules can be set up which make an action the default and effort must be made to cancel it.

Risky choice: The experimental evidence suggests several tendencies (Kahneman and Tversky 1979; 1982):

1. There is risk aversion for gains with moderate or high probability.
2. Lotteries are attractive with large gains of low probability.
3. Insurance is attractive for large losses of low probability. (True of fire but not flood because of greater familiarity with fire.)
4. Sure things are given much weight.
5. There is risk loving over losses when the probability of losing nothing is increased.

Much of the seminal work in this area was done by Allais. He gained his insight working for the Algerian Office of Mining Research where the problem was to make "a reasonable compromise between the mathematical expectation of the gains that might be expected and the probability of ruin" (Allais 1979: 451). Mining exploration is like "a lottery with the tickets costing several hundred million and prizes of several hundred billion francs . . .". If you could explore long enough you could get your money back handsomely, but run the risk of ruin before. Allais observed a very strong preference for security in the neighborhood of certainty once the sums become substantial (441). This behavior is quite different from the maximization of expected value computed by weighting outcomes by their probability and summing. It is common to find that "The ultra-cautious will purely and simply eliminate all random prospects for which the probability of ruin exceeds a certain threshold value" (92).

Allais concludes, "it would be wrong to consider a game as psychologically attractive if the mathematical expectation of the monetary values involved is positive" (50).

It may not be so if cardinal utility does not rise linearly with monetary gains. People care about the shape of the probability distribution of psychological values, and in particular, of their dispersion (second moments). To understand behavior, analysts must consider the "pleasure – or aversion – inherent in the fact of taking a risk, i.e. in taking part in games in which different shapes of the distribution of the psychological values are possible." "The pleasure or aversion attaching to risk-taking constitutes an additional element which modifies the results derived from the pure calculation based on a simple probability weighting (objective or subjective) of the psychological values to be drawn from the different outcomes possible" (52–3).

The dispersion of psychological values is the key fact of the psychology of risk. Maximizing the mathematical expectation of a monetary gain is often irrelevant. The psychological value of the dispersion of values is important in itself. "Most individuals are, in practice, sensitive to the existence of the possibility of great losses or great gains." "The mere existence of these losses or gains is an intrinsically important fact in itself" (54). Conclusion: "It would be wrong, therefore, to neglect the dispersion of psychological values even in the frame of a first approximation; indeed, I contend that this factor is the specific characteristic of the psychology of risk" (55).

Thaler (1996: 229) observes, "Most people can be fooled into violating the substitution axiom in the Allais paradox, but few would agree to a long series of bets that risk bankruptcy, no matter how attractive each bet looks." "Following the rule 'don't accept an offer that looks too good to be true' protects people from disaster (at the cost of passing up an occasional really good deal)." Here the role of cultural institutions is demonstrated. Thaler uses this observation to destroy the argument that people must be rational to survive in the long run.

There appears to be some multiple selves operating in risky choices. On the one hand there is a high risk aversion and on the other people display an optimism bias and take a lot of risks in some areas such as exhibited by the high rate of small business failure.

Loss aversion is subject to framing. Allais observed that people make inconsistent choices between probability weighted outcomes in some cases. The following choice situation developed by Robin Dawes illustrates what has become known as the Allais Paradox, though Allais regarded it as something to be expected and not paradoxical. A person is offered two pairs of choices. In the first there are 100 balls in an urn of which 89 are red, 10 blue and 1 black. With choice A, the blindfolded person gets a one million dollar payoff if she draws a ball of any color. With choice B, the person gets one million if the ball is red, 2.5 million if blue and nothing if black. In the second game the payoffs are slightly different. Choice C gives red, nothing; blue or black, 1 million. Choice D gives red, nothing, blue 2.5 million, and black, nothing. In repeated experiments, most people choose A in the first game and D in the second. Choice D in the second game maximizes expected utility (probability weighted outcome), but the popular choice A in the first game does not. This is consistent with the generalization that people have difficulty utilizing probability weightings. Since the payoff if red is drawn is the same in both games, it should not logically affect choice. That leaves only the blue and black payoffs. Since they are equal in both games, if a person prefers A to B in game one, they should prefer C to D in the second. The typical inconsistent choice suggests that the difference in the red payoff between the two games is affecting the way the choice is framed. The difference is presumed to be one of possible regret that is created in B of game one and not in D of game 2 since there is another zero payoff possibility in that game. People might feel ashamed to get nothing while going for the extra payoff in game one, but less so going for it in game two. The consequences of drawing the black ball are numerically the same in the two games, but psychologically different.

The result is consistent with the idea that people try to avoid regret, and regret appears much larger when you forgo a sure thing while seeking a large gain (related to the weighting of omission and commission and loss aversion noted above).

3.3.8 Perception of differences

One regularity that seems hard-wired is that the minimally perceptible difference of an absolute change in magnitude is proportional to the original magnitude. This hard-wired regularity is known as the Weber-Fechner Law. A given change in the intensity of light may be imperceptible from a bright light and easily discerned when the change is from a dim light. With respect to economics, we may ignore a saving of $10 on a $1,000 item but travel across town to save the same amount on a $30 item. The psychological value of a dollar depends on the context.

3.3.9 Sunk costs

Teachers of freshman economics delight in showing students that sunk costs should be ignored. For maximum monetary gain, bygones are bygones and the only thing that counts is the return to the margin of further effort. If marginal revenue is less than marginal cost, the investment should be abandoned. In spite of the lesson, people find it very hard to do. There is something more at stake than monetary gain. One would have to admit to a mistake, and that is hard to do. Robert Frank (1997: 245) tells the story of the faculty member who has reserved an indoor tennis court by paying a fee. When the time arrives, the weather is beautiful. While the professor prefers to play outside rather than in, he nevertheless plays inside. If asked, the professor would probably say that his standard operating procedure is to always get his money's worth. He gets more for the sunk cost by playing inside. This behavior is exhibited in the stock market when a stock suffers a loss and the prospects for recovery seem dim. Nevertheless, many will hold on in the rather vain hope that their original judgment will be vindicated. Most of us feel that we have not suffered a loss until the stock is sold, so the loss can be postponed.

Something of the same phenomenon occurs in what Boulding (1973) called the "sacrifice trap." A case in point is a bloody war that can't be won. Nevertheless we struggle on because to stop would be to admit that we made a mistake upon entry. Worse, it cheapens the sacrifice we have already made. To stop is to signal that the past deaths were in vain. Better more deaths than to admit a mistake seems to prevail. Self-regard is a powerful motivator.

3.3.10 Confirmatory bias

Some selective perception is unavoidable. However, there are systematic biases. "A range of research suggests that once forming strong hypotheses, people are often too inattentive to new information contradicting their hypotheses. Once you become convinced that one investment strategy is more lucrative than another, you may not sufficiently attend to evidence suggesting the strategy is flawed" (Rabin 1998: 26). (See also Bruner and Potter 1964.) As noted above, this may be related to the maintenance of self-image (identity) as a person who is quick in sizing up a situation and gets it right the first time. It is a social relationship when it involves saving face. Many are subject to "hindsight bias." "We knew it all along." (Fischoff 1975.) This has implications for predicting future happiness (see section 3.3.5 above).

3.3.11 Selfishness and regard

Humans may like themselves best, but the extent is an empirical question. And, the definition of self is learned. We make transfers and do not exploit our advantage to the fullest to let others have more. We tip in frequently visited restaurants about as much as restaurants in another city. Tipping is a learned institution where most of us do not calculate advantage, but do what fits the situation. As noted above (section 3.2), when we play ultimatum games, the modal split of the pot is 50:50 (Andreoni and Miller 1996; Guth and Tietz 1990). If the controllers were completely selfish, they would offer only a token. Norms and moral judgments are made.

People donate to the provision of high exclusion cost goods and volunteer to conserve natural resources (Train, McFadden, and Goett 1987). Leaders emerge to provide a high exclusion cost good when there is little personal reward except the feeling that the cause is good (Schmid and Soroko 1997).

Many entitlements are learned over time. When enough people begin to regard an outcome as their right, it is often respected by others even if not officially enforceable. These rights are reinforced by shows of indignation and other subtle punishments often with the help of third parties. Equity theory suggests that people feel that those who put in more effort should have more claim on output (Berscheid, Boye, and Walster 1968). But, it is institutions that shape what we regard as "more effort."

Human association can be sought in itself and not only as a means to other goods. "As social animals we humans have a powerful urge to belong – to feel attached to others in close relationships. . . . When needs for close relationships are met, through supportive friendships or marriage, people enjoy better physical and emotional quality of life" (Myers 1999: 374). "People in every human society belong to groups and prefer and favor 'us' over 'them'" (375). We may be self-regarding, but our sense of self can include others. While we seek the regard of others, it is curious that something that appears to be cheap to supply is so carefully hoarded by those who could give it.

3.3.12 Fairness

Market conditions often create a situation where demand or supply changes abruptly from some base point. This base point contains some understanding that a firm is entitled to a profit and workers and consumers are entitled to reasonable wages and products. When the conditions occur where the firm could reap a large gain, there are widely held rules and expectations of what is fair and moral behavior (Kahneman, Knetsch, and Thaler 1986). These are: (a) a firm should not impose losses on others to gain itself; (b) a firm need not share its gains otherwise; (c) a firm may impose losses on others to protect itself. These rules are exhibited in the following experiments. A particular automobile model is in short supply. There is some general reference point price for the model. If the firm eliminates a prior discount, 42 percent regard it as fair, but if the firm adds a surcharge, 71 percent regard it as unfair.

In the case of a firm whose profits have stopped rising, only 20 percent regard it as unfair to eliminate a bonus, but 62 percent regard it as unfair to reduce wages by 5 percent. In the case of a profitable firm that finds itself in a labor market with much unemployment, 77 percent regard it as unfair to cut wages 5 percent. In contrast, a firm that has been losing money and cuts wages 5 percent is regarded as unfair by only 32 percent. This institutional norm will be investigated further in another chapter where labor markets, sticky wages, and business cycles will be explored.

With respect to the rules for making rules, there is experimental evidence that people prefer decision-making procedures that give all parties equal opportunity to influence outcomes (Tyler 1990).

3.3.13 Satiation

Can we ever be too rich? For some the answer is no, but for many there are limits. A study of New York City cab drivers shows that drivers work shorter hours on good days (Camerer 1997). The drivers report that they have income goals and when they are reached, they stop. The behavior is consistent with the model of asymmetrical gains and losses. Any gain over the goal is not regarded as an opportunity cost, while shortfalls stimulate extra effort. There are not many jobs where the worker can choose hours worked. Some argue that modern capitalism and industrialism were invented to prevent people from choosing the length of their own work week and force people into a take it or leave it choice (Marglin 1974).

3.3.14 Surprise and boredom

Much effort goes into reducing uncertainty, but in the mixed bag that constitutes humanity we also prize surprise. Scitovsky (1976) observes that humans exhibit a need to relieve boredom by pursuing activities for their own sake. Alfred Marshall mentioned science, literature, the arts, sports, and travel as examples. The problem with these is that they require skill to enjoy. How do you know if some skill is worth acquiring until after you have acquired it? It is easy to try sweets to see if you like it, but a quick bite of literature or chess tells little. Scitovsky (1998) argues that as modern technologies have made life easier they have also made it less challenging and thus boring. He cites the increase of adventure sports as a seeking to re-inject danger and challenge to relieve boredom. He and others also suggest that aggression of all types from wars to gangs to watching crime on TV is an attempt to relieve boredom that requires little skill to utilize. Boredom may be part of a hedonic treadmill in which some demand greater and greater increments of income or other experiences to overcome boredom. (See below, section 3.5.4.)

3.3.15 Framing inputs

The human brain is constantly facing new experiences and is challenged to fit an action to it. There is often no directly applicable experience to rely on. We have to make a jump from the new situation to something similar where we know what to do. This jump may be conscious or unconscious. In which box (category) will the new experience be placed? This process can be quite different from one individual to another, but there still seem to be regularities. Different frames for a choice problem are like new experiences. If they go in one box, a certain value and action gets attached, but if put into a different box, a different action ensues. From some of the examples above, we know that preference reversal is exhibited when the same objective choice is presented in different frames. For example, experiments have presented people with the following paired choices of health programs with different consequences:

A. 200 people will be saved.
B. 1/3 probability that 600 people will be saved.
   2/3 probability that no people will be saved.

Or,

C. 400 people will die.
D. 1/3 probability that nobody will die.
   2/3 probability that 600 people will die.

Experiments consistently exhibit people choosing A in the first set but D in the second. In terms of outcomes of living and dying, options A and C are equal and if A is preferred in the first set, C should be preferred in the second. Living, dying, and dread cues may be placed in different boxes and different experiences and emotions may come to bear.

The agenda or menu affects choice even when containing what objectively appears to be irrelevant alternatives. While people are often unaware that the menu of choices influences their decisions, (Simonson and Tversky 1992) note that at other times decision-makers explicitly rationalize their choices with references to their choice sets. For instance, people may state explicitly that a given choice is a compromise between two other choices. Indeed, such findings suggest an alternative to the utility-maximization framework that may help explain framing effects, preference reversals, and context effects: people may make choices in part by asking themselves whether they have a "reason" to choose one option over another (Shafir, Simonson, and Tversky 1993). An apparently irrelevant alternative can provide that reason. Recall the role that reasons play discussed above in section 3.1.2.

Rabin (1998: 37) concludes, "More than confusing people in pursuit of stable underlying preferences, the 'frames' may in fact partially determine a person's preferences." The basic processes of learning to make sense of our environment are explored in the next section.

To summarize, some of the above behavioral regularities involve mistakes and biases, such as estimating frequencies that are knowable. Even here, use of the term bias may not be appropriate. Some regularities such as weighing losses more than gains are valuational and while violating the strict rational choice model, it seems presumptive to say this behavior is biased any more than other valuations a person makes such as attitudes toward fairness or satiation. Some economists (Thaler 1992) refer to departures from maximization as "anomalies." Far from being a deviation from the common, they are to be expected. When what constitutes maximization is clear and can be pointed out, people will choose it and the anomalies often disappear (Frey 2001: 12). But, if you point out that they weight losses greater than gains, they may reply, "So what?"

3.4 Behavioral Law and Economics

Many of the behavioral tendencies noted above have implications for the behavior of judges, juries, and citizens (Korobkin and Ulen 2000; Sunstein 2000). These include such things as complexity, ambiguity, availability and representativeness, anchoring and adjustment, overconfidence and self-serving biases, and hindsight bias. The context of judicial decision makes a difference for judges, juries, and citizens.

A behavioral approach to law and economics produces some different hypotheses than the standard model. For example, if people are only motivated by self-interest they will violate laws when there are not effective sanctions. But if they are motivated by a moral standard or care for others, they will follow the law even if it is not in their narrow self-interest. For other applications, see Jolls, Sunstein, and Thaler 1998; Scott 2001; and Dallas forthcoming.

3.5 Learning

Humans in their daily lives as consumers and producers have the same problem as a research scientist, that is to make sense out of their environment and to act upon it (Mantzavinos (2001) following Popper). Things happen, we act, things happen. We are taking in sense information, acting, taking in more sense information and are either at rest, continuing, or escaping. Two basic psychological processes will be explored here: a model of stimulus, behavior, and reinforcement; and a complementary model of cues and patterns. Both are consistent with human evolution and what we know about the brain.

3.5.1 Stimulus, behavior, and reinforcement

The learning process may be conceptualized in terms of stimulus, behavior, and reinforcement (SBR) (Skinner 1971). Stimulus might be hunger, a change in price of a consumer or producer good, a change in inventories, market share, stock prices, a labor strike, or refusal of a child to eat her dinner. Behavior is forthcoming which may change something in the environment. The feedback either reinforces the behavior or alters it. People learn.

Skinner was an experimentalist who altered the content and timing of the feedback and observed the change in subsequent behavior. He was satisfied if he could learn how to modify behavior. He could teach pigeons to walk a maze or make a figure eight or children to stop bedwetting by altering the way the environment responded to the subject's behavior. Skinner felt that the way the brain worked to connect environment and behavior could not be observed so he did not try to explain why one type of feedback worked and another did not. He did, however, observe a difference between positive and negative reinforcers.

Skinner took advantage of the natural variation in behavior. When a segment of action occurred that he wanted to have repeated, he would experiment with delivering different reinforcers until he found one that worked. This "Thomas Edison approach" did not appeal to many researchers' sense of science. Skinner did observe that things we generally regard as good are stronger reinforcers than when our environment punishes us for a behavior. Giving a subject food after a behavior desired by the experimenter was more likely to cause the previous behavior to continue than a punishment would cause the undesired behavior to cease. This is consistent with the observation above that a dollar is not a dollar. A dollar reward is psychologically not the same as a dollar fine in its effect on subsequent behavior.

Punishment for a behavior does reduce that behavior. But, it frequently only suppresses it with the subject being resentful, devious, looking for ways to continue without detection, etc. On the other hand, reward for a behavior is more likely to continue that behavior. We can speak of the behavior being internalized in the habit of the subject.[5] It seems natural and the thing to do. The subject is less likely to calculate how the prior behavior could be continued and still in some sense get away with it. The reward can't be too obvious as people resent being manipulated even with good things.

The SBR model is a backward looking model in the sense that current behavior is a product of past experience. It is unconscious learning. This has fundamental implications for public policy. Much policy to alter behavior is designed to alter the flow of cost and benefits. (One felicitous phrase is the challenge to find incentive compatible institutions.) So we fine and jail drug dealers, firms with unsafe working conditions, terrorists, etc. Nations threaten each other with atomic bombs hoping to change their behavior. Or we subsidize a certain activity such as hiring the unemployed to make it more profitable. Contrary to SBR, these policies are built on a conception of behavior that is based on a calculation of advantage that would occur in the future. It involves "reasoning why" one behavior might be better than another in its future payoffs. Humans can make these calculations, but only some of the time. And, when they make them is in part habit.

In contrast to "reasoning why," the SBR model observes that behavior is in part unconsciously shaped by past experience – direct, vicarious, or imagined. Present behavior is not by chance, but the result of reinforcers supplied by the environment and given meaning by the person. Change the environment if you want to change behavior. When the person does what the policy designers want, follow with a positive reinforcer. So in the case of present or possible drug dealers, provide positive reinforcement when they exhibit non-dealing behavior. It works better if the reinforcement only comes with the desired behavior. If gold chains and designer jackets are reinforcers, then they must come from the environment when a young person is a serious student and not a drug dealer. This is not easy, which probably explains why punishment is so popular even if not very effective. This model leads to the hypothesis that if the firm with safe working conditions is praised and rewarded, more of this behavior will be forthcoming than if the same effort is directed to fines for unsafe conditions.

Behaviorism (that is, stimulus–response, which is not the same as SBR) is now out of fashion and labeled as reductionism. But, Skinner did not deny that there was a cognitive processing of information, he just thought he could not observe it, so he spoke little of motives and emotions. Now with PET scans of the brain, we have more insight into cognitive processes. We know what parts of the brain are active when the person says they are in a state of anger or fear for example. We have reason to believe that people are making cognitive evaluations of their relationship to things and other people. But, how does that help design behavior-changing institutions? For example, suppose a low-skilled person has experienced continuous lay-offs, low pay, and no respect from employers. After some time they are often depressed; they withdraw and stop trying to find work or improve their skills. (Incidentally, they are not counted as unemployed in US statistics.) They may not respond to stimulus of new opportunities that another person with different experience would run with. Penalizing a depressed person with threatened withdrawal of welfare benefits if they do not seek work or training may have no effect or even lead to mental breakdown or criminal activity. Skinner would try to find some variant in their behavior that is going in the right direction, small though it might be. Then he would experiment with various types and timing of feedback from the environment to find something that would reinforce and enlarge the desired behavior. When we are stuck in the limited policy options of increasing costs or subsidizing benefits, SBR at least offers other alternatives even if they proceed by trial and error. Can cognitive scientists proceed less blindly in altering the subject's learning?

An animal experiment with some parallels to the chronic unemployed above suggests the difficulty (Seligman 1975). A dog is placed in one side of a divided box. A shock is applied to the side where the dog is and the dog can escape by jumping the barrier. They quickly learn to avoid the shock. Other dogs are tied in a hammock and then subjected to a shock they cannot escape. When removed and put in the divided box, they do not quickly learn to escape. It is difficult to train them to jump even when not tied.

Seligman suggested that the animal had a mental image of hopelessness. The same might be said of the chronically unemployed. Is it useful to then say that the image causes the behavior? "The specifics of both feelings and behavior are determined by environmental circumstances. Both 'feeling good' and 'working hard' can be controlled by positive reinforcers, such as adequate pay, praise from supervisors, regular promotions, good relations with co-workers, and ability to do one's job effectively" (Nye 1992: 68) SBR findings are consistent with the conception that "preferences" evolve and change. Changed behavior can be created by more than a change in incentives (prices). Reinforcers and learning can change the underlying mental constructs that interact with prices. An adequate institutional economics must accommodate instinct, habit, learning, and conscious and unconscious reasoning. Implicit learning of a habitual character is ubiquitous in humans and higher animals (Reber 1993). Deliberation and consciousness evolved later and on top of more basic processes of learning (Cosmides and Tooby 1994a: 327). Mind, body, and environment are interdependent; so are intent and materialist causality. Action produces feedback and what might be termed belief, and belief provides the foundation for action. Reinforcement links the material and mental worlds.

Institutions shape individual behavior via reinforcement. Informal and formal institutions affect expectations that people have of an individual's behavior in a particular context. Thus, institutions shape the flow of reinforcers from the environment that either increase the probability that the behavior will be repeated or extinguished. This process can operate with different degrees of consciousness. Reinforcement is the process by which a society's dominant institutions are reproduced from one generation to another.

3.5.2 Cues and patterns

A widely known visual experiment involves a picture with small blocks of varying shades of gray. A first glance, the picture is like a lot of new experience, not meaningful. But all of a sudden, the image of Abraham Lincoln comes to mind. The blocks have cued a pattern to which meaning and action are attached (Margolis 1987). We leap to the conclusion of its meaning and act (verbalize its name). Many thought processes are like that. The incoming sensory information is organized by the brain into chunks, and meaning and action emerge without any conscious calculation of the pieces or alternative possibilities. There is nothing that might be termed "looking up choices." The world is simply too complex and our brain's processing capacity too limited to have a complete belief system and preference ordering like a book in our brain ready to be read. Thankfully, our brain takes in what it can and leaps to a conclusion. "The triggering of prior mental categories by some kind of input – whether sensory or more abstract – is," Hofstadter (2001) insists, "an act of analogy-making." Seeing Abraham Lincoln just "fits." It is not a matter of good enough or optimal search. It just fits. This leaping is our great strength and, of course, our great weakness, for often the leaps are into a chasm. These pattern responses can be in some sense quite dysfunctional, but nevertheless persist until something jolts us and the brain reorganizes. This leaping is often quite creative and imaginative. We can make up a meaning and our actions can create a world to make it in some sense come true.

Our brain tries to make sense out of complex new sensory inputs that it cannot possibly compare in detail to prior experience. It sees a pattern and in some sense fits an old understanding and habit to the new situation. For example, the role of public debt in an economy is a complex phenomenon about which even experts disagree. For many, a parallel is seen between private debt where they have some experience and public debt where they have none. This cued association probably explains why so many think public debt is undesirable. Opinion leaders seek these cues and intensify them. But while we can apply logic and observation to such phenomena, we really have no choice but to rely on these leaps of "understanding" for the great bulk of the world. Economists who specialize in such matters can use their scarce processing capacity to deconstruct this phenomenon, but this means they are using their cued imagination for a whole host of other phenomena just like everyone else. The process of "cues and fits" is consistent with satisficing.

The construction of meaning and order given to the environment can emerge from two processes. One is by making comparisons across what appear to be similar cases with similar characteristics. For example, public debt has some characteristics of private debt for which the individual has learned certain responses. The response to private debt is extended to the public. Or, the brain can construct meaning from the same entity over time, a kind of biographical process. If the phenomenon in question has a history, then certain behaviors are forthcoming related to an expected future of the event (often regardless of its specific characteristics). Sometimes the knowledge of a phenomenon is very incomplete and knowledge of its history is a substitute basis for action. For example, a good may have high information cost, but people transact based on who made it or how it was made. Which process the brain uses affects outcomes. Heimer (2001) suggests that "biographical analysis tends to be emergent, the result of an inductive process, while the analysis of case streams tends to be more deductive, arising from comparison of each new case with an imposed and pre-existing cognitive system embodied in routines and protocols." She further observes that the phenomena under question are more likely permitted to play an active role in the construction of meaning when biographical processes are used compared to case analysis. In the latter process, other people get treated as objects rather than subjects. Categories that cue behavior are social constructs and emerge from transactions and actions.

Schlicht (1998: 2) sees custom as "emerging from the individual's desire to align behaviour, conviction, and emotion with one another. Individuals have a preference for patterned behaviour, for acting according to their convictions, and for forming their convictions in accordance with what they are experiencing." As noted above in the discussion of the modular brain, humans like to think they have reasons for their actions. Customs provide reasons by reference to what is perceived as normal and natural. Schlicht observes, "routine and habit build on spontaneously perceived regularities which escape our regular deliberation" (2). When people embrace a customary property right, it carries an emotional charge where violation of something viewed as an entitlement engenders righteous sanctioning.

Models of stimulus, behavior, and reinforcement and of cued behavior are similar in that people are not "reasoning why" to do something, but unconsciously "seeing that" a behavior fits.

3.5.3 Belief persistence

Experience or feedback from the environment reinforces or extinguishes behavior. It is easy to understand how an act followed by food and other pleasant goods might increase the probability of the act being repeated. But, reinforcers are themselves perceived and interpreted. Not only is some experience filtered out, but some is misrepresented. When strongly held beliefs are confronted with evidence, the evidence is sometimes misrepresented. If you favor a certain action, the same evidence that further persuades you may equally support an opposite conclusion in someone who initially opposes the action. Lord, Ross, and Lepper (1979: 2099) observe that when our current beliefs are faced with complex and ambiguous evidence, we emphasize the strength and reliability of confirming evidence, but the weaknesses and unreliability of disconfirming evidence.

This phenomenon applies to the readers of this book. "With confirming evidence, we suspect that both lay and professional scientists rapidly reduce the complexity of the information and remember only a few well-chosen supportive impressions. With disconfirming evidence, they continue to reflect upon any information that suggests less damaging alternative interpretations" (Lord, Ross and Lepper 1979: 2099). Rabin (1998: 28–9) summarizes findings relative to human skill at informal correlation inferences as follows: "Richard Nisbett and Ross (1980) argue that the inability to accurately perceive correlation is one of the most robust shortcomings in human reasoning, and people often imagine correlations between events when no such correlation exists. Jennings, Amabile, and Ross (1982) argue that illusory correlation can play an important role in the confirmation of false hypotheses, finding that people under-estimate correlation when they have no theory of the correlation, but exaggerate correlation and see it where it is not when they have a preconceived theory of it." In spite of these path dependencies, we do alter beliefs over time. It is a bit of a tautology to say that strongly held beliefs are slow to change, since we have no independent way to define what is a strongly held belief. We have much to learn about learning.

Rabin (1998: 31) asks when and how learning takes place. He concludes that research "does not support the strong versions of the experts-get-things-right and in-the-real-world-people-learn hypotheses. Research also suggests we should use extreme caution in defining the relevant notion of learning, because many people who do learn general principles do not apply those principles in particular situations."

"Any enduring custom requires an explanation in terms of stabilizing forces and transmission processes" (Schlicht 1998: 20). In the context of bounded rationality, imitation provides a guide to complex situations. Social approval can be as reinforcing as material rewards. These processes will be further explored in section 11.2.

3.5.4 What's your pleasure?

Current happiness correlates: What underlies our behaviors? When we seek something, we say we like it. Where does this come from? Some things seem hard-wired and instinctual. Our bodies react to certain inputs that can be measured in hormonal and autonomic nervous system response (Frijda 1986) such as burns, stabs, pangs, and sinking feelings (Elster 1998). Facial expressions in response to some events are quite universal as are electrical, chemical and blood flow changes in the brain. Thinking is not something apart from the chemistry of the brain. Happiness makes a chemical and so does pain. Real events leave a chemical and so do imagined ones (Franklin 1987).

When we are hungry, food gives pleasure. But what food? A negative avoidance behavior is rather universally associated with slimy soft tissue meats. Some evolutionary biologists think this was imprinted as survivors avoided these likely bacteria infested parts (Pinker 1997). But, some people eat grasshoppers and others find them repulsive. Much is learned. And much of that learning arises out of transactions with other people, especially those we have some affinity for. Also see Korsmeyer (1999).

What goods, services, and conditions are correlated with happiness (utility)? Much of the data popularly associated with happiness concerns money incomes. But when we ask people what makes them happy or to indicate their present level, income is not primary. "Income has complex and generally weak effects on happiness. Cross-sectional studies find a small positive effect but only at the lower end of the income scale" (Argyle 1999: 354). On the other hand, relative income is important (Easterlin 1995). "Comparisons with the income of others are important in wage negotiations and more important than absolute income values" (353). What then are major factors in happiness? Social relationships (particularly marriage), social support, being employed, leisure, health, sport and exercise, social clubs, music, voluntary work, and church attendance. Argyle (369) suggests a redirection of policy, "Governments often behave as if increasing incomes and the standard of living is their main policy, though we have seen that income is a fairly minor predictor of happiness, has almost no effect for the richest half of the population, and has no historical effect at all."

Being unemployed is a major cause of unhappiness. For the employed, job features associated with well-being are opportunity for personal control, opportunity for skill use, externally generated goals, variety, environmental clarity (for example, task feedback), availability of money, physical security, supportive supervision, opportunity for interpersonal contact, valued social position (Warr 1999: 396–7).

What is known about welfare functions as more income or other experience is added or subtracted? The Law of Decreasing Marginal Utility (concave function) is so entrenched that many take it as a given. However, Praag and Frijters (1999: 420) reason, "Concavity implies that individuals are risk averse, but scientific experiments with insurance and gambling behavior show that this is not always true; it therefore follows that a utility function may be convex in certain regions."

Individuals differ in their experience and genes. "A major finding of our empirical research, although intuitively plausible, is that individual welfare functions differ between individuals" (421). There is evidence of shifting welfare functions because of adaptation of norms to changing income. People are at first happy with more income only to become accustomed to it and raise their standard and thereby become unsatisfied, a kind of "hedonic treadmill" (Brickman and Campbell 1971). Praag (1999: 421) observes that "income satisfaction for any income level, not only for an individual's own current income, depends on an individual's own current income. It implies that two individuals with different current incomes will evaluate any given income differently."

Expected utility theory inspired by Bernoulli assumed that people think in terms of levels of wealth. But, past outcomes and reference points matter. The prospect theory of Kahneman and Tversky (1979) noted in section 3.3.7 above is based on observation that "the carriers of decision utility are gains and losses relative to a reference level, which is often the *status quo*" (Kahneman 1999: 17). And losses from that *status quo* are weighted more than equivalent sized gains. The *status quo* can shift over time and create a hedonic treadmill as noted above. Kahneman argues that the proper measure of well-being should be the objective reporting of good or bad at the moment something is experienced and not at the point of decision (decision utility looking forward) or recalling of the past. People can be made happier even if on a satisfaction treadmill.

Consumer theory guides research whose results can be used by consumers, voters, business, and politicians. People may have been making progress and experiencing goodness, but people buy goods and vote in part looking forward (conditioned by the *status quo*). Perhaps politicians and parents of demanding children should remind people of their progress. This may not be effective as witnessed by politicians (or labor leaders) with a solid record of delivering income growth being voted out of office. The reason is captured by the phrase, "What have you done for me lately?"

Does economic research provide any useful information to consumers? Does it suggest thinking harder about progress, getting off the treadmill and heading for the mountains, or attempting to get more satisfaction from existing goods by learning more and improving skills is use? Business of course is by advertising and planned obsolescence trying to speed up the hedonic treadmill.

The above type of behavioral economics is necessary for informed consumer choice of goods and public policies and better prediction by business of how to satisfy consumer demand. It is not necessary if you merely want an apologia for whatever consumers and producers do. If consumers reveal prior preferences by choice in markets, then whatever they do is optimal. This is empty of analytical content as pointed out by many economists including Sen (1977).

Predicting future happiness (consumer theory): Preferences are expectations. Humans can develop a goal (preference) and predict the direction of future happiness from choosing alternative goods and services as a function of their relative prices and expected satisfaction. But they can't do it for all choices, and even where calculated prediction is used, people often get it wrong. The evidence is summarized by Loewenstein and Schkade (1999: 85) as follows: "1. People often hold incorrect intuitive theories about the determinants of happiness, which in turn lead to errors when predictions are based on them. 2. Different considerations may be salient when predicting future feelings than those that actually influence experienced feelings. 3. When in a 'cold' state people often have difficulty imagining how they would feel or what they might do if they were in a 'hot' state – for example, angry, hungry, in pain, or sexually excited. It may also be the case that, when in a hot state, people frequently have difficulty imagining that they will inevitably cool off eventually. Such 'hot/cold empathy gaps' can lead to errors in predicting both feelings and behavior."

Can the contribution of present choices to future happiness be improved by learning? Loewenstein and Schkade (1999: 85) are pessimistic: "Learning from experience does not seem to offer a broad cure for prediction errors because intuitive theories are often resistant to change, memories of experience are often themselves biased or incomplete, and experiences rarely repeat themselves often enough to make diagnostic patterns noticeable." Loewenstein and Schkade (1999: 99) suggest the presence of a "confirmation bias." People focus on evidence that confirms their priors and ignore contrary evidence. Also "If people don't remember what they originally predicted when an outcome is realized, they will be unaware of, and thus unable to correct for, prediction errors."

How do people make decisions in the face of bounded rationality? They decide based on rules (Anderson 1987); (Prelac 1991), habits (Ronis, Yates, and Kirscht 1989), and gut feelings (Damasio 1994). "The most common source of experiential surprises could therefore be the absence of an explicit prediction in the first place" (Loewenstein and Schkade 1999: 100). In addition, people underestimate their adaptive response to conditions.

3.5.5 Preference formation and change

Economics has been preoccupied with the question of how the economy could be arranged so that people with given preferences got as much utility as possible from their resources (constrained maximization). Sen (1977) has chided us with the phrase that we have been obsessed with improving the means to unimproved ends. Some thought it was sufficient to take preferences as revealed by choice in markets. But it is now clear that the institutions and performance of the market or any choice situation feeds back on behavior (Bowles 1998). What any institution or any particular structuring of a market reveals is only one of several possible selves. An evolutionary perspective is more appropriate than that of a single optimum equilibrium.

Learning is not just about how to best serve a given end. Much of the behavioral literature cited above expresses itself in terms of biases and mistakes in a context where the analyst knows the truth. But, many of the problems that the brain has to solve are not like that. The problem is what to make of ourselves and how to get along with other people in the process. Emotions underlie behavior. By emotion I mean that the process is not a calculation of how best to serve some end or objective, but is itself the setting of that objective. This is not a deductive process subject to error and bias, but a creative process with many possible creations. Elster (1998: 70) suggests that "emotions provide a meaning and sense of direction to life. . . ." To say that behavior is emotional is not to say that learning is absent, but only that the responses are not calculated (LeDoux 1998).

"Learning is more than the acquisition of information; it is the development of new means and modes of cognition, calculation, and assessment" (Hodgson 1998: 175). "Learning entails developing a structure by which to interpret the varied signals received by the senses" (North 1994: 362). Part of the structure is genetic, part the result of experience, part physical environment, and part cultural. Categories evolve to organize perceptions. North emphasizes, "The capacity to generalize from the particular to the general and to use analogy is a part of this rediscription process" (363). It is the source of creative thinking, ideology, and belief. "Ideologies are shared frameworks of mental models . . ." "Institutions are the external (to the mind) mechanisms individuals create to structure and order the environment" (363). While external, they can become internalized in habit and patterns of thought.

Holland et al. (1986) argue that deliberation "is not a process of discovering what we want, but a process of reflecting upon what there is most reason to want." Actions consequent upon deliberation are themselves inventions – processes by means of which we invent our projects, make our values, redesign our future selves and make sense of our past selves. Preferences are shaped by social interaction. "Consumption comprises a set of practices which permit people to express self identity, to mark attachment to social groups, to accumulate resources, to exhibit social distinction, to ensure participation in social activities, and more besides" (Warde 1996). Also see Chwe (2001).

De gustibus semper disputandum est: Institutional economists question Stigler and Becker's (1977: 76) assertion that tastes are "stable over time and similar among people . . ." From this they deduce that "all changes in behavior are explained by changes in prices and incomes . . ." (89). Stigler and Becker try to save the theory by assuming that utility is a function of investments in knowledge. Knowledge allows one to appreciate a good more and thus get more utility from it. People invest in knowledge (or advertisers do it for them) so that they can more efficiently transform market goods into household goods and utility.

The authors assume that firms are equating the marginal returns from advertising with those from other resource combinations to produce the market good. If they make money and sell more product after advertising, it must be because the consumer's stock of appreciation capital has increased. Global equilibrium is again established, consumption has changed, but tastes have not – only prices of household goods have changed (even if prices of market goods have not). So say Stigler and Becker without talking to anyone. Do people really want to increase their stock of appreciation capital? If resources can be used to change preferences or appreciation capital as well as to produce goods, it raises a question about welfare conclusions.

Another way the neoclassical theory can be preserved is to assume that market commodities are grouped into meta-categories, the taste for which is constant. The content of these categories might change as a result of learning which specific products best serve the meta-category. But even if meta-preferences are constant, firms in business and politics have some success in getting people to place a given product into one category (mental account) rather than another. The popular term is "spin doctoring." For example, Stigler and Becker acknowledge that humans are status conscious. So they argue that the taste for status is fixed (and similar for all) but different fashions fill the taste over time. If A's status is decreased as others spend more on similar goods, Stigler and Becker "expect wealthy countries like the United States to pay more attention to fashion than poor countries like India, even if tastes were the same in wealthy and poor countries" (89). This may explain consumption patterns in the two countries, but Stigler and Becker's logical assurance that meta-categories are stable is of little help to businesses who want to know whether rings in one's nose or navel will be perceived as status enhancing or just plain stupid.

Tastes among people are continuously disputed. That is why human interdependence produces so much conflict and why groups are trying to persuade others to their point of view or arrange rights so that others' tastes can be ignored. Tastes within a person's multiple-selves are continuously disputed. People struggle to define themselves and second-guess their choices. *De gustibus non est disputandum* must in light of the evidence be revised to *de gustibus semper disputandum est.*

3.6 Conclusion

Key words in describing how the mind works include: bounded rationality, unconscious reinforcement, multiple-selves, emotion, status and regard seeking, care for others, imagination and creativity, intuition, cues and fits, cognitive restraint, use of heuristics, learning, and evolving complex adaptive systems. The brain's ability to reform connections among elements is part of creativity and institutional change. The fundamental implications of bounded rationality and other tendencies of the brain suggest a world marked by fragile equilibrium or disequilibrium, necessarily incomplete markets, and where competition may not have the expected results. Lexicographic choice, mental accounts, rules of thumb, etc. are consistent with the limited information processing capacity of the brain. Laws and habits that constrain choice are consistent with the modular brain, as are preference reversals, intransitivity, and inconsistencies. Not all values are commensurable, and behavior is influenced by contingencies and context; history and imagination. Frames are influenced by institutions. The implications of these will be spelled out in the following chapters. An analysis of the impact of alternative institutions and institutional change must be built on a firm base of behavioral science. In the next chapter, the way the brain works will be put in the context of culture and the formation and evolution of institutions.

NOTES

1. The word "brain" will be used for convenience in referring to the body's whole nervous-sensory system including literally the brain as well as the enteric nervous system (Pert 1997).
2. "Valuation on the fly" is not consistent with construction of prior payoff matrices in game theory.

3. Neuroeconomists have found that when respondents are made low offers, a part of the brain associated with disgust is activated (Postrel 2003).
4. Behavioral scientists dispute the extent of innate tendencies. One that is widely accepted is universal structures in language found in all peoples researched by Noam Chomsky.
5. We can also speak of behavior being intrinsically motivated – done for its own sake. But this may imply more consciousness than is actually present. Intrinsic motivation may be a poor term for it implies value intrinsic in the good itself, rather than simply valued by some as an end, not a means. When a behavior has been unconsciously reinforced, introduction of an explicit monetary reward may reduce the desired behavior. Frey (2001) refers to this as "crowding out." For example, when blood may be purchased it reduces the value of volunteer giving (Titmuss 1971).

Chapter 4
Individuals and Institutions

4.1 From Individual Experience to Institutions and Back Again

The previous chapter focused on how the individual brain works. But, to understand behavior, we must examine systems of brains – the brain in a social setting. "Culture, context and history . . . are fundamental aspects of human cognition and cannot be comfortably integrated into a perspective that privileges abstract properties of isolated individual minds" (Hutchins 1995: 354). The basic task is one of "locating cognitive activity in context, where context is not a fixed set of surrounding conditions but a wider dynamical process of which the cognition of an individual is only a part" (xiii). Human cognition is a cultural and social process. We are not just affected by culture, we are part of a system and process of shaping culture and being shaped. *Neither individuals nor institutions are a starting place for analysis. Both are an outcome of a process.*

The proper unit of observation is again the transaction – the interplay of learning individuals and their environment. "Culture is an adaptive process that accumulates partial solutions to frequently encountered problems" (Hutchins 1995: 354). For example, a firm's culture evolves over time as its members create solutions to repeating problems. These are saved in the procedures of the firm and in the minds of its members. They are part of the firm's competencies. New members are affected by the existing structure of relationships and, over time, become part of the spiral of being shaped by the structure and shaping it. When the routines in various parts of the firm interact, something new may emerge at a higher level. The process and transformation involve evolution, uncertainty, individual and society interaction, and emergence – in sum, learning.

4.2 Evolutionary Theory

North (1994) asks, "How comparable is the learning embodied in intentional choice to the selection mechanisms in evolutionary theory? The latter are not informed by the beliefs about the eventual consequences; the former, erroneous though it may be, is driven by perceptions of downstream consequences." Both are operating.

The natural environment shapes institutions. For example, North (1997: 5) argues "the origins of some norms, including those embedded in religious beliefs may have had their ultimate source in basic features of primitive agriculture with diverse climatic, soil, and product characteristics imposing organizational imperatives on the players." The term imperatives may be too strong. Institutions in some manner must fit the goods situation, but there are many possibilities. Harris (1974) suggests that the Islamic prohibition of pork may have protected a desert oasis from spoliation. The sacred cow of India may have insured survival of breeding stock in a drought. However, a functional role does not posit a unique institution.

Belief structures filter the information derived from experiences (North 1994: 364). "Given the fact that the knowledge of the rules is socially shared, in the sense that the rules are common knowledge in the society, these actors can be confident that they can with reasonable accuracy formulate the necessary beliefs about what other economic actors are going to do" (Knight and North 1997: 222).

Following a stimulus, a person acts, and others react to that behavior. The feedback (reinforcers) from this environment must be interpreted. Patterned behavior (feedback) of others constitutes institutions. Beliefs affect the way the mind interprets the information it receives. The interpretation of this feedback from the environment is not mechanical, which is why "institutional mechanism" is not an apt metaphor. This possible slippage in interpretation and perception is a source of variation playing the same role in institutional evolution as mutation does in biology. People can go out of their way to be deviant and reject the feedback that others find reinforcing. If this reaches a particular threshold, institutions are destabilized and change. Thus, collections of challenger individuals change institutions by changing the feedback to the incumbent holders of the previous institution.

While the behavior of person A engenders feedback from B, C, and D that may reinforce that behavior, A may be joined by others to give a different interpretation to the feedback and in turn provide sufficient feedback to B, C, and D to create new institutions in a continuing evolution. The challengers (deviants) may not be aware that in the aggregate they are changing informal institutions. Alternatively, they may consciously organize to change formal law to defeat the incumbent. These themes will be taken up again in chapter 13 on institutional change. Social evolution is necessarily consistent with the inherited tendencies of the brain such as bounded rationality. Some of the behavioral regularities were noted above in section 3.3.

4.3 Uncertainty

Rationality is not the product of the individual alone. Perceptions of others are a part of one's rationality. "A demand curve is more complex than a price. It involves knowing about the behavior of others" (Arrow 1986: S391). In order for a monopolist to set price, it is necessary to know how consumers will shift demand for other products and in turn how this will affect demand for the monopolists's product and perhaps input prices. The problem of oligopolists in understanding the reaction of other oligopolists is well known. Strategies including sending false signals are relevant. The oligopolist struggles with the problem, "I think that he thinks that I think, etc." This "outguessing problem" can create multiple equilibria. "Closure becomes elusive" (Mirowski 2002: 511).[1] Even in a competitive world, the individual needs to know a large number of prices to make optimal decisions. All of this seems beyond the limited information processing capacity of the human brain. Arrow (1986: S392) states, "under these knowledge conditions, the superiority of the market over centralized planning disappears. Each individual agent is in effect using as much information as would be required for a central planner." Individuals fill in holes in their knowledge with conjecture. It is institutions both formal and informal that provide the habits and mutual expectations that make coordination possible. Forecasts can be self-denying or self-fulfilling. If enough people share a forecast, their behavior in response to it can be self-fulfilling. The forecast can work even if based on false premises. "We can have situations where social truth is essentially a matter of convention, not of underlying realities" (Arrow 1986: S396).

The evaluation of investments that pay off in the future is done in the face of fundamental uncertainty (Littlechild 1986). Entrepreneurs must imagine the future, and not just one, but a number of complementary investments by others. Knight and North (1997) observe that if the dreams are not shared sufficiently, then the investments will turn out to be inefficient. But the inefficiency is not a prior fact but something created in the process. It is not that the information feedback is insufficient to produce the correct investments in economic and political areas, but rather there is no feedback from something that does not yet exist but is being created. It is possible that there can be a whole series of insufficiently shared expectations and dreams so that each round of first investors goes broke and changes in the laws bear no fruit. In one sense that is what happens when poor countries pass laws that look like the rich countries', but get no results. While the formal law is one signal of a shared expectation that invites others to join in, it may not be sufficient.

Systematic choice may be made by conceiving of probability distributions. "But in the case of uncertainty no such probability distribution is possible, and, in consequence, to quote two of economics' most eminent practitioners, 'no theory can be formulated in the case' and again 'in cases of uncertainty, economic reasoning will be of little value'" (Knight and North 1997: 213). But human beings do construct theories all the time in conditions of pure uncertainty – and also act on them and sometimes die for them. The big question is "how and why they develop theories in the face of pure uncertainty, what makes those theories spread among a population or die out, and why do humans believe in them and act upon them?" (214).

Expectations, plans and institutions are interrelated. "Institutions are a response to uncertainty. They economize on the scarce resource of cognition" (Loasby 1999: 46). Even where knowledge of the past might inform the future, our limited information processing capacity suggests that it may be reasonable to ignore some information. Heiner (1983) has identified a competence–difficulty gap where people may rely on standard operating procedures when incomplete and faulty calculation would lead to mistakes. He argues that prediction is most possible when most people are relying on their culturally learned rules of thumb.

Institutions exist to structure human interaction in a world of uncertainty or, as Heiner puts it, arise from the effort of individuals in the face of pervasive uncertainty to reduce that uncertainty by limiting the choices available to the players and thereby making behavior predictable. "Without institutions there would be no order, no society, no economy, and no polity" (Knight and North 1997: 214). This is a strong statement. I interpret it to mean that it is only by shared expectations that we can make sense of the world and thus the concept of the isolated individual is nonsense. While institutions contribute order, that order emerges from differences in the mental models held by different individuals and these differences are a source of continued evolution. Models built on a representative individual miss the essential character of network complexity.

Bounded rationality implies that the list of all possible future states is incomplete. Nevertheless, if events are specified and the analyst asks people to assign probabilities, they will do so. But, this does not mean that they make decisions in this additive way. "If the probability space itself is undefined (unbounded) then it is meaningless . . . to attach prior probabilities to imagined events" (Potts 2000: 170–1). G. L. S. Shackle's (1949; 1979) concept of subjective potential surprise is more meaningful for non-ergodic open systems. Emergent conjectures are more than some projected function of lagged historical variables. Whether a state occurs in the future is not a given shrouded in mist, but a matter partly determined by the interactions of the network of multiple agents.

Shackle and Ford (1990) suggested a role for intuition and imagination. Knowledge of the past is an input into imagination, but does not fully constrain or determine it. The creative act of imagination supplements the list of possibilities for the future. Since only a few possibilities can be imagined, the creative and selective process is influenced by the frames of culture and ideology.

The selected and partially created list of possibilities can be ordered by what Shackle called "degrees of disbelief" or "potential for surprise" when additive probabilities can't be attached. Successful individuals have good intuition and are quick to adapt to new information. This does not mean that personal or collective plans are worthless, but only that they must be flexible. In Perlman's (1984: 585) words, "Dammed is the man whose plan freezes his imagination." Related to the concept of surprise is the concept of disappointment. Even if the state of nature we envisage occurs, we may not be as happy with it as we anticipated. This can lead to reflection on our preferences for preferences. And as Hirschman (1977) suggests, it may lead to a shift in concern between individual welfare and public affairs, and constitute the fuel for political movements. (More on uncertainty in section 6.7.4.)

4.4 Individual and Society

We care about the welfare of others. We care about not only our absolute level of consumption but also our relative standing. We suffer the pain of envy and the pleasure of showing off to others (Frank 1985; 1999). As part of the learning process we copy others and conform. At the same time we seek our own identity and try to differentiate ourselves. The choices of others that differ from our own challenge us by demonstrating that other things are possible. When people try to remove this discomforting challenge by regulations, the charge of paternalism is raised. One person's freedom to choose is another's discomfort, which may be more debilitating than inadequate food and shelter. On the one hand we want to belong and have others' choices support and legitimate our own. That gnawing fear that I may not understand the world is made bearable by the fact that I am doing what others are doing. Rizzello (1999: 160) answers the question of why people follow rules by saying that "There are reasons concerning belonging, consideration, and approval."

Organizations are the dominant fact of our social and economic existence. (See chapter 5 below.) Most of us make our living in organizations. The multiple selves that simultaneously want to conform and be different can have it both ways when we join an organization. There is a limited field of conformity where our behavior is reinforced at the same time we maintain a distinction from others on the outside who are different. Some distinctions such as race, language, and religion are probably popular because they are so easy to make. Others in the organization reinforce our loyalty and require it.

"Social preferences over other people's consumption depend on the behavior, motivations, and intentions of those other people. The same people who are altruistic toward deserving people are often indifferent to the plight of undeserving people, and motivated to hurt those whom they believe to have misbehaved. If somebody is being nice to you or others, you are inclined to be nice to him; if somebody is being mean to you or others, you are inclined to be mean to him" (Rabin 1998: 21). Contributions toward high exclusion cost goods are not the result of simple altruism. Crosson (1995) found a strong positive correlation between subjects' contribution levels and their beliefs about how others were contributing. Communication greatly increases the contribution to high exclusion cost goods (Dawes 1988). This will be explored in more detail in chapter 6.

The perceived motives of others also affect contributions to high exclusion cost goods (Goranson and Berkowitz 1966). People also have a tendency to retaliate against the negative actions of others (Blount 1995). They will hurt themselves to hurt others who they regard as undeserving (malevolence). It is clear that people are not just concerned about physical or monetary outcomes, but also about relationships (socio-emotional goods).

Understanding status relationships is relevant to institutions of taxation. "If all similarly situated individuals are required to pay comparable tax increments, each taxpayer may feel relatively just as well off" (Vickrey 1994: 509). He notes further that if A and B are of similar status, B's gain may be negative for A; while a much poorer X's gain may beneficial to A. "The net result of these considerations seems to be that it is not possible to say anything very definite from a strictly behavioral point of view on the relative subjective sacrifice involved in making of a gift and the payment of a tax, though on balance the evidence may seem to point to the tax as more painful than the gift, but not by anything like the amount of loss suffered, say, if the same quantum of resources had been destroyed by some uninsured catastrophe" (510–11).

There are many situations in economic life where cooperation increases the total payoff to a potential group over what they could do individually. The achievement of this outcome is a "coordination problem." Institutions are the essence of coordination. The situation is represented experimentally by giving subjects an endowment. If some amount of this endowment is invested in a common pool, the experimenter adds value to it. Realization of this larger payoff depends on rules of thumb that the participants utilize. One such rule is to always begin with cooperation and then follow what others do (tit-for-tat). This behavior might be the result of calculation, but is probably learned, internalized, and habitual. In that case the context and frame where this rule is seen to fit is critical. It is not necessary that the parties care for each other's welfare being enhanced (altruism), but it is certainly helpful. Malevolence is certainly a hindrance.

Solving the commitment problem for the provision of high exclusion cost goods has many complementary components. Narrow short-run individual maximization of easily observed benefits is not enough. Lengthening the time horizon helps. Caring for the welfare of other persons in the group helps. Caring for the regard of other persons in the group helps. Social approval and disapproval are routinely transferred among individuals in the course of their daily routines. Homans (1950) observed spontaneous monitoring and enforcement among workers in the Western Electric bank wiring room. People respond to reinforcement from status and regard as well as monetary reward. Nee and Ingram (1998: 28) argue, "Conformers have an interest in monitoring the norms of the group insofar as it reinforces the criteria upon which their higher status is based." Actors are located "in a network of personal relationships characterized by certain norms, in accordance with which they evaluate – and reward and punish – each other" (40). To say that people exchange emotional goods has a connotation of forward looking conscious calculation. But since the dispensing of approval may be partly conscious and partly unconscious, a better conceptualization may be a mutual flow of reinforcers of various kinds.

Humans can reflect on past or projected benefits and costs to decide whether or not to support a social norm or formal rule. But we can't do it for all our behavior. Most of the time, we don't ask ourselves if a particular institution is worth supporting. We just see a situation and an action seems to fit and we do it. This mindset is a result of experience, but not all at a conscious level. It is part of the formative socialization of the individual (Stanfield 1979: ch. 7).[2]

The transformation of informal norms into formal law often requires solving the same commitment problem wherein some people work to pass legislation even if their personal benefit–cost calculation is negative in terms of wealth (spend more time than the specific benefit of the legislation to themselves). Another supporting process in common law countries is the use of best practice as the basis for court rulings. The observations of judges may be selective, but they are reflecting practices that have been developed by trial and error in the population. However, in a fast changing world, not all formal law has its origin in informal norms.

In situations that are somewhat unique and separated in time and players, various formal institutions are used to achieve coordination, such as majority rule to pass a bond issue to fund improved sanitation systems. The fact that some participants do not regard their net share of costs and benefits to be fair is always a problem, even when objectively every one appears to gain.

4.5 Emergence

Hayek (1975) makes the point that we do not and cannot know enough to consciously plan institutions. He calls it our "fatal conceit" to think otherwise. From this he concludes that the market is superior to central planning or any kind of intentional collective action. Superior in the sense that it makes better use of the sum of human knowledge. He is right that the human brain cannot comprehend the world in its complexity and will necessarily make leaps and extensions. This will be true whatever variety of institutions we choose. We will make this leap whether the subject is what kind of automobile to buy, firm to organize, or legislation to support. Whether we share these leaps informally or formally does not make them better or worse, just different. The planner brain with its knowledge seeks the help of other planner brains to win out over other multiple selves with their knowledge. This is the underlying basis for formal institutions. As will be demonstrated in subsequent chapters, individuals making their best choices within their opportunity set may not achieve the performance they want. Sometimes, conscious collective action is necessary to alter the opportunity set. Democratic processes also selectively aggregate human knowledge. Some trials of new institutions must necessarily be conducted at the aggregate level (Vanberg 1992: 114).

The relationship between actor and both formal and informal institutional structures is central to any social science theory. Structure has precedence in time over the acts of a living person. But that person is one of many whose behavior is shaping the evolving structures over time. Action and structure are interdependent, but distinct and separable over time. Each has some autonomy and stability, but nevertheless form a nexus where each defines the other as does the yin and yang. Each level emerges from the other, but each is not explicable solely in terms of the other. "An entity or aspect found at some level of organization is said to be emergent if there is a sense in which it has arisen out of some lower level, being conditioned by and dependent upon, but not predictable from the properties found at the lower level" (Lawson 1997: 176). (Also see references to Holland and Potts in chapter 13 on evolutionary change.)

Complex adaptive systems are characterized by a global structure that emerges from local activity rules. Lewin (1999: 202–3) suggests four rules by which complex adaptive systems operate. (1) "The source of emergence is the interaction among agents who mutually affect each other." (2) "Small changes can lead to large effects." (3) "Emergence is certain, but there is no certainty as to what it will be." (4) "Greater diversity of agents in a system leads to richer emergent patterns."

Adam Smith's famed "invisible hand" concept is a kind of emergence theory. The local activity rules are individual greed plus the market. The emergence is a performance of the economy claimed to be the best possible. We shall see, however, in subsequent chapters that what emerges may not only be unanticipated by the participants, but undesired by many.

4.6 Conclusion: Learning and Evolution

People's learning is shaped by institutions, and their learning shapes evolving institutions. What is common in the feedback that one individual receives from many others can be conceptualized as an informal institution. Whether business or consumer, we act according to routines that have been reinforced by feedback from the environment and evolving interpretation thereof. We solve new problems by adjusting already known routines and rearranging data and meanings in a creative fashion. We use what we have learned in the past, our cognition of the present environment, and select and create alternatives. Selective perception is unavoidable. Human ability to reform connections among elements is part of creativity and institutional change. Learning is much more than simply choosing from given alternatives according to prior value weights. Alternatives, values, means, and ends are forged together in ongoing learning and can be different for different people, but are common for many for a period of time. Institutions, both informal and formal, are repositories of knowledge.

NOTES

1. "To know a state includes knowing, not only everything there is to know about the state of the physical world, but also everything there is to know about everybody's state of mind, including their knowledge and beliefs. The self-reference implicit in such an interpretation brings Gödels's theorem to mind" (Binmore 1999: 120). Everything must be known and connected, but both completeness and consistency are logically impossible. Binmore's answer to this problem was to imagine an evolution of machines so that only one type remained so that one machine plays another just like itself. All players would have the same algorithmic version of rationality. "Fortunately, operating within a computer context torpedoes most of the difficulties that arise when trying to model players as people" (Binmore and Vulkan 1999: 4). People have to go in order to maintain the core of neoclassical economics. People are turned into cyborgs in Mirowski's (2002: 564) felicitous language: "The quest to elevate humanity to deserve the vaunted honorific of 'rationality' by painting humans as prodigious machines would seem so neurotically misplaced as to be scandalous. . . ."
2. Humans can also reflect on how their image of themselves fits into the various social structures that they are a part of (Davis 2003). Since the various social structures are not necessarily consistent with each other and people's perceptions of them are not mechanical, there is a continuous tension out of which evolution emerges.

Chapter 5
Institutions and Organizations

Institutions are an independent variable in institutional impact analysis and a dependent variable in institutional change analysis. An adequate theory then must specify the institutional variable carefully and provide a basis for how the institutional variable relates to other variables identified by theory. This is the task of this chapter. It is preliminary to the detailed development of hypotheses in chapter 6 on impact analysis and chapter 13 on change analysis.

5.1 Human and Physical Relationships

When the recipe for production of a good or service is written, it does not contain institutions in addition to land, labor, and capital goods. Physical things are produced by physical things. Institutions and organizations are mental constructs. They influence what things humans put together to produce physical things, but they are not some magical extra ingredient.[1] Some years ago, economists were baffled by the fact that their measures of changes in physical inputs could not explain observed changes in physical outputs. Many tried to add a residual variable and called it technology. But this was a name for our ignorance rather than an identification of an input. The technology can be represented in a sub-function explaining the inputs to produce a specific technology. But it would be double counting to include the new machine and the research expenditures to produce it in the same function.

Take an agricultural example. The production of corn requires seed, land, labor, and machines. Surely over time technology changed. Open-pollinated seeds were replaced by hybrid seeds. How shall this be specified? Shall we add a magical variable called technology to the production function? No, it will be much clearer if we properly specify the seed input. Hybrid and open-pollinated seeds are simply two different inputs. And the hybrid seed and the research expenditures to create it cannot be added together as inputs to corn production.

Economists had the same problem with the labor input. Over time the quality of the labor input changed. Labor was specified simply in terms of hours. Shall we add a magical input called human capital or education to the production function? No, it will be clearer if we properly specify the labor input according to its skills and delivered intensity and timeliness.

What about the motivation of the labor? Shall the production function include hours of college-educated labor plus an institution related to motivation, monitoring, and incentives? No, the only thing entering the production function is the physical labor carefully specified. We can, however, ask how a particular labor quality was actually present and got combined with other inputs in a timely fashion. This is an institutional question. The content of a particular production function is in turn a function of institutions. So we might have:

- **Production function**
  Corn output = f (hybrid seed, man hours of literate labor, land acres of
         specified quality, tractors of specified horsepower, etc.)

(The hours of literate labor can be further specified as punctual, attentive, etc.)

The institutional sub-function then might ask how any of the above factors actually came to be present. This sub-function would explain why the labor variable in the production function was attentive or looking out the window. For example,

- **Institutional impact function**
  Hours of literate labor actually applied = f (labor institutions including formal
         rights and informal habits of
         workmanship and professional standards)

In an institutional theory, the relationship of the dependent variables is not a deterministic function but is rather one of facilitation so that "f" here should be read as the independent variables facilitate the realization of the dependent variable.

Each explanation must in turn be explained. Why are certain labor institutions present and not others? This is the domain of institutional change analysis.

- **Institutional change function**
  Labor institutions = f (situation of mass production, exclusion cost, ideology,
         political rules, $n \ldots$)

While institutions are not factors of production, there is no production function independent of institutions. Likewise, the firm is an organization and is not a production function, though it's processes affect the actual content of operative production functions. Likewise, management is not an input into a production function, though again, managers affect the content of the operative physical production function. In this sense, it is confusing to speak of "organizational capital" (Tomer 1987).

Opportunity sets and rules: An institution is a structured transaction, a structured human relationship. It is often described in terms of rules and positions that define opportunity sets. Rules can be interpreted as "if X, do Y (or don't do Y), under conditions Z." For example, we say person A owns a physical object. But the thing of interest here is not the relationship between A and the object, which is a matter of the physical production function, but rather the implied cognitive relationship between A and person B. If we take Veblen's definition of an institution as a way of thought or action of some prevalence and permanence, the ownership relationship translates as B avoids certain acts relative to a physical commodity. This is the source of A's opportunities. The B in this case may be composed of lots of people. The relationship may have some permanence if the rule is hard to change.

The rule may be formal and created by some explicit collective process of legislature or court. Or, the rule may be informal and created by some implicit cultural learning process. To summarize, a statement of an institution as A owns thing T translates into action as B avoids T, and A may act on T without consulting B. This relationship between A and B creates a set of opportunities for A and exposures for B. So when we specify an institution in terms of a rule category, it is a shorthand for a relationship, transaction, and opportunity set.

Rules constitute constraints. But if the transaction is made the unit of analysis, it is easy to see that one person's constraint is another's opportunity. Thus, a rule is also an opportunity and liberation. This conception does not start with an unlimited field of action that is then constrained. It starts with an interdependence to be sorted out and opportunities are then created by limits.

Rules are often attached to positions and the positions constitute a networked system. Positions are best understood as elements of a transaction. "Practices routinely followed by an occupant of any position tend to be oriented towards some other group(s)" (Lawson 1997: 164). Each position takes on meaning in relationship to another position. Examples are landlord and tenant, teacher and student, CEO and corporate board of directors, parent and child, and plaintiff and defendant. "Social rules associated with specific positions are not merely reproduced and transformed by the immediate occupants of the positions in question but by the actions, inter-actions of a far wider grouping – basically all of those in a position to be affected by or to influence them" (172). The expected behaviors of occupants of informal positions are often described as roles. We speak of playing the role of mother. The expected behavior of occupants of formal positions within an organization are often expressed in job descriptions. Or it is expressed in fields of action described as privileges, such an owner may sell a resource or capture its surplus; or a firm may use its superior savings when negotiating with labor, but may not refuse to bargain with the union.

Mutual coercion: From a transactional view, institutions are simultaneously a constraint (on B) and a liberation (for A). In a world of scarcity and interdependence, a transaction is necessarily a matter of mutual coercion (Samuels 1992b: 35–7). If A can't coerce B, then A has no arena for action and no opportunity to receive bids from B. Likewise, if B can't coerce A, B has nothing to bid with (nothing to exchange). The opportunity sets of A and B may be mutually agreed to but that does not deny that rules are meant to give opportunity to some by denying it to others. If A could not call upon the sheriff or neighbors to reinforce (sanction) A's opportunity, A would live only by B's forbearance and charity. The ability to keep others off (avoid) is as coercive as the ability to command a performance.

Cost is institutionally defined: Cost is the value of opportunities given up when any action is undertaken. This is a physical phenomenon. But, what is given up is always a selective perception. And the value of the things given up is a matter of whose preferences count, which is an institutional phenomenon. Is the value what else an owner might have done with the resource (for example, use the land for corn rather than soybeans)? Is it what the owner might have received if sold to another? Or is it the value that another person puts on the resource that the non-owner then must bid for or do without? Institutions determine the answer to these questions (Samuels and Schmid 1997).

The costs that are attached to a production function to derive a cost as a function of output are the surface phenomena of a deeper underlying institutional structure. This can be illustrated with an environmental example. What is the cost of producing corn? It is the alternative uses of the inputs of land, labor, and capital. But whose interests are in the opportunity sets of others that must be acquired by the entrepreneur growing corn? The entrepreneur may own the land, but does she own the ground water into which excess nitrates and pesticides leach? If those who consume ground water have to buy the right to be free of these effects, the bid price becomes the entrepreneur's opportunity cost. If the consumers of ground water have the right to be free of interference, then the entrepreneur must make the bid. These bids are not always the same depending on transaction costs and wealth effects. Thus, cost is fundamentally a matter of institutions. What the world will ultimately look like is a function of these institutions. Are we to have lots of cheap corn or lots of pure drinking water? The very definition of what we mean by total productivity is at stake. These are the fundamental non-marginal decisions of institutional choice.

Interdependencies, not externalities: Interdependence of people is a fact of scarcity. One person's acts affect the welfare of another. This has to be sorted out and given order, or there is merely brute force and war. The candy maker's noisy machines cause a problem for the doctor next door (Coase 1960). If the machines were not there, the doctor would have peace. If the doctor was not there, the machines are no problem. It is not helpful to say that there is an external effect of the machines, because one could also say that there is an external effect of the doctor. It is more straightforward to say they are interdependent in a world of scarcity. (If there were only one person per square kilometer, there would be no scarcity of air space; but of course there would be no one to buy candy or medical services either.) Externalities are ubiquitous.

Air space is just as much a physical input in the production function of candy as is labor, sugar, and machines. Likewise, air space is as much a physical input into the production function for medical services as is labor and medicine. The unavoidable institutional issue is in whose opportunity set is the scarce commodity. If there is to be a market for this opportunity, the issue is who is the buyer and who is the seller. Whoever is made the owner, they will listen to the bids and pleas of the non-owner. If the bid is insufficient, the non-owner suffers. That someone suffers from scarcity is inevitable. This suffering cannot be remedied by any institutional cleverness whether tax, regulation, or market. These just make manifest the underlying rule-created opportunity set distribution.

Power and economizing: Institutional economics is not about calculating advantageous exchanges and resource combinations. It is about the non-marginal questions of whose interests count via distributions of opportunity sets. At any given time, there is some set of opportunities in place and the parties go about trading and economizing as best they can. Depending on the socially conditioned knowledge of the physics involved, the candy maker will economize on the use of air space and consider substitutes as a function of the prices she faces. But these prices are in turn a function of institutions. The damage that each causes the other is not a fact independent of institutions.

To have an opportunity in your opportunity set is to have power. Power is the ability to visit costs upon others (Samuels and Schmid 1997: 227–31). Power is "The ability of one actor to alter the decisions made and/or welfare experienced by another actor relative to the choices that would have been made and/or welfare that would have been experienced had the first actor not existed or acted" (Bartlett 1989: 30). Power is the ability to have your interests count.

In impact analysis, if we compare the performance of two different institutions (sets of opportunities) in terms of the income received by A, the difference is a measure of power. After transacting, A and B have made all the economizing choices that are open to them as a function of power distribution. If they do not inquire into why the opportunity sets are as they are, they will say that their transaction was voluntary and mutually beneficial. They would rather have the resulting set of commodities than the pile they started with. But, if you asked each whether they would have preferred to have a different set prior to the transaction, each might want more. To alter institutions is to alter power, and if it makes a difference in performance, there is a measure of power.

Power as used here is much more than market power. It is not just a question of affecting price via preventing competition and entry of other suppliers. It is a question of affecting price by being one of the sellers rather than a buyer of an opportunity. There are some instances where it is hard to distinguish. For example, if a firm is free of unions, there may be a different wage than if it must bargain with a collective. This is partly a matter of eliminating the marginal worker who would work for less from setting the wage of all. It is partly a matter of the right to recover any fixed investments that the worker might have in their skills and homes. Power is also involved in preference formation.

Just as one can economize on physical inputs in a production process, one can economize on those sub-relationships that are within your power to choose. Thus a firm may have the power to choose whether to pay employees by a piece rate or annual salary, but not to refuse to bargain with a union. It may have the power to organize on a regional or functional basis. It may have the power to enter into a contract with a supplier or to buy out that supplier and make it a subdivision of the firm.

5.2 Administrative, Bargained, and Customary Transactions

The relationships between persons (or organizations) may be between legal equals or between a superior and an inferior. When the parties are legal equals it is a bargained transaction. Legal equals are not economic equals. Legal equality just means that each party has an opportunity set and may only exchange if both parties agree. One person may have many opportunities such as a large employer and the employee only a few. One may have large savings and another few. Agreement to trade should not be mistaken for agreement of what one has to trade.

Administrative transactions imply a superior and an inferior. The superior may issue a command within some range of choice and the inferior is obliged to carry it out. This may be the order of a government administrator or a corporate manager. The structure of administration may be put in place by a higher order act of administration or by prior negotiated agreement as in the case of a labor contract. The contract may specify a range of options available at the discretion of the foreman. Likewise, legislation may specify a set of discretionary options open to a government agent. The inferior in that transaction may not bargain. Such bargaining would be an illegal bribe. However, the agent's discretion may have been the subject of bargaining when the authorizing legislation was passed.

The distinction between bargained and administered transaction is subtle. Just as the administered transaction is embedded in a higher order transaction (such as a labor contract or legislative action), the bargained transaction is embedded in a higher order transaction which established who has what to trade. The parties bargain after the basic institutions are established. Buyers make voluntary bids because of the ability of the owner to coerce them and prevent access. (Recall discussion of mutual coercion in section 5.1 above.) Thus bargained and administered transactions are nested within each other.

There is a sub-class of administration that may be called a rationing transaction. The manager of a corporation may ration the budget among different entities and functions. The American presidency is often referred to as the administration. In some regards it functions as does a corporate management.

In customary transactions, the party whose behavior favors others, making a grant (transfer) to another, does not see it as an obligation to a rights holder. It can be a subconscious response to a cue provided by the actor's relative position and role in a network of expectations. "Humans collectively construct meaning upon environments and behavior" (Jennings and Waller 1994). "Perception is an act of categorization" that enables actors to make sense of the world (Hodgson 1994: 59). These cultural patterns are not constraints on an otherwise natural set of tendencies, but constitute those tendencies (Mayhew 1994).

To summarize some of the behavioral themes of chapter 3 (especially section 3.5 on learning), in addition of subconscious reinforcement, "Conformity pressures in groups result from normative influences because group members seek to obtain rewards and avoid punishment, to identify with attractive others, and to construct an ideal public image. . . ." (Dallas 1997: 108). This will be further developed in explaining informal institutional change in section 13.2.

5.3 Organizations (Firms), Institutions, and Boundaries

An organization is "a system of consciously coordinated activities or forces of two or more persons" (Barnard 1948: 73). (In contrast, individual action may be also coordinated unconsciously via shared habits and values. Individuals may be coordinated by market exchange within a set of institutional rules.) An organization is a means for collective action for individual members within a boundary (who is in and who is out). In common parlance, we know what it means to be organized. It means some shared notion of where people in the organization are going and how the individuals might collectively act to get there. An organization is some boundary of people with shared institutions and mutual recognition of opportunity sets. Organizations are systems of relationships for coordinating individual actions according to some decision rule or persuasion – a mix of authority and custom. Organizations contain positions and a hierarchy (bureaucracy), and the members act together with something less than unanimity. When people join an organization, they expect their actions to be predictably ordered with that of other specific persons. Still, some acts are not calculated and these habits learned in interaction with others are a major contributor to outcomes and constitute a reason for joining. The individuals in an organization in part suspend calculation with respect to designated actions. The situation implies a rule-like behavior (possibly a habit) that fits an environment.

To reiterate: organizations embody a set of institutions (human relationships) to which a group of people subscribe. Some of the institutions are unique to the organization, some are chosen from a set available to others, and some are obligatory and given as a result of a larger rule-making organization. For example, General Motors uses corporate law given by the state, but makes its own organizational chart, contracts, and alliances with others. Over time it forms its own informal corporate culture with varying degrees of consciousness. It plays by corporate law given it by the organizations of the nation state as well as influences these laws. Its corporate culture is in part shaped by the broader culture and its practices combine with others to shape that broader culture. Generally, if one capitalizes the name, it is an organization, but if it is lower case, it is an institution. For example, GM, The International Coffee Organization, the City of Genoa, and the Schmid Family are organizations. The corporation, the family, the balance rule, and zoning laws are institutions. As with all generalizations there are exceptions.

What is an organization? We all know one when we see it, but it is hard to describe precisely. There would be agreement that the following are private organizations: General Motors, Harvard University, Church of England, and the Sierra Club. They all have an executive/administrative structure, but some have employees who are paid and others have members who pay in money or in labor. An organization is composed of members who have met some membership requirements. Their actions are coordinated; that is to say there is collective action.

Organizations may be defined as "groups of individuals bound by some common purpose to achieve objectives" (North 1990: 5). This is true at some level, but not in detail. While benefits may exceed costs for all individuals, it simply is not true that employees of GM share objectives in any detail. What can be said is that GM constitutes some boundary of people with shared institutions and mutual recognition of opportunity sets. The employees and stockholders utilize institutions formed in a larger boundary such as the laws of incorporation that give corporate stockholders limited liability and the system unlimited life. The collectivity makes institutions within itself that apportion opportunities to its members and employees. An organization is collective action within another boundary of collective action.

"Empirical organizations are not the same as institutions. Organizations sometimes represent arenas for amalgamations of the rationales of a whole repertoire of institutions, and sometimes arenas for competing rationales. Thus, the members of a particular empirical organization usually express in their actions norms and values associated with several institutional forms" (Sjostrand 1993: 23).

There are people who share objectives who do not form organizations. They are what Olson (1965) refers to as "latent groups." An important topic of analysis is why some people with shared objectives form groups and others do not. A person may belong to some cohort defined by some characteristics such as gender, race, age, occupation, etc., but people with these characteristics may or not form an organization.

Members of an organization act collectively and with various degrees of consciousness within a larger system of opportunity sets created by other organizations such as a nation state or by unconscious cultural processes. (The conscious and formal processes are complements and substitutes with the informal cultural processes.) And, organizations are players in those larger collectivities as well. For example, GM is an organization, not an institution. However, it can be considered a collection of applied institutions – a group of institutions with some boundary of application. It utilizes corporate and contract law and also tries to influence these laws. In studying institutional change, North (1990) argues that organizations must be conceptualized separately from institutions because organizations are the engine for changing formal institutions that do not suit the dominant members. North uses a metaphor of the rules of a sport. "Modeling the strategies and the skills of the team as it develops is a separate process from modeling the creation, evolution, and consequences of the rules" (5). The strategies and competencies of the team are themselves molded by other institutions.

There is a sense whereby we may speak of organizational knowledge. Winter (1982) explains, "The coordination displayed in the performance of organizational routines is, like that displayed in the exercise of individual skill, the fruit of practice. What requires emphasis is that . . . the learning experience is a shared experience of organization members . . . Thus, even if the contents of the organizational memory are stored only in the form of memory traces in the memories of individual members, it is still an organizational knowledge in the sense that the fragment stored by each individual member is not fully meaningful or effective except in the context provided by the fragments stored by other members" (76). Harris (1971: 136) suggests, "Cultures are patterns of behavior, thought and feeling that are acquired or influenced through learning and that are characteristic of groups of people rather than of individuals." The individual–social relationship is complex. "Although tacit or other knowledge must reside in the nerve or brain cells of a set of human beings, its enactment depends crucially on the existence of a structured context in which individuals interact with each other" (Hodgson 1993: 174). Further, "Individuals have an incentive to conform to the group and gain access to its knowledge" (175). This individual–group interaction was the reason that the transaction was chosen as the unit of observation in chapter 1.

Some define an organization as a process by which "individuals are persuaded to set aside their individual purposes or goals and pursue those of the organization" (Galbraith 1967: 130). This conception may lead to making the organization something apart from individuals, rather than a process by which individual purposes are formed and conflicts in purposes are worked out. Organizations are systems of relationships for coordinating individual action according so some decision rule. That decision rule may be unanimity, but, because of decision costs, is usually some form of majority (Buchanan and Tullock 1962). Organizations usually have some administrative process wherein rules are applied and collective action taken. It is common to speak of the goal of an organization, but this is often the goal of the winning coalition within an organization. The person who objects may have the option of leaving the organization or working to change it. A dissident may later learn to identify with the winning coalition (March and Simon 1958: 65).

Boundaries are relative to function. In the US, only stockholders can vote for corporate directors. Non-managerial employees are not "members" but they are nevertheless stakeholders. They may have certain opportunities because of custom, internal corporate rules, or bargaining ability. In Germany, labor has formal representation on corporate boards by law. If a corporation forms an alliance with another firm short of formal merger, it retains its identity, but certain functions are now subject to consensus with the alliance partner.

Why organizations? Why firms? Organizations are the norm, and markets are a secondary connector of human action. Given the dominance of organizations, one might better ask, why isolated individuals? The question might even better be, why one boundary to collective action rather than another? The most basic boundary is one of how many people recognize a property claim. I might have an understanding with my neighbor as to what land uses are in my opportunity set and what are in hers. On this collectively established basis we may trade. Someone outside of this boundary may, however, not agree and assert a claim rather than make a bid. Likewise, I may have an understanding with my boss and fellow employees as to promotion criteria.

It is convenient and relevant to human purpose to report performance by collectivities. So we speak of the profitability of a corporation or the accomplishment of a university even if it represents the work of its members. There is always an element of artifact in the groupings and boundaries chosen for reporting. A firm is at one level an artifact of accounting, a collection of activity and assets represented by a balance sheet and net worth.

A firm is not just a cheaper way to put together known inputs to produce a known product according to a known recipe. A firm is a collective of people organized to create a product and recipe (including market demand and creation). It is a collective imagination and vision. It is not merely an economizing process, but an envisioning process. You can't economize on an unknown (Hardin 2003). The organization must deal with fundamental uncertainty. The firm is not just a place or nexus of contract where known inputs with known productivity are bought, but more fundamentally a collectivity where competence is built (Hodgson 1999b: ch. 11). See section 6.7.5 below.

In the public sector, conflicts of interest cannot be resolved with reference to economizing since that assumes whose preferences count. In the world of business, the process of conceiving of a new product and process cannot be described in terms of economizing since that assumes what is to be created.

Loyalty and calculation: Any grouping of relationships has the potential to inspire loyalty. Loyalty is the suspension of calculation. Participation in an organization may create loyalty and affinity (sympathy). Members may identify with the goals of the organization and the welfare of other members. A member acts consistent with the opportunity sets expected by other members. Loyalty is about learning and internalization, not just the manipulation of costs and benefits to the calculating mind. It involves a broad set of reinforcers and not just that of material punishment. An organization is the arena of suspended calculation. If the members grow to care for each other (have social capital), they will act in accordance with their perception of the group's objectives even when they do not fit their own. They will not be opportunistic and take advantage of others even when no external sanction can be applied. Members may make grant transactions (gifts) inside the firm going beyond minimum work standards. An example is a case study showing some account clerks in a utility company that produced more than the average worker even when receiving average wages (Akerlof 1982). These fast workers were making a gift (grant) to other slower workers and to the company.[2]

Objectives, boundaries, and information flows: It is difficult to speak of objectives of an organization and often obfuscating to speak of some mythical center that independently knows what it wants and tries to get others to go along. In complex organizations, the CEO can't know how to maximize profits or anything else independently of the flows of information from the members. And this information flow is a matter of organizational structure. The mythical center can't calculate what structure would be the most efficient because of bounded rationality. Nevertheless, we can speak of the decision of a firm to make or buy an input needed for its production process. Out of an existing hierarchy may come a set of actions to add employees, functions, and inputs to the hierarchy. Shirking is not the biggest problem of organizations. Rather it is deciding what is best to do in a world of uncertainty.

The boundary of organizations is quite unstable (Simon 1991: 29). Firms with quite different structures survive in the same industry. Still there is empirical evidence of some patterns (Williamson 1985). This will be discussed in the next chapter. Here we only want to describe possible ways to categorize the institutional alternatives.

Boundaries: The boundary is perhaps the most abstract and general way to describe an institution or an organization. It is a way to ask who participates in a decision. When a factory is to be closed, who gets to participate? Is labor on the board of directors? Does a supplier have anything to say in the decision to terminate purchases or refuse to pay when quality is questioned? Is the downstream water user included in a decision to dispose of waste? Is a voter included in voting district A or district B? Likewise, who is in and outside an organization and what are the qualifications for membership?

Markets, hierarchies, and alliances: The archetype of a market is an auction involving individuals and everything else is to some degree an organization. But, institutional economics is not an equilibrium price-auction market analysis (Thurow 1983: ch. 1). The degree to which transactions are auctions is as fundamental for performance as is the degree of competition. When two individuals or two organizations agree (contract) to a sequence of timing of mutual actions (often only vaguely specifiable), there is an organization, albeit transient and without a registered name that a consumer would recognize. In this age of strategic business alliances and sharing of information there is a blurring of boundaries even if there is an exchange. We distinguish arms-length transactions of an auction from those transactions that are closer and kin to an organization with floating boundaries/members. Contractual relationships used in "just-in-time" manufacturing are plans negotiated in a market, but it is not an auction market. Price is negotiated, but the coordination depends on much more than the communication of price. Suppliers are not just looking at price and then deciding how much to produce. Rather, price, quantity, and timing are agreed to up front and continuously evolving.

Unorganized collectivities: Most people are born into a collectivity called a family. They did not choose to join depending on how well the costs and benefits of membership worked out. They simply learned its habits and its associated opportunity set. Each element of this total opportunity set has a boundary. People may share a language, food habits, hunting customs, etc. The boundary of each may be different. There is no completely isolated individual who can choose to stay isolated. Those who fall into various groups and cohorts will often be treated in some common ordered way by others. For many of our opportunities, we can't decide to join and we can't keep others from joining. If others want to learn our language or follow our food habits, we can't stop them. And if others treat us in a certain way because they see us belonging to a group, it is hard to stop them. People can't exit from many of these institutional collectivities though their collective action may change the opportunity sets. Just as we find ourselves in formal positions and memberships that confer rights (opportunities) and obligations, we are "members" of informal differentiated social classes, life-styles, racial and ethnic groups, age cohorts, and mythic and symbolic representations of the past to the present which also apportion opportunities, even if we are mostly unaware of them.

5.4 Making Rules: The State

While institutions may be described in terms of positions and rules, there are higher order institutions that create lower order institutions. To explain the impact of alternative rules for making rules, we shall have to carefully specify the state as a variable. Economists are quick to provide an exchange theory to explain everything. An exchange theory of the state envisions a bargain between rulers and constituents wherein the ruler offers protection and settlement of disputes for a fee (North 1990: 48). We need not go back in the mists of time to imagine how peace was obtained among human animals with the ability to kill each other. Suffice it to observe that any negotiation beyond bodily threats assumes something that each legitimately brings to the transaction. Even the warlord enlisting people for raids on neighbors took advantage of the emotions distinguishing us from them. And, chiefs and kings did not invoke the spirits for nothing. The learning of mental models containing relationships of authority is integral to having something to exchange. The manipulation of symbols remains a part of the modern political process.

5.4.1 State and market

The state is antecedent to the market (Schmid 1999b). There is nothing to trade without some institution for deciding who is seller and who is buyer and what each may do to get the agreement of the other to a price. The formal rules of commodity transactions are created by government. As Coase (1992: 717) puts it, "what are traded on the market are not, as is often supposed by economists, physical entities, but the rights to perform certain actions, and the rights which individuals possess are established by the legal system." Samuels (1989) refers to the necessary conjunction of state and market as the "legal–economic nexus."

The highest order of rules for making rules are constitutions or things that function like constitutions. These provide the basic rights of individuals and groups as well as the broad framework of legislative and judicial bodies. For example, at this level we decide that people may not be enslaved, there is universal suffrage, proportional representation, rights of *habeas corpus*, etc.

The legislative and judicial bodies themselves formulate rules for their own conduct. For example, the detailed committee structure, agenda formulation, voting district boundaries, degree of unanimity required for action, rules of evidence and procedure, and rules of standing before a court. Again, there are rules for what resources individuals and groups can use to influence this process such as limits on campaign contributions or withholding of evidence.

5.4.2 Informal institutions for making informal institutions

Are there alternative structures for making informal institutions? The question seems strained. Informal institutions are formed out of purposive individual choices, but their emerging structure is largely non-deliberative. So how can we think about alternative evolutionary structures? As each person acts, some collective structure emerges, but no one actually chose it or none may have even envisaged it. What then is the role of research and analysis? It can raise the level of the argument. There is a process of persuasion that goes on informally as well as formally. Metaphors are employed. A powerful one is to make an institution seem natural and perhaps inevitable. A major question is when to leave the informal evolutionary structure alone and when to replace it with deliberative collective choice. See Hirschman (1991) and Vanberg (1989).

The arguments of economics as a discipline are those of the inputs into cultural learning. Marx's argument of the inevitable victory of the proletariat and withering of the state became part of popular political movements around the world. Contemporary theories of the automatic emergence of the best of all possible worlds from "free markets" are another example.

Formal and informal institutions affect the evolutionary path of each other and the performance of each at the moment. A particular relationship may be neutral, complimentary, substitutive, or conflicting (Ellickson 1991). Interacting institutional change will be explored in chapter 13.

5.5 Social Choice (Conflict Resolution)

5.5.1 Specifying the state as an institutional variable

Social choice refers to the process of aggregating individual preferences. Societies are constantly facing new conflicts (interdependencies) and forging new institutions to apportion opportunities. For example, with invention of TV satellite dishes there is a clash between neighbors who want the reception and those who consider the dish an ugly blot on the landscape. In the heat of political debate it is tempting to say, "let the market decide." Is the institutional variable properly specified in this proposition?

Let the market decide has two interpretations. One is that the opportunity should be sold to the highest bidder (or given to what is expected to be the highest bidder). This is hardly neutral or natural. Such a method for distributing new rights just makes them an extension of existing rights. Those that have a lot will get more. The deeper meaning of "let the market decide" is that rights should be given to those who already have many.

The second interpretation is that some person A is seen as the natural owner and if anyone else wants to have the opportunity, they must buy it. The question is well illustrated in a debate between Buchanan and Samuels (1975) over the interdependence created by a rust disease that travels from ornamental cedars (where it is harmless) to apple trees (where it is disastrous). The Virginia legislature passed a law that allowed an apple tree owner to petition the state to destroy any offending cedars. This was seen by Buchanan as the heavy hand of the state destroying human freedom. He proposed a market solution to the governmental regulation. Let the orchardists buy out the cedar grower if they can. If they can't, then orchardists will have to economize as best they can. He worked with an institutional variable specification that separated the state from the distribution of ownership. It seemed natural to him that the cedar grower owned not only the land upon which the tree was growing but also the surface of neighboring apple tree leaves where the associated disease spores generated on the cedars come to rest. The physical production function for growing cedars has inputs of land, labor, and space for the spores. All of these things are necessarily consumed in the process of growing cedars.

Samuels turned the assumption of initial ownership of apple leaf surfaces on its head. There is nothing natural about who owns this opportunity. Rather it is a matter to be decided. The state creation of rights is antecedent to the market, not an alternative to it. The market just carries out the implications of ownership. The market can work with either party being the buyer or seller. But it cannot be the process by which ownership is created. The conception of the state and market as alternatives is a mispecification of variables. One can have state owned or privately owned orchards, but one cannot have a market without a state. This statement must be modified in the sense that the process of making rights (who is seller and who buyer) can be informal rather than a matter of explicit legislative or judicial choice. When new interdependencies are discovered, one party may assert ownership and, if accepted, trading begins. In this process the party that can make its interest appear more natural may become the de facto owner and in fact later be confirmed by the common law or formal statute.

Note that production functions are never complete and are themselves matters of selective perception. Did you find it strange to hear that the inputs of cedar production include apple leaf structures? Or the reverse; inputs of apple production include the amount of cedar trees in the vicinity. Before science discovered the habits of this parasite, apple trees died but their owners did not understand why. They were ignorant of their interdependence with cedar growers and therefore there could have been no formal or informal ownership of the opportunity at stake. Specification of the resource opportunity (input) at issue is as important for the evolution of institutions as is the specification of institutional components and alternatives.

Compensation is no answer to a dispute over rights. The issue is who will compensate whom. When the state process decides who is owner it simultaneously decides who must compensate whom. That's what it means to be an owner of a tradable opportunity. A political choice that all change in the holders of a right must be compensated is to say that rights are fixed forever and the status quo reigns. Later in the book, the decisions of American courts to alter rights and owners under what is referred to as the 'police power' will be examined.

The implication of the above for theory and hypothesis formation is that we may conceive of two levels of analysis. One has the *rules* of commodity transactions as the dependent variable with alternative rules for making rules as the independent variable. The second has *performance* of the workaday economy as the dependent variable and the above alternative rules for commodity transactions as the independent variable. Both are impact analysis of alternative institutions.

5.5.2 Specifying performance variables

It was suggested in the introductory chapter that the performance of alternative institutions be specified in substantive terms of who gets what. This allows each interest to answer the question of what is good for them. It does not allow the analyst to say what is best for everyone. This must be worked out in the political process as groups contend for power. But, there is a demand for science to supply an answer to the question, "What is the best institution?" Can the political process be replaced with science? Are there tests that can be performed which can instruct politics and raise it above the fray? We will look at some of the main contenders for this honor below.

Efficiency. Can we test institutional alternatives by which one is more efficient? No.[3] Efficiency is a derivative of the institutional choice, not the other way round.

Institutions select whose interests are a cost to whom. Institutions shape cost and thus relative prices. To use efficiency as a basis for institutional choice is to be caught in a "value circularity problem." Efficiency is not a unique outcome. Out of many possible efficiencies, one is selected by institutional choice. The point can be illustrated by observing that the point on the contract curve that is reached via bargaining depends on the initial distribution of resources. (Economists portray this in what is known as an Edgeworth Box.) It can also be illustrated by the well-known microeconomic fact that a demand curve depends on the distribution of income. If preferences differ, a change in the distribution of income (because of policy or normal working of the market) changes relative prices and thus destroys the basis for summing the value of the total product that might be produced in response to that demand. Models of a representative consumer cover up this fact.

Arrow (1963: 40) puts it this way, "There is no meaning to total output independent of distribution. . . . In a world of more than one commodity, there is no unequivocal meaning to comparing total production in any two social states save in terms of some standard of value which makes the different commodities commensurable; and usually such a standard of value must depend on the distribution of income."

The problem with efficiency is that there are too many of them and thus efficiency gives no basis for choosing among them. We are necessarily comparing efficiency *E*1 with efficiency *E*2. Within each there is of course a set of efficient and inefficient outcomes. This just says that once you decide whose interests count, stick to it. But that says nothing about choosing *E*1 or *E*2. That takes a moral choice of whose interests count. Make no mistake, institutional economists have no quarrel with efficiency – they just recognize that it necessarily has an institutional context (Vatn 2002). This is not an "efficiency vs. other values" argument. Unless distribution is chosen, there is no subsequent calculation of efficiency. Likewise, institutional economists have no quarrel with markets – they just recognize that the issue is who is buyer and who is seller.

Aggregate welfare analysis covers more than it reveals. Just one example for now. Some economists argue that taxes are a deadweight loss that distorts market allocation (Breton 1989; Mankiw 2004: 163). This can be true only if taxes are wholly tribute. If taxes are a payment by firms and households for publicly provided inputs into production, they are no different than payment for any inputs. There is no natural market independent of the rights determining what is a legitimate cost to whom. As noted above, cost is institutionally defined. Further, to call all redistribution of rights a deadweight loss (rent seeking) is only to sanctify the *status quo* rent earners.

Freedom: If efficiency cannot be the test for which institution is better, perhaps freedom can. Freedom sounds like something that all could agree on. But it is empirically impossible in a global sense. Specification of the transaction as the unit of analysis has already shown us that in a world of scarcity A's freedom is B's limit and exposure. As Isaiah Berlin put it, "Freedom for the pike is death for the minnow." When a person demands freedom, they are really demanding that they have a scarce opportunity rather than someone else. Freedom as a performance variable must have an interest group subscript on it.

Freedom to trade what you have for what someone else has, begs the question of who has what to trade. Knight and Bonner (1947: 4) make the point saying, "The fatal defect in the utilitarian doctrine of maximum freedom as a goal of social policy is its confusion of freedom and power. Its advocates overlook the fact that freedom to perform an act is meaningless unless the subject is in possession of the requisite means of action, and that the practical question is one of power rather than of formal freedom."

Democracy and unanimity. Can rules for making rules be devised so that individual preferences can be aggregated without violating some widely agreed on principles such as non-dictatorship? Arrow (1963) in his "impossibility theorem" has formally demonstrated what other institutional economists have long intuitively understood, namely, no such constitutional and political rules are possible. One easily understood element is provided by what Arrow calls the voting paradox. If you change the agenda in a series of political choices, you change the winning coalitions that emerge. The setting of an agenda is another kind of "boundary" institution. Arrow (1963: 59) concludes, "If no prior assumptions are made about the nature of individual orderings, there is no method of voting which will remove the paradox of voting . . . , neither plurality voting nor any scheme of proportional representation no matter how complicated. Similarly, the market mechanism does not create a rational social choice. . . . If we exclude the possibility of interpersonal comparisons of utility, then the only methods of passing from individual tastes to social preferences which will be satisfactory and which will be defined for a wide range of sets of individual orderings are either imposed or dictatorial."

What about unanimity? It would appear that unanimity would protect the freedom of each individual since the individual could always prevent any change that was not mutually beneficial. Buchanan and Tullock (1962) note that there is an individual calculus such that a person protected by such a constitution might agree to a subsequent social choice rules of less than unanimity when the costs of getting others to agree to some change that a person wants is greater than the costs of accepting some unwanted change initiated by others. More fundamentally, "under such a rule, the status quo is a highly privileged alternative" (Arrow 1963: 120).[4] "There is no special role given to an alternative because it happens to be identical to or derived from a historically given one" (119). Arrow concludes, "Collective rationality in the social choice mechanism is not then merely an illegitimate transfer from the individual to society, but an important attribute of a genuinely democratic system capable of full adaptation to varying circumstances" (120).

Decision processes are sometimes valued in themselves in which case the institutional variable is both an independent variable and a dependent performance variable. Arrow (1963) notes that the stability of political systems depends in part on allegiance to a process and willingness to accept some results contrary to the person's self-interest. But he denies that this can be wholly independent of outcomes. Social welfare judgments require both. He finds it hard to believe that "individuals ascribe an incommensurably greater value to the process than to the decisions reached under it" (91). See also Waligorski (1990), who makes the same point. We learn that a certain decision process seems to produce outcomes that serve our interests and they may constitute a habit that is hard to break even when the flow of outcomes seems to be running against us.

In summary, the rules for making everyday rules as well as the everyday rules themselves must be worked out and require a moral judgment of whose interests count. This theme is further explored in chapter 12 "Political Institutions."

Minimize transaction costs: Can the minimization of transaction costs be taken as a performance variable and test of institutional adequacy, as Williamson (1985) suggests? If two people find a transaction beneficial it would seems that the elimination of any barrier and friction preventing the trade would be universally approved. The metaphor conceives of institutions as grease that make all beneficial transactions possible. Some go as far as saying that transaction costs are the sole reason for institutions and that if transaction costs were zero, no institutions would be necessary.

"Of course, 'efficient' institutional changes that reduce transaction costs or increase productivity or economic growth may do so only at the expense of certain individuals or groups" (Rutherford 1994: 161). Interdependence theory tells us that there is more to transactions than two parties. The failure of a transaction between two parties is often the opportunity for a third party. For example, the failure of many ranchers to sell air pollution rights to a phosphate miner or a coal fired electricity producer is an opportunity for other breathers. These third parties could themselves be included as joint owners of the air. If they refused to sell, we would not say the result was transaction cost hindering Pareto-better trade. While for reasons of transparency it might be clearer if all rights were thus explicit, it serves some to have a *de facto* right protected by transaction costs and it is not the analysts' portfolio to presume whose interests should count. One person's friction is another's opportunity. Institutions are about apportioning opportunity. Colby (2000) reminds us, "when cap-and-trade policies are being introduced, property rights themselves still are a subject of contention." Markets are often touted as the solution to environmental conflicts, but can only operate after the effluent cap gives property rights to one party or another (Stephenson 2003).

Coase rule: Coase (1960) deduced that if transaction costs were zero in markets, the use of a resource would be the same regardless of who had the property right. Some ran with this theoretical proposition and applied it to the policy world and concluded that property rights did not matter. Coase in his Nobel Prize acceptance speech (Coase 1992) explicitly observed that since there are commonly positive transaction costs, economists must analyze the impact of alternative property rights. Coase was aware in passing that while resource use might be the same, income distribution would be different. And for this reason, institutions are important even in the imaginary world of zero transaction costs. Because of transaction costs, Coase (1992: 717) said, "the rights which individuals possess, with their duties and privileges, will be, to a large extent, what the law determines" and can't be contracted around. "It is obviously desirable that these rights should be assigned to those who can use them most productively" (718). That puts us back into the calculation of what constitutes efficiency or total product maximization, which as we have already seen is presumptuous of whose interests count. Damages are not independent of institutions and thus can't guide choice of institutions.

Liebhafsky (1973) says Coase considered only the presence or absence of liability (assessment of damages) and not an injunction. Liebhafsky did not accept Coase's proposition that the farmer causes "damage" to the rancher (if the cows can't stray) as well as the rancher's stray cows damaging the farmer's crop. He points to the value circularity problem when he says, "in evaluating a change by making use of the Pareto optimality test, . . . it is necessary to select an initial position or a starting point from which to measure the change" (658). Liebhafsky as citizen prefers to start with ownership and right of injunction held by environmental interests rather than those he regards as laying waste to resources.

People as product: If economics is grounded in improving human life, then we must include in performance measures more than GNP or even who gets what. The "what" must include more than physical things. Human relationships are not just instruments, but ends. What kind of people are being produced? Crime, suicide, family dysfunction, drug use, intolerance, wars, and terror plague us (Caplow, Hicks, and Wattenberg 2001). Must work and leisure be separated? Institutions are not just ways to relate people to each other to solve commitment and coordination problems, but also to create relationships that are peaceful and feel good.

Some institutionalists have not been shy in suggesting the performance variables (conception of the good society) that they think should be accounted for and in some cases serve as preferred criteria for choice of institutions. For example, Mark Tool (1979: 293) argues for an "instrumental value principle." An institution is better if "it provides for the continuity of human life and the noninvidious re-creation of community through the instrumental use of knowledge." See also Liebhafsky (1973: 627). Without taking sides, an analyst can cast a broad net in imagining substantive performance variables to document that will be of interest to different stakeholders with different views of the good society.

5.5.3 Necessity for moral choice

"Empirically, we can reject the idea that the consensus can be found in the expressed individual wills" (Arrow 1963: 84). Because of conflicting interests and conflicting views of the good society, some moral judgment is inherent in any social choice of whose interests count. There is not some set of data out there that already contains the answer. It has to be worked out in the political process. If we are to avoid war, some degree of altruism is necessary, some willingness to regard others as subjects (ends) and not just objects to be manipulated. This general will or consensus is not something to be found, but to be created. "It requires a definite value judgment not derivable from individual sensations to make the utilities of different individuals dimensionally computable and still a further value judgment to aggregate them according to any particular mathematical formula" (Arrow 1963: 11). It does not take a formal model to come to the conclusion that each and every citizen cannot be sovereign if they have conflicting interests. If we do not allow a dictator to choose among these conflicting interests, we shall have to do it ourselves by imposing self-restraint. Morality is about self-restraint. Arrow's rationality conditions show that social outcomes are among other things a function of boundaries (agenda). Whose preferences count is a function of institutions and when we choose institutions, we choose among interests. There is not some pre-existing resolution of conflicts out there that directs the choice of institutions to express that resolution with fidelity. Institutions are not something to be derived, deduced, and discovered, but rather the prior to be created from which efficiency and apportioned freedom derives. "Politics is not a process of fact finding or identification of truth but rather of conflict resolution between individuals" (Sandmo (1990: 52), summarizing Buchanan).

5.5.4 Reasonable value

As human wills clash in the everyday struggle for survival and realization as they see it, people attempt to persuade (or force) others to accept their view of who should have opportunities and who is exposed to those opportunities. Some will reason from religion, others from natural law, economic efficiency, process, etc. The law and economics movement has attempted to find a guide to court decisions that rests on economic theory. One proposed test is that the cheapest avoider of a cost should bear it. But as one of the reformed originators of the law and economics movement suggests, "who is the cheapest avoider of a cost, depends on the valuations put on acts, activities, and beliefs by the whole of our law and not on some objective or scientific notion" (Calabresi 1985: 69). He insists that efficiency must ask the prior moral question of whose interests should count.

Let us admit that there is something attractive in the hope that something prior to the struggle exists that can be discovered; something so powerful and self-evident that all would be persuaded. The divine right of kings to make these decisions for us has fallen and the role of religious leaders has likewise declined, though still influential. "Pragmatists insist that we have now outgrown our need for external truth rules to tell us what is the better thing to do" (Bromley forthcoming). Ends "must inevitably be experiences by imaginations or anticipation and not by external occurrence. Choice, inescapably, is choice among thoughts and thoughts . . . are not *given*" (Shackle 1961: 273).

In the US, the Supreme Court is the ultimate arbiter, albeit influenced by the social milieu. Most parties accept the court decisions after making their case, even if they contest how the general language of the Constitution relates to the particular decision. The words are subject to different interpretations. Whatever the general principle that may prove persuasive, the detailed meanings are worked out as people learn and debate within existing and evolving rules for making rules.

Robinson (1962) suggests that, "The Keynesian revolution has destroyed the soporific doctrines, and its own metaphysics is thin and easy to see through. We are left in the uncomfortable situation of having to think for ourselves." Hayek wanted to find the principle for settling conflicts in custom. But, there are usually competing customs as there are competing interpretations of a constitution. Commons observed that the courts selected "best" practices from custom, but best was always debatable.

For Commons, "The word 'reasonable' has no intrinsic meaning when modifying the term 'value'" (Ramstad 2001: 264). For Commons, the regime of prices resulting from a particular set of rules formulated by the legislature and affirmed by the courts "is not intellectual or rational – it is the valuation of stupidity, passion and ignorance, and the dominant collective action that controls individual action" (Commons 1934: 763).

What is reasonable is to be created, not found.[5] This is a heavy existential burden, too heavy for some who prefer to "escape from freedom" (Fromm 1941). The philosopher, Taylor (1966: 265) says, "In the exercise of that freedom lies whatever is human in ourselves, and if you are diffident of that freedom, that is a delusion of the ignorant or a sentiment of the forum, then, whatever it is you discuss, you do not discuss the historical condition of men. Which is simply to have said, you do not discuss politics."

5.6 Conclusions

It is not necessary to conceptualize institutions and organizations as factors of production to see how they affect economic performance. Rather this can best be understood as how institutions and organizations affect which production function actually exists in time and space. Cost is an institutional artifact determining whose interests count as a cost to others. Interdependence means that someone will always suffer the external effect of the exercise of rights by others. Rights give their owners the power to make these preferences count by apportioning opportunities. When the power question is settled for the moment, each party (individual or organization) can economize within its opportunity set. The apportionment of power requires a moral choice – a public choice, either formal or informal. Efficiency and freedom as performance measures beg the question of whose interests count when interests conflict.

In spite of the rhetoric of individualism, the dominant decision unit in modern society is the organization, a collective. While an organization has individual members/employees, there is some institutional structure that aggregates the individual decisions. Organizations are a process for making rules for its members and influencing the rules defining its relationship with others outside the organization. The governance and boundaries of an organization are not simply the result of economizing by its members or transaction partners. It is both a power struggle and a process for learning and working out individual and collective identities. State, market, and organizations interact to define each other.

NOTES

1. Williamson (2002) contrasts the neoclassical firm as a production function and the firm as a governance structure.
2. Collins (2001) found that managers of firms that went from good to great had a strong identification with the firm and were less motivated by personal monetary rewards. They tended to credit others for the firm's success.
3. Many answer yes, such as Cooter and Ulen (1988).

4. Buchanan (1992) in his autobiography laments that his rule enshrines the *status quo*.
5. Is the argument of this book nihilistic and one of moral relativism? No. Nihilism is defined as "total rejection of established laws and institutions" and philosophically as denial of an objective basis for truth. For what it is worth, I do not reject all present laws or the possibility of widely shared concepts of truth and values. If I thought there was no role for reason and knowledge, I would not bother to write this book. I do reject the pseudo-scientific claims of social welfare maximization that hide the speaker's preferences for alpha over beta. I accept the necessity to choose in alpha–beta conflicts and cannot lie to myself that I have not done so by hiding behind the high priest's robes. This is my value judgment.

Chapter 6
Sources of Human Interdependence

6.1 Introduction

Human interdependence is conditioned by the inherent characteristics of goods (resources). The possibility for one person's actions to affect the welfare of another person is a function of the physics and biology of goods and services. For the purpose of analyzing the impact and change consequences of alternative institutions, these inherent characteristics are a given, even though over time, technology may change them. Institutions, both formal and informal sort out the potential interdependencies and provide order and predictability to the parties. One can describe how institution "X" compared to "Y" facilitates the interests of person or group A. Once the power issue is settled, economizing is possible. Second order institutions for economizing and mutual gain may also be analyzed.

The opportunity sets created by formal and informal institutions are related to the environment in a mental process. An opportunity seen by the analyst may not be perceived by an actor, or the opportunity may be forgone. The actor may make a mess of it and realize little advantage. The actor may not apply the institution that the analyst has in mind, but rather another to a given situation. This makes empirical work difficult. In every case, institutional economics works in terms of behavioral regularities applicable to most people.

This chapter is organized by different categories of the sources of interdependence. These sources are the inherent characteristics of goods and will be referred to as the "situation." These include the degree of incompatibility, exclusion cost, cost to provide the good for another user, cost to produce another physical unit, and various kinds of transaction costs. The kinds of institutions that affect performance in the context of each source of interdependence are identified and hypotheses suggested of how alternative institutions facilitate the interests of one group or another. Theory specifies the relevant variables and relationships among them.

Several themes will emerge from the analysis. The institutional resolution of the interdependence requires a moral judgment of whose interests count. No feature of a good dictates the appropriate institution. Every interdependence creates an externality and the policy issue is who creates externalities for whom. Where interdependent interests exist, choice of whose interests are to count is a power issue. To have a right is to be able to coerce others to do without or to meet the owner's terms. Where there is interdependence there is a formal or informal right to direct the interdependence and thus affect performance. However clear the right appears, it creates *de facto* opportunities.

6.2 Incompatibility

Uses and users of many goods and opportunities are incompatible. If one person has the opportunity, another must do without. If someone uses a parcel of land for corn, it is not available for another person's use. Alpha's use of land for rearing pigs is incompatible with neighbor Beta's enjoyment of sweet smelling air. (See table 6.1.) Alpha's right to vote reduces the influence of Beta's vote. When most people think of property rights, they are thinking of these incompatible use goods (IUGs). When combined with markets, the ownership of an IUG means that its owner's preferences count and she is a potential seller, rather than a buyer, of opportunities. An owner has the power to create costs for others who want but do not own the opportunity. Cost is a function of rights distribution. The poor have little that is a cost to others.

The institutional structure that gives opportunities to some and necessarily exposures to others is varied. A person may be an owner by act of legislation. Examples are ownership of off-shore oil deposits or radio frequencies in the electromagnetic spectrum. In the common law countries, one is an owner if the court fails to enjoin others when they infringe on one's opportunities. So if Alpha builds a house that blocks Beta's view or sunlight, Alpha is the effective owner if Beta does not challenge. And if challenged in court, Alpha is the owner if the suit is decided in Alpha's favor. Regulation can also be the source of an effective right. If Alpha is prohibited from building near the shoreline, then Beta owns the right to be free of Alpha's incompatible use. In this case, Beta has a use right but perhaps not an exchangeable right.

The performance impact of a right to an IUG is relatively easy to predict. If environmentalists own the air, then the air is likely to be cleaner than if industry owns it, even if the right is exchangeable (see table 6.1). If a poor person is given land, they will be richer than before. There are some fine points to be argued such

Table 6.1 Incompatible use: situation, structure, and performance

Situation	Structure	Performance
Land – between farmer A and farmer B	1. Farmer A is factor owner, may trade	1. Farmer A sells to B whose bid > A's reservation price
(or air between industry and breather)	2. Farmer B is factor owner, (a beneficiary of regulation)	2. Farmer B keeps and A goes hungry (has lung disease)

as the effect of land reform on land yields, but the income distribution effects are usually obvious. Private property in land and other opportunities does have incentive effects. It is common knowledge that when rights are insecure users are afraid to make long-term investments. Still, the value of opportunities changes and societies either confirm or deny the new values created by environmental changes.

Pareto-worse changes in rights are essential for some varieties of economic development. The problem is to find a balance between enough security to foster investment and enough loss of value to those who otherwise would extract such a price for their consent that innovation would be stifled. Consider the Supreme Court case where a bridge was to be built across a river. The landowners near the abutments of the bridge sued fearing that the construction would cause some erosion of their land. The effects of lots of innovations are uncertain and if those who might be damaged could enjoin, there would be much less innovation. Distribution of the costs of economic change is a factor in the speed and kind of economic development (Horwitz 1992). The location of ownership has an income effect as well as affecting transaction costs (Field 1991). The income effect causes willingness to pay and willingness to sell to diverge. The "takings" issue in US law is one place where these issues bite (Samuels 1992a). There is no doubt that sometimes regulation decreases the value of some rights holders. The empirical question is how much taking an old owner can absorb before incentive to invest is destroyed and how much taking a would-be owner needs to make a new venture feasible. At some point, the buying out of old owners could stop innovation whose fruits are initially uncertain.

New interdependencies are created and discovered by changes in technology. No one thought about air rights over land until the airplane was created. Then landowners claimed the right to sell air space and the airplane industry claimed the same right. The courts decided in favor of the airlines and that had much to do with the growth and cost of air travel. Likewise, no one argued over the rights to describe a sporting event until the age of radio and TV. The broadcaster claimed that buying a seat and space for their equipment entitled them to broadcast a description of the game. But the team owners claimed the description was their right to sell and the courts sided with them, making team owners and eventually the players millionaires. The direction of these performance impacts is relatively straightforward even when the source passes into the mists of what is taken for granted.

6.2.1 Externalities (interdependence)

There are two ways to conceptualize externalities. The most common is to view externality as a by-product of some production process. So there is intended steel and unintended air pollution. Alternatively, externality may be viewed as simply the lost opportunity occasioned by the incompatible use of a good. Instead of the pollution being seen as a by-product, it may be seen simply as another input necessary to produce an output. We do not usually say that labor (expenditure of effort), iron ore, energy, and machines are by-products of steel. They are simply inputs. And so is a space to put waste. All are necessary inputs. The question for all of them is who owns these inputs and therefore is in a position to make their use by others a cost. Iron ore is paid for because the mines are owned. Likewise, the land for the steel plant is paid for because someone owned it and the steel plant had to buy it. The steel plant will pay for a place to put its waste (in the air, water, or land) if that resource is owned by others. If it already owns it, the steel company will listen to bids of others who would like it, but do not own it. If the farmer rejects the bid of the steel company, the company will have to find a more expensive substitute. Its costs go up. Or if the steel company already owns the land, it may reject the farmer's bid. Likewise, if the steel company owns the air or water and uses it for waste disposal, the farmer or any other neighbor may offer the owner a bid for something it likes but does not own. If the bid is rejected, the farmer and neighbor turn to more expensive substitutes including doing without.

A negative externality is inevitable (ubiquitous) if goods are scarce and use by different parties incompatible. This is why people contend to be owners. Ownership defines who has the opportunity and who is exposed to the exercise of these opportunities. The ability to create negative externalities produces income for the owner. The bid persuades the owner of the opportunity to forgo her preferred activity and defer to the bidder. A poor person is one who has few owned opportunities that produce income. An owner who cares for a non-owner and derives utility from that person's welfare will transfer ownership to that person to reduce that person's exposure to the owner's opportunities. E.g. a person with a lot of land may share produce with the hungry and a person with a lot of pollution rights may share those rights with the contaminated by reducing the polluting activity and finding more costly substitutes for the owned inputs.

Ownership rests on a consensus of legitimacy. This willing acceptance of the distribution of opportunities rests upon some moral judgment. Expenditure to enforce ownership against those who contest or deny ownership ranges from police to guerillas to armies. Legitimacy of ownership requires some minimal threshold of respect, if not care, for the owners. A despised owner is an insecure owner. Without respect and willing participation by non-owners, the expenditures to maintain putative ownership can be very high.

6.2.2 Sustainability

If person A uses land for corn, it can't be used at the same time by B for corn or something else. If A uses land for corn such that it is not eroded and exhausted, it is possible for B to use it for corn or something else in the future. The capacity for a flow of services of biophysical resources can be sustained or run down. Air can be used for waste disposal, which is incompatible with healthy breathing. But, when disposal ceases, the capacity for breathing is restored.

However, in the case of oil and minerals, when they are burned or otherwise transformed from low entropy to high, throughput can't be sustained or restored. Daly (2002) defines throughput as "the entropic physical flow from nature's sources through the economy and back to nature's sinks."

The inherent character of oil and minerals (and other natural stock resources) is incompatible use through time. This creates interdependence among generations.

What alternative structures are relevant? One, the owners of value added inputs also own any value of nature. Or, all citizens of a nation or world can be regarded as factor owners. An example of the first is when OPEC restricts output enough to earn a return above the opportunity cost of pumping and exploration. An example of broader ownership is the Alaska Permanent Fund wherein all Alaskan's receive royalties from oil extraction. Daly advocates a world-wide tax on natural resources to be paid to the poor.

The performance variables for this IUG interdependence are income distribution, the relative amount of wealth and ilth, and the degree to which physical throughput is sustained or diminished. Daly makes a moral judgment in favor of distributing the value of nature to the world's poor and passing on to future generations the same access to nature enjoyed by the present. He opposes World Bank, IMF, and WTO emphasis on economic development that ignores the sustainability of throughput.

6.3 Exclusion Cost

If a factor owner is to receive revenue to cover production costs in the market, it must be possible to exclude those who do not pay when the good is provided to those who do. A high exclusion cost (HEC) good is one where if the good exists for one user, it is costly to exclude others, even if the users can be identified. The exclusion cost is greater than net revenue. A useful metaphor for HEC good is that of a fence. If the fence that keeps people out is too costly relative to the value of the good, the good may not be produced or at least not in the quantity that would be indicated by the summation of demand. Of course, knowing the demand is the problem, for people do not reveal their demand if they are hoping to ride free, that is to use without paying.

HEC is not primarily a detection or policing problem though this adds to it. A producer of cleaner air knows that many breathers are using the improved product, but still if the product is produced for one payer, the non-payers can't be excluded. The non-payers can claim they would pay nothing and this cannot be tested by denying access. Of course, no one can be excluded if their use is unknown or costly to detect, such as the person digging clams on a beach at night or surreptitiously dumping chemicals in a drain. But, detection is not enough in any case.

Environmental goods generally are HEC. What institutional structures affect performance with HEC goods? Will nominal factor ownership produce income as in the case of a low exclusion cost IUG? Theory should indicate the relevant kinds of institutional structures that control the interdependence created by the situation and suggest the performance associated with each (see table 6.2). Note that these goods are labeled HEC, not "public goods." The latter term has within it a suggested policy conclusion, namely public provision, but that is just one of the institutions that could be chosen and it is prejudicial to have the name of the good contain a policy conclusion.

Air is an IUG *between* industry and breathers. Consider factor ownership of the IUG by industry – the right to dispose of a certain chemical in the air. They are the sellers. Air is HEC among breathers and those wanting cleaner air are buyers. If

Table 6.2 High exclusion cost

Situation	Structure	Performance

Good = Air
High exclusion
  cost among
  breathers
Low exclusion
  cost among
  industries
	1. Industry owns
	a. Market. Bargaining
	  • Breathers must bid
	  • Industry A bids to
	    industry B
	b. Admin. – tax on breathers
	  to buy industry rights
	c. Customary (internal
	  motivation). Breathers
	  boycott polluting industry
		
		• Free-riders. Bid fails and
		  would-be riders do without
		• Rights traded; firms economize
		No free-rider. Unwilling rider is
		  coerced
		Few free-riders. Bid is successful

	2. Breathers own
	a. Administration: standards,
	  regulations. No trade
	  allowed
	b. Market. Bargaining. Who
	  sets price? If one owner
	  sells, all sell
		
		Breathers use all. If industry steals,
		  court orders pay
		
		Offer to sell some. Tort liability.
		  But some people want ∞ price.
		  Who counts among breathers?

the structure is market bargaining, the result may be free-riders defeating a successful bid. If the structure is a tax on breathers, there are no free-riders, but rather some unwilling riders.

Note that waste disposal *among* industries is low exclusion cost. One firm can use and others can be excluded. Rights may be traded and firms economize comparing the cost of buying disposal rights or using treatment technologies (line 1a in table 6.2).

Knowing how the brain works is especially important in understanding the performance of different institutions applied to HEC goods. If people were in fact calculatingly selfish, we can predict free-riding – people who use the available HEC good, but do not pay.[1] Two kinds of free-riders can be distinguished. The free-rider with guile is calculatingly opportunistic. She is maximizing her own utility by taking advantage of those who pay. The unwitting free-rider uses any available HEC good, but has no guile as she just reasons that her action can't make a difference. This is especially true with costly goods with many beneficiaries. One person contributing to the cost can't make a difference in provision.

Accompanying the free-rider is the frustrated would-be rider who perhaps is willing to pay (forgoes opportunism), but because of too many free-riders, there is little or no good to enjoy. The would-be rider thinks that her share of the cost is just, but has not the opportunity to enjoy the good. Olson defines a "latent group" as containing individuals who "cannot make a noticeable contribution to any group effort, and since no one in the group will react if he makes no contribution, he has no incentive to contribute." "Large or 'latent' groups have no incentive to act to obtain a collective good because, however valuable the collective good might be to the group as a whole, it does not offer the individual any incentive to pay dues . . ." (Olson 1965: 50). Of course, the incentive is a matter of one's state of mind. If one cared for the would-be riders, one would not be opportunistic.

If people are opportunistic with guile, the institutional alternatives for provisioning HEC goods are limited. Olson suggests two. One is administrative, rather than market. People are taxed to provide the good (structure 1b in table 6.2). Workers in a union shop are forced to pay dues to the union even if they disagree with their program. Farmers are forced to pay part of their sales to finance advertising for their generic products. Typically the government imposes these check-off programs after approval by a majority of the producers. Administration eliminates the free-rider, but at the cost of "unwilling riders." Unwilling riders are those who in the situation of HEC and the structure of administration must pay but do not have a utility from the good equal to their share of the cost of production. Where there are HEC goods, there is a necessary tradeoff between the interests of the would-be riders and the unwilling riders if the only choice is market or administration.

The second way to avoid free-riders is a tie-in sale (selective incentive). The HEC good is tied to a low exclusion cost good and the buyer of the latter is forced to pay for the HEC good when buying the low exclusion cost good. Olson describes several examples. Lobbying organizations such as the American Farm Bureau secure legislation which benefits all farmers whether or not they are members and helped pay for the lobbying (Olson 1965: 153–9). So the Farm Bureau sells goods and services to farmers such as insurance. A farmer cannot buy the insurance or get patronage dividends without being a member and paying dues. Insurance profits may not go directly into lobbying, but there are opportunities for sharing overheads in the organization. Another example is the Sierra Club that uses profits from magazine and photographic sales to finance its lobbying. The American Medical Association can use profits from pharmaceutical advertisements in its journal. The tie-in sale creates unwilling riders as well in the sense that the buyers of the products first choice would not be to finance lobbying, etc. Tie-in sales are questionable under anti-trust law, but non-application in this case is a valuable property right for the groups who utilize it to provide HEC goods.

Empirically, a lot of free-riding can be observed. But, the fact that all beneficiaries do not needs explanation. If some forgo opportunism, it suggests that more could learn to do so. This opens up many more institutional options, some of which are informal and reinforced by social sanctions. Some people act out of habit, sense of moral obligation, ideology, or care for others. They see themselves as occupying a certain status or position with attached behaviors (structure 1c in table 6.2). People learn to value an action for its own sake, rather than as an instrument to achieve other goods. It becomes part of their identity. "Analysis of horizontal (nonhierarchical) relations leads to discussions of trust or solidarity – states of relationships or groups that lead to cooperation beyond that to be expected from decision dilemmas such as the 'free-rider problem' or the 'prisoner's dilemma'" (Granovetter 2002: 38). People may forgo opportunism because they "want sociability and hope to be liked, approved of, and admired by others" (37).

6.3.1 Prisoner's Dilemma and other games

The interdependence created by an HEC good is similar to that in the Prisoner's Dilemma (PD) (Poundstone 1992). Its distinguishing feature is a payoff function that produces a dominant choice to a calculating and selfish individual. A choice is dominant when it maximizes the payoff to an individual no matter what the other party does. Still when all players chose the dominant choice (don't cooperate), they find themselves in a low level equilibrium that is not attractive. Nash Equilibrium is defined as where no player can improve their position by acting alone if others stick to their position. This has been described as a social trap (Platt 1973). The only way out of the trap is to act collectively and to be confident of the cooperation of others. Confidence (trust) is learned in successful transactions with others over time including general learning of norms of behavior. People have some ability to recognize whom they can trust (Frank 1988). Dawes has found that groups with five minutes of conversation before playing a PD game had higher rates of cooperation (Dawes 1990). See also Frey (2001: ch. 8).

Schelling's (1978: 36) conception of interdependent binary choices has PD characteristics. He illustrates it with students striving to achieve an even number of males and females in a dorm. Each student observes the mix and moves to his advantage only to discover that others also move and destroy the mix that everyone agrees is desirable (see table 6.3).

Table 6.3 Interdependent binary choices

Situation	Structure	Performance
Interdependent binary choices Consumer's action affects supply and demand simultaneously	1. Markets – Marked by individual, piecemeal marginal choice	1. The aggregate result preferred by most is not achieved (e.g. 50:50 mix of genders); but no one will move
Hard to predict actions of others Hard to contract to control others' choices	2. Administration – e.g. students assigned to dorms. Explicit collective action	2. Achieve some desired dimension, but unwilling riders and loss of individual choice
Schelling's examples of mixing and sorting: dorm, gender. Racial mix Problem is not IUG resource scarcity. More similar to HEC	3. Status – e.g. some cultural habit of gender (class) pairing. Learned – just the way things are. Slow to move	3. Achieve desired aggregate, and few unwilling participants

The dorm case parallels the commonly observed phenomenon of segregated housing in US cities. Schelling demonstrates that even if most prefer some integration, a simple decision rule to move if the neighborhood has more than a certain percentage of another class may result in almost complete segregation. The speed and degree of migration and resulting segregation is very sensitive to small changes in the migration rule. The result may be quite stable without any explicit collective action. This is typical of complex systems wherein "each system gets transformed from a state where individual elements follow their own local rules to one displaying an emergent, global pattern" (Batten 2000: 19).

The Chicken Game is a relative of the Prisoner's Dilemma, but is marked by the absence of a dominant strategy (Goetz 1984: 1–37). In small groups, the individual can see that her contribution makes a difference (no unwitting rider). Still, she may choose strategic behavior hoping that others will contribute and she can ride free. While people may be more likely to respond to social pressure in small groups, the person who has no regard for others will not respond to their threat to withhold regard. The non-cooperator gambles that most others will contribute. If they do not, all lose. The Chicken Game is often characterized by some parties who bluff their unflinching willingness to defect, hoping that others will go ahead and contribute rather than do without the good. Persons making this gamble in the small number case might be called gambling free-riders. Olson (1965) suggests that those with small interests may exploit the large who can afford to contribute and have much to lose if the project fails. This does not account for people getting mad and becoming willing to forgo gains to teach the undeserving a lesson.

Some high exclusion cost goods exist in nature and the question is not how they will be produced, but who gets to use them. A person may be made the nominal exclusive owner, but not be able to actually exclude. Any good is exposed to thieves, but some more than others. A case in point is forests. The Brazilian government only permits logging of mahogany in designated areas. But in practice it is hard to police extensive areas and when logs are floating downstream or incorporated into finished products, it is hard to determine if they were harvested from approved areas. Unless people learn to cooperate willingly, the cost of policing and certification may be prohibitive.

A number of other payoff situations have been identified by game theorists (Bergstrom 2002). In two-person "stag hunt" games, the best response to the other's defection is to defect, but to cooperate if the other cooperates. The metaphor is of two hunters who can cooperate to kill a stag or defect and kill only a hare. Bluffing is irrelevant. Unless the parties are antagonistic, they can probably talk themselves to cooperation. "Haystack models" have been used to understand evolutionary dynamics. Random group formation creates groups with different proportions of people inclined to cooperate or defect. The payoffs are such that cooperators do not do as well as defectors within the group, but a group with more cooperators does better than groups with fewer. The metaphor pictures two mice inhabiting haystacks. The payoff is such that a cooperating mouse is eliminated by a defecting mouse, but two cooperating mice do better than their neighboring groups composed of defectors. The logic of the game suggests that if people can select their partners, they can prosper. In practice, when cooperators seek cooperators, they can compete success-fully. Frank (1988) suggests that in fact people can tell who is likely to cooperate, so cooperators can go into business partnerships with cooperators.

The "folk theorem" demonstrates that a self-policing norm can sustain any behavior. Self-policing involves a learned willingness to sanction defectors in repeated games. But sanctioning others is costly and the result is subject to high exclusion cost. This can only be solved by social capital concern for the welfare of others or by an emotional response where people do not calculate, but act to avenge a wrong. The folk theorem has its name perhaps because no answers can be deduced from the payoff matrix, but rather we must inquire into the minds of the players. Analysts have to talk to people.

6.3.2 Ways to unseat the free-rider

In summary, the various formal and informal institutions that might unseat the free-rider are:

1. Leviathan (administration such as taxes), tie-in sales, a federation creating small sub-groups within larger organizations. (Olson 1965.)
2. Look for whom you can trust. Take advantage of emotions. Personally, reinforce your own cooperative behavior so you will be seen as trustworthy. (Frank 1988.)
3. Learn whom you can trust (reputation) in other experiences and apply to a new situation as needed. (Hirschman 1984.)
4. Play tit-for-tat, which maximizes returns in repeated games. (Axelrod 1984.)
5. Rearrange current reinforcers (for example, Christmas Clubs). (Platt 1973.)
6. Learn "docility, i.e. receptivity to social pressure and custom." (Simon 1991: 35.)
7. Create environments in which people learn to follow a moral norm and perform an activity for its own sake (Etzioni 1988; Taylor 1966). Invoke the sacred (Harris 1974). Learn to sanction others who ignore the norm.
8. Create environments in which people learn to care for each other (social capital) (Robison and Schmid 1994). Make time for people to talk to people (Dawes 1990). Recall section 3.3.11 on selfishness and regard.

6.3.3 Common pool resources

An important variant of high exclusion cost goods is the common pool resource (CPR). It has the following inherent characteristics, following Ostrom (1990). It is critical to distinguish the resource system from the resource units. The resource system or pool is a high exclusion cost good. And, inputs to improving the pool have higher returns than if applied to only some portion of the pool. For example, it is better to let one owner's cows graze with those of another owner and move together across an alpine pasture rather than to keep each person's cows on a fenced portion of the pasture system (Netting 1981). It is the fruit of investment to sustain or increase the yield of the resource system that is HEC. Exclusion cost (fencing) may be possible, but because of the response to system-wide management, it may be uneconomical to exclude even where possible. It may also be costly to monitor use and detect when resource units are being harvested. This is the case of some dispersed resources such as ocean fisheries or forests. It may also be costly to obtain information about the productivity of the system and availability of the resource units over time and space (high information costs to those not close to the resource). Note that use of resource units is usually incompatible. For example, if one person harvests a bunch of alpine or veld grass, tree, or an ocean fish, it cannot be used by another. Free harvest of the units means that no one will invest in the system.

When do people involved in a CPR act voluntarily to sustain the system that produces the good (resource units)? The answer is generally the same as for high exclusion cost goods: when they do not make individual calculations of advantage; that is, when they forgo opportunism in the context of building trust, identify with others, feel an obligation to others, and don't feel good about being opportunistic. The inherent characteristics of common pool resources are often controlled by the chosen structure of common property institutions. Common property with clear rules for who can use and to what extent should not be confused with a free for all resulting in the tragedy of the commons (Bromley and Cernea 1989).

Rural infrastructure, including small-scale irrigation projects, has characteristics of CPR. There are efficiencies in system-wide management. It is costly or undesirable to limit use to those who contribute to the maintenance of these systems. The farmer at the head of the water distribution system can maximize individual returns by contributing little to maintenance but at great loss to downstream users. In studying the success and failures of a large number of rural infrastructure projects around the world, Ostrom et al. (1993: 225) observe the following characteristics of successful projects: "Beneficiaries are aware of the potential benefits they will receive; recognize that these benefits will not fully materialize unless facilities are maintained; have made a firm commitment to maintain the facility over time; have the organizational and financial capabilities to keep this commitment; and do not expect to receive resources for rehabilitating the facility if they fail to maintain it." Obtaining a firm commitment and creating an effective organization is of course the problem.

6.3.4 Institutional change analysis

The benefits of institutional change often accrue to the members of a group and if accomplished, no one can be excluded whether they contributed to the change or not. Reference has been made above to the problem of financing political lobbying. The same point can be made about political participation in general such as voting. The individual cannot affect the outcome (unwitting free-rider is possible). While many do not vote, many do. They do not calculate their individual net benefit but act out of learned habit and ideology. Political participation often is the result of emotion and people feel that their identity is at stake. In this context they may not calculate individual cost and benefit. When people feel deprivation and injustice, they may bear large costs to reform institutions, a kind of "reform utility" that differs from ordinary goods.

6.3.5 Policy implications

No situation characteristic of a good tells people what they must do to direct the interdependence. HEC goods may not be produced at all or in the quantities that are implied by suspected demand. The would-be riders may be frustrated. But, to reduce their frustration is to create unwilling riders. Collective action may eliminate free-riders but at a cost. The free-rider reduces the welfare of those who volunteer to pay. If the latter use collective action to obtain the good, they reduce the welfare of unwilling riders. It is collective choice of institutions that determines who is the thief. To choose among the conflicting interests requires a moral judgment. A moral judgment is a class of decisions that substantially affects the distribution of opportunities. The point is not to label some as moral and others as immoral, but to note a category of choice.

6.4 Non-Rival Goods (Marginal Cost of Another User/Use = Zero)

There are often substantial gains available from joint production. The cost of another *user* or *use* may be zero – sometimes referred to as goods in joint supply or non-rival goods. Institutions determine how the gains are to be divided, and the division may influence whether or not the potential gains are realized.

6.4.1 Cost of another user

The cost of another user of some goods is zero. Once any physical quantity of the good is produced or available to one person, it can be made available to another (up to some threshold). Another physical unit has a positive cost, but the cost of another user of whatever physical units are available is zero (MC = 0). The classical example is national defense. Once the physical boundaries of a country are protected at whatever quality, adding another citizen within that boundary has no extra cost. One person may consume these goods without decreasing the physical amount potentially available to others.

For example, once a cable TV system of a given size and quality is built, adding extra subscribers along the line adds little to cost. See table 6.4. Adding a competitive second line doubles the cost (average cost to all subscribers) which some will regard as a waste and others as worthwhile variety.

Institutions which define pricing rules are instrumental for MC = 0 goods. They are going to have a consequence for income distribution as they affect the prices faced by different persons. It is possible for group A to pay the cost of production and group B can be allowed to use the good without paying anything or causing A's

Table 6.4 Marginal cost equals zero

Situation	Structure	Performance
Cable TV	1. Many cable firms	1. AC up – waste vs. variety tradeoff. Unstable
	2. Monopoly, no regulation	2. AC down – no duplication or variety. P > AC
Interdependent parties: customers, broadcasters, cable companies	3. Regulated monopoly. Who pays fixed cost? a. P = AC = AR b. Price discrimination Who chooses quality? Different rules for making rules	3. Different effects on wealth distribution Different interests count
	4. Government monopoly. Incidence of taxes and fees	Same issues as in (3) above

AC = average cost; AR = average revenue; P = price

cost to increase. But, A's cost could be less if B helped pay. Several informal rules of thumb might apply. Many accept the idea that everyone should pay for any costs that their use creates. But this has no meaning in this case since cost is invariant with any particular person's use.

People could contribute to the cost of a MC = 0 good according to their income. There is a taxation concept in public finance called "ability to pay." There are many examples in both publicly and privately provided goods of differential pricing. Some may be calculated to maximize profits, reflecting differences in willingness to pay and elasticity of demand (Ramsey or Lindahl Pricing). But, some reflect widely held ideas of fairness. Seniors and students are given discounts to the halls of the performing arts. Once the costs of the hall and the performance are covered by those buying tickets at the regular price, additional persons may be admitted without extra cost. They can be charged nothing or a discount. The basis for the price difference can be whatever the seller desires or customers find acceptable. Differential pricing is labeled "discriminatory pricing" when we disapprove of price structure.

For some goods, the marginal cost of another user may not be zero, but relatively minor compared with the average cost. For example, once a length of TV cable is laid, the cost of other users along that length is only a minor hook-up cost. Similarly for a satellite system. There is a major cost to establish the system and relatively minor cost for another individual receiver. The same is true for the telephone line that enters a home or business. In the US, regional phone companies own the line. It costs little for them to carry a competitor's long distance signals. Public policy sets the cost sharing.

Goods with relatively insignificant marginal costs are a source of great wealth in the private sector. For example, once enough music records are sold to pay for the production cost of the record, additional copies are cheap to produce. Generally these are sold at a fixed price to all. Large sales make the producers and artists rich. The same is true of printed material. Record companies are very upset when entrepreneurs in poor countries do not honor copyrights and make and sell copies at their marginal cost. They are also upset when people exchange copies over the internet. Owners of sports teams and the players have become rich as TV makes the marginal cost of another person viewing the game nearly zero. It is the power of informal habit that we take the ownership of the right to sell the radio or video description of an event for granted. Yet, as mentioned earlier, this was a matter of formal litigation in the US and the court gave the right to the owners of the sport teams. They became the seller and the networks became buyers even if they only took up the equivalent of a only few seats in the stadium. This is an extreme example of rights to differential pricing.

What is the definition of the unit to which MC = 0 applies? Buchanan (1968: 54) suggests that it refers to units "which are jointly supplied" and notes that the final consumption units of different individuals may be widely different. He emphasizes the question of divisibility. A "public good" is one where individuals may not adjust the quantity available (can only try to adjust price they pay). He never mentions MC = 0, but it is what makes a good indivisible. A non-rival good may have low exclusion cost: for example, a bus of a given size over a given route up to capacity. Thus, "public good" is not a useful term and can't distinguish different combinations of exclusion cost and non-rivalry.

The usefulness of the situation, structure, performance (SSP) framework in showing similarity in the conceptions of different authors is illustrated in table 6.5, which outlines the impact of exit, voice, and loyalty structures in the context of MC = 0 goods as developed by Hirschman (1970).

Foreign policy, for example, creates an environment that is difficult for a country's citizens to avoid (or other nations to avoid) and where there is no extra cost for another citizen or country to benefit from whatever environment exists. A member of NATO (or WTO) might exit, but would still be affected by the general impact of NATO policies. Or, they might stay loyal to the organization and try to reform it from the inside. Or, they might exit and voice their protest. The cost sharing issue also arises, for example, when the US withheld payment of UN dues because they thought their share was too high and in protest against UN programs on population policy, etc. Some MC = 0 goods are unavoidable and incompatible among those with different preferences (see section 6.4.3 below). The effect of a given level of education in a community is another example noted by Hirschman. Everyone can enjoy the general level of literacy without extra cost.

6.4.2 Policy implications

For goods where the marginal cost of another user is zero, "Equilibrium may be consistent with almost an infinite number of sharing schemes for the costs over inframarginal units" (Buchanan 1968: 37). Equilibrium is defined in terms of marginal prices while the shares of total costs to each party can be anything. Recognizing this, he proposes a uniform tax-price regardless of quantity. "This assumption or

Table 6.5 Exit, voice, and loyalty

Situation	Structure	Behavior	Performance
Non-optimal MC = 0 He calls them "difficult exit from public goods" e.g. foreign policy. Exit not available, not because of institution, but because of inherent character of the good (pp. 101, 104) e.g. effect of level of education in the community (p. 102)	a. *Loyalty* Voice from within b. *Exit* Could resign membership in the organization, but not be able to escape its effects b-1 *Voice* from without b-2 Cop out	a. Individual stays with organization, but tries to reform it. The greater the crisis, the greater the loyalty b. Resign: can stop being member producer, but not consumer b-1 Resign, but protest	a. Recuperation of organization is possible. Individual bears "shame" b. No recuperation. Organization and public not aware of reasons for resignation b-1 Individual feels "relief." May stimulate recuperation b-2 No recuperation, Individual thinks they can escape, but are confused. "Malaise"

Quotes from Hirschman (1970)

convention, which is admittedly an arbitrary even if a reasonable one, allows income effects to be included in the model, but it does so only by guaranteeing one particular division of the gains from trade that are secured in producing the public good" (44). "Such a sharing scheme must be arbitrarily introduced or 'constitutionally' agreed upon by all participants" (44). Here he clearly sees the institutionalist theme that the outcome of bargaining is a function of institutions beyond competitive markets. There are interdependencies not directed by the distribution of factor ownership and competitive markets. "In utilizing this convention as a means of shoring up the usefulness of Marshallian geometry, we are implicitly selecting the final position on the Pareto welfare surface. Other positions of final equilibrium embodying different distributions of the taxpayers' surplus may be equally relevant in any given real-world situation and no 'efficiency' attributes characterize the arbitrary position that the convention produces" (46). He suggests that, "we simply confront each individual with the opportunity to 'purchase' or to 'vote for' a most preferred quantity at each price (marginal = average)" (44). There is nothing simple about having each person record their demand schedule. Without this information, the Pareto-optimal quantity cannot be known which is necessary for the bargaining over the different tax prices each is to pay. Elsewhere he advocates transparency in informing taxpayers of the cost of public services, but how can this be done if we are yet to bargain over cost allocation?

Coase objects to marginal cost pricing *cum* government tax subsidy on income distributional grounds, but ignores that private multi-part pricing is also inherently an income distribution matter. Coase observes "there is a redistribution of income in favour of consumers of goods produced under conditions of decreasing costs" (Coase 1946: 176). Hotelling (1938) had argued that the benefits would be widely diffused, so the issue could be ignored.

Others advocate charging different prices to different people with different valuations (Lindahl 1958). Samuelson (1969) derisively calls them "interpersonal 'Robin-hood pricings'" (122). Hayek (1960: 206) opposed price discrimination. A moral judgment is required whether everyone is charged the same price or a differential price.[2] Projects with favorable benefit–cost ratios may nevertheless fail when interest groups cannot agree on cost sharing (Park and Shabman 1982).

6.4.3 Avoidance and pre-emption costs

Two other characteristics of a non-rival good (NRG) affect human interdependence – cost of avoidance and the degree to which the availability to person A limits the choice of quality or quantity available to B who has positive but different utility. The interdependence issue focuses not only on cost sharing but also who gets to choose the quantity and quality of the non-rival good when a physical unit is to be produced or purchased. A non-optional or high avoidance cost non-rival good is one whose quantity of use can't be varied by an individual, but is determined by the available physical unit. The quantity available becomes the quantity used. The avoidance dimension of quantity is measured in such things as frequency and time of use in reference to people.

Quantity is always with reference to a set of quality characteristics that defines the good. One variety of interdependence depends on whether people can simultaneously utilize different qualities. A pre-emptive non-rival good is one whose qualities used can't be varied by an individual independent of the use of others. The pre-emptive dimension is measured in physical characteristics of the good such as size, weight, speed, etc. These characteristics define quality.

- If NRG and *optional* (avoidable), the issue is who pays how much, a matter of cost sharing. If also *pre-emptive*, there is the additional issue of who chooses the single available *quality* if preferences differ. Persons with different preferences can adjust *quantity* taken even if only one *quality* is available, as shown in table 6.6.
- If NRG and *non-optional* (unavoidable) and *pre-emptive*, the issue is not only cost sharing, but also who chooses the *quality*. The interdependence is greater and the "who chooses rule" is more important if the good is unavoidable since the person whose preferences are not fully met at least has the opportunity to adjust quantity taken if the good is avoidable.

Who chooses the quality of NRGs is a function of rules for making rules. The decision rules of a legislature in the case of national defense or flood control will influence which interest determines the kind of military forces and their deployment or the kind and quality of flood control (dimensions such as dam safety). Private organizations such as labor unions have rules for deciding when to strike and the benefits demanded. All of these goods are pre-emptive and unavoidable.

These distinctions can be illustrated by the case of one landscape view and set of conservation practices pre-empting another (table 6.6). Suppose hunters and environmentalists (tourists) derive benefits from landscape and conservation features such as wildlife habitat. Further, suppose that each user's benefits exceed average costs of persuading landowners to practice conservation. Suppose the landscapes that hunters prefer differ from those preferred by tourists. There are two interdependencies: one is who pays the fixed cost, and the second is who gets to choose the quality of the good when one pre-empts another. If the hunters pay the fixed cost with license fees (line 1a), the tourists and hikers can view at no extra cost. The reverse is also true – if the tourists pay the fixed cost (perhaps in a hotel tax), the hunters' use adds nothing to cost (or the cost can be shared as in line 1b). Institutions determine who is the marginal user.

Again, factor ownership and degree of competition does not control all kinds of interdependence. The character of the good's cost functions affects how one person's choice affects another, and thus the kind of rights that control and direct the interdependence and thereby influence the performance measured in terms of what goods exist and who pays for them (income distribution).

6.4.4 Cost of another use

Just as the cost of another user may be zero, the cost of another use may be zero (the different use usually has a different set of users as well). There may be some

Table 6.6 Non-rival interdependencies inherent in landscapes

Situation	Structure	Performance
The landscape view is MC = 0 (among hunters and environmentalists-tourists)	Landowners are factor owners. In the purchase decision: 1. Cost sharing Rule	Income distribution:
	a. Hunters pay fixed cost and tourists only MC	a. Tourists benefit at no or little cost
	b. Hunters license fees + tourist hotel tax share cost equally	b. All pay average cost
Pre-emptive(only one quality can be present)	2. Who chooses quality level to be purchased? a. Government voting rules favor those with preference for quality #1	a. Those with pref. #1 win. Those with pref. #2 enjoy the quality #1, but can't get their preferred quality independently of the choices of others
	b. Rules favor those with preference for quality #2	b. Opposite of above

marginal costs of another use, but different uses utilize the same basic fixed invest-ment. Consider the case of a large dam and reservoir. This common investment in water storage can be used for flood control, irrigation, and generation of electricity. Each of these requires additional investments in irrigation channels and generators, but there are substantial savings from joint production rather than separate single purpose dams. The institutional issue is how to share the advantages of joint pro-duction. Vickrey (1994: 198) says "More serious problems arise in the increasingly widespread cases of joint production of several distinguishable products or services. Where competitive markets exist, the market conditions dictate the allocation of joint costs among the various products, as when a meat-packing establishment pro-duces steaks, hides, glue, and offals. There is no way in which one can determine a meaningful average cost of hides by considering only the production process." He regards the common practice of average cost pricing over the whole output as arbitrary. These rules of thumb are one sense of administered prices.

Vickrey suggests an "optimal" decision-making sequence as follows: "first estab-lishing a pricing policy to be followed in the future . . . then planning adjustments to fixed capital installations according to a cost–benefit analysis based on predicted demand patterns and predicted application of the pricing policy, subject to whatever financial constraints may be applicable, and then eventually determining prices on a day-to-day or month-to-month basis in terms of conditions as they actually develop" (199). This requires a lot of information, which is never market tested, and a possible government subsidy to cover the fixed cost. He refers to the common practice of setting a high initial toll to cover amortization charges and then no toll when the facility is paid off as inappropriate in part because a positive price is necessary to avoid congestion and defer the necessity for additional facilities.

Electricity, gas, and telecommunications are marked by high fixed investments and a network of generation, transmission, and reception of multiple products. "Significant common and joint costs will yield important economies of joint service or joint product development. Networks permit the development of multiple ser-vices at a lower cost than if each service were to pay its stand-alone cost" (Trebing 1995: 226). What is the impact of regulation versus market competition and unbundling of functions? Some of the performance measures are reflected in Trebing's challenge "to achieve high levels of utilization and network optimization without recourse to undue price discrimination, cross subsidization, or risk shifting" (226). Public regulation of energy monopolies was the dominant institution, but poor performance in the 1970s resulted in the Federal Energy Regulatory Commission requiring the separation of natural gas as a commodity from pipeline transport and the unbundling of generation and transmission of electricity in the 1990s. In general, concentration in natural gas and electricity increased as did prices and price discrimination. The most dramatic case was the California energy crisis in 2000–2001. Wholesale electricity prices skyrocketed as did peak/off-peak prices and supply was restricted. The causes are hotly contested. Winners were new owners of generation and losers were residential/small business customers and incumbent investor-owned utilities (Trebing 2001: 397). Auction markets are not conducive to large fixed investments in generation. The discussion continues below in a sec-tion 6.5 "Economies of Scale."

6.4.5 Summary of non-rival (MC = 0) goods interdependencies

It is useful to specify the dimensions of MC = 0 goods as follows:

Situational dimension	Variables
1. Quantity of the good	Physical units
2. Quantity of use	Frequency and time of year
3. Quality of the good	Size, speed, weight, concentration of an ingredient

Examples

Dimension	Variables	Degree of avoidance and pre-emption costs
Road example		
1. Quantity of the good	Miles of road	low avoidance cost
2. Quantity of use	Person A 1 trip/day	
	Person B 2 trips/day	
3. Quality . . .	Two lanes, hard surface;	high pre-emption
	Both persons use same quality	

The cost of another user of a 10 mile, two-lane, hard surface, well-maintained road is zero

Air quality example		
1. Quantity of good	An airshed (square miles)	
2. Quantity of use	Everyone breaths all the time	high avoidance
3. Quality . . .	Everyone must use some given quality	high pre-emption

The cost of another user of an airshed with 10 ppm sulphur dioxide is zero

6.5 Economies of Scale

Economies of scale (EOS) refer to the cost of another physical unit declining. This is in contrast to MC = 0 goods which refer to the cost of another user, not physical unit. While this difference is critical to understand, EOS goods have many of the same interdependencies as MC = 0 goods. Again, there is the issue of who pays fixed cost and who pays marginal cost, which is falling (line 3, table 6.7). Again, there is the question of who chooses the quality of the good (line 2). There is a price–variety tradeoff (line 1). Some will want little variety (monopoly) to achieve maximum economies of scale and others will give up some of those economies to get variety (many firms).

Industries with increasing returns tend to be unstable (line 3). Firms may cut prices to marginal cost or below even if they are not covering total costs in the hope of driving out competitors, and then raising prices again (predatory pricing). The

Table 6.7 Economies of scale

Situation	Structure	Performance
Any good with economies of scale, e.g. air lines	1. Monopoly vs. many firms	1. Price–variety tradeoff
	2. Rules specifying who chooses quality, if little variety (e.g. grades and standards)	2. Advantage to some producers and consumers over others
	3. Rules of price differentiation and competitive strategy. International trade dumping rule. Predatory pricing rules	3. Income distribution. Who pays fixed cost and who only marginal cost. Instability possible
	4. Rules of demand alteration (e.g. advertising)	4. Pay-off to similar tastes
	5. Rules determining the extent of the market (e.g. Commerce clause of US Constitution and International trade treaties – WTO)	5. Realize potential economies of scale. Degree of globalization

airlines are a good example. The problem of wide variation in prices over time was the context for the creation of the Civil Aeronautics Board. They regulated which firms could fly which routes and set prices. This created stability, but also the lethargy of monopoly. Forgetting why regulation was created in the first place, the Board was abolished in 1978. For a while many new firms entered the industry and prices fell. Then a period of consolidation occurred and many lines disappeared bringing the industry back to a small number of national firms with periodic price wars.

Many industries have constant or decreasing marginal costs. No factor of production is fixed since inputs can be reallocated among industries. If marginal cost becomes less than marginal revenue, there is nothing internal to the firm that determines output (Sraffa 1926). The supply curve is essentially flat. "Output will be constrained, not by marginal cost, but by the cost and difficulty of expanding sales at the expense of competitors" (Keen 2001: 74). Sraffa suggested that firms will have a target output and target markup that they will try to maintain by product differentiation. Widely shared informal institutions may influence what a firm (and its bankers) expect its rivals to do as each seeks its market niche.

Some nations try to cover fixed costs with domestic sales and then charge marginal prices on exports to the detriment of firms in the receiving countries. International trade agreements have anti-dumping provisions.

When a good has economies of scale, it pays to have the same tastes as everyone else (line 4). Business understands this and spends huge sums on advertising. One result is the homogenization of tastes on a global scale. This is part of the tension between western firms and fundamentalist peoples who object to what they consider as intrusion of mass consumerism into their culture. Some industries need global markets to achieve economies of scale. Trade policies affect the extent of the market (line 5). Western nations seem to be more enthusiastic about gaining access to markets in poorer countries than in opening their markets to imports from these same countries.

A good produced under increasing returns has an advantage over competing substitutes in the early stage of its production. As demand grows for a product with economies of scale, its costs fall as larger, more efficient plants and distribution systems are built. A new product could be seen by consumers as superior, but at small introductory volumes its price can be too high to attract buyers. This produces a kind of lock-in or path dependence (Arthur 1990; 1994). An alternative institution that can break the lock-in is some kind of collective action to require the new technology, protect the infant industry with a tariff, or otherwise subsidize it during scale-up. The problem with many of these is that a short-term support can turn into a long-term subsidy for a lethargic industry. An example is the development of new energy sources. When the energy plants or energy-saving cars are in small-scale production, the per-unit costs are higher than traditional sources. Only collective action guarantees some minimum demand can the new product be produced at a competitive price. Subsidies for wind and solar power and government purchase of alternative energy vehicles are a case in point.

Increasing returns lock-in is part of a more general situation of circular and cumulative causation as depicted in the last row of table 6.8 below. The success in selling a good with economies of scale in one period feeds back (circular) on the ability to invest and achieve even lower costs in the next period. The circularity is reinforced and amplified (cumulative). The interacting complex systems have the property of emergence where the whole is more than the sum of the parts. Where economies of scale prevent equilibrium, standard operating procedures and behavioral norms emerge from evolutionary processes.

The production of some commodities has economies of scale (and network economies) to the extent that the low point on the average cost curve is not reached unless only one firm supplies the good. These super-ordinary economies of scale present a dilemma in institutional design since low production cost calls for a monopoly, but monopolies can set a price above average cost. These industries are sometimes prejudicially termed "natural monopolies." But this prejudges whose preferences count if the name suggests the appropriate policy. The two major institutional alternatives are public ownership or franchise bidding by private firms. Presumably, the monopoly public firm could achieve economies of scale and would not price above average cost. Still, it has less incentive than a competitive firm to keep costs low. Alternatively, private firms can bid for the right to supply the good specifying quality and price. This achieves the benefits of competition initially, but requires continual monitoring and, at franchise renewal, all possible entrants are no longer on equal footing (Williamson 1985: 326–51). Different groups prefer different tradeoffs among the consequences of institutional alternatives. The causal relationship between alternative institutions is often difficult to untangle and in the end perception is heavily influenced by ideology.

6.6 Circular and Cumulative Causation

The concept of circular and cumulative causation was developed by Myrdal (1944) who was studying the interaction of Black poverty, education, and expectations in America. Blacks were discriminated against leaving them poorly educated and with low incomes. As a result, Blacks had low expectations and may not have made the most of the poor options they had. Their poverty justified the discrimination to many white supremacists. This is a vicious circle not unlike the lock-in described above. To generalize, "Cumulative causation describes a relationship between an initial change in an independent variable and the dependent variable, whereby the dependent variable in turn causes a change in the formerly independent variable in the same direction as the initial movement" (Schmid 1999a). Also see Skott (1994).

The interdependence of economies of scale can create circular and cumulative causation and lock-in as noted above. The situation Myrdal describes involves the interaction of poverty, education, and expectation. Other sources are the interaction of expectations, investment, and aggregate demand. Macroeconomic fluctuations exhibit vicious circles. A decline in aggregate demand feeds back and reduces employment that feeds back and reduces aggregate demand again. This will be explored in chapter 9. Another case is the interaction of past income and lobbying for legislation enhancing future income. The powerful become more powerful as success in the economy provides the means of success in politics. Any process involving feedback, reinforcement, and amplifiers can create circular and cumulative causation. Sequential decision-making in markets and civil affairs may produce unwanted consequences that can only be avoided by explicit collective action. The several examples of the phenomenon are summarized in the SSP table 6.8.

Table 6.8 Circular and cumulative causation (feedback, reinforcement, and amplification)

Situation	Structure	Performance
Interaction of expectations, investment, and aggregate demand falling	1. Market 2. Planning, including fiscal policy	1. Deep depressions 2. Recovery
Interaction of poverty, education, and expectations	1. Informal rules of discrimination 2. Civil Rights Act	1. Minorities stay poor 2. More equality
Interaction of income, lobbying, and legislation	1. No limit on contributions to politicians 2. Campaign finance limits	1. Rich get richer 2. More equality
Interaction of economies of scale in one product with another	1. Market 2. Collective action to scale up a new competing product	1. Lock-in, path-dependence 2. New product replaces the old

6.7 Transaction Costs and Benefits

Transacting with others is not free. It takes time and resources. Four determinants or varieties of transaction costs are distinguished: information or measurement costs, contractual costs, the commitment problem in the context of asset specificity costs, and the costs of fundamental uncertainty. Each variety is inherent in goods (factors) and creates a particular interdependence that is controlled by different alternative institutional structures each with a hypothesized performance. *A transaction occurs when the rights to a good or service are transferred across hands (across people).* (This is not to be confused with the transport costs of physical movements of goods that may or not be accompanied by a transfer of ownership.) Rights or ownership is used in the broadest sense to mean the acknowledged opportunity to participate or withhold consent. Williamson's (1985: 19) metaphor of friction is not apt because the rights to be transferred among whom are problematic. A machine is purpose built and anything that obstructs the purpose is undesirable. But in the world of human organization, one person's friction is another's opportunity. A dictator has zero transaction costs, but this is hardly in the interest of the objects of the dictation. Transaction cost can be economized like any other cost, but it is fundamental institutions that determine who has what to economize and thus who counts in decisions and who pays irreducible transaction costs. Whose interests are to be a cost to whom? Some transaction costs are given, a part of the inherent situation, while others are what Ramstad (1996: 416) calls "instituted phenomena." Recall discussion of cost being institutionally defined in section 5.1. Only when the basic rights are established can the actors economize within their opportunity sets.

6.7.1 High and asymmetric information costs

Information asymmetry between transacting parties creates interdependence.[3] If you can't tell the quality of a good or persons by using your sense organs, there are information or measurement costs to some degree. This is part of bounded rationality. High information cost (HIC) means that it is difficult for buyers to match quality to price. The producer seller knows more about the product than the buyer. What are the relevant structural alternatives and hypothesized performance? The theory will be developed and applied first in the context of consumer goods and then in terms of insurance. (The application to labor quality including moral hazard is discussed in chapter 11.) *Caveat emptor* is one possibility and is equivalent to buyer liability. The buyer may make mistakes. Given HIC, it is difficult for buyers to know what their best alternative is. For example, they might purchase a contract for repairs if needed. But this can be hard to judge if the quality of the product is costly to measure.

Labels might be required if the seller has lower costs to provide the information than the consumer. The label might indicate product content, how made, etc. Not all consumers will have the same interest in label content since it adds to the cost of the product. There are conflicts among consumers with different interests and ability as well as between consumers and producers.

Producers of high-quality products want buyers to be able to discern the quality so that a premium price can be obtained. But if buyers can't determine quality, bad goods will drive out quality ones. Producers of quality goods spend huge sums of money for celebrity endorsements, again adding to the cost of production without actually contributing to the product itself. Some refer to this as a "social waste" (Milgrom and Roberts 1992: 156). Some economists do not assume that consumers believe the endorsement, but argue that the spending is a signal of quality (Spence 1973). The producer would not spend such large sums if they did not have a quality product, for if buyers became disappointed, the advertising would be wasted. Are there more economical signals? Some manufacturers subscribe to a semi-independent agency that establishes standards and allow the use of their label if the product is certified to standard. Alternatively, the government could make tests and publish the results, as in the case of auto gas mileage.

Another set of alternatives is the common law rule of merchantability vs. explicit governmental administrative regulation. Both involve setting a standard, which not all consumers value the same. The rule of merchantability says that for a good to be called "X" it must conform to certain standards, usually some kind of average of what is available, which is what most producers do. If the consumer brings suit, the court decides if the standard is met and what, if any, relief the buyer is entitled to. Alternatively, a government agency may set a standard and set fines if not met. For example, it is costly for a consumer to detect salmonella in meat. If the standard for negligence or government inspection requires the absence of salmonella, those who cook it carefully and kill the organism have an unnecessary expense and include it in the product price. Some prefer cheap shit and others prefer to reduce the risk via strict liability or regulation. The popular press often ridicules the volumes of regulations, but HIC means that if there are quality issues they are settled with reference to administrative rules or the volumes of case law on the subject. The extent of possible human interdependence determines the details of rights to be worked out. These alternatives and hypothesized performance consequences are summarized in table 6.9.

Policy implications: Can the best institution be specified? Some suggest that product liability should rest on whoever agreed to it when the product was purchased. "Sellers will presumably start accepting responsibility for mishaps that they are in a good position to control, while buyers will accept the liabilities that they can bear more cheaply than they can persuade sellers to shoulder them" (Heyne 1994: 185). But in the face of HIC, how will buyers know what they are in a good position to control? These are tragic choices. There is no doubt that some people will use a product recklessly and the careful do not want the price of their restitution built into product prices. Deciding who is the reasonable person is the issue at law.

A person who jumps from a stalled ski lift will appear to many as unreasonable. But a young Orthodox Jewish woman did exactly that, as she believed that being with her boyfriend after dark even on a broken lift was a sin. Do ski lift owners have to build in a high level of no-failure (and of course charge every user a corresponding price)? Guido Calabresi was an early proponent of benefit–cost analysis to establish liability. But in later work he argued, "who is the cheapest avoider of a cost, depends

Table 6.9 High information costs for products

Situation	Structure	Performance
High information costs about product attributes	*Caveat emptor*	Buyer makes mistakes
Asymmetric – seller knows more than buyer	Voluntary or required labels. Warranties	Buyer makes fewer mistakes
	Brands, endorsements and certification	Ditto
	Rules of merchantability	Ditto, but not all will agree on the standard
	Product standards and liability	Ditto
	Require provision of information by lowest cost provider	Lowest cost provider depends on whose interests are regarded as a legitimate cost

on the valuations put on acts, activities, and beliefs by the whole of our law and not on some objective or scientific notion" (Calabresi 1985: 69). "What is efficient, or passes a cost–benefit test, is not a 'scientific' notion separated from beliefs and attitudes, and always must respond to the question of whom we wish to make richer or poorer" (69). "Then the problem becomes one for judgment by responsible men of the significance of the competing social interests involved, in the face of strong advocacy of reasons for favoring one party or another in light of available evidence concerning probable consequences of deciding one way or another" (Liebhafsky 1973: 628–9). See discussion of minimizing transaction costs and the Coase Rule in section 5.5.2.

Adverse selection: Sellers of insurance have high information costs in discerning the risk of a potential buyer. Information asymmetry favors the buyer. Adverse selection (precontractual opportunism) arises when buyers have more information than sellers prior to the purchase. For example, health insurers cannot easily determine which person over 65 will have the most claims in the future. They do know the average, but as they raise premiums to reflect the average claim, those potential buyers who estimate that they will remain relatively healthy, begin to self-insure. This leaves a pool of buyers who are high risk. Again, insurers raise the premium to cover the now higher risk, and then more potential buyers depart. This leaves only the worst cases or "lemons" as Akerlof (1970) calls them and there may be no price at which the insurer is willing to serve the set of customers who wish to buy. Changing the price not only affects revenues of the seller, but also the cost of supplying the product as the risk pool changes (Stiglitz 1987). Akerlof cautiously suggests that this adds a major argument in favor of Medicare. Forcing everyone into a common pool enables a low premium to be charged. Some will applaud and some object. The decision to act collectively is contentious.

In the case of auto insurance, insurers reduce the problem by offering different rates for different degrees of deductible coverage. Discounts are offered those who buy a policy with a high deductible before the insurers pays for damages. This is attractive to people who believe they are relatively safe drivers as they self-insure for the remaining uncovered damage risk. The hoped-for self-selection in this case provides useful information to the seller. Do these structures chosen by insurance companies provide a bloodless performance? The self-assessed low-risk buyers may have made the best choice from available alternatives, but would have preferred full coverage at a cost fitting their risk class. Is this second best? Keep in mind that if buyers could be trusted, the risk classes could each be charged their appropriate rate. The first defense against opportunism is the internalized sense that it is wrong.

It is well known that young drivers on the average have more accidents than experienced adults. Even though some young drivers are very careful, the insurance company faces high cost to distinguish them, and thus charges all young drivers the same high rate. This differentiation may be optimal for the seller, but some buyers may regard it as discriminatory. The problem is compounded when the buyer lives in a certain part of the city where accidents and damages are more common. The insurance company knows the average risk and charges all in the area accordingly. Especially when the buyers in that part of town are in a racial minority, the practice will appear discriminatory. The so-called "red-lining" of auto and fire insurance is prohibited by some states. The means of one group's cost saving is objectionable to another group. Another conflict arises when some buyers in the high-risk pool refuse to buy insurance on their cars. This means if they damage another car or driver, the damage is not covered. Going without insurance may be illegal, but many car owners risk detection which itself has high measurement costs. Again, the law determines whose preferences count when interests conflict. Assertions of optimality cover up the conflict.

Labor: The rules for organizing labor also interact with information (monitoring) costs. An employer is uncertain as to a job seeker's competence. This will be dealt with in detail in chapter 11 on labor institutions, and is just noted here. Also to be discussed there is the problem of moral hazard when an employer is uncertain as to an employee's effort. Simon called attention to the conflict between making sure agents are obedient to command and the benefits of delegation.

Product prices: Sellers and buyers need price information from different locales to make the best deal. For example, asymmetry in information can disadvantage farmers selling to more informed buyers. The United States created a federal price reporting service during World War I initially to serve its administrative needs. Developing countries such as Mali created public price information in 1989. Such information helps reduce regional price differences to the cost of transport.

Table 6.10 Contractual cost

Situation	Structure	Performance
Contractual cost among consumers	Class action law suits for consumer products	More suits filed
Political contractual cost	Rules for making rules: a. simple majority b. two-thirds majority	 More rules changed More status quo

6.7.2 Contractual (negotiation) costs

The cost of getting the agreement of another party to a transaction is a function of the number of necessary parties and the complexity of the agreement. For example, if a large parcel of land is needed for a private urban development, it will be costly to get agreement to sell from a large number of owners (table 6.10). There may be strategic holdouts. These contractual costs may prevent the project from going ahead if all individual sellers must be dealt with. Alternatively, the city government could threaten condemnation if the project is deemed to serve a broad interest. In a sense, transaction costs are reduced, but these inherent costs are still there. They are transformed into lost opportunities for the individual landowners. Shifting of these costs affects performance.

Another example of contractual costs involving large numbers is that of consumers who feel that their purchase did not perform as advertised. A large number of buyers have a small loss and it does not pay any one of them to bear the costs of a court suit. There are economies of scale in preparation of the evidence. The court may accept a class action suit (see table 6.10). Lawyers may accept the case for a contingent fee so that the buyers need not put up any money initially. There is a conflict of interest between buyers and sellers that is decided by the grant of class action standing. There is a further conflict between groups of buyers, some of which do not want to be in the class and wish to pursue a different settlement.

Complex business arrangements mean that contracts are necessarily incomplete. It is impossible to anticipate and specify all the possible contingencies. When the problem becomes obvious, there must be some way to settle disputes. In the US, this is done with reference to the Uniform Commercial Code and the common law of contract. Courts apply various principles, one of which is their sense of its contribution to their sense of economic development. These principles evolve over time in the context of the environment (Friedman 1965; Schmid 1992). In some gross sense, the law of contract saves transaction costs. It fills in the holes that the parties did or could not anticipate. But, the costs are there and the law distributes them.

Consider the coordination of investments to obtain a high definition TV (HDTV) system. There must be compatible program content, broadcasting studios, and

Table 6.11 Contractual business costs

Situation	Structure	Performance
High contract negotiation costs to acquire a needed input	1. Grab and pay court assessed damages	Pay market price rather than unique value of owner
	2. Breech contract and pay damages	Ditto
	3. Grab and claim reasonable use	Harmed party receives nothing
	4. Grab and have government declare you owner because you would have bought it at zero transaction cost	Income distribution favors new initiative

receivers. There is no conceivable nexus of contract possible here. There are just too many people to form an explicit commitment to have the necessary pieces in place at the same time. Yes, there are fixed assets involved, but even if there were not, there are simply the *ex ante* costs of getting everyone on board if each party makes an independent market decision. Alternatively, and the policy of the US, the system can be mandated as of a given date. This is a power decision when interests conflict. Some may be content with the existing system, but will have to make the investment if the other parties are to have the option of enjoying HDTV.

When an entrepreneur thinks she has a better idea for the use of a resource owned by others, transaction costs would be reduced if she could just grab it and pay damages (table 6.11). Or if there is a better use for assets committed in a contract, just break the contract and pay damages. Alternatively, the court could enjoin the grabber (equitable remedy) or hold the person to the contract. Can we do a total benefit–cost analysis and decide which is better? (Compare Polinsky (1980) and Schap (1986).) Not if the rules themselves affect prices and what is a cost. In the case of injunctive vs. damage relief, the right of injunction gives the beneficiary the ability to demand their own unique valuation whereas if only entitled to damages, they must accept the going market price determined by the court. The rules determine whose valuation counts. Recall policy implications in section 6.7.1 above.

Politics: The rules for making rules must explicitly deal with contractual cost. This will be discussed in detail in chapter 12, "Political Institutions" but just noted here (see table 6.10 above). For example, these rules specify what proportion of the electorate must agree to initiate a collective action (similar to the class action case above). The larger the percentage, the higher the costs of getting agreement. Buchanan and Tullock (1965) called attention to the tradeoff between the cost of negotiating agreement to change a law and the costs of having to accept a law you don't want (political externality). Requiring a large percentage agreement makes it hard to get a change you want, but hard for your opponents to get a change you don't want – obviously a power issue. One individual's calculus of the degree of unanimity needed for collective action is not likely to be the same as another's.

6.7.3 Asset specificity

Some technologies are specific to a particular set of trading parties. Some are specific to a particular use or industry. For example, firm A may deliver some material to firm B in a package or transport that only fits the acceptance technology of firm B. If firm B ceases the trading relationship, the specialized equipment is only worth its scrap value. Likewise if a machine is especially developed to make a certain product, it will not produce another. For example, a machine that is designed to dig potatoes cannot harvest wheat. If the purpose-built potato machine is invested in, it is only worth scrap if demand for potatoes drops and the firms must leave the industry. A truck, on the other hand, can haul many different commodities and if demand for any one of them changes, it can haul another without loss of asset value.

The loss of asset value from a change in demand is an *ex ante* loss which the firm will try to avoid if it has options. If it has no assurance of continued demand, it will invest in general purpose technology. The general purpose technology has higher per unit costs. Since both trading parties are aware of this, it is in their mutual interest to achieve the special purpose technology and share the benefits. This is the story of so-called "transaction cost economics" of Williamson (1985). It is hypothesized that the transacting parties will agree on some safeguards to protect specialized asset values. The buyer would like the option to desert an old supplier if a new one comes with an even better deal, but will forgo it to obtain today's best specialized technology with low per unit cost. This is an information problem only in the sense that one party lacks information on the commitment of the other party. It is not a problem of measuring product quality as discussed in section 6.7.1 above.

Assurance may take the form of mutual investment by buyer and seller whose value would be lost if they ceased trading. Williamson refers to this as providing a "hostage," something like the practice of warring leaders to marry a child to the enemy as a pledge against attack. An alternative is to expand the firm and acquire the other firm. This makes the input formerly purchased in the market an input provided by a subsidiary subject to command. This is conceptualized as the decision to produce internally and coordinate by hierarchical command or to buy externally in the market. Williamson thus predicts that the more industry is marked by specific assets, the more transaction cost saving integration will occur. In the situation of specific assets, integration is efficient and any attempt to prevent it would be unproductive. (See table 6.12.) Care must be taken to specify the background institutions such as corporate law within which hierarchy and market alternatives operate. In the framework of Coase and Williamson, technology determines the governance structure. But economic historians North and Wallis (1994: 622) deny the fixed relationship between technology and institutions. "Institutions do not exist to minimize transaction costs."

Table 6.12 Transaction cost *à la* Williamson

Situation	Structure	Performance
Ex post high transactions cost: Specific assets between input suppliers and output processors	1. Hierarchy Hostages and other safeguards	No loss of specific assets. Specialized low per unit cost technology used
Commitment problem when contracts are necessarily incomplete	2. Market	Potential loss of specific assets. High cost, general purpose technology used. Fundamental transformation leads to hold-up

The possibility of bargaining over the potential gain of specialization is plausible, but limited in application. A small supplier to GM or Ford does not have the real opportunity to bargain and obtain assurances for the recovery of specific assets. They either meet the buyer's demands or lose the business. Suppliers gamble on an uncertain future. If they do not, they are out of the game for sure. Another case is that of contract animal feeding. The processor and feed supplier deliver baby pigs to a feeder who must build housing to the integrator's specification (Martin 1997). No assurance is offered of a long-term contract that would allow recovery of the investment. Take it or leave it is the game. If these short-term contracts are in the opportunity set of GM or the pork integrator, these firms will economize and use them and minimize their own transaction costs. But the transaction costs inherent in specific assets are still there, and the only choice is who bears their consequences. Opportunism is possible on both sides. In the case of pork contracting, the farmer is unlikely to defect from the processor since they would lose the value of their buildings. But the processor may defect from the farmer if they find another farmer and building more to their liking. The farmers either are foolhardy gamblers with few better choices or have some non-contracted reason to trust the processor.

Galbraith suggests that the "enemy of the market is the engineer" who keeps inventing new goods that cause defection of consumers to new products and subsequent losses to specific assets in the production of old goods (Galbraith 1967). The planning firm does not just dump stuff on the auction market and wait to see what happens. The issue might be reframed as the enemy of the market is the fickle consumer. The firm's economizing answer to this problem is to plan and spend a lot of money on advertising and image making to keep the consumer loyal. Another option is to buy out innovating firms and their patents and suppress them until the original assets have been recovered. The availability of these options has implications for the kind of world we live in.

Lots of firms accept the gamble of the innovating engineer and the fickle consumer without assurances. Farmers are the prime example of a sector where each generation of new technology is embraced at the margin and spreads even when many lose the value of their assets in the previous technology – a process referred to as the "agricultural treadmill" (Cochrane 1958). The competitive process requires that they either play the game or quit even when no assurances are available. Johnson (1997: 107) developed the theory of fixed assets to explain why farmers continued to supply outputs even when prices did not cover average costs. A resource remains fixed in use as long as "its marginal value productivity in its present use neither justifies acquisition of more of it or its disposition." Farmers make investments without assurances, it becomes a mistake, and the mistake persists (Johnson and Quance 1972).

Whereas Williamson (1985) used the idea of specific assets (transactions costs) to show that firms would choose an efficient form of private governance, Johnson emphasized that farmers would keep on producing even when returns did not cover acquisition prices as long as the marginal value product was greater than variable costs plus salvage value of capital assets. These assets were specific to the industry (rather than to a particular set of transacting parties) and became fixed in production (did not exit) under the above conditions. So while Williamson's theory gave a rationale for the best of all possible worlds, Johnson saw a troublesome "overproduction trap" (Johnson 1986). Williamson argued that if left alone, firms would negotiate private arrangements that would protect against losses to specific assets caused by the opportunistic behavior of trading partners. Johnson argued that without collective action, farm firms making their best choices at the margin could not escape continuing asset losses as each wave of cost-saving technological adoption became fixed in the agricultural sector. Self-adjustment was impossible.

The problem of the overproduction trap is a variety of circular and cumulative causation. It is not caused just by transaction costs, but primarily by the change in output prices caused by the aggregate effect of investments in the industry. The best decisions by individuals turn out badly in the aggregate. On the "agricultural treadmill," the harder each firm strives to maximize profits via innovation, profitability escapes them.

One-year forward contracts are increasingly common in animal feeding – either directly between farmers and processors/retailers or indirectly in futures markets. The one-year forward contract assures farmers that the price will cover planting (or feeding) costs, but does nothing to assure recovery of long-term capital assets such as machines and buildings. Forward contracts give more assurance that spot markets, but less than vertical integration (Jaffee 1995).

The overproduction trap has led to costly agricultural subsidies in all western countries that seem to go on without end. Failure to understand the inherent situation of agriculture has led to the wishful thinking that the problem is temporary. If some of the public money had been put into buying unnecessary land assets for permanent retirement, the problem could have been solved for less money and less human stress. Farmers have gone bankrupt and left agriculture, but the land has not. Farm lobbies have succeeded in avoiding major losses to specific assets at the cost of keeping them in unwanted production. An alternative is to share the losses of removing the assets from production.

Some sectors fail to adopt low-cost technology because of the structure of institutions combined with transaction cost. Periodic energy crises are the setting for policy debate on alternative energy sources such as solar or oil shale. Firms hesitate to invest even when current prices make the investment look profitable because they can't be sure that the prices will last. So consumers are still vulnerable to energy shocks as no substantial practical alternatives are in place. Some consumers might be willing to make a contract with alternative suppliers so that their investments might be recovered even if market prices fall. Contractual costs make this impractical. Alternatively, the government as their collective agent might contract to buy a certain amount from new source suppliers as a kind of insurance against the next crisis. Conflicts of interest arise out of the situation and no institutional structure can abolish it.

The SSP framework facilitates comparison of authors who are talking about the same thing but with different language. Hirschman (1970) focuses on alternative structures (exit, voice, and loyalty) in the context of how a firm might recover from mistakes that displease customers. Depending on institutions, the dissatisfied consumer may exit (stop buying), voice their concern (persuade and complain), or remain loyal customers giving the firm time to recover. This would be no problem if assets were not specific. Table 6.13 combines the language of Williamson and Hirschman using SSP.

Hirschman (1970: 2) seems to imply asset losses as a reason why firm "wipe out" is undesirable. He contrasts his concern with the traditional model where recovery of a particular firm is not essential because its "factors are hired by others." The case could be strengthened by more attention to specific assets. Hirschman does not talk much about rights, but rights can affect the relative costs of exit vs. voice. He describes cases where exit is impossible. This could be a matter of institutional policy prohibiting exit or just a lack of available substitutes in the economy. He doesn't give a lot of explicit attention to public policy, but does refer to collective action making exit more costly and voice cheaper. What influences the relative cost of exit and voice?

What do we get from different paradigms? While Hirschman never used the term specific assets, his situation fits that category. Hirschman raises questions in terms of exit and voice and generalizes from firms, political parties, to unions. Williamson examines producer goods where firms can integrate or find other means to assure each other of continued exchanges. Hirschman examines consumer goods where firms can't contract with consumers. Consumer loyalty is the only possible assurance. If opportunism with guile is assumed (Williamson), researchers will never look for loyalty. SSP allows us to find the commonality and differences in related conceptualizations that let us learn the consequences of alternative kinds of institutions in many different cases that have the same kind of interdependence (situation).

Institutional economics can add new variables to empirical studies and provide the basis for reformulating the dependant variable. Institutional economics suggests that perceptions and uncertainty of the consequence of specific assets count in choosing governance structures rather than only what the analyst sees. Further, network embeddedness (multiple relations between buyers and sellers in an industry) may affect the sense of dependence of a supplier, as will trust. Trust will be explored in detail in section 7.2.4. In an empirical study of transactions between a large firm and its many suppliers, Berger, Noorderahaven, and Nooteboom (2002) found no

Table 6.13 Transaction costs à la Hirschman

Situation	Institutional structure	(Conduct/activity)	Performance
Specific assets	1. *Exit right*	Exit chosen	1. Firm given no time to recuperate. Loss of specific assets
"Standardized durable consumer goods requiring large outlays" (p. 42)	2. *No exit right* (Exit costly)	**Voice**	2. Specific assets saved
	3. *Loyalty.* Mix of alert and inert customers. Status and custom	Voice chosen. Keep buying	3. Specific assets saved
Recasting Williamson in Hirschman's terms:			
Specific assets with uncertainty	4. *Hierarchy.* Vertical integration or use of hostages and non-standard contracts	Exit foregone	4. Specific assets saved. Low per unit cost
Producer goods	5. *Market.* (Exit right)	Exit occurs. Opportunism	5. Assets lost. Avoidable only if high per unit cost technology used

Quotes are from Hirschman (1970)

Table 6.14 Risk

Situation	Structure	Performance
Risk Search cost. More information available, but at increasing cost	*Search* Stopping rule; Forecasting; Insurance	Equilibrium possible; Forecasting errors

significant relationship between safeguards and asset specificity. "Thinking further, it seemed to make most sense not to look at safeguards as dependent variable, but at perceived dependence" (83). Managers of the buyer and the many sellers were asked about how dependent they felt they were. It was found that asset specificity was significant in explaining felt dependence, but so was negative network embeddedness and trust.

6.7.4 Risk and fundamental uncertainty

The interdependence created by risk, fundamental uncertainty, and complexity differs. The institutional structures relevant for each differ. Probability can be attached to known categories of future events, but not to events that have no name. In the case of complexity, the future is in principle knowable, but the difficulty of calculation can create errors to which no probability can be attached.

Economizing on search costs is relevant only for risk (uncertain specified future events). When more information of known value is available at an increasing cost it is possible to calculate optimal stopping rules that can produce an equilibrium. Entrepreneurs invest in forecasting, but are often wrong when other firms make the same forecast and the opportunity disappears. Firms base action on projections of the past and revise as new information becomes available. The situation and relevant structures for risk are shown in table 6.14.

What do consumers and firms do in the face of complexity? They simplify and use some standard operating procedure (SOP) or rule of thumb cued by certain characteristics of the environment. There may be good reason behind this practice whether or not people actually think about it. (Heiner 1983) identifies a competency–difficulty (C–D) gap. People do not have the competency to make sense out of complexity. Rather than calculate, they rely on routines. If others rely on the same SOPs, the routine becomes custom and the world becomes more predictable than if you have to guess how others are going calculate. Arrow refers to this as rationality not being a product of the individual alone (Arrow 1986). Following a rule means that the decision maker is not flexible in adapting to new circumstances. But flexibility in using all possible information may not enhance performance. If everyone tries to realize all the gains from trade, it creates a further uncertainty that prevents achievement of these gains. It may pay to ignore complex information even when available.

Table 6.15 Complexity

Situation	Structure	Performance
Complexity. Bounded rationality. High information processing cost even if info is available Competency–difficulty gap* Different cognitive errors are possible: Morphological, sensory, etc. Event categories are known, and subjective probability may be attached	Individual strategies: 1. Try to use all available information. Attach numerical probabilities? 2. Use SOPs (habits learned in business or social culture/networks): e.g. advertising budget, inventory control 3. Change has been so rapid that no SOPs have emerged	1. Errors. Partly because can't predict others' behavior when making complex calculations 2. Acts of others are predictable 3. Chaos. Can't predict. If SOP is wrong, does feedback correct the structure?

*Heiner (1983)

Some empirical evidence of the C–D gap is provided by (Mazzotta and Opaluch 1995). For additional insight see Wilde, LeBaron, and Israelsen (1985). The situation and impact of Heiner's C–D gap is framed in SSP terms in table 6.15.

SOPs do change. Competitive pressure may provide a strong selection process. Still, appropriate decision rules are not automatic since there is often no corrective feedback and reinforcement. People miss the opportunity for gain by not buying insurance against rare, but disastrous events (Kates 1962). In the case of floods, calculating expected utility would pay, but in the larger class of such events, people are not sure, so they adopt a rule of ignoring this class of events altogether. This turns out to be rational given the risk of making a series of big mistakes, but the practice could persist even if wrong.

Heiner (1983: 579–80) provides an alternative conception of the "Law of Demand" without any resort to calculation from indifference curves. When prices rise, consumers face a competency–difficulty gap and the decision rule is to reduce purchases. In some cases this will not maximize utility, but then an elaborate consideration of preferences and prices for all goods can also produce mistakes. Arrow observes that many theories are consistent with a budget constraint. "For example, habit formation can be made into a theory; for a given price–income change, choose the bundle that satisfies the budget constraint and that requires the least change (in some suitably defined sense) from the previous consumption bundle" (Arrow 1986: S386).

Radical uncertainty of the yet-to-be actions of others is a quite different situation of interdependence than risk or complexity (Littlechild 1986). No subjective probability estimates are possible for unique and non-repeating decisions. Consumers use advertising to gain information. If preferences do not change, the main public policy issue is truth in advertising. Advertising is one way to control the fickle consumer and direct demand to imagined new products. If preferences can change consumers' imagination, there is a public policy issue of what we want to become as a society. "Issues of efficiency blend very quickly into issues of morality" (Littlechild 1986: 34).

In the Austrian view, an agent can invest in more information, but does not know what to search for. Entrepreneurs have private hunches about unexploited opportunities not seen by others. This view predicts that taxes and regulations will make the search more expensive and reduce the discovery of opportunities. The Austrians are thus skeptical of regulation. But in a learning situation, where entrepreneurs can't know all alternatives, environmental regulation such as a scheduled mandatory reduction in waste and emissions could lead the firm to discover new technologies for profitable recycling that escaped attention before. We can't assume that all profitable alternatives are known independently of institutions.

With fundamental or radical uncertainty, there is nothing out there to be discovered. Rather the manager's problem is to imagine the future, and any particular future is a function of how many others have the same imagination and act upon it. The future is created, not discovered. Consider a hypothetical scenario. A firm like Microsoft has a vision of a new information technology system with pieces needed from other firms. It invites other firms to invest in research to supply the pieces. The supply firms have no assurance that the total system will work, but Microsoft lets it be known that if you are not on board early, you can't play in the future. There are other institutions that coordinate visions. One is the Japanese *keiretsu*, a combine of related firms and a main bank that takes a long-term view of new product development (Aoki 2000). (The Korean *chaebol* has some of the same features.) Another is the German banking practice of giving loans to firms who have a vision of interconnected investments. (See table 6.16.) They have found this to produce more secure loans than the best forecast of demand and profitability of an individual firm.

Where is power and conflict in all this? Is it in persuasive images of the future? Investments are tied to expectations formed in the face of fundamental uncertainty. This relates to macroeconomics. Chapter 9 will explore what happens when actors are pessimistic about the future as in a downward business cycle.

Fundamental uncertainty means "Choice is in the first place origination, the creation of choosables" (Shackle 1992: 509). The future is not unknown as much as non-existent (Shackle 1979; Wiseman 1983). The agent is vulnerable in a world where others are making independent choices. Collective action in the form of shared imagination can reduce that vulnerability. Management consulting is a huge business. Do these consultants know the future or do their images get propagated and thus become reality? The future is largely what we make it. Just reducing transaction costs of achieving a deterministic outcome is not enough. Metaphorically, friction is not the only enemy and grease is not the only answer.

A firm contemplating a large investment in a new product wants to predict consumer demand. An example would be a biotechnology firm that can produce a genetically modified organism that lowers food production costs. But will consumers regard it as the same product as before, only cheaper? Does it make any difference

Table 6.16 Fundamental uncertainty

Situation	Structure	Performance
Fundamental uncertainty: Radical subjectivity* Instability Future can't be represented by subjective probability distribution. Agent does not know what to search for Names of variables are unknown Unique, non-repeating situation	1. US firms related by contract but outside is fickle consumer and new product maker. Banks at arm's length 2. Japanese *keiretsu* Firms are loyal to each other. Banks extend loan repayment if necessary 3. German bank loans to firms all along the supply chain	1. US loses market share to other countries 2. Working together to *create* an *imagined* future 3. Ditto
Fickle consumer (learning) "Fickle" technology and possible new products	*Collective action* to create the future. Advertising to create and maintain consumer demand Williamson's hostage between firms is not helpful against consumer defection. Allow firms to suppress new technology? Private hunch. Consultants Rules for sharing unanticipated cost Strategic management	Value of an opportunity and likelihood of finding it New products and industries fail or succeed Survival of the firm and its trading partners
Uncertainty of yet undetermined action of others	*Imagination to create the future* Strategic alliances Public policy on advertising because it can affect imagination	Create futures Firms have shared visions A firm may fail because not consistent with behavior of others

*See Littlechild (1986) and Potts (2000: ch. 7)

whether consumers have stable underlying preferences *or* learn that a new product serves these preferences better than an old product as argued by Stigler and Becker? (Recall section 3.5.5.) Both involve cognition and learning, and resources are used in that learning as well as in the production of goods. Whether people change their preference for food safety over time or learn that GMOs are less safe is of little importance to Monsanto. Econometric models based on past price and quantity behavior will not predict if there is structural change in basic preferences *or* in human skills and understanding of how a particular product achieves those preferences. Just (2001: 1147) argues that analysts will have to depend more on talking to people now rather than looking at past behavior. "Representing unfolding events likely requires a great deal of judgment, which invalidates the precision of econometric forecasts and confidence intervals. Perhaps, in the midst of unanticipated change, no purely scientific approach can substitute for dialog with the agent decision makers who will determine ultimate reactions."

The above raises fundamental methodological issues. The underlying structure of nature is the basis for event regularity – A is always associated with B. Further, the presence of A is obvious and cognition invariant. In that case, association is predictable without knowledge of deep structural causes (Lawson 1997). But, if human affairs are marked by learning that changes connections between variables, then the analyst must inquire of deep cause (Schmid and Thompson 1999). Economics then needs psychology.

There are enough unanticipated structural changes to warrant putting resources into designing institutions to share the consequences of unanticipated events (both costs and benefits) and into organizing the firm and the industry to adjust faster as the future reveals itself.

6.7.5 Evolutionary and competence based theory of the firm

When the best action is not knowable, but has to be invented, an evolving competence theory of the firm is useful. When the best action is not deducible from the past, present (or forecasted) facts, a learning organization is necessary. Learning is the discovery and development of aspects of the problem being solved, as discussed in chapter 3. In the face of uncertainty, the firm is an organization for collective action and learning within which its members learn and create the production function and make decisions relative to its customers and input suppliers. The firm is a set of social relations, conversations, and persuasions that offer a richer context for learning than does arm's length transactions. An arm's length transaction in an auction market may tell the producer that something is wrong if the supply does not clear at the cost of production. But it tells precious little about why and what will happen next. If costs of inputs are rising, the auction market does little to suggest what the buyer might do in cooperating with the supplier to reduce costs. The path of innovation must be created.

When a firm's boundaries expand to include more functions and people, both command and delegation are expanded. If the future product and its production function are yet to be created, the firm is much more than a locus of contract. The problem is more than getting others to do what the center wants done. The center does not know what to do independent of information and visions of others. Delegation is essential to utilize the knowledge of everyone in the organization. Close supervision and high-powered incentives could be counter-productive if the benefit of delegation is lost (Simon 1991; Teece and Pisano 1994: 539). Edwards Demming argued that driving out employee fear releases creative energy (Walton 1986).

The different members of the firm have different perspectives on what will further firm profits because of their particular work experience. The big problem is to utilize the knowledge of the members in choosing what to do in the context of fundamental uncertainty. An evolutionary perspective wherein exploration of an end-in-view may change the originally conceived objective is what strategic management is all about. Firms are not only reacting to a given environment, but are part of making that environment.

Shirking can only be defined when the central authority has clear knowledge of what should be done. Where images of the future are critical, shirking is not the big problem in a firm. "Doing a job well is not mainly a matter of responding to commands, but is much more a matter of taking initiative to advance organizational objectives" (Simon 1991: 32). People will have different and conflicting images of the future. They are not shirking when they withhold their enthusiastic participation, but have different ideas of what will contribute to the bottom line. People can conflict over the meaning of the environment without guile or opportunism.

When all parties in a firm agree on what constitutes maximum profitable actions, then the only contest is distribution of that profit after the fact. But when there is disagreement on subjective opportunities, there is a contest over competing visions of the future. "The essence of power effects is not so much *ex post* distributional considerations but rather *ex ante* control over strategic developments" (Dietrich 1994: x).

Businesses speak of their core competencies. A firm's ability to innovate is much more than hiring pieces of a puzzle whose finished appearance is already known. Employee knowledge and creativity are intrinsically social and arise within an organizational framework that is larger than the sum of its parts. Competence, the ability to make new connections, is a property of systems and networks including firms (Potts 2000: 139; Foss and Knudsen 1996: 1). Something is lost if the individual is separated from the organization which produced that person's tacit knowledge. "Existing managerial personnel provide services that cannot be provided by personnel newly hired from outside the firm . . . because the experience they gain from working within the firm and with each other enables them to provide services that are uniquely valuable for the operation of the particular group which they are associated" (Penrose 1995: 46). "Production costs cannot be independent of social relations" (Hodgson 1993: 257).

There are simple firms with contractable functions that can minimize transaction costs of opportunism and shirking by integration compared to an auction market. They are producing standard products with known production functions for the moment. But, this is not the way for complex firms to survive in the long run. Shirking and opportunism are not the main problem for an innovating firm. Rather it is how to achieve growth of knowledge and competence.

Table 6.17 Review of all transaction cost sources

Situation (and good)	Structure	Performance
Good = e.g. blood, coffee beans *HIC*– measurement of labor or commodity quality	Labeling regulation Labor identifies with firm	Consumers make few mistakes. Labor does not shirk. Ditto for borrowers
Good = e.g. machines, human capital Uncertainty of the behavior of trading partners + *asset specificity*	Integration; hostages Non-standard contracts *Keiretsu*; German banking Plantations. Farmer must buy inputs from processor Status, conventions	Value of specific assets not lost. Trade-off between flexible technology and low cost per unit of output Degree of opportunism
Contractual Cost (Cost of negotiation) Related to number of and access to parties	Integration; the firm Contract enforcement Damages vs. injunction Class action rights Eminent domain	Ability to trade impersonally at a distance Who gets rent?
Good = future state of world *Fundamental uncertainty:*	Advertising. Consumer co-op	Consumers stay loyal
Fickle engineers and consumers who make old products obsolete	Public subsidies to investment in new technology	Consumers stay until investments are recovered
C–D Gap: can't process all available information	SOPs	On the whole, get it right more than wrong. Acts of others predictable
Radical subjectivity: (no names for variables)	Learning the culture *Keiretsu*, alliances, joint-ventures	Work together to imagine and create the future

6.7.6 Conclusion and summary of transaction costs

Information as a good is not the same as a high information cost good. Information often has HEC and non-rival characteristics and the relevant structures addressing that were identified in sections 6.3 and 6.4 above and included such things as copyright, trade secrets, and private vs. public provision. But, this section on transaction costs is different.

As summarized in table 6.17, the source of transaction cost interdependencies include: the costs of contract negotiation, the uncertainty of the behavior of trading partners, the uncertainty of future states of the world (particularly the general level of demand and new technology), and the competency–difficulty gap of the brain. The performance variables useful to describe the impact of alternative institutions are noted in the table. Human transactions are costly. Some are subject to economizing (reducing total cost) and some can only be shifted among the parties (power issue). Without theory, the source of the interdependence can't be identified and the alternative structures to affect performance can't be seen since an institution to control for asymmetrical information on product quality is not the same an one to control for general uncertainty.

6.8 Rent and Rent Seeking

Economists use rent differently than people in the street who speak of the price they pay for an apartment as rent. "Economic Rent" is a return above opportunity cost due to natural limits to supply. So that part of apartment rent that is above the cost of building and maintaining the apartment is economic rent. In this case it is mostly the location advantage. Apartments near centers of economic activity have more "rent" in what people pay than apartments further away that are of the same quality and size. Governments can control contract rent with no consequence for investment and maintenance as long as the controlled price covers opportunity cost. But if the market is not used to allocate land with a location advantage, an administrative transaction is required to ration the limited supply. (See table 6.18.) Henry George advocated the taxation of rents and hoped it would cover a large portion of governmental expenditures (Gaffney and Harrison 1994).

The other source of a return above opportunity cost comes from monopoly and other artificial restrictions against firms entering a line of business. Sometime both of these sources are called rent and trying to maintain them is called rent seeking. In principle, monopoly profit can be competed away and anti-trust law can help. Entrenched monopolists may prevent this through effective lobbying and thus preserve their extra profits. New would-be monopolists are rent/profit seekers.

Rent coming from locational advantage and supply limited in nature (good farm land or land within walking distance of a major university) cannot be competed away. The only policy choice is who gets the rent. One "rent seeker" is trying to replace another rent recipient. When someone condemns rent seeking, they are just saying that they prefer the *status quo* rent holder over the groups trying to get it (Samuels and Mercuro 1992).

Table 6.18 Economic rent

Situation	Structure	Performance
Inelastic supply of land close to center of economic activity creates rent (a return above opportunity cost)	*Market* – (Factor ownership of land not an issue, but right to rent is) 1. Anti-trust (competition)	1. Rent still earned (above opportunity cost) Price rations fixed supply
	Administration – 1. Rent control at opportunity cost (Allow some rent to be earned to be sure opportunity costs are covered)	1. Excess demand requires non-price rationing No effect on supply or maintenance of buildings Less distortion of public land use planning and investments
	2. Tax some of the rent	2. No effect on supply. Market price still rations limited supply. Reduced pressure to frustrate public land use plans
Plus economies of scale in creating centers of economic activity	3. Build new town. Hard to develop at large scale (similar to introducing a wholly new computer operating system)	3. New town successful. Creation of new centers reduces rents at old centers

Rents are created by public investments in highway interchanges and subway stops. Effort by landowners to capture these rents by influencing public decisions is often a source or great wealth and corruption. Governments often want to distribute land uses to obtain a particular landscape. If zoning is used, the low-density zones receive little rent while land granted zoning permission receives much. Again, efforts by landowners to capture these rents often frustrate public land use planning. If the rent were taxed away, this pressure would be reduced.

6.9 Fluctuating Demand and Supply

The demand and supply of some goods is subject to cyclical fluctuations. The demand for transportation and electricity fluctuates with the time of day, day of the week, and the seasons. The supply of some foodstuffs fluctuates with the seasons and the weather. Pricing rules affect how the costs of meeting peak demands and allocating reduced supplies affects whose interests count. For example, if electric generation capacity is built to supply peak demands, there is excess capacity at other times. The users at the two periods may not be the same. If average cost pricing is the rule, then the user who uses electricity at the peak times pays the same as the person who only uses at the slack time. Peak-load pricing makes the peak user pay for the capacity necessary to meet the peak demand. Different users have different elasticities of demand and if some using electricity when priced at average cost shift to non-peak periods in response to higher peak-load pricing, less capacity will be needed.

6.10 Socio-Emotional Goods

Some goods and services cannot be separated from the "producer" without changing their character. This intrinsic character is a source of interdependence whose outcome is influenced by the institutional structure. The transfer of goods from one person to another can carry some emotion with it. Depending on the social relationship, the physical good or service symbolizes feeling between the producer and the recipient. It communicates that A cares for B and usually that B has regard for A. It can communicate mutual respect, admiration, and trust. Trust is putting resources at risk of the opportunistic behavior of others when one attributes to them a motive of sympathy and concern for your welfare (Tyler 2001). The emotional content makes the good more valuable to the recipient than if the good were separate from the producer. For example, a rose from your spouse is of different value than the same physical rose given by your boss or won in a lottery.

Gifts of socio-emotional goods can create (and express) the sympathy that one has for another. This sympathy is social capital that gives its holder resources and opportunities not available in the *quid pro quo* of market exchange (Robison, Schmid, and Siles 2002).

History shows a steady commodification of goods that once were deeply embedded in human relationships (Polanyi 1944). Land was once a part of a spiritual relationship among people and with their gods. It could be used but not alienated.

Peasants were tied to each other and the feudal lord and there was no labor market. This contrasts with the modern conception of individual ownership that can be traded to others at will.

One of the last major economic activities where the person is not fully separated from the good or service is care for children and the elderly (Folbre 2001). This is not to say that there is not significant hired care, but it cannot produce the same value. A gift of oneself intrinsically carries an emotional message that is destroyed if the same service is paid for. This is not to say that a bond of mutual regard may not evolve from a paid caregiver. It is not without meaning to note that the words care and giver are often combined. The gift and giving make a difference. In practice, custom has given much of the responsibility for caregiving to women and it is organized outside the market.

If there is no feeling between the caregiver and the recipient, there is possible motivation to shade quality. Since care of children and the elderly is a high information cost good as well, it may be difficult for the third party buyer to monitor quality, and opportunism is possible. Feelings of bonding and caring are often combined with a learned sense of obligation and norm-following. Sympathy and social norms are complements in practice and an over-reliance of one or the other is probably not sustainable. Both need reinforcement by a return of emotional goods from recipients or others in the community expressing approval of the acts.

Labor is intrinsically embedded in human relationships. Labor power comes with a head that can be loyal and forthcoming or grudging. Labor union negotiators ask for dignity and regard as well as money and benefits, though each can suggest the other. If labor thinks they are not being paid and treated fairly, they are opportunistic and non-cooperative. More on this in chapter 11, "Labor Institutions."

Some blood is bought and sold and some is gifted. Some of its qualities are high information cost thus creating the possibility of opportunism. Some sell blood but do not volunteer their medical history making it more costly to determine quality. People who make a gift of blood have no incentive to lie about its quality (Titmuss 1971). If some blood is sold, it reduces the satisfaction of the giver, since the recipient has alternative sources; and purchased blood reduces the satisfaction of the recipient from knowing that someone cared enough to make the donation. Some empirical studies involving socio-emotional goods and social capital are reviewed below in sections 7.2.4, 7.3.4, and 7.4.1.

6.11 Overview

This chapter has outlined some of the major inherent characteristics of goods that create human interdependence. A good may have more than one situational characteristic and thus multiple varieties of institutions directing the interdependencies. The theory presented suggests the kinds of institutions (structures) that control and direct that interdependence. It also suggests the kinds of substantive performance variables that are relevant to describe the outcomes of that interdependence. The theory is summarized in table 6.19. The hypothesized relationships among these SSP variables can be empirically tested so that good advice can be given to different interest

Table 6.19 Institutional economics theory: variables and relationships (impact analysis)

Situation	Structure	Performance
Incompatible use good (IUG)	1. Factor ownership. Use or exchange rights 2. Degree of competition if market	1. Who creates externalities for whom? 2. P = MC. No one affects price

High exclusion cost (HEC)	1. Markets
	  a. Tie-in sales
	2. Administration (tax)
	
	3. Status
		1. Free-riders frustrate would-be riders
		  a. Fewer free-riders
		2. Reduced free-riders, but some object
		  Unwilling riders
		3. Neither of the above

Interdependent binary choices ("mixing and sorting")	1. Markets – isolated individual choice at the margin 2. Collective choice – administrative rule 3. Status	1. Aggregate result (mixtures) preferred by most is not achieved. Tragedy 2. Achieved, but some may feel forced 3. Achieved, individuals regard process as natural

Prisoner's Dilemma (PD); existence of a dominant choice	1. Market
	  a. (If repeated, play tit-for-tat)
	2. Collective; discussion
	3. Status
		1. Defection. Result no one wants
		  a. Trap avoided
		2. Cooperation
		3. Cooperation

Economies of scale (increasing returns)	1. Rules of demand alteration; herd mentality
	2. Price differentiation rules
	  a. Average cost pricing
	  b. Marginal cost pricing
	  c. Predatory pricing. Anti-dumping rules in international trade; infant industry protection
	3. Rules for who chooses quality if only few large-scale standard products
	4. Intro of new products into market or by collective action
	5. Rules determining the extent of the market
	6. Monopoly or many firms; with or without price regulation
		1. Advantage to those with similar tastes
		2. Who pays fixed or only variable cost? Instability. No equilibrium
		
		Relative growth of nations
		
		3. Whose preferences count?
		
		4. Path dependence; cumulative causation. Lock-in
		
		5. Realize economies of scale
		6. Unit cost vs. variety tradeoff

Table 6.19 (*cont'd*)

Situation	Structure	Performance
Marginal cost = zero (MC = 0) a. Avoidable, i.e. optional b. Unavoidable and pre-emptive	1. Cost-sharing rule 2. Cost-sharing plus who chooses the single available quality 3. Regulated monopoly or many providers	1. Who pays fixed or only variable cost? 2. More important than in (a.) because can't adjust quantity taken and only one quality will exist. Whose preferences count? 3. Unit cost vs. variety tradeoff

Transaction cost:
 1. High (asymmetric) information cost (HIC) (measurement) (monitoring)
 	
 2. Uncertainty + specific assets
 	
 3. Uncertain future states of the world
 4. C–D gap
 5. Radical subjectivity
	1. a. Labeling regulation Products liability ... Penalties for failure to reveal quality
	    b. Market vs. status
	 2. Integration; hostages; non-standard contracts
	 3. Advertising. Subsidies to investment
	 4. SOPs; culture
	 5. Keiretsu; alliances. Learned fads of conjecture and speculation
		1. a. Cost of producing info paid by different parties with different costs of obtaining information. Who makes mistakes?
		    b. Labor shirks or identifies with firm
		 2. Value of specific assets not lost. Tradeoff between flexible technology and low cost per unit of output
		 3. Consumer loyalty. Recovery of investment
		 4. Predictability of the acts of others
		 5. Work together to imagine and create the future

Surpluses (rents) (Returns above opportunity cost.) Natural limit to supply	1. Factor ownership Corporate ownership Co-ops. Worker owned firms 2. Markets + investor owned firms	1. Who gets the rents? Will rents be maximized? 2. Factors paid MVP and employer gets the surplus
Fluctuating demand and supply	1. Peak-load pricing 2. Markets or administrative rationing	1. Who pays for periods of unused capacity? 2. Market clearing; no lines. Buyers regard it as gouging
Socio-emotional goods	1. Markets 2. Status	1. Reduces value of socio-emotional goods 2. Enhances values of socio-emotional goods

groups as to what institutions make their interests count. If you do not know where the interdependencies are coming from, you can't design institutions to direct them.

Some common themes emerge. Knowledge of the sources of interdependence identifies areas of potential conflict as well as opportunities for cooperation. It identifies the distinction between issues of power and economizing. Contested opportunities are governed by rights, which in a market make a person a seller rather than a buyer. After the power issues are worked out, economizing may proceed. The resolution of power issues contained in formal and informal institutions is antecedent to the market. Resolution involves the making of moral judgments about distribution by the participating parties whether they realize it or not.

ANALYTIC STEPS FOR AN IMPACT METHODOLOGY

1. Ask what is the physical good central to the case being analyzed?
2. What is the inherent characteristic of this good (its situation)? The character of the good suggests the source of human interdependence. Identify the interest groups (stakeholders).
3. From the theory summarized in table 6.19, specify the structural variables (institutions) that direct each source of interdependence to suggest the kind of property rights that are likely to be important for each situation.
4. Select performance variables suggested by the theory and a survey of interest groups.
5. Formulate testable hypotheses relating situation, alternative structures, and their contrasting performances (outcomes – who gets what).
6. Test using methods outlined in the next chapter.

NOTES

1. Breton (1989: 732) says "A person free rides whenever he or she participates in the benefits of a good or service, but does not share proportionately in the costs." But, it is just the recipient's valuation of the good that is impossible to measure in the market for HEC goods. Under Breton's definition, holders of consumer surplus not subject to differential pricing would be free-riders.
2. Welfare theorists have searched for characteristics of goods that would justify a particular institution. Private goods would be optimally allocated by a market while public goods might not. Paul Samuelson (1969) defines a "public good" as "one that enters two or more persons' utility." Since most goods have a degree of "consumption externality," Samuelson can't find a clear guide to policy. "If the experts remain nihilistic about algorithms to allocate public goods, and if all but a knife-edge of reality falls in that domain, nihilism about most of economics, rather than merely public finance, seems to be implied" (109). By "consumption externality," Samuelson refers to the interdependencies created by MC = 0 and economies of scale that have a game-theoretic or bilateral monopoly element of indeterminacy that is not solved by exclusion even if feasible. Samuelson insists, "For the $(n + 1)$th time, let me repeat the warning that a public good should not necessarily be run by public rather than private enterprise" (108n). If he had avoided the use of the term "public good" in the first place, he would not have to continually make the point.
3. Asymmetry is the source of interdependence, not absolute costs of information, which is a standard production economics economizing problem.

Chapter 7
Methods

<hr>

7.1 Introduction

<hr>

Institutional economics is not limited to any particular method of investigation. All of the tools usually used in economics are relevant. This chapter will present illustrative examples of empirical research in three broad categories: experiments, case studies, econometrics, and simulation. The purpose is to illustrate how different methods can be used to test some of the hypotheses developed in previous chapters. The chapter will sometimes show how previous empirical work might have been improved with better theory. The *situation*, *structure*, and *performance* (SSP) framework will be used to provide a common framework for the empirical studies even when it was not explicit in the original work. Studies of social capital are chosen as one application where several different methods can be contrasted.

7.1.1 Specifying alternative institutions

To test the impact of alternative institutions, the institution must be carefully specified so that the differences in human relationships are clear over time and space. Shall they be described as patterned, regular behavior, a mental state (expectations), or rules (an abstract object)? Since physical behavior at some level is the performance we want to explain, it can't be used as an explanatory variable. It is often convenient to describe human relationships in terms of rules, either formal or informal.[1] For example, in a situation where several people want to be served, access could be auctioned or offered on a first come, first served basis. The presence of an auction can be observed (a bargained relationship between an access owner and buyers). Further inquiry might determine the presence of a formal rule of first come, first served, with sanctions for violation. If not, an informal rule/custom might be operating. It is tempting to say if a behavior of honoring queues is observed, the rule must be "honor queues." Social pressure sanctions can be observed suggesting that people expect others to follow a rule and are willing to bear cost to enforce it. The honoring of queues may be so internalized that the actor is not aware of having made a choice. The environment and past experience simply cue behavior.

Formal institutions (rights) are written and it is tempting to say there has been a change when the statute changes. But, we know that citizens (and sometimes officials) are often unaware of formal law. In this case, perception of "what the law probably is" is operative. The formal law may be regarded by the obligated parties as illegitimate, and the rights holder may be unable to enforce it. The degree of willing participation matters. Conversely, people often limit themselves even when the law does not require it, and people accept the behavior of others even if the law does not support it. Formal law is often embedded in complementary informal institutions. Two jurisdictions with the same formal law, but different informal rules, may perform differently. Sometimes, a major rule change is offset by unchanging economic power.[2] Considering all this, the expectations and mental images of relative opportunities and obligations would appear to be the best way to describe institutions.[3] But, as a practical matter the analyst has to use whatever descriptors are available – often beginning with simple abstractions and probing deeper if possible. The researcher's problem is not unlike that of a new employee in a large firm who asks, "What is my role and what are the rules?" The employee reads the manuals and talks to people.

Some contrasting structures (institutions) are highlighted for analysis (hypothesized performance of each alternative). However, there are background institutions that have accumulated through time (up to the point of the present analysis) that are common to the contrasted structures. For example, two alternative private governance choices by firms take place within general corporate law and informal routines. If this background had been different, the highlighted alternative structures each might be expected to have different outcomes. This is especially important if we hope to transfer our understanding of the performance of these institutional alternatives to a different setting.

7.2 Experiments

7.2.1 General

The laboratory provides an opportunity to test the impact of alternative institutions. Institutions and situation can be varied and the effects observed. Smith (1989: 154) one of the leading experimentalists, argues that the laboratory provides greater control over variables than can be obtained in the field. He further argues that experiments encourage better theory specification since the variables must be explicit in the experimental design. What are the elements of a theory to be tested? Smith suggests three that have some similarity to SSP. They are environment, institutions, and behavior. Under environment he includes the characteristics of the people and commodities, namely preference and production functions. The key characteristics are willingness to pay and willingness to accept. Environment is roughly equivalent to situation in SSP. Environment usually includes the payoff matrix to various actors depending on their actions.

Smith (1989: 153) defines institutions in terms of the "language of communication" (bids and offers) and the "characteristics of the commodity." However, the SSP framework includes the character of the good in situation (environment). Institutions specify the order in which actors move and the rules under which a bid becomes a contract. Smith describes it as "the institution specifies the rules, terms or conditions under which components of market demand make contact with components of market supply to produce binding allocations." In SSP, institutions describe the property rights (opportunity sets) of the interdependent parties. These rights are often simplified in many experiments in terms of starting place allocations of budgets and the rules for making and accepting bids.

Behavior for Smith is the agent's choice of messages (bids and offers) that result in allocation outcomes. The standard theory of market choice describes behavior in terms of the outcomes of market clearing and equilibrium. Institutional theory emphasizes how different institutions affect whose preferences count and vice versa. Experimental design for Smith involves insertion of controls such that any inconsistency between predicted and actual behavior denies the behavioral assumptions of the theory (154). Institutional theory takes human motivation as a variable rather than an assumption to be tested in a dichotomous fashion.

For example, from Olson (1965) we have the theoretical prediction that people will free ride in the presence of high exclusion cost goods (no bids are forthcoming). (Similar logic is used to predict the outcome of Prisoner's Dilemma games, namely movement toward the Nash equilibrium.) Subjects are presented with a group payoff matrix such that the experimenter adds to a pot to be shared by all subjects as a function of total contributions from the subjects from their given budget. Further, subjects are presented with a personal payoff matrix where they benefit from any contribution to a shared pot regardless of their own contribution, which in effect creates a HEC good. If any contribution to a HEC good occurs, Olson's standard theory is falsified, more specifically, the assumption of narrow-self utility maximization. An institutional theory might be that free riding will vary with the degree of social capital. Subjects can be assembled that are thought to vary in social capital (Marwell and Ames 1997). Or, as part of the experiment, the subjects might be subjected to various learning experiences (see section 7.2.2 below).

In general, Smith and many theorists are satisfied that "The experimental evidence is often consistent with the predictions of market theories" (1989: 163). Some are more interested in theory than in how to change behavior and secure different outcomes (Smith 2000). The evidence that many people free ride for example may persuade readers that lots of people are selfish. But, for others, they note that if some do not free ride, it raises the possibility that others can learn similar behavior. These analysts want new behavioral theory to identify potentially new instrumental variables (Camerer 2003). Experiments related to Prisoner's Dilemma, transaction costs, and social capital will be discussed below.

7.2.2 Prisoner's Dilemma experiments

In Prisoner's Dilemma (PD) games there is a dominant strategy that has a higher payoff for a subject regardless of what others do. Dawes designed an experiment that has PD characteristics (Dawes 1990). Each player is given $5 that she may keep or contribute to a joint pot. The institution is varied as follows. Under the non-contingent rule, if four out of the nine players contribute their money to the pot, everyone gets $10. No individual can make a difference to her payoff. The institution is then varied to a contingent rule wherein if five of the nine (and the individual must be one of them) contribute, all get $10. Further, the rights of participants are circumscribed by a prohibition of side payments and everyone is anonymous after the game begins. The rules eliminate reciprocal altruism and reputation as motives. The institution is further varied by having some groups proceed immediately to the game and others to have five minutes to get acquainted before the game begins. This introduces an opportunity for learning. Under the non-contingent rule, the dominant strategy is for all individuals to keep all their initial money.

What behavior resulted from the variation in institutions? Without discussion, and with the non-contingent rule, 30 percent contributed to the common pot. With the payoff of each person contingent on their contribution, 45 percent contributed. Self-interest has an effect shown by the higher contribution when payoff is affected by own behavior. With discussion, and with the non-contingent rule, contribution jumped to 75 percent and increased even more to 85 percent with the contingent rule. The opportunity to pursue self-interest makes a difference, but even more difference is associated with discussion. Interviews indicate that in the absence of discussion, cooperators cite doing the right thing. With discussion they cite the group welfare (sympathy) as the reason. This research is an example of an institutional approach where motive is not assumed, but treated as a variable. The objective here is not primarily to test old theory, but to develop new insight into how alternative institutions affect behavior.

Did the five minutes of conversation trigger sympathy or norm following? Dawes designed another experiment to distinguish these motives by varying the identity of the beneficiaries of cooperation. "If discussion triggers conscience, and our contributing subjects are acting to satisfy its demands, then discussion should enhance contribution to strangers. If, however, discussion elicits caring about group members, then it should enhance contributions only to people in the groups with whom one interacts" (Dawes 1990: 103). Groups of seven were each given $6. For each $6 given away, the experimenter added $12 to the total pot to be divided among the players. Again, there is a dominant strategy because if a subject gives her $6 away and no one else does, the subject gets nothing. If all give, then each gets $12. Half of the groups were told that the pot would be divided among the seven in their group, and half were told that the pot would be divided among six comparable members of another group (strangers). Similarly, what the subject receives is a function of the behavior of the strangers.

Again there was a big difference in the rate of cooperation with and without discussion. But, discussion made little difference when the benefit went to strangers. Dawes is not afraid to get out of his armchair and talk to players about their motives. "In the absence of discussion, most cooperators cite 'doing the right thing' as their major motive; with discussion the majority cite 'group welfare.' In contrast, defectors cite their personal payoffs" (109). Dawes believes that group identity is key, but "group identity does not equal morality. It is fragile, easily manipulated, and at times draconian . . ." (110). Note that his groups are small. We can't talk with distant people and look them in the eye as real persons. If we do not include distant people in our sympathy or groups to which our normative obligations apply, cooperation will be low and we are doomed to low payoffs.

Inferring the presence of group identity and motives of sympathy vs. norm following can be done by clever experimental design. But ultimately, to describe the operative structural institution, we must make direct inquiry and work with what people say, with all its interpretative problems. For example, a survey was made of the reasons that people might return a hypothetically found wallet (Schmid 2002). Subjects were asked to indicate the importance of various reasons if they would return the wallet by distributing 100 points among feeling sympathy for the owner, it is the ethical thing to do, and expectation of a reward. Different communities differed in the patterns of reasons. Another way to measure the structural variable (what institution is operative in a community) is to ask people what others would do and why. The expected rate of wallet return for others is dramatically less, and people tend to regard others as more motivated by personal reward than they are. The difference between attitudes toward local people and more distant people was tested by asking subjects how they would distribute their charity to victims of disasters. Differences in the patterns of motives among communities (structure) can be correlated with differences in cooperative community activity (performance).

7.2.3 Transaction costs

In the game described above, the institution ruled out market exchange. The so-called Coase Rule says that if the parties can bargain at no cost, they will agree to an allocation that maximizes total net benefit. Consider the usual interdependence of incompatible use goods such as use of a stream for waste disposal or for fishing. Consider a hypothetical payoff matrix as shown in table 7.1. The industry can maximize net revenue (12) by choosing high pollution level 1. The fisher would have zero revenue at that level. They would prefer level 3 where their benefit is 12, but the industry has zero revenue. At an intermediate level 2, the fishers have 4 and the industry 10 for a maximum total group benefit of 14, which is greater than the low or high levels. In an experiment conducted by Hoffman and Spitzer (1982) (H&S), the game (institution) was designed so that the winner of a coin toss had the property right to choose a non-cooperative outcome. The question is whether naming the owner (either the fishers or industry) would affect the outcome. In legal terms, does the placement of the liability affect resource use?

The efficient total joint profit-maximizing pollution level is 2. If the industry owns the right to level 1 (factor ownership), it can be made better off by a bid of anything greater than 8 from fishers. Fishers can afford to pay just up to 10 to achieve level 2 and be better off than before. The Coase Rule predicts that the parties will make bids such that level 2 is achieved. Standard selfish preference theory further predicts that if industry owns the right to level 1 it will not agree to any trade that makes its revenue less than 12. Yet in the experiment, the parties most frequently agreed to a 7 and 7 split of the aggregate net revenue of 14 at level 2. H&S concluded that the Coase Rule rules and the efficient result will be obtained.

Table 7.1 Externality game (Hoffman and Spitzer)

Situation	Structure	Performance

IUG *between* fishermen and industry
HEC *among* fishermen
Transaction cost to organize bid?
Group size up to 38
	Markets – factor ownership alternatives:
	1. Fishers own injunctive rights can choose pollution level 3.
	  e.g. Industry gets 0
	  Fishers get 12
	2. Industry owns; can choose pollution level 1
	  e.g. Fishers gets 0
	  Industry gets 12
	Hypothesis:
	a. with internalized sense of fairness
	b. selfishness of preference
	Experimental design:
	c. Coin toss to determine owner
	d. Hashmark contest to determine owner
		Resource use:
		Coase rule predicts resource use is the same with structure 1 or 2: i.e. pollution level 2
		Total value max. at 14
		Experiment confirms
		
		Distribution:
		a. 50:50 even split.
		b. Owner takes more. Not confirmed.
		
		c. 54% of trials had even splits
		d. 29% had even splits

Payoff matrix

	Industry	Fishers	Group net benefit
Level 1	12	0	12
Level 2	4	10	14
Level 3	0	12	12

Bargaining costs between two parties (and within groups) is apparently low enough not to interfere with the efficient outcome. A given level of environmental quality is a high exclusion cost good among fishers. Whatever fishing is available for one is available for all fishers. At some point, a larger group will have transaction costs so large as to wipe out the gains from trade. Hoffman and Spitzer (1986) repeated their experiment with groups up to 38 people and found that the efficient result was still predominantly chosen even if each member of the group had veto power (unanimity rule). The point at which transaction costs prevent achievement of gains from trade remains untested. Still, the even split of the gains from trade was observed.

H&S were curious about the split. In the two- and up to 38-person experiments, ownership was determined by a coin toss. They hypothesized that this appeared arbitrary and unjustified to the subjects. So they repeated the game with a "game trigger," namely the right to accept or reject a bid was "earned" by the winner of a tic-tac-toe (hash mark) game. The parties were informed that they had earned the right. This reduced overall the percentage of even splits of the gains from trade from 54 percent of the trials to 29 percent (Hoffman and Spitzer 1986). For more background see, (Hoffman and Spitzer, 1985). The inference is that people who believe they have a right to the lion's share take it. H&S did not try to confirm these inferences with interviews as did Dawes above. The empirical results are summarized in an SSP chart in table 7.1. This facilitates comparison with the earlier theoretical chapters and other experiments. The commonly observed even splits are consistent with evidence of inherited altruism (Field 2001).

Searching one's own experience, it seems incredulous that 38 people with different preferences can reach the aggregate maximum. If one or a few persons demanded most of the joint gain, would not the rest of their group begin to object? Why would a member of the group bother to help achieve the group maximum if she gets little from it? Anticipation of this possibility may account for the observed even split of the gains. From the example given in the article, all members of each group had the same payoff from a given pollution level. The starting place reference is equality and the person who asks for more stands out. But what if some fishers place a higher value on fishing than other fishers? Does that justify asking for more of the joint gain? Could they persuade others?

Institutional theory gives attention to distribution and does not assume that all members of a group have the same selfish preferences. It does not assume that the structure of the institution does not affect attitude toward the relative gains of others. Fishers don't all put the same value on a clean environment and some, if they were owners, would not sell at any price and thus deny other fishers a gain from trade. The experimental payoff and other institutional structures might be constructed to test this.

The payoffs in the above experiment had no negative numbers and no place for immobile assets. If industry had zero profit even at a high level of pollution and would suffer losses to immobile assets if it shut down, there may be no gains from trade and the initial rights distribution will determine use.

H&S strongly conclude, "the courts need not choose rules because of worries about the inefficiency that might be generated by disputes over the division of surpluses" (Hoffman and Spitzer 1985: 297). The question is further explored below.

7.2.4 Social capital: ultimatum and dictator games[4]

Games can be designed to test for existence of self-regard vs. regard for others and the role of distribution in achieving gains from cooperation. A person who has the regard and sympathy of others can be said to hold social capital that may result in benefits not expected in impersonal and narrow self-interested transactions. *Ultimatum games* are constructed so that one party (the controller) is given a pot of money and may propose a split with another party. If the split is accepted, the pot is distributed thusly, but if it is rejected, neither party gets anything. *Dictator games* are constructed so that the controller realizes whatever is proposed regardless of the actions of others. Experiments with ultimatum and dictatorship games have provided economists with a rich set of empirical observations that shed light on economic behavior. Camerer and Thaler (1995) have provided a meta-analysis of this literature. The literature provides overwhelming evidence that controllers *offer* positive sums to split a pot of money with a partner who may reject the offer in which case neither person receives anything. People will not *accept* Pareto-better gains from trade if deemed unfair. It is indisputable that people are doing something more than maximizing their own incomes even in one-shot cases. What is disputed is whether the behavior can best be modeled as sympathetic and altruistic (inter-dependent utility function) or as an expression of manners and etiquette. Camerer and Thaler prefer the latter explanation.

The authors argue that the altruistic utility function explanation is not satisfactory because "it is not possible to say whether the average participant puts a positive or negative value on the other subject's payoffs." (Could they not be asked?) In dictator games where the controller may keep all of a windfall regardless of the acceptance by others, the offer of money to the other party appears to be consistent with a positive relationship (sympathy) to the other party's payoffs. In contrast, in ultimatum games, respondents who reject the proposed split which denies any income to the controller may be interpreted as receiving no utility from the controller receiving some income. If I cared about someone, I would both offer a large share of the pot and accept any proposed split from them. The dollar amount of the gift could be the same in both cases. A dollar is a dollar. On this reasoning, the authors conclude, "that the outcomes of ultimatum, dictatorship and many other bargaining games have more to do with manners than altruism."

However, caring need not be invariant of other's actions. If I am making the proposal and care about the other party, I offer a fair split. My prior feeling about my partner is not affected by the transaction itself. But if someone I initially cared for (and would have offered a fair split) sends a signal that they do not care for me by offering a poor split, I may change my attitude toward them and will not be willing to use the proposed split as an opportunity to make a gift. Large differences in the affinity each feels toward the other are unstable. So, contrary to Camerer and Thaler, the fact that I may have a positive interdependence with the other's utility as a controller and a negative interdependence as a responder does not call the altruism concept into question. Altruism is predictably different depending on the occasion and opportunity of others to signal their care for the controller. The evidence is consistent with a model that says the average player (1) puts a positive value on other's payoffs if that person has not signaled negative feelings toward the player and (2) puts a negative value on other's payoffs when the other person signals lack of caring. The average player does not feel close (altruistic) toward a person making an unfair proposal.

There is other evidence that is consistent with this interpretation. Robison and Schmid (1991) conducted a mind experiment in which people were asked to set a price for selling a used car of known value to people whom the subject might be expected to have varying degrees of affinity such as family member, friend, stranger, and nasty neighbor. People indicated willingness to lower the price to those close to them (make them a gift). When the game was switched from selling to buying, a different pattern emerged. If you pay more for a friend's used car, you have the opportunity to give them a gift of the same dollar amount that you made by accepting a lower price for a good you are selling. The data however revealed that people did not offer the same break when buying as when selling to the same affinity group. Here as in the ultimatum and dictatorship games, there is an asymmetry. We reasoned that in the used car experiment, the gift was much more obvious when you paid more than the market price and one risked being labeled a chump and evoking embarrassment and a negative reaction from the beneficiary. The beneficiary can more easily accept a gift via a lower than market price when buying by chalking it up to clever negotiation on their part, but a gift resulting from someone paying the beneficiary more than the market price stands out like a sore thumb. Camerer and Thaler use the term "insulting" to describe an unfair proposal in an ultimatum game. Likewise, a gift that is too obvious may spoil the relationship.

Both sets of games exhibit an asymmetry that could be caused by the difference in the actual or expected behavior of the other party. This behavior is not necessarily incompatible with the concept of manners. An unfair controller in an ultimatum game is both rude and undeserving of the recipient's care and benevolence (exempts the individual controller from the general feeling recipients have toward their fellow humanity that is held until proven otherwise). The unfair controller is no longer the average neutral person who the dictator had agreed to share with. Rudeness (lack of manners) could be the term for anyone who indicates they have little affinity for the actor signaled by unfair (or embarrassing) proposals.

There may be other reasons to prefer an explanation of manners to altruism. Learning of manners is emphasized by Camerer and Thaler. Young children are found to accept minimal offers in ultimatum games that older children and adults reject. This can be attributed to experience in repeated games that unfair offers to others result in your forgoing gainful opportunity. This seems to root the experimental data in more familiar selfish rationality. The authors speak of learning that "long-run concerns outweigh the short-run costs" (1995: 218). But then this can't explain the benevolent behavior in one-shot games or leaving tips in restaurants you never expect to visit again. The authors "prefer to think that people have simply adopted rules of behavior they think apply to themselves and others, regardless of the situation" (218). Why can't this be applied to altruism as well as manners? Surely behavior can be reinforced by more than monetary payoffs. From the responses of other people, we can learn to like other people as well as to like money.

The concept of social capital may provide a better explanation of the evidence than either manners or altruism. Altruism is often used in the economics literature to refer to a taste for giving, which as the authors note in the introduction of their article is often assumed to be stable. However, the authors clearly believe that people learn and preferences change. Their reference to hotel room cleaners who leave their names in the room is an example of an attempt to change the guest's preferences as applied to a specific individual. Social capital is a coefficient of others' welfare in one's utility function, which is an evolving function of the relationship and affinity between the parties. Social capital is consistent with the observation that controllers in dictatorship games offer more of the pot to friends than strangers. The value of others' income in the controller's utility is a function of affinity. And, if the other person signals their lack of affinity for the controller or the responder, the behavior is different. People learn and are reinforced within the transaction as well as outside.

What are the lessons for economics in general? An owner of a factor is like a dictator who says in an offer to sell, take it or leave it (do without). An owner who is aware of the consumer surplus of another may bargain for it in a take-it or leave-it fashion even when the owner's reservation price is less than the buyer's willingness to pay. Such an owner runs the risk of the buyer walking away even from Pareto-better trades. What the experimental research suggests is that splitting the gains from trade is likely and that the achievement of the gains will not fail due to arguments over distribution. Still there are notable exceptions, especially where the parties are not faceless.

7.2.5 Summary of factors affecting cooperation

Some of the variables controlled in experiments have been shown to be associated with the percentage of contributions to high exclusion cost goods. Ledyard (1992: 143) groups these into: (1) Environmental variables that are easy to control: marginal per capita return, common knowledge, homogeneity, and thresholds. (2) Systemic variables, but hard to control: beliefs and group identity. He suspects that altruism, effort and risk aversion might be relevant, but remain not measured in his view. (3) Design variables: communication, rebates, and moral suasion. He offers these conclusions upon review of the literature (172–3):

1. Hard-nosed game theory cannot explain the data.
2. Contributions are, however, certainly responsive to marginal selfish payoffs.
3. Altruism or group-regarding preferences cannot explain the data.
4. It is possible to provide an environment in which at least 90 percent of subjects will become selfish Nash players.
5. It is possible to provide an environment in which at least 90 percent of subjects contribute toward the group interest. Why and how often this all works remains a mystery.
6. There are three types of players: dedicated Nash players who act pretty much as predicted by game theory . . . ; a group of subjects who will respond to self-interest . . . if the incentives are high enough but who also respond to decision

costs, fairness, altruism, etc., and a group who behave in an inexplicable (irrational?) manner.

Can a better understanding of how the brain works make this more understandable? Are there informal institutions that are present in the field but not modeled yet experimentally?

7.2.6 Field experiments

Some experiments are possible outside the laboratory. A field experiment was designed to test for racial discrimination in the new car market (Ayres and Siegelman 1995). Standard theory predicts that personal preferences cannot persist in competitive markets. Anyone who discriminates would lose customers and profits to other sellers. Yet, there are many reports of Blacks being charged higher prices. To test this systematically, potential buyers of different races were carefully trained to approach sellers in the same way. More than three hundred paired audits at new-car dealerships revealed that dealers quoted significantly lower prices to white males than to black or female test buyers using identical, scripted bargaining strategies. This experiment demonstrates the effect of informal cultural institutions.

With respect to social capital, the *Reader's Digest* placed wallets on the street in cities around the world to determine the rate at which they would be returned with money intact (equivalent to $50). The overall rate of return was 56 percent, with 100 percent in Norway and 21 in Mexico (Felton 2001). Those returning the wallets cited reasons of general devotion to honesty, religious principle, and empathy.

7.2.7 Framing

Psychology experiments reported above in section 3.3.15 demonstrated that the framing of choices affects decisions. Framing is a kind of institution whose effects were illustrated by a thought experiment asking citizens in a suburban Michigan community about their attitudes toward alternative wetland preservation policies (Pierre 1999). When one sub-sample was asked, (1) "*If someone destroys a community resource, he/she should compensate the community for the community's loss,*" 75 percent agreed. When another sub-sample was asked, (2) "*If the state wants private on-site owners to preserve wetlands, the state should compensate the property owner,*" only 26 percent disagreed. Both samples had the same high majority of people who thought wetlands provided important off-site benefits. These inconsistent responses are consistent with framing effects. The first phrase puts the person into a perspective of a community owner whose rights are affected by developers. The second phrase implies that the landowner is being deprived of something and the benefit to the community is not mentioned.

Sometimes experimental results can be compared to actual voting containing similar alternative frames (Kendall and Dorman 2001). A 1995 initiative in the state of Washington presented voters with this choice: (3) "*The Washington State Legislature has passed a law that restricts land-use regulations and expands governments' liability to pay for reduced property values of land or improvements thereon caused by certain regulations for public benefit: Should this law be approved or rejected?"* The law was rejected three to two.

The same issue of compensating for the affects of regulation arose in a proposal brought to the voters of Oregon in 2000. The ballot title was as follows: (4) *"Amends Constitution: Requires payment to landowner if government regulation reduces property value."* The amendment was approved by 53 percent of the voters.

The wording in Washington (3) was similar to the experimental question (2) in that it put the voter into a frame of mind of being a community owner of something valuable that unregulated development would violate. The wording in Oregon (4) was similar to the experimental question (1) in that it put the voter into a frame of mind of being a private owner whose assumed rights would be reduced without any reference to possible community benefits. It made it easy for the voter to categorize the problem as one of "the individual vs. faceless government."

7.2.8 Conclusion

Experiments provide one important method for warranting the impact of alternative institutions. The advantage of experiments lies in the control of relevant variables and clear specification of the alternatives. The disadvantage lies in threats to external validity, namely whether the experimental conditions mimic the real world. Economists try to design experiments so that the incentives embodied in the institutions are clear. In doing so, the designer may inadvertently send a cue to the subjects that signals the experimenter's intent. "The problem is that clear incentives provide subjects with an understanding of the experimenters' intent, and such intent is most clearly conveyed through clear incentives" (Dawes 1994). The conflicting objectives of clear incentives and not signaling intent are not easily reconciled. Clear payoff matrices eliminate dirty looks of other players from consideration, but it is just those reinforcements from others that constitute society.

A payoff matrix in dollars makes calculation of maximum advantage easy. But in life, people's payoffs are often vague and they have to supply the values from an often conflicting base. The environment throws up vague information and people have to intuit relative magnitudes, a cognitive process. And, we know from psychological experiments that they have great difficulty doing this.

Hard nosed game theorists like Binmore (1994: 24) say, "Love and duty are [not] the cement of modern societies. . . ." He rejects the results of Prisoner's Dilemma experiments illustrating the effects of prior conversation such as done by Dawes (see above). The money offered was not large enough and the game not repeated enough. He prefers calculations based on the superior results of repeated games, such as tit-for-tat. While experimenters can tell subjects whether a game is to be repeated, in real life whether games are *expected* to be repeated is a cognitive matter of interpretation. Binmore says, "Greed and fear will suffice as motivations; greed for the fruits of cooperation, and fear of the consequences of not reciprocating the cooperative overtures of others" (24). "My model of man . . . is unashamedly to be [homo economicus]" (25). To explain voting, he invokes the idea that voting is fun. But if we can learn that voting is fun, we can learn that it is our duty or believe in a myth. We form ideas that enable our self-respect and the respect of others. This feedback is hard to formally model, but plays a role as well as the dollars in the payoff matrix. We intellectuals glory in our calculated rationality. Sen (1977) refers to the rational pursuit of irrational preferences. Why is it more rational to pursue a narrow concept of self than a broader concept of self? If we can learn to like goods, we can learn to like people.

How do we explain the process of institutional change whereby the elite rich give more rights to the poor? Binmore again, "If the affluent are willing to surrender some of their relative advantages in return for a more secure environment in which to enjoy those which remain, or in order to generate a larger social cake for division, then everybody can gain" (1994: 5). It appears that all his vaunted rationality can offer is something to keep the rabble from revolution. In this view, the rabble are constrained only by the costs of revolution. "Change by mutual consent" (7) puts a sanitized face on what is a mixture of force, seeing things as natural, and other acts of evolving cognition. Binmore's story of selfish calculation is just as likely to increase the recalcitrance of the rich and increase their feeling that they deserve all they have and therefore it is better to fight to the death than give in to the undeserving and hated rabble.

Plott (1995: 217) expresses his discomfort with the concept of external validity. "The word 'validity' sets a standard that is impossible to meet in policy contexts." There are always unobserved parameters. Plott argues that, "Simple judgment cannot be avoided. The experiments simply shape the thought processes, the data, and the arguments that form that judgment" (217). Experiments provide one kind of input into that judgment. Case studies and econometrics provide additional input.

The results of actual experimental games and of game theory can be compared. Game theory most commonly includes a specification of the rational, selfish actor who maximizes utility based on expectation of other players' strategies. In the case of ultimatum and dictators games for example, this leads to a prediction that responders will accept even a small distribution, which is contradicted by experiments. North (1994) is critical of game theory because it lacks a description of players' reasoning and learning. Instead of the demanding conceptions of the probability distributions of the actions of others, people may employ myths, taboos, prejudices, habits, and norms that are cued and given meaning by interpretations of the environment.

7.3 Case Studies

Case studies take advantage of naturally occurring experiments where some decision makers are applying some institution to a set of existing situational variables. The analyst describes selected situation variables and the structure of the institutions guided by the theory outlined in chapter 6. The analyst is either implicitly contrasting the performance observed with what was expected to be the case with another institution, or explicitly with some comparison case (over time or cross-section). For example, suppose the object is to learn something of the impact of two alternative voting rules on the formation of winning coalitions. The two voting rules are used in two different states. The analyst uses theory to suggest what other situational or structural variables might affect the performance and makes a judgment that these other variables are sufficiently similar in the two states that the difference in performance can be attributed to the two voting rules. Since no comparison or econometric analysis can include all variables, some necessary selection of what to include is made. Critical for SSP analysis is that the situation (characteristics of the good which create the interdependence) be similar in the comparison.

Let's turn to some case studies that both illustrate the case method and provide some test of the theory of this book.[5] Case studies relating to trade, infrastructure investment, economic development, and social capital will be discussed below.

7.3.1 Mediterranean trade

Long-distance trade in the Mediterranean reemerged during a Commercial Revolution from the eleventh to the fourteenth centuries, after a long period of decline. Long-distance trade presents a problem in commitment. Local rulers have a monopoly of physical force and are in the position to confiscate the goods of foreign traders. The threat of withdrawal by any one merchant provides no incentive for the ruler to respect the trader's property. Without going into the argument, Greif, Milgrom, and Weingast (1994) present evidence that bilateral and multilateral reputation processes were insufficient to solve the problem. They argue that the problem was solved by the development of merchant guilds in large Italian city-states; large enough to exact penalty on any errant foreign lord. These guilds allowed the merchants to act collectively and non-marginally. A further question can be asked about how the guilds in turn solved the free-rider problem among their members, but suffice it here to note that Greif attributes it to a host of social and political factors and not just caused by the appearance of new gains from trade.

A further commitment problem existed between merchants and their overseas agents. Distance and information costs meant opportunism by agents was possible. It was impossible to write complete contracts and impossible to enforce in any kind of court. Two alternative institutions emerged and their performance can be contrasted. The Jewish Maghribs of North Africa depended on familial ties (Greif 1992). A Maghribi would employ only another Maghribi who would be disciplined by other Maghribi if he were opportunistic. "Multilateral punishment enabled the employment of agents even when the relations between a specific merchant and agent were not expected to repeat" (130). On the other hand, it was presumed that a Maghribi would cheat a non-Maghribi. So if he offended any member of the tribe, he could not get work within the tribe or outside. This limited the extent of the market to members of the tribe who happened to immigrate to various trading centers.

The Italian Genose on the other hand could find trading partners anyplace. The Genose traders acted as patrons and paid unrelated agents a premium "efficiency wage" to ensure their commitment (higher than the wage in comparable work). The "efficiency wage" was made possible by a trading monopoly operating out of Genoa. "This monopoly was utilized to provide agents with the stream of rents required to keep them honest by conditioning agents' future trade investment on past conduct." Greif describes institutional change thusly, "The *patron system*, based on a bilateral reputation mechanism, evolved to govern agency relations" (130). Further, his impact analysis was based on the fact that Italian traders eventually dominated Mediterranean and Far East trade suggesting that their institutions were superior to those of the Maghribis. Greif's conclusions rest on his ability to persuade that the situation (high information cost) faced by the two trading groups was essentially similar and the only difference between them was in structure, the use of familial ties vs. the efficiency wage.

Greif has his own theoretical framework called "Historical and Comparative Institutional Analysis" (Greif 1998). There are useful contrasts and similarities with SSP. Greif sees institutions primarily as constraints – providing incentives for behavior by altering payoffs. SSP adds institutions as enablement and the possibility of learning non-calculative habits. Greif's theory primarily addresses institutional change and incidentally impact analysis. He identifies the informal structural forces (variables) such as strategic interactions, evolutionary processes and limits on cognition. These variables then determine the resulting prevailing institutions (rules of the game, values, norms) as performance. Similar to SSP, he does not presume that the prevalence or appropriateness of an institution is determined by efficiency or equity. Also similar is the attention to learning. "The extent of knowledge, rationality and cognition is to be evaluated rather than assumed" (81). While the focus is on "emergence" of institutions (change analysis), he also addresses the performance of alternatives (impact analysis) as noted in the comparison of Maghribi and Genoese success above.

Greif emphasizes outcomes (what institutions emerge and prevail) that are endogenous and self-enforcing (no external enforcement). This would appear to limit his analysis to informal institutions. However, as in the case above, the Genoese could pay the efficiency wage because the formal government of Genoa enforced a monopoly sufficient to generate funds to pay the wage. So the two are never in practice separate in spite of the language of spontaneous order.

Several insights from his empirical work deserve mention. "Complementarities among past economic institutions impact institutional evolution." "Society's institutions are a complex in which informal, implicit institutional features interrelate with formal, explicit features in creating a coherent whole." "This institutional complex is not a static optimal response to economic needs" (82).

7.3.2 Infrastructure investments

Infrastructure projects such as roads and irrigation systems in developing countries are notorious for their poor maintenance. What about these goods creates interdependence? They are high exclusion cost goods. Users are tempted to be opportunistic and not contribute to maintenance. Ostrom and colleagues documented the performance of an irrigation system rehabilitation and extension project in the Philippines. Since the people are poor, donors must contribute most of the cost, but the proportion may vary. Ostrom observed some unique features of the administration of this project that set it apart from the usual (the comparison group). This project required the beneficiaries to initially contribute 10 percent of the project cost in the form of labor, material, cash, and rights of way. "The policy was based on the presumption that irrigators who pay for system reconstructions will be more likely to operate and maintain them" (Ostrom, Schroeder, and Wynne 1993: 56). In fact, the ditches were maintained better than in many other projects and the farmers began to refer to them as "their ditches." The initial contribution may have served as a fixed cost and the farmers may not have wanted to waste their initial sunk cost. It is not clear, however, from the documentation exactly how the free-rider problem was overcome – why the farmers contributed to the initial cost. When making cross-sectional comparisons of the impact of alternative institutions, it is important to make sure the situation (for example, exclusion cost and group size) and the institutional structure are comparable in each observation (Poteete and Ostrom 2003).

Irrigation projects often suffer from poor physical design. The engineers can't easily know as much about unique features of the fields as do the farmers themselves. It might be hypothesized that farmers eager for the benefits would share their information. But this is not true in practice as farmers report that it is the government's project and it is their problem. In this project the engineers were given an incentive to seek out and respect local farmer knowledge. The engineers were rewarded and promoted on the basis of farmer acceptance of the project rather than only on the basis of their technical skills and qualifications. The farmers felt respected and involved and shared their information. The physical performance of the project was exceptionally good and was attributed to participatory institutions of the project. (See table 7.2.)

One case study by itself can warrant little of the connection between alternative institutions and performance. A meta-analysis of many cases can look for patterns that seem to be confirmed by the weight of the evidence. The work of Ostrom is exemplary in that regard. She had collected from all over the world cases of how people have behaved with respect to common pool resources (Ostrom 1990). See also Agrawal (2001). Ostrom has her own theoretical framework, again with some similarities and differences with SSP (Ostrom 1986). She speaks of the configuration of rules (structure), the state of the world (situation), and community variables such as norms and culture. The state of the world includes many of the variables described in chapter 6, "Sources of Human Interdependence," such as information availability, information processing capacity, non-rivalry, and feasibility of exclusion. Under rules (institutional structure) she distinguishes those that require, prohibit, and permit. Configuration includes boundary, scope, position, authority, information, aggregation, and payoff rules. The "action arena" links the transacting parties with the rules and the state of the world to produce "results" (performance). When cases of common pool resources are collected, these variables are used to organize the evidence. In addition to cases and meta-analysis of cases, Ostrom also utilizes game theory which could be used to design experiments (Ostrom, Gardner, and Walker 1994). Also see Kiser and Ostrom (1982).

Table 7.2 Philippines irrigation case

Situation	Structure	Performance
Good = information on the terrain. – design problem HIC of local conditions – cheap to farmer, costly to engineer; "information asymmetry"	1. Farmer treated as part-owners and buyers – not gift recipients, i.e. people who can exit or command. Agency is accountable to an owner-buyer (not to gift recipient). 2. Central agency makes all decisions. It is the government's project and people's demand doesn't count.	1. Farmers volunteered information; saved money on ditch design 2. Farmers withhold information. Ingrates!
Good = construction material storage. Low EC for locals, but HIC for government.	1. Farmer is part-owner? Pay 10% of cost. a. But if fully decentralized … 2. Gov't owned. No learned self-restraint.	1. Farmers build fence and monitor supplies so not stolen. a. Local officials may steal the materials. 2. Supplies stolen.
Good = construction charges. HIC	1. Central – poor auditing incentives. No sealed bids?	1. Contractor is opportunistic and over-charges.
Good = infrastructure (irrigation system) HEC on total system. Non-contributing labor can free ride.	1. Part owner – pay 10% of total cost. Create a sunk cost. High initiation fee à la Hirschman. 2. Grant; learned psychological effect of grant.	1. Maintained "their" ditches. 2. No maintenance.
Good = work of engineers. Low information cost to supervisors.	1. Promote (pay) on basis of technical skill. 2. Promote on basis of farmer acceptance of system.	1. Farmer knowledge wasted. 2. Engineers ask farmers for local knowledge.

Based on Ostrom, Schroeder, and Wynne (1993: 56)

7.3.3 Economic development: England and Spain

The case method is illustrated in the work of North (1990) when he compares the institutions of England and Spain in the sixteenth and seventeenth centuries. While Spain had an early lead in wealth, England spurted ahead. The problem of interdependence that North focuses on was the fiscal crisis of the king as the cost of warfare increased. Physical assets are ultimately high exclusion cost goods in the face of the military power of the king who can confiscate property as needed. But such confiscation suppresses investment and growth. What were the contrasting institutional structures in the two countries that interacted with the situation? (1) England had relatively secure property rights that the king granted in exchange for relatively predictable grants from his lords while Spanish kings confiscated property at will. (2) England had the Magna Carta that limited the power of the king and eventually led to a parliament sharing in policy making while the Spanish Cortes was seldom used at the same time that a large centralized bureaucracy flourished. (3) England instituted a decline in mercantilist restrictions and its textile firms avoided guild restrictions while the Spanish instituted rent ceilings on land and wheat. Exchange was much more personal in Spain than England. These variables are summarized in table 7.3.

Table 7.3 Comparative case analysis: England and Spain in the sixteenth and seventeenth centuries

Situation	Structure	Performance
Fiscal crisis to finance war. Physical assets are ultimately HEC against the King. Investment requires secure expectations.	1. Britain a. Secure property rights (paid for in grants to King). b. Parliament shares in policy making. c. Decline of mercantilist restrictions. Escape of textiles from guild restriction. d. Depersonalized exchange.	1. Economic growth. Dominated western world. Capital market evolved.
	2. Spain a. Insecure property rights (confiscation) provided revenue for the King. b. Cortes seldom used; large centralized bureaucracy. c. Rent ceiling on land and wheat. d. Personalized exchange.	2. Three centuries of relative stagnation. State bankruptcies. Underdeveloped capital market.

Based on North (1990)

The performance contrast of these institutions was dramatic. England had rapid growth and dominated the western world while Spain suffered three centuries of relative stagnation and frequent state bankruptcies. Capital markets evolved in England but lagged in Spain. North extends the analysis to suggest that the English path extended to the United States with superior results to the Spanish path which was extended to Latin America.

7.3.4 Social capital

There are substantial economies of scale in many industries and achieving those economies is a factor in comparative economic development. Francis Fukuyama argues that some countries have institutions that facilitate the creation of large firms and others do not (Fukuyama 1995). Fukuyama uses a comparative case analysis to contrast the performance of different institutions. Large firms make it difficult for a central manager to monitor the performance of employees. It also makes it difficult for owners to monitor agents. High information cost (HIC) creates room for opportunism. Fukuyama argues that large firms are made possible by trust. He tests this hypothesis by comparing the institutions and performance of the United States and Japan on the one hand and China on the other.

The US, Germany, and Japan are similar in that they have dense networks of voluntary organizations that are not rooted in families (Fukuyama 1995: 53). In this context, unrelated people learn to trust each other. Further, people in these cultures learn a set of moral obligations that apply to all beings, not just family. These attitudes make possible the use of professional managers in large firms. In contrast, China had few networks of voluntary organizations. "The lack of trust outside the family makes it hard for unrelated people to form groups or organizations, including economic enterprises" (75). The family was central to Confucian thinking. This meant that Chinese firms were primarily family owned and managed by a strong central figure. Management was very personalistic. There was a tradition of equal male inheritance that split up any large firm.

The performance impact of these alternative institutions has been quite different. Industry is very small scale in Taiwan compared to Korea or Japan. The networks of firms are different. The six largest Japanese *keiretsu* average 31 firms per group, the Korean *chaebol* have 11, and the Taiwanese network organization only seven and the firms are smaller and largely based on family (73). The Japanese have a tradition of *banto*, the professional manager brought in from outside to manage the family business while there is no equivalent in traditional Chinese life (75). The Chinese are very good at assembling capital from family members which gives them an advantage in starting a new business and often leads to their dominance in small business in many countries. But the family obligation cannot raise the sums necessary for large firms, which must rely on capital markets. The institutional and performance differences are summarized in table 7.4.

The Orma people of northeastern Kenya recently became more sedentary, but remain pastoralists. Since the herds must be kept at some distance from the village, the herd owners are subject to opportunistic behavior by hired herders if there is

Table 7.4 Economies of scale and trust

Situation	Structure	Performance
Economies of scale potential. High information cost (HIC) Large firms subject to employee opportunism. Transaction cost to assemble capital.	1. US, Japan and Germany High level of trust for non-kin. Professional management; moral obligation to all persons. 2. Chinese – Low level of trust outside family. Family management. Moral obligation only to family. Equal male inheritance.	1. Large firms, large networks. Achieve economy of scale. Innovative. 2. Small firms, small networks. Advantage in assembling capital for start-up firms. Less delegation within firms leads to less innovation

Based on Fukuyama (1995)

a labor shortage within the family. Ensminger (2001) observes the herd owners calculating the construction of incentives to avoid opportunism. Some of these take the form of "efficiency wages." Ensminger interprets these transactions as each party building a reputation that is more profitable to maintain than interrupt. "This is not so much about the creation of trust as it is about calculated self-interest" (199). Still, she reports that after many years of transactions, the herd owner may formally adopt the hired herder as his own son. One owner reported, "I don't even remember how much I have paid him" (199). Is this not evidence of a change in self-identity? One would expect that initially the relationship is calculated *quid pro quo*, but after years of investment in building social capital, the parties develop sympathy for each other. Could we inquire whether the parties would report a loss of socio-emotional goods if the relationship was interrupted all else equal? (Recall section 6.10 above.)

7.3.5 Other

The case literature is immense. Some notable examples are: Alston et al. (1996); Braudel (1981); Chandler and Hikino (1990); Collins (2001); Diamond (1997); Harris (1974); Horwitz (1977); Olson (1996); and Schmid (1987: ch. 12).

7.4 Econometrics

The difference between case studies and econometrics is often small (McCloskey 1985). Econometric results are often not robust with respect to model specification, lags, functional form, choice of proxies, etc. (Leamer 1982; Mayer 1992). We may not know what variables to include in a model and some may not be measurable (Sutton 2000). These are also problems in case studies. Both require a judgment on the weight of the evidence and level of significance necessary to accept a hypothesis. How shall institutional variables be included in regression equations? A physical production function has no place for institutions. For example, corn output is a function of land, labor, seed, etc. The institutional question is how do the relationships among people affect the quality and presence of land, labor and capital (recall chapter 5 where it was argued that institutions are not factors of production). Econometric models relating to social capital, slavery, and air pollution will be discussed below and another relating to worker cooperatives is included in chapter 11 on labor.

7.4.1 Social capital

In the previous section on case studies, an application to social capital was described (Fukuyama 1995). Social capital resulting in trust had an effect on achieving economies of scale and economic development. A similar question was investigated econometrically by Knack and Keefer (1997) (K&K) with cross-sectional data from 29 countries. The measure for trust came from the World Values Study that asked, "Generally speaking, would you say that most people can be trusted, (or that you can't be too careful in dealing with people)?" Nations differed in the response of their citizens to this question with a mean value of about 36 percent agreement.

The dependent variable was per capita income over 1980–92. Other independent variables were proportion of eligible students enrolled in secondary and primary schools in 1960; per capita income at beginning of period; price level of investment goods relative to the US. "The social capital variables exhibit a strong and significant relativity to growth" (K&K 1997: 1260). This is consistent with the results of Fukuyama's comparative case study though Fukuyama's time span is much larger.

Knack and Keefer also investigated factors associated with trust. Fukuyama (1995) and Putnam (1993) in their case studies had found that group membership was related to trust, but when K&K controlled for gross domestic product, schooling, and a measure of inequality, group membership was not significant. Why the difference? Are the case and econometric studies using the same concept of trust? For Fukuyama, "Trust is the expectation that arises within a community of regular, honest, and cooperative behavior, based on commonly shared norms, on the part of other members of that community. Those norms can be about deep 'value' questions like the nature of God or justice, but they also encompass secular norms like professional standards and codes of behavior" (1997: 26). Knack and Keefer in their search for data used the response to the World Values Study about agreement with the statement, "would you say that most people can be trusted?" Fukuyama uses historical accounts and studies that indicate a lack of trust outside the family in Hong Kong (1997: 75) and a "lack of spontaneous sociability" in Latin Catholic countries. Unfortunately, K&K did not have data for Taiwan. As Fukuyama argued, Japan and the US were similar on K&K's trust scale, but Germany ranked much lower. But, Fukuyama would perhaps be surprised to find K&K's placement of the Latin countries of Mexico and Argentina on a similar level with the US and Japan. If we put Fukuyama's cases in rank order of trust, Japan, Germany, and the US would be at one end, with France in an intermediate position followed by Italy, Taiwan, and the Latin Catholic countries. K&K's (1997: 1285) order of many of the same countries shows Norway and Canada at the top, with the US and Japan in the middle, and Mexico, Turkey, and Brazil at the bottom. The low placement of Germany and France, plus the placement of Argentina with Germany, Italy, and France makes one think that these two indices are measuring somewhat different things.

Are the case and econometric studies defining group membership the same? For K&K the membership in groups ranging from churches, cultural groups, unions, to political parties is counted. Fukuyama also speaks of cultural groups, religious to political, and professional organizations for example (1995: 54), but unions are not listed in his index. Fukuyama does not detail memberships, but moves to the presence of non-family business and size of business networks that he presumes are facilitated by other "spontaneous sociability." K&K do not have variables for these latter organizations. K&K emphasize that not all organizations are the same and disaggregate them into Putnam type (social) and Olson type (political).

Fukuyama tells a story of a chain of causality that runs from degree of spontaneous sociability (outside the family), to trust, large non-family firms, and growth. K&K jump from memberships to growth. The two studies together raise the question whether trust and large firms necessarily result from sociability. And while sociability may be associated with growth, the connection may be varying content.

The purpose here is not to reconcile the differences in these two studies but to indicate some of the problems and tradeoffs in the two methods. Much judgment and interpretation is involved in both. Both methods require theory to indicate what variables to include and whether the specific measure and examples used track the concepts of the theory. And both methods considered together may be more revealing than any one.

7.4.2 Slavery

There can hardly be a more contrasting institution than that of free vs. slave labor. Many observers hypothesized that free labor, being self-motivated, was more productive. Fogel and Engerman (1977) set out to test that hypothesis. Rough comparisons of output per person showed that output was higher on large southern plantations with slaves than on northern farms. But would this picture hold up when other variables thought to affect productivity were held constant? Some of the other variables had to do with the quality and quantity of other inputs (capital and land), economies of scale, organization of production, prices, product mix, and omitted outputs. Fogel and Engerman estimate production functions for southern plantations with slaves and without, southern slave owning plantations, and northern non-slave farms. These are compared and used to compute the geometric index of relative total factor productivity. One of the key issues is possible difference in labor intensity. The difference in the econometric estimates is interpreted as the different impact of the slavery institution.[6] The authors conclude, "Greater intensity of labor per hour, not more hours of labor nor more days of labor per year, is the reason why the index of total factor productivity is 48 percent higher for slave than for free farms" (Fogel and Engerman 1977: 293). Other evidence suggests that the gain in efficiency came from a speed-up of labor functions obtained by the carefully monitored gang system of specialization in hoeing, planting, etc. applied to cotton and sugar. (This supports Marglin's (1974) case analysis that the function of bosses is to get people to work harder than they would with free choice.)

Efficiency is relative to the inputs and outputs considered. Fogel doesn't include the costs of preventing escape and the legal systems that enforced it. Any econometric model is subject to data availability and that is especially severe in the case of historical analysis. While the slavery studies have their critics, more data is available for a specific industry than for a whole economy's development such as the story that North tells of England and Spain in the above case study section. For Fogel's own analysis of the limitations of econometrics in history see Fogel (1975). For Fogel's comments on the methods of North, see Fogel (1997) and on the methods of Kuznets, see Fogel (1989). Mirowski (2001) offers a rare comparison of econometric and case study results in an industrial history.

7.4.3 Air pollution

Florida phosphate mining and processing creates a dust that settles on citrus trees and pastures decreasing yields. A study estimated land value as a function of citrus prices, land quality, and phosphate dust on the trees (Crocker 1971). It is institutions that affect the miner's choice of releasing the dust and the ability of different groups to have their interests served. If the air is owned by growers, the pollution variable should be significant, but the hypothesis was not confirmed.

For a summary of how institutions were conceptualized in the several econometric studies above, see table 7.5.

Table 7.5 Selected econometric studies

Air pollution (phosphate mining) Interrupted time series design
$$O_1 \ O_2 \ O_3 \ X \ O_4 \ O_5 \ O_6$$
Each observation (O) over time is an econometric estimate of sign and significance of the pollution variable explaining land value. The X refers to the institutional change.

Social capital (trust) and development
Per capita growth rate = f (degree of trust, education, inequality, size, group membership, civic community).

Slavery
Equation for slave owning farms: factor productivity = f (scale, product mix).
Equation for owner operated farms: factor productivity = f (scale, product mix).

Plywood co-operatives (see section 11.2 for details)
Equation for co-ops: hourly earnings = f (output prices, input prices, etc.).
Equation for stock firms: hourly earnings = f (output prices, input prices, etc.).

7.5 Simulation and Computation

Simulation is increasingly used to build up from a micro foundation of individual and organizational behavior to macro performance. A landmark work is that of Nelson and Winter (1982). Firms act on the basis of habits and routines rather than assuming they can process the information necessary to maximize profit. Nelson and Winter's model is able to simulate the fundamental facts of western growth, namely "the rising output per worker, growing capital intensity, rising real wages, and a relatively constant rate of return on capital" (Nelson 1995: 70–1). The evolutionary approach reveals "considerable variation among firms in the technologies they are using, their productivity, and their profitability" (71) that is not consistent with neoclassical theory.

The Santa Fe Institute has proposed a common language for simulations that is available on their web site (Stefansson 2002). Other materials are available at Tesfatsion (2001). The inductive approach of agent-based modeling is particularly useful to understand the emergent features of complex systems to be discussed in chapter 13. Some applications to economic situations are surveyed in Luna and Perrone (2002) and Luna and Stefansson (2000). For example, the classic Prisoner's Dilemma game can be simulated. Each agent may begin with a random choice to cooperate or defect. A decision rule is specified so that each player compares its payoff from its initial action with the payoff from its opposite. If it can do better, it tries the opposite or, if not, repeats its former action. The simulation stops when neither player can do better. The simulation shows that equilibrium is reached in no more than two moves. Simulation models contain environments, rules, and agents. In the PD example, the environment is the payoff matrix, the rule is to compare payoffs and execute accordingly, and the agents are the players who receive the payoffs and employ the rules.

Simulation incorporates agent heterogeneity (different motives) rather than assuming the representative agent. An evolving utility function can be specified and learning can be incorporated. For example, there is a large literature on tax evasion based on mathematical models incorporating expected utility, experiments, and more recently, simulation. Mittone and Patelli (2000) specify three varieties of taxpayers who attempt to maximize their utility: honest, imitative, and perfect free rider. The simulation demonstrates that in the absence of governmental auditing, the honest and imitative behaviors are extinguished. In principle, some of the behavioral regularities discussed in chapter 3 could be incorporated in simulation models, but much of their determinism would be lost. Whether these regularities, history, and genuine human creativity can be tractable remains to be seen (Mirowski 1996; Mirowski 2002). There is a parallel between tightly regimented experiments with human subjects and computational economics. Humans are reduced to automata.

In conclusion, each method explored above can be appropriate given the questions and the data. Each complements the others, and if a common picture is confirmed by more than one method, more insight is gained. Can general theory be built and tested in the social sciences, particularly when people learn? As a starting place, I adopt the stance of Przeworski and Teune (1970: 13). "Our position is that the characteristics of particular systems can be expressed as general variables, such as the presence or absence of student participation in university decision making, and as such would be applicable across all systems. In fact, whenever there is a system specific factor that seems to be necessary for explanation, the conclusion should not be that systems are unique but rather that it is necessary to identify some general factors so far not considered." The inherent situational characteristics such as economies of scale or exclusion cost can be expected to be found in a large number of instances in history and place. While some general hypotheses can be formed about the performance of institutional alternatives, the difficulty of specifying the actual cognition in time and place keeps us modest.

NOTES

1. Authors differ in the breadth of what is meant by a rule. "By 'rules' we mean the routines, procedures, conventions, roles, strategies, organizational forms, and technologies around which political activity is constructed. We also mean the beliefs, paradigms, codes, cultures, and knowledge that surround, support, elaborate, and contradict those roles and routines" (March and Olsen 1989: 22). Whether these are included as instrumental institutions or variables to be held constant, these all seem relevant, but lead to empirical indigestion. Selection and simplification are inevitable. Given this complex reality, one can understand the urge to develop an economics without institutions.
2. For example, one might think that an extension of the voting franchise would make a big difference in who counts. But, if economic power can be used to finance elections, the old elite may continue their influence.
3. North (1990: 3) and Soltan (1998: 46–9) prefer to define institutions as rules. Krasner (1983) defines institutions as principles, norms, rules, and decision-making procedures around which actor expectations converge in a given area. Soltan (47) further requires that "the institution influence action, not just the actors expectations converge on it."
4. This section was written in interaction with Lindon Robison.
5. For a review of the methodology of case studies in institutional economics see Wilbur and Harrison (1978).
6. Using econometric estimates to compare two institutions is essentially the method used by such studies as Crocker (1971) and Ahlbrandt (1973), which are analyzed in Schmid (1987: ch. 12).

Chapter 8
Markets

It is simply not true that scarce resources are allocated among alternative uses by the market. The real determinant of whatever allocation occurs in any society is the organizational structure of that society – in short, its institutions.

Clarence Ayres (1957: 26)

8.1 Introduction

Now that we have an institutional theory to guide inquiry and have examined various methods of empirical research, we can begin a series of chapters that describe representative applications of theory using different methods. They are grouped by subject matter. The first chapter in this section is a look at the institutions creating markets (bargained transactions). This is followed by chapters on financial and macroeconomic institutions, technology, labor, political systems, and finally studies of institutional change.

No one can escape the constant drum beaten for markets, privatization, and security of ownership, and contract enforcement. However, these terms need to be unpacked. There are alternative market rules that serve different interests and define the content of economic development in different ways.

Each person is interdependent with others if we are to move beyond self-subsistence and take advantage of specialization and economies of scale. If coordination fails, we are back to self-subsistence. Economic activity can be coordinated by talk among legal equals; that is, bargained transactions among resource owners who are buyers and sellers of a particular opportunity. Agreements are reached as to who will do what, when. Markets can be described in evolutionary terms. Human ingenuity throws up variety in terms of products and production methods and these are selected by buyers. But selection is not done by some vague abstraction called competition or consumer sovereignty, but by institutions that constitute the rules of competition and rules that structure the environment and what fits (survives). Change the institutions and you change what survives.

Property rights (who has what to trade) are antecedent to the market. The market is not a single thing. There are as many different kinds of markets as there are different market rules and starting place distributions of opportunities. Who owns the firms in the market? How are they organized? What products are allocated in markets vs. administrative transactions? What are the detailed trading rules? How do firms price their products? The United States, Japan, and Germany are all market economies, but have quite different market institutions (Whitley 1999). The former communist centrally administered economies have much more to decide than their initial commitment to the market. What kind of market will they evolve? Some of the results of empirical comparative performance of alternative market institutions should inform this and other debates.

This chapter begins with the question of who owns and controls whatever organizations exist. Next is the question of the internal structure of the organization. Then what are the consequences of using bargained or administrative transactions? Within this question are the issues of firm integration, what is subject to a use or tradable right, and what exactly does a firm have to sell. If bargained transactions are used, what are the specific rules of the market? If bargained, how are prices determined? Are profits institutional artifacts? Finally, all of these questions come together in the decisions accompanying the transformation of the former Communist countries to markets.

8.2 Who Owns?

Who owns and controls whatever organizations exist? Large-scale firms are typically stock firms owned by fragmented investors with hired managers. But there are also cooperatives, a few worker owned firms (see chapter 11), and many not-for-profit firms. Not-for profit hospitals, for example, exist alongside for-profit hospitals. Germany requires workers' representation on corporate boards of directors. There is a world-wide movement to privatize many previously provided public services such as prisons, water supply, transport, communication systems, and schools (Sclar 2000). To illustrate how SSP theory applies, the case of privatization of formerly government produced goods is examined.

8.2.1 Privatization

Take the case of trash pickup. It could be individually purchased by consumers from private firms. But, economies of scale would be lost if several private firms served the same route. There is the usual variety vs. unit cost tradeoff. Further, some individuals may decide that the service is not worth the cost and leave the garbage in the back yard. This could be controlled by nuisance law or regulation but these have transaction costs. Several trucks down the same road increase maintenance costs. Unsightly garbage cans are on the street for a longer time if different firms pick up on different days. Details matter and just declaring for privatization and markets is not enough to speak to all of the interdependencies. In the light of this, many local governments whose citizens want a tidy town provide the service paid by a general or specific tax. While paid for by taxes, the single service does not have to be done with public employees. The local government could hold an auction for the franchise, but once the private service is in place there may be lock in and specific asset problems upon future renegotiation of the contract. "As with most complex economic problems or organization, it turns out there is no single, all-purpose, best solution" (Williamson 1985: 327).

Private firms in principle have a greater incentive to economize as any savings accrue to the owner (if the agency problem can be solved). But, there are two ways to economize: find cheaper production methods or reduce the quality of the product. Where the product is a high information cost good the owner has an incentive to reduce quality. This is subject to the cost of monitoring by the local government or the individual consumer. This may be relatively cheap in the case of garbage, but costly in the case of nursing homes, nuclear power stations, or prisons. Student achievement tests can be designed, but not all agree on the content of the tests, nor the incentive of the teachers to teach to the test.

The incentive to economize also applies to labor. The union movement has had a long time to organize public employees. Many small private contractors are not unionized and their cost savings come at the expense of workers.

The hottest issue in privatization in the US is the use of public money to finance vouchers that can be used in private schools. This is promoted by many as an expansion of freedom. But, whose freedom? The students of parents with less initiative and money remain in their local public school that loses economies of scale. While local schools are often segregated they are often the only place where people of various backgrounds (including religion) have a chance to come together. Vouchers mean that a school can be organized for any specialized tastes and parents find it easier to keep their children from being exposed to ideas and people they do not approve of. One person's freedom of choice narrows the choice of others who want a more polyglot experience. Information cost is also relevant. Some may be able to determine the quality of various schools, while other would like to leave the monitoring to an elected school board.

Public money for church schools is the rule in France. Do we know the comparative performance of this institutional alternative? The US Supreme Court ruled the use of publicly funded vouchers in religious schools was constitutional in *Zelman v. Simmons-Harris*, 122 S.Ct. 2460 (2002).

People are searching for easy remedies to poorly performing systems whether education in the US or development in Africa. Rather than facing the hard choices, markets and privatization are advocated. From the perspective of this book we know that the market is not a single thing and detail matters. See "trading rules" below in section 8.5. We also know that the public firm (or private for that matter) is not a single thing and organizational detail matters. See "internal organization" below in section 8.3. Internal incentives matter. There are well-run public firms and agencies and poor ones. Same for private firms.

8.2.2 Shareholders and managers

Economies of scale and technology seem to require more capital than a few investors can assemble. Is this the functional reason for fragmented small stockholdings who can't directly influence professional managers? "Savings could also have moved through large-scale financial intermediaries – the banks, insurers, mutual funds, and pension funds that gather people's savings and invest them" (Roe 1994: xiv). Roe argues that US formal law inhibited financial intermediaries from acting collectively as is more common in Germany and Japan. This will be discussed further in the context of macroeconomic fragility in chapter 9 as some of these laws are changing. See also Aoki (2000: ch. 5). Germany, Japan, and the US with their distinctive forms of capitalism go through cycles of relative success. It is very hard to relate ownership structure to long-term performance since controlled experiments are not possible.

Managers, owners, bankers, financial firms, and other publics via government struggle to control the corporation at the same time that they hope to stabilize the relationships among themselves to manage uncertainty. If any party wants to control a firm, it is not enough to excel at production, sales and marketing. Corporate history is full of cycles of acquisitions and mergers with new organizational inventions coming along such as leveraged buyouts, stock repurchasing, and strategic use of debt, not to mention some of the newer creations of closely held joint ventures and clever bookkeeping. Fligstein (2001) documents recent US history where control goes to those who can maximize shareholder value. It remains to be seen whether this has been carried to extremes and instability leading to still newer themes of control. Fligstein concludes, "Efficiency is socially constructed rather than constructed by markets. And there may be many ways to organize 'efficiently'" (190). And, these serve different interests.

8.3 Internal Organization of Firms

What are the alternative internal structures of an organization (firm)? Though much of the research is abstract and deductive, some is empirical. We shall only consider a few dimensions to illustrate how theory might guide research: internal organization of the firm; multinationals; joint ventures and alliances; and hierarchy vs. markets.

Much has been written about the M-form (multidivision, such as branded products within GM or geography of sales) of corporate organization vs. the U-form (functional such as engineering or marketing). The problem is not unlike that in writing this book. Are the chapter titles and subheadings to be theoretical concepts, methods, or commodities and applications? The same problem occurs in a legislature. Are the committees to be by agency, by problem areas such as poverty, or by budgetary or regulatory function? What are the consequences of combining the water resource functions of the US Department of Agriculture, Corps of Engineers, and Interior rather than the more commodity and client interests that now distinguish these agencies? (Schmid 1971.)

The problem is that everything needs to be coordinated with everything else, but that is impossible. There are inevitable tradeoffs. For example, defining divisions technologically makes it cheaper to coordinate research and development and manufacturing, but it is not particularly related to customer needs. Defining divisions by products does not answer the question of what constitutes a product. Is it cars separate from buses or Chevrolet separate from Buick? And what if both have the same sized and powered base, but are designed to convey a different image to different market segments. Better fit with one dimension tends to make a worse fit for another dimension. While certain forms seem to persist in certain industries, there are cycles of managerial reform with new managers creating new organizational forms to distinguish themselves and show they are doing something even if its consequences are hard to predict (or one problem reduced and another enlarged).

Corporate law is perhaps the set of rules that has most to do with internal organization. The concepts of limited liability and life beyond particular individuals were one of the great institutional inventions of all time and its evolution is discussed in chapter 13 on institutional change.

8.4 Bargained vs. Administrative Transactions

Several interrelated questions can be usefully seen as a choice between bargained and administrative transactions, sometimes described as markets vs. hierarchies (private or public). The parties can be categorized in various ways and alternative institutions relate them to each other. Conflicting claimants on various inputs can be given a use or exchange right and that right can be reallocated over time. Ownership is often made effective by regulation, which appears to be an alternative to the market, but is actually prior to the market, if it is allowed. What does a firm have to sell, or have they only a use right? Once ownership is determined and markets allowed, what is the consequence of relating the following parties via markets or private administration (ownership): producers of different products (multi-product or economies of scope question); producers of the same product to producers of the same product in the same country (economies of scale question); producers of the same product with producers of the same product in different regions or countries (multinational question related to economies of scale); and producers of an input with the producers of an output.

8.4.1 Conflicting claimants

The market vs. hierarchy alternative is usually framed as whether two owners are related to each other by markets or are jointly owned and the parts related by administration. But ownership itself is a right to administer some opportunity. Where did this right come from? As has already been discussed, the market cannot settle this question. The right obtains by collective administration or custom. When someone wants to be free of regulation, they are really claiming that they are the owner and then entitled to exchange it at will, but the questions can be separated.

What goods can be traded and what does a firm have to sell are closely related. An almost universal complaint about government is that there is too much administration; too much red tape – too many forms, too many rules, too many. . . . Poor countries seem to be the worst in this regard. One example was documented in a case study by de Soto (1989) who pretended to be a new entrepreneur creating a clothing manufacture in Peru. (See table 8.1.) He kept track of the hours it took to

Table 8.1 Market rules. Contrasting conceptions of the functions of institutions: constraints vs. enablement and giving direction to interdependencies

Situation	Structure	Performance
Good = clothing machines and human bodies. Workplace safety is *IUG*. Sewing factory "experiment." Gains from trade.	*Institutions as constraints* 1. "Red tape" created by requiring government permits. 2. No permits required. No liability for workplace hazards.	1. Empirical "experimental" result: creates opportunity for officials to collect a private tax. Time is wasted in getting permits. Or is it? 2. New business; gains from trade. Workplace hazards.

Good = urban buses and pedestrians using the street. *IUG* at high speed.	*Institutions as enablement and interdependence direction*
	 3. Informal sector, competition among private jitneys –
	  a. No liability for damages.
	  b. No permits required.
	 4. Formal sector. Law is not just red tape but provides opportunity for pedestrians.
	  a. Judicial liability decisions.
	  b. Regulation and permits.
	  c. Delegate to informal organizations (NGOs?).
	
	 Maybe the bus drivers association sets standards for its members.
		3. Jitneys hit pedestrians who can't recover damages.
		
		 4. Reduced accidents, and when they happen the cost is spread.
		  a. de Soto predicts good results.
		  b. see 1 above.
		  c. ?

Economies of scale Complex goods. Inherent transaction cost to pool labor, capital, ideas, and to trade at a distance. Specific assets.	*Institutions as enablement* 5. Informal: family, reputation, personal trust and threat. Underground economy. 6. Formal: Contract enforcement. Limited liability. Integrated firms. Judges are not individual profit maximizers (status).	5. Small scale. Risk is concentrated. Little investment in specific assets. Markets are thin and local. 6. Pooling of capital, diversification, convert debt to shares, spread risk. Markets extended. Trade at a distance with strangers.

Based in part on de Soto (1989)

obtain all the necessary permits, licenses, etc. He argued that the red tape slowed the development of new firms and drove business underground, and also becomes the basis for bribery of officials. The problem with the informal economy is that underground firms cannot use government institutions like enforcement of contract when they need them. Underground firms are necessarily small and rely on family relationships. They can't capture economies of scale, with the exception of the drug trade. They cannot aggregate large sums of capital on an informal basis because of high transaction costs.

There is no doubt that government officials create rules that only serve to provide them employment and bribes. But, in many cases, one person's regulation is another's opportunity. Constraints on one party are enablement for others. Many of the licenses that de Soto complains about are for the protection of workers and consumers. For another example, street space is an incompatible use good between drivers and pedestrians. De Soto observed that private urban buses (jitneys) frequently operate without licenses and insurance. When buses hit pedestrians, the injured cannot recover damages in court. There is a literature that regards laws that let some capture the benefit of the work of others as undesirable "rent seeking." This is distinguished from protecting the productive property of persons. The distinction is not easily made and often involves a value judgment of who is worthy and productive (Samuels and Mercuro 1992). Informal organizations sometimes can be substitutes for formal law.

De Soto hypothesizes that statutory law is more likely to be rent seeking and antithetical to development than court made law. So he would prefer that the courts develop liability law in the case of urban jitneys rather than the legislature making regulations. This begs the question of the self-interest of judges, which is a problem in many countries. The above interaction of situation, structure, and performance is summarized in table 8.1.

Is a court made rule assessing liability for injury to workers by employers or pedestrians by bus drivers an administrative interference with the putative natural and "free" market? Is a law requiring a permit and training by bus drivers an interference with free markets? Court made liability rules and administrative regulations have functional similarities in that they define relative opportunity sets. They both determine who has what to trade. Must the worker pay the employer to provide a safe workplace or a pedestrian pay the bus driver not to run her over? Or must the driver pay the pedestrian damages (or pay to get trained and certified to reduce the probability of accidents)? Rights are antecedent to the market, not an interference with some state of nature.

The same issues arise in product liability when the consumer is dissatisfied with product quality. Prior to the Consumer Products Safety Act of 1972, these conflicts were settled by the courts at common law. Since the law differed among the states, comparative impact analysis was possible. Some had strict liability in tort, and some had only negligence. Manufacturers in those states with strict liability (manufacturer pays regardless of fault) purchased more liability insurance than those in states with negligence rules (manufacturers pay only if they did not follow commonly accepted manufacturing practices) (Croyle 1979). All of this would be unnecessary if information costs were zero and consumers could tell quality easily.

8.4.2 Use or exchange rights

What rights are the owners to only use and what can be traded? For example, the right to put a certain amount of material into the air was a use right in the United States. Then firms were allowed to buy and sell these rights. What are the consequences? If one has only a use right, there is no incentive to economize except to consider internal opportunity costs. But, if a firm has a cheap way to avoid disposal it will do so if offered a greater return from another firm with a more expensive alternative. Making rights tradable can thus lower the total cost of meeting any level of air quality as low cost of control firms sell their rights to high-cost firms. The market, of course, begins with the allocation of air use among industry and environmentalists. This is a question of power. Once the cap on total disposal is set and allocated among firms, trading can begin. Basic rights distribution is prior to the market. Some claim that markets are an alternative to the contentious administrative choices among competing claimants. But, the claims of competing groups must be settled before trading can begin (Samuels and Schmid 1976).

There is also the issue of who owns the future gains from technological change. The environmentalists would like any gain in treatment efficiency to result in further environmental improvement, while industry would like to hold the air quality constant while reducing its costs of achieving it. Industry argues that unless it captures the gains it has no incentive to improve the technology. Still, some of the technological change is the result of publicly financed research.

Another example of where performance including income distribution is affected by tradability is the case of land development rights. Local governments have typically issued rights to convert open land to housing and commercial use. If your land is zoned commercial it is worth much more than if zoned agricultural or another low-density use. This creates great incentive for landowners to influence zoning decisions in order to capture the appreciation in land value. Some are enriched while others nearby are not. A relatively new institution is transferable development rights. All landowners are given development rights but not enough to build high-density projects. To do so requires the purchase of another owner's rights. This means that all landowners get a portion of the land appreciation even if their particular parcel is zoned for a low-density use.

8.4.3 Integration

What are the consequences of firm A becoming a multi-product firm by buying Firm B? Chandler (1977) has described the history of the development of the conglomerate multi-product firm whose divisions are profit centers. Various stories can be told to fit the facts, but it is difficult to show that alternative forms actually had different long-term profit performance. Chandler attributes the long-term revolution from individual proprietors related to each other via markets to multi-divisions coordinated by hired managers to transaction cost and coordination savings with emphasis on the latter.

What are the consequences of a producer buying the firm supplying an input (integrating output and input)? Milgrom and Roberts (1992: 556) offer this summary: "The advantages of simple market procurement are greatest when particular circumstances prevail. These include the use of standard inputs, the presence of several competing suppliers, economies of scale in the supply firms that are too large to be duplicated by the buyer, economies of scope that would force the vertically integrated firm into unrelated business, and the absence of specific investments on the part of either the buyer or the seller."

Williamson uses the degree of asset specificity in an industry to predict which industries will be organized hierarchically (integrated) and which will not. As laid out in chapter 6, asset specificity creates a motive for "opportunism with guile." The avoidance of this sort of transaction cost has a different emphasis than Chandler's coordination advantages of the integrated firm. Williamson's hypothesis has been confirmed empirically to some degree by Masten (1996) and Williamson (2000), but large exceptions occur such as in agriculture. There are other models explaining the firm and its acquisitions. Williamson's model assumes that somehow the manager(s) know where they are going and the firm is governed to achieve it efficiently. Here the institutional problem is one of optimization and efficiency. But in an uncertain world, this is not possible. In this context the firm can be seen as a strategic process that creates its future over time (Dietrich 1994: 174–81; Kay 1982; Kay 1999). It evolves with its environment in ways that are not fully predictable. Creation of and reaction to technological change is critical and explored further in chapter 10 on technology.

Grossman and Hart (1986) observe "given that it is difficult to write a complete contract between a buyer and seller and this creates room for opportunistic behavior, the transaction cost-based arguments for integration do not explain how the scope for such behavior changes when one of the self-interested owners becomes an equally self-interested employee of the other owner" (692). They use the insurance industry as a case study. The sales personnel or the insurer can own the list of clients. They predict, "in products in which the renewal is not guaranteed and is sensitive to the agent's actions, the agent will be more likely to own the list . . ." (714). They argue that the property casualty sector is more sensitive to agents' action in fitting policy to client and servicing clients than is life insurance. In fact "65 percent of the premiums are generated by agents who own the list" (714). Whether you find this convincing probably depends on your taste in theory. The fact that a substantial percentage of sales are not predicted suggests efficiency must be defined and is not the only consideration. There appear to be agents who want to be independent and some companies accommodate them and find their niche accordingly. Other companies want to control the sales process and find employees who are comfortable in being simply employees. Both types coexist and one does not drive the other out of business. Theories that emphasize transaction costs (relative to specific assets) or incomplete contracts both point to relevant variables.

Grossman and Hart emphasize "the symmetry of control – namely, that when residual rights are purchased by one party they are lost by a second party – and this inevitably creates distortions. That is, integration shifts the incentives for opportunistic and distortionary behavior, but it does not remove these incentives" (716). This is consistent with the theme of this book that externalities cannot be eliminated, only shifted. Grossman and Hart are firmly in the efficiency mode of analysis, which needs to be expanded to the evolutionary perspective noted above.

Empirical work in the efficiency mode tends to justify whatever exists if it is not specifically mandated by government. The substantive performance perspective of this book is different. Using the insurance case above, we would ask about the size of incomes of sales personnel when they own the client list or not. Are there companies that have decided to abandon sales via independent agents, and what tactics have they used to acquire the client lists? Are clients actually better served when agents own the lists? Much of the transactions costs and incomplete contracts literature argues that apparently restrictive practices of firms are really means to efficiency and only incidentally means to market power. Thus, things like the infamous company store are deduced to be an efficient way for the firm to protect its specific investments in human capital. This conclusion is reached without talking to workers.

What are the consequences of a producer of a given product buying another producer of the same product (scale of firm)? One of the keys to economic development is the realization of economies of scale inherent in many evolving technologies. This has been understood at least since Adam Smith's famed idea, "the division of labor is limited by the extent of the market." This was updated by Young's (1928) "Increasing Returns and Economic Progress." The Commerce Clause of the US Constitution was a major institutional innovation that prohibited states from creating local monopolies that would not be able to realize economies of scale. The debate continues to this day as western rich countries through the WTO, World Bank, and IMF pressure poorer countries to open their markets to imports. However, the "everybody wins" mantra of so-called free trade is essentially static and ignores the possibility that rich countries achieve even further economies of scale as their exports increase while poor countries find it difficult to catch up. Kaldor points to "the principle of cumulative causation whereby some regions gain at the expense of others, leading to increasing inequalities between relatively prosperous and relatively poor areas" (Kaldor 1985: 74–5).

The same questions explored above apply to the issue of multinational firms. Economies of scale and opportunities for combining technological knowledge may not have been exhausted within one country or region. Joint ventures are thought by some to be a middle ground between market coordination and administration by merger. This is disputed by Kay (1999: 187) who observes that joint ventures "generally exacerbate hierarchical problems rather than reduce them." The European Commission claimed that market fragmentation impeded industrial cooperation within the Community. It hoped that removal of trade barriers would stimulate more joint ventures across national frontiers rather than mergers that raise more questions about loss of competition. Research by Kay (1999: 249) however, finds that the ratio of merger to joint venture activity has increased rather than decreased over time. Further, there is no evidence that mergers increase profitability that potentially could result from market power or efficiency gains (Mueller 1988). The economies of scale, if any, may be lost to problems of internal management. Kay suggests that the popularity of mergers is "easier to reconcile with managerial theories of firms in which growth and size are managerial objectives, than with traditional neoclassical profit-maximizing perspectives" (1999: 225). For other institutionalist studies of European integration see Schneider and Aspinwall (2001).

8.5 Trading Rules and Market Formats

There is much more to market rules than anti-trust to maintain competition. The conception of markets vs. hierarchy is misleading in that there are many kinds of markets as well as many kinds of hierarchies. There are first-price or second-price auctions, English (ascending price) and Dutch (descending price), double auctions, sealed bid, cost-plus, and the most common of all, posted-offer markets. Experimental work suggests that they differ with respect to the speed and ability to reach Marshallian price and quantity equilibria (Smith 1989). Different results are obtained depending on the risk attitude of agents. Mirowski (2002: 558) challenges experimentalists to investigate other performance measures suggesting, "that different market formats might exist to facilitate differing objectives."

There are many other dimensions to markets. The law and economics movement claims that it has an objective means to assess the performance of alternative institutions such as the rules of contract. It would test alternatives for their efficiency characteristics. The subject matter is suggested by some topics highlighted in Cooter and Ulen (1988), a popular textbook widely used in law schools: "What Resources Should Be Protected by Property Rights? What Contracts Should Be Enforced? Optimal Punishment?" Note the use of the term "should." The field is dominated by what Coase called "blackboard economics," and deductive analysis rather than comparison of actual substantive impacts of alternatives on who gets what and what the world looks like. It is argued that the analysis of law is just a problem of economizing. This position is still dominant even after one of its founders, Calabresi (1985), changed his view and pointed out the circularity problem caused by costs being a function of rights. "What is efficient, or passes a cost-benefit test, is not a 'scientific' notion separated from beliefs and attitudes, and always must respond to the question of whom we wish to make richer or poorer" (69).

With respect to the economics of breach of contract, Cooter and Ulen define "an efficient breach as follows: a breach of contract is more efficient than performance of the contract when the costs of performance exceed the benefits to all the parties" (1988: 290). The facts of the case are judged sufficient to reach this verdict without the necessity to go to the field and determine what happened next in jurisdictions that used one rule vs. another. Harrison, however, points out that the conclusion ignores information costs, requires reliance on an objective outside standard for the determination of the non-breaching party's expected utility, and the degree to which the parties can communicate (Harrison 1995: 126–30). There is also the distributive issue of whether buyer or seller is to share in the benefit of the breech.

There are many areas of law and economics that cannot be discussed here. Reference has already been made above, sections 7.2 and 7.3, to the impact of alternative liability rules. See also (Croyle 1979).

Commercial code and development: Poor countries look at the institutions of the rich and are tempted to copy them. For example, Mali has copied the commercial code of France. But France did not have the same code when it was at Mali's current stage of development (Schmid 1992). Take the case of a builder whose work is destroyed before completion through no fault of his own. Does the builder have to be paid in whole or in part, or must he absorb the entire loss? The commercial code and court action might be different in countries where there are or are not efficient insurance markets.

8.6 How Firms Price Products

One of the functions of markets of course is to determine prices. The standard model has price determined by supply and demand.[1] Competition forces price to equal marginal cost and firms just respond to the emerging prices. No one sets prices, the only thing the firm can do is get in or get out at the optimal output level. The only exception is monopoly and artificial restrictions on entry. In this view, the only institution that matters is anti-trust. But, we have seen that there are more sources of power (interdependence) than barriers to entry. The interdependencies of constant costs and economies of scale are quite different than those associated with diminishing returns.

"Costs, revenues and the elasticity of demand for the product are not facts but forecasts" (Streeton 2000: 422). In the face of uncertain demand schedules, firms often practice mark-up pricing (Lee 1984). "Businesses distinguish costs that vary directly with the flow of output, then calculate the average overhead cost (including an allowance for depreciation) at a standard rate of operation of plant, and, finally, add a margin for net profit more or less according to their judgment of what the traffic will bear. Thus the full-cost principle and the degree-of-monopoly principle are combined" (Robinson 1979: 42). Supply and demand have a weak effect in industry as opposed to primary commodities. "Prices of manufactures are quite insensitive to swings of demand, but react quickly to changes in costs" (42). Firms prefer to cut output rather than prices. Kaldor (1985: 31), summarizing various econometric studies, observes, "in the vast majority of cases (which means in practically all cases except for certain staple products of agriculture and mining) the sellers are price-makers and quantity takers, and not as Walrasian equilibrium theory supposes, price-takers and quantity-makers. This means that prices are mainly cost-determined; demand has virtually no influence on prices (except of course by an indirect route in that demand determines the quantities produced, and changes in the latter may have an influence on unit costs)." The latter point refers to economies of scale (section 6.5 above). Pricing depends on many standard operating procedures such as a markup above cost at a target utilization of plant capacity. The standard is related to firm and industry culture.

Costs of production are normally constant or falling. There is no natural equilibrium in the case of goods with economies of scale, and prices are unstable. A firm may act strategically. It can price based on the marginal cost of today's volume, or it can price on the basis of what marginal cost would be if volume were greater. Of course, the firm hopes that the strategy will in fact result in the higher volume or today's selling at a loss will be disaster. Firms sometimes will price on an average cost basis in the home market, but marginal cost price in foreign markets. The international rules of anti-dumping affect performance. Institutions matter.

"The size of the firm is constrained by the size of its niche within the given market, and the difficulty of raising finance for a much larger scale of operation" (Keen 2001: 75). Some products are bought for status, and price is part of the status (Frank 1999). In that case, a firm does not try to gain market share by lowering price, but rather adjusts quantities to whatever can be sold at the target long-term price.

There are non-marginal changes in pricing practices that have little to do with supply and demand. Institutional economics becomes especially relevant to understanding them. An example is the discount store. For years the standard appliance store had a low rate of turnover and priced accordingly. Then a venturesome retailer decided to sell at a very small margin, but hoped to earn a higher rate of return on capital via a higher turnover. This was a change in thinking, an informal institutional change.

Pricing can affect consumption, and consumption can affect repeat purchases. For example, people who pay for an exercise program by the month rather than annually are most likely to steadily use the facilities and thus more likely to buy another year even when the total cost is the same. Initially, those paying the yearly fee experience a sunk cost effect, want to get their money's worth, and use the facilities more than those paying monthly. But the effect wears off and in the final months of the year those who paid yearly seemed to regard the service as free, used the equipment less, and were less likely to renew their memberships (Gourville and Soman 2002). Perceived cost is as important as actual cost.

Price competition is a Prisoner's Dilemma with a dominant choice and Nash equilibrium. This no-profit equilibrium is unstable in the face of fickle consumers and mistaken investments by competitors (excess capacity and below-cost sales). Firms engage in strategic behavior, including mergers, alliances, product links, etc. to avoid price competition. Some efforts fail; some succeed for a while, fail, and re-emerge in different form. Transaction cost economists (Williamson) urge us look at this through the "lens of contract." Institutional economists invite us to look through the lens of property rights, and economic sociologists ask us to conceptualize a social system (Fligstein 2001). How do these fit together?

Consider the example of Microsoft. When it enjoys a copyright monopoly, it is easy to describe it as a government-created barrier to entry. When it enjoys the competitive advantage of economies of scale with application software, it seems like laudable cleverness and natural order of things. When it bundles applications to its operating system, it raises traditional anti-trust questions. When it buys other firms (hierarchy) is it a matter of transaction cost economizing or monopoly power? These are some alternative and complementary ways to stabilize a market and avoid price competition over commodities. They construct opportunity sets of present and potential parties and can be described as opportunity sets, property rights and a social system. The lens of contract seems only a part of the picture, and property rights are a social system, so are different words for the same thing.

8.7 What Is Profit?

Much is written about maximizing profit. However, profit is not a self-evident fact, but rather an institutional artifact. All corporate financial statements in the US note that it has been prepared in accordance with generally accepted accounting standards. These standards are promulgated by a private organization of accountants, though occasionally formal government intercedes. When time is accounted for there are many alternative ways the flows of costs and returns can be expressed. There are alternative rules for amortizing capital expenditures. During the Enron bankruptcy scandal, questions were raised about the rule that allows the prospective flow of income from leases to be listed as current income. Are stock options issued to managers a charge against present income? Equating marginal cost and revenue to maximize profit is not straightforward.

8.8 Communism to Markets

Administrative transactions are an alternative to bargained transactions. In China, the former USSR, and its satellites, the state was the owner of resources and decided what to produce and how. Laborers were offered jobs and could allocate their income among consumer goods as available. The fall of communism and the shift from centrally administered economies to market economies is the largest social science experiment of our time. The experiment allows us to consider all of the market dimensions discussed above. It is as if all of the issues above came up for grabs at one time, instead of being the result of years of evolution. It demonstrates that reform is not as easy as just declaring that markets are now legal (Schmid 1994). What kind of markets? Details matter. While all the former communist countries moved toward market institutions, they did so at different speeds and content, thus allowing an opportunity for comparative analysis. Stiglitz (1999: 2) compares the performance of Russia and China over the period 1989–99. He argues that the advisors to Russia "underestimate the importance of informational problems, including those arising from the problems of corporate-governance; of social and organizational capital; of the institutional and legal infrastructure required to make an effective market economy." Also see Murrell (1991).

There are high monitoring costs associated with corporate management and asymmetric information between agents and stakeholders. Stiglitz observes that the benefit of monitoring corporate managers is a "public good" (1999: 13), a high exclusion cost good in SSP terms. All stakeholders share in the results of good performance, but have little individual incentive to provide input. See section (1) in table 8.2. The structure that Russia (and its neoclassical advisors) chose to deal with this interdependence was private ownership with separation of ownership and control. But, in an economy without a well-functioning public regulation providing transparency and accountability, the managers stripped assets from the privatized firms and sold them for their own gain. This was furthered by the institution of "loans for shares" whereby private banks loaned money to their favorites to buy firms. When this was combined with exchange convertibility, there was an incentive to strip assets and put the money from their sale into foreign banks rather than invest in new enterprise. The performance results were disastrous – in ten years GDP was half of what it was at the beginning and there was much greater inequality. Still, a review of privatization at the firm level shows efficiency gains from privatization (Megginson and Netter 2001). Part of the gain is reduced employees who become a cost to society rather than the firm.

The reform institutions in China were significantly different. Initially, "China achieved its transformation without adopting private property rights, let alone privatizing its state enterprises" (Rodrik 2002: 30). China put great emphasis on Township–Village Enterprises (TVE). Ownership was still public, but decentralized. These firms were related to other firms via markets. The local party officials had a stake in the success of these enterprises because they could keep much of the new revenue for both reinvestment and for the development of public infrastructure (Qian 1999). This resulted in substantial peer monitoring. Many new firms were created rather than assets being stripped from existing firms. Local governments supervised three-fourths of publicly owned industrial output. They coordinated industrial development with investments in infrastructure. Local government provided a secure expectation that firm assets would not be confiscated. This made banks more likely to make loans (16). Purely private firms grew more slowly, but did so via new firms and not changing ownership of old firms. China did not privatize for the sake of privatization, but followed a dual-track to market development. Special economic zones were part of the dual strategy. Its financial markets were largely closed until it joined the WTO in 2001. This helped it escape the financial crisis that crippled many East Asian countries in 1997.

The performance results are in sharp contrast to Russia. Chinese GDP quadrupled. The performance was associated not only with institutions that provided incentives for investment, but also for coordination of these investments. Stiglitz emphasizes the situation of high information costs associated with having complementary industrial and infrastructure investments on-line together. Price alone is not enough information. Qian observes that, "the community government can reduce information asymmetry involved in market transactions by integrating a number of investments, since market observation drawn from the transactions are much more informative than they are when drawn from transactions resulting from unorganized private investments" (1999: 16). Local governments had access to the books of the industrial firms and that made taxation efficient and synergistic with success of the firm.

When the national government provided incentives for the local government by letting them keep much of the new revenue, national tax revenues fell dramatically. Not only were local governments provided incentives, but individual savers as well. Savings accounts were anonymous so that government could not easily confiscate the assets of people out of favor. Governmental predatory behavior was thus reduced. How then can the national government meet its obligations? Qian mentions, "indirect revenue through the banking system" (1999: 19). If the banks make money, they can be taxed. The cost is spread rather than being assessed at the margin of individual and local government initiative.

Uncertainty and bounded rationality are further key situation variables in the transition context. No one has done it before and can be sure of what will work. The Russian reform seemed predicated on the assumption that wholesale privatization will automatically provide the answers. The assumption was that it did not matter who owned the resources as long as it was private and markets were allowed. Greed would produce the answers. The Chinese put more emphasis on incremental learning. A popular metaphor is "crossing the stream one rock at a time" which contrasted to the earlier Chinese "Great Leap Forward" or the Russian shock therapy. The Chinese kept the state-owned enterprises functioning (even if poorly, it is better than stripping the assets) while they added new initiatives. Decentralization to local governments allowed regional experimentation and adaptation to local conditions. Today, the state sector is in disarray, marked by corruption and resulting in massive unemployment.

The Russians had a further interdependence arising from the transaction costs of enforcing contracts. When they relied on self-interest in the context of a weak legal system and the demise of informal reciprocity of favors (Ledeneva 1998), it was hard to get non-opportunistic behavior by parties to complex transactions. Stiglitz (2002) argues that some social capital would have been helpful, but the "blitzkrieg" destroying old informal institutions put nothing in its place (10). (See analysis of social capital in chapter 7 above.) The average citizen did not regard the new owners as legitimate, which did nothing to secure their willing participation, but rather provided incentive for sabotage and getting yours while you can.

There are also lessons for institutional change, which will be the subject of chapter 13. It is noted briefly here to illustrate the different levels of analysis. Change in everyday formal institutions is a function of the rules for making rules illustrated in section (2) of table 8.2. Change in everyday informal institutions depends on functional, power, isomorphic and learning processes illustrated in section (3). Change in the rules for making rules is illustrated in section (4). Stiglitz points to the Russian failure to acknowledge the interdependence of "human fallibility." The ideology among former Cold War warriors was that the communist system was totally worthless and must be quickly destroyed, thus the centrally directed shock therapy. Stiglitz observes that the prevailing ideology was similar to the former Bolshevism that had earlier destroyed capitalism with a hubris that communism had all the answers. The Chinese were more insulated from dominant western thinking and did not want to repudiate communism, but rather reform it incrementally learning along the way. They were willing to start from where they were and emphasize self-education of the citizenry. See section 4 in table 8.2 below.

Russia had earlier experimented with leasing as an institution for reallocating resources, but this was wholly abandoned in favor of voucher privatization (Stiglitz 2002: 27). The Russian mood reinforced by western advisors was not interested in improving the old system, but rather replacing it wholly with private property however distributed.[2] The rationale was that if reform proceeded slowly the old elites and bureaucracy would stifle change. The political process (the rules for making new rules) also played a part. Yeltsin accepted campaign money from the new owners who wanted the old party managers out of the way. Government did not go away, it was just used by some as before for their own narrow purposes. They used

Table 8.2 Alternative institutions for transition economies

1. Impact theory (everyday formal and informal institutions)

Situation	Structure	Performance

Results of monitoring corporate management is HEC.
 	
High information cost. Info asymmetry. Uncertainty.
 	
Transaction cost to enforce contracts.
	1. Russia – *formal* institutions
	  a. Privatization vouchers.
	  b. Open capital accounts and loan-for-shares.
	  c. Weak legal system.
	2. China – *formal* institutions
	  a. Public ownership (TVE).
	  b. Closed capital accounts.
	  c. Weak legal system.
	
	1. Russia –
	  a. Private ownership.
	2. China –
	  a. Local government coordinated industrial and infrastructure investments.
	
	1. Russia – old *informal* habits destroyed, including social capital. New owners illegitimate.
	2. China – dual system combining old and new.
		1. Stakeholders are free-riders and managers strip assets. GDP half of 1989 level. Great inequality.
		
		2. Peer monitoring. Investment in new enterprises. GDP quadrupled. Relative equality; no big losers.
		
		1. Little coordination.
		
		2. More coordination of investments.
		
		1. Few new complex industrial networks. Sabotage.
		2. Better coordination.

Table 8.2 (*cont'd*)

2. Institutional change (everyday *formal* institutions). Which *formal* structure (1) above will be chosen and prevail is a function of the constitutional rules (4 below) for making the everyday rules. The independent (structure) variable in (1) above is the dependent variable (performance) in (2) below.

Uncertainty on institutional impact. Bounded rationality.	*Rules for making rules:* 1. Reform dictated by center. 2. Decentralized (federated) government. Regional experimentation. No democracy. Constitution specifies markets, but with socialist face.	*Everyday rules:* 1. Privatization in hands of the few. 2. Township–village enterprises.

Which alternative structural rule above for making rules prevails depends on process (4) below.

3. Institutional change (everyday *informal* institutions). Which *informal* structure in (1) above emerges? The informal independent (structure) variable in (1) above is the dependent variable (performance) below.

HEC. IUG, between old elite and challengers.	Functional, power, isomorphic, and learning processes. (Described in chapter 11.)	Russia – old informal habits destroyed. China – new added to old. Dual system.

4. Change in the rules for making rules. Which constitutional rule emerges? The independent (structure) variable in (2) above is the dependent performance variable below.

HEC. IUG between old incumbent elite and challengers.	Functional, power, isomorphic, and learning processes. 1. Russia – Cold War warriors thought communism was all wrong. 2. China – more isolated from West.	Rules for making rules: 1. Reform dictated by center. 2. More decentralized government. Constitution specifies markets, but with socialist face.

government to further and protect their property interests, but as seen above, that was to protect their right to grab assets in the new market economy rather than provide incentive for new enterprise. Just what it was about the contrasting formal and informal processes that created new institutions in Russia vs. China can only be hinted at here and analysts are necessarily modest. A sketch of the variables of situation, structure, and performance in impact and change analysis are outlined in table 8.2.

8.9 Conclusions

The market is not a single thing. There is as much variation in the performance of different markets as there is in markets vs. non-markets. Different market rules interact with different sources of interdependence to produce different perform-ances. Failure to understand this in the West has made market implementation in former centrally planned economies more haphazard. Institutions to facilitate trade are important, but it also matters who has what to trade. On the international front, the World Bank is beginning to examine a broader set of institutions. The distinc-tion between markets (bargained transactions) and hierarchies (administration) is becoming blurred. Hierarchies have plenty of bargaining inside and internal organ-ization matters. Firm boundaries are becoming blurred. What there is to buy and sell starts with collective/administrative decisions. Privatization creates new incentives, which depending on the situation may produce unexpected results. Uncertainty destroys simple pricing rules. Profit can be an institutional artifact.

NOTES

1. For a critique see Keen (2001: ch. 3) who follows Sraffa in pointing out that without diminishing returns, supply and demand are not independent. Price then depends to a major extent on a variety of institutions.
2. Stiglitz (2002) suggests that Russian policy was mistakenly based on an extension of the Coase rule. "Even if one distributed assets to someone who did not know how to manage them well, in a society with well-defined property rights that person would have an incentive to sell to someone who could manage the assets efficiently."

Chapter 9
Macroeconomic Institutions

It is not a correct deduction from the Principles of Economics that enlightened self-interest always operates in the public interest. Nor is it true that self-interest generally is enlightened; more often individuals acting separately to promote their own ends are too ignorant or too weak to attain even these. Experience does not show that individuals, when they make up a social unit, are always less clear-sighted than when they act separately.

John Maynard Keynes (1926)

There are markets not only in real goods and resources, but also in the financial assets that represent them. The paper economy of financial assets contains symbolic references to real goods that signal human behavior (Bazelon 1963). To understand performance, it is necessary to understand how the creation and ownership of financial assets structure the interdependence created by specialization (non-subsistence production). When the institutional paper economy collapses, the most sophisticated plant and human skills are for naught. Further, the owners of physical assets can find their value enhanced or destroyed, not only by bombs and rust, but also by change in financial assets. At the heart of the coordination of economic activity is the institution of credit and that is a power issue just as much as the ownership of land and equipment. It will be useful to distinguish between capital goods and financial capital – the former is a physical thing and the latter represents an institution and a social relationship.

9.1 Money Matters

The previous chapter discussed the role of markets in coordinating the use of resources – capital goods, natural resources, and labor. Implicit in the discussion was the institution of money. Money is not a neutral symbol that merely lowers bargained transaction costs (Peterson 1996; Wray 1996). Money is an institutional artifact that has no fixed relationship to the capital goods of machines and plant or their output. The fact of uncertainty (not just risk) means that investors cannot posit a probability distribution about some normal trend. Individual investment decisions cannot be based on a probabilistic income stream, but rather on expectation of that stream, which may not occur. Such decisions alter and amplify the actual stream that does occur, creating a path-dependence. Shackle (1955) coined the term "crucial decisions" to refer to acts which change the conditions under which the decisions can be repeated. "The very performance of choice destroys the existing distribution functions" (Davidson 1982–83: 192). This is the essence of circular and cumulative causation. "Keynes rejected the neoclassical view of a 'real-exchange economy' where goods exchanged for goods and money is neutral and just a convenience. He saw that the separation in time of selling goods and purchasing them meant the real value of sales can't be known and every transaction is a speculation" (Chick 1983). Keynes rejected Say's Law and its conclusion that involuntary employment was impossible. The conventional wisdom was that unemployment was caused by real wages being too high (sticky wages) because of market imperfections.

Economists have been quarreling over the neutrality of money for some time. Commons (1934: 605) noted that the classical and hedonic economists "had eliminated money as a mere 'form,' a 'medium of exchange' having no effect on the exchange-values previously determined in the processes of production, pleasure and pain. But money, says Wicksell, is not a mere difference in 'form,' where it plays only a passive part, but in 'reality,' with money playing an active part." Commons agreed with Fisher (1932: 82) who said booms and depressions are rooted in the transactions that create debt. The factors include the currency problem, price level, net worth of business assets and liabilities, the profit margin, the production index, currency turnover, and the "psychological causes and effects of optimism and pessimism" (Commons 1934: 608).

Contracts are made in terms of money and not in real terms (Davidson 1972). The relationship between money and things is not just a matter of the stock of money, but also human valuations as a function of expectations. These cognitive elements can change without any change in the money supply and thus are a source of involuntary unemployment. The demand for monetary (financial) assets does not automatically convert into real things. When expectations decline, the prices of monetary assets are bid up and new borrowing declines. There is no necessary conversion of savings into real investment if valuation changes. Unemployment can occur if savings do not find an outlet in real reproducible assets. Davidson (1982: 115) referred to this as a violation of the axiom of gross substitution.

The value of business assets is also a matter of expectations. A firm that is borrowing based on the market value of its capital goods (past successes) and financial assets may suddenly find that a change in expectations of others destroys its ability to borrow. Again, cognition changes the relationship of things and money. As firms borrow less, they lay off workers. This can set in motion the vicious circle of depreciation. "A shortfall of validating cash flows relative to payment commitments can set off an interactive and cumulative downward process" (Minsky 1986: 166).

9.2 Credit and Coordination: or "The Fable of the Missing Hoe"

To understand the role of credit in addressing the coordination problem, let's look at parts of the world where it does not function well. There are some countries where the credit system was never very active or has broken down. Every one in the marketing chain insists on cash. This slows economic activity greatly as production begins only if it is paid. Money can't be made on money. Let's look as what credit does and its alternative in a command or familial system. Let's imagine a simple system of production involving labor and land plus a capital good such as hoes, and one intermediate step, perhaps transportation or some minor processing before sale to consumers. Consumers are also the suppliers of the capital good, namely labor to make hoes. If these parties were a family they would simultaneously agree to make hoes, grow corn, transport corn, and eat corn. The person with land would not insist that he be paid before handing the corn to the truck driver, and the truck driver would not be paid before handing it to the eater, and the eater would not be paid before supplying the hoe. They would agree to participate and wait to share the product as the circle of production is closed.

In a non-family situation, this contracting is expensive. So in capitalism, the coordination is done with credit. What we observe in many poor countries is that some production capacity potential exists which is not being realized. The guy with the land says, "I need credit to buy a hoe so I can produce more corn." The trucker-merchant says "I need credit to buy grain from farmers." If the trucker-merchant had an order from consumers (or retailers) he could go to a bank with their promise to pay and obtain credit with which to pay the farmer who in turn pays for the hoe and begins production. The corn is produced, trucked and delivered, and eaten. If the eater got paid for the hoe, he can pay for the corn and the debt is validated (paid off). But the problem is that the merchant has no actual order from the consumer-eater since he is unemployed – no demand for hoes. Instead they all sit there planning desperate revolution and thievery.

The bank hesitates to grant credit perhaps because it has seen so many of its previous loans unpaid. The production didn't materialize and the debt could not be validated. So all wait for evidence that anyone in the system has a real order from someone with the existing capacity to pay (savings). But there are few of these people because of unemployment. How do we get this system going better and faster? The parallel between the fable of the missing hoe and modern recessions will become obvious below.

Because some countries could not solve the coordination problem (and for other reasons), they turned to administrative transactions. In a command system, the central planner would order each of the participants to perform their tasks and supply each other with services and sell the corn to consumers. The system was energized by creating credits in a government bank for each firm to transfer to each input supplier. Coordination was achieved but other problems were created as is well known. Part of the problem in the ongoing transition from communism to markets is that markets in physical goods are not enough.

Let's turn now to the essence of the credit system as it exists today.

9.3 Banking and Property Rights

An owner of real incompatible use goods in use or idle can loan them to another who can coordinate these goods for production. Institutions and associated organizations relate borrowers and lenders. Much of the connection is done by financial intermediaries such as commercial and investment banks, money funds, and savings and loan associations. But, commercial banks can do something more than move existing funds around. They can create new money. Someone with a better idea for the use of resources needs authority to reorganize them. Money creation is the coordinating institution. An entrepreneur having been given credit comes to resource owners and says, "follow me." "I can make something of these resources that does not now exist. I can add knowledge as well." To understand this process, we must understand money and credit.

Money is debt; there is no other kind. Even the bills in our purses are evidence of debt. But this is peanuts compared to the total money supply. How then is modern large-scale debt (money) created? A property rights perspective is useful. How does an entrepreneur get in a position to obtain resources without borrowing them from their owners (or from savers)? Historically, entrepreneurs were armed with a big stick to back up their orders, literally a big stick for beating or a symbolic totem of authority. The modern equivalent is money and debt. How does a would-be entrepreneur get the right to order resources around? A loan from a bank is instrumentally such a right. The bank creates symbols after the entrepreneur's name that are used to pay for resources, without the necessity for borrowing real resources or savings. Money is created when loans increase, and destroyed when the debt is repaid. Legislatures create rights when they change laws and regulations. Banks create rights to command resources and thereby to control the resulting new production if any. Commercial banks in turn received this authority from the Federal Reserve System that got it from Congress. Congress was given authority to create money by the Constitution. To summarize:

- *Money* – Symbol for what is and what can be. It is debt of someone that others accept as payment.
- *Money creation* – Make a loan by writing numbers (an electrical charge) after people's names. All money is debt.[1] No printing press needed.
- *Commercial banker* – Creator of a property right for a fee. Seller of the right to hire resources. Creates new symbols so people can organize unused resources. They also act as an intermediary between owners of existing money and borrowers.
- *Central bank* – Creates the right of banks to create money. Regulates money supply along with the Treasury. Gives banks standards for what constitutes a good portfolio of loans (including what is good collateral, as noted below in section 11.2.2). Creates rights as much as any legislature or court.

9.4 Business Cycles and Capitalist Development

Investment and borrowing are not deterministic phenomena. They are essentially a product of expectations, which are a cognitive matter. One invests if the rate of return exceeds opportunity costs. But returns and costs are subjective estimates of the future. Current spending validates past debts. Whenever it does not, the value of capital assets declines and new investment drops.

Any system is subject to random change. The change can be simply a slight decline in expectations. Enthusiasm for anything is hard to maintain. Firms may not borrow and invest at previous rates that had sustained full employment in anticipation of declining demand. Or, declining aggregate demand does not validate yesterday's investment causing financial losses. A firm looks at expected and actual demand and expects or realizes a decline in profits. It adjusts current employment, output and borrowing. This cost cutting is expected to restore profitability. (It would if the world were mechanistic.)

However, in a world of circular flows, one firm's cost cutting is another person's or firm's reduced income and subsequent reduction of aggregate demand. The firms who cut costs in response to declining demand subsequently find that demand has again declined and output and employment are too high again. This feedback process with amplification is the essence of *cumulative and circular causation.* "The cumulative path taken by an economy becomes dependent upon, rather than being independent of, the totality of those very individual decisions at every moment in time" (Rotheim 1996: 30). Recessions and depressions are vicious circles. They can also be characterized by the Prisoner's Dilemma metaphor. Each firm acting alone in its best interest faces a set of dominant choices where non-cooperation (reducing employment) is always better regardless of what other firms do. If all or some threshold of firms would maintain their employment and output, the shock would dissipate. The output and payments of other firms constitute the demand for any given firm. But while any firm understands this, they also understand that if they cut their costs while other firms do not, aggregate demand will be maintained at no cost to the non-cooperator. As Keynes noted above, "individuals acting separately to promote their own ends" may not succeed. Their best efforts may only result in a low level Nash equilibrium.

A recession can be self-reinforcing as explained above. In time it may also be self-limiting if it leads to falling prices and increased real money supply (Krugman 1996: 5). Most people don't want to wait that long.

Businesses are not the only borrowers. Changes in consumer expectations affect consumer borrowing (measured by The Conference Board's Consumer Confidence Index and Expectations Index). Consumers who become more pessimistic about their employment and salaries reduce their borrowing to solve anticipated individual problems. But, when this reduces aggregate demand, employers in fact reduce labor use and wages, if they can, insuring that the consumer's fears were well founded. Consumer loans repaid decrease the money supply. Banks, fearing non-payment, reduce consumer credit outstanding just as they reduce business credit by calling loans earlier and making fewer new loans.

Changes in the valuation of financial assets also affect consumer borrowing, as it does business borrowing. For example, a drop in stock or real estate prices reduces collateral as well as demand for credit. Expectations cause changes in the ratio of private expenditure to income. Net saving in the US by the private sector fell from 5.5 percent of GDP in 1992 to minus 6 percent at the end of 2000. When consumer borrowing returns to normal after a credit boom, it can create a decline in aggregate demand and recession (Godley and Izurieta 2001). Cycles are also a function of real factors such as technology, labor productivity, and wars that are also interdependent with expectations.

9.5 Expectations: Psychology and the Fed

The Federal Reserve Open Market Committee adjusts short-term interest rates to control inflation and avoid recessions. This choice is not just a technical matter of finding the appropriate intersection of the supply and demand for money. As noted above, business investment is a matter of expectations, and expectations are a matter of image and interpretation. Federal Reserve Chairman Greenspan tried to understand investor psychology. For example, when Iraq invaded Kuwait in 1990, oil prices surged. Greenspan was quoted as saying, "I would suggest that perhaps the greatest positive force that we could add to this particular state of turmoil is not to be acting but to be perceived as providing a degree of stability." "Some bank presidents wanted to lower interest rates slightly, arguing that it might give a psychological boast and create confidence that they were acting to prevent a recession." (Woodward 2000: 69.)

Greenspan chose his words and timing carefully. During inflationary periods, the size, sequence, and timing of each interest rate change was calculated for its psychological impact (Woodward 2000). During recessions, a lower interest rate or tax cuts cannot increase expected profits and investment if expectations are falling at a faster rate. During expansions, successful investments reinforce more investment even if interest rates are rising. Investors may reason that it is better to borrow now before the rates go up even more. The optimism and pessimism of the human brain feeds on itself. Macro policy is more complicated than finding the equilibrium between some known marginal productivity of capital and its cost. Also see Mayer (2001). There is no doubt that hyper-inflation can be halted by high interest rates stopping investment and creating recession. The other popular alternative is wage and price controls that create black markets and reduced output. Neither alternative is attractive. Institutions to dampen extremes in expectations have not yet been found.

The language of academia and the financial press often uses the idea of sin to explain declines in business activity. It is said that a recession is caused by over-optimism and over-building in the previous period that must be corrected with painful medicine. What does this mean in substantive terms? Can any economy over-build and have too much capacity in real terms? What does it mean to say we have too many factories in the aggregate? This is surely a failure of institutions more than physics or the niggardliness of nature. Scarcity has to be created for our own good.

Conventional wisdom has it that monetary policy must be made by an organization independent of politics and staffed by technicians. But, as Marglin (1999) points out, "There are winners and losers from any monetary policy, and it remains the art . . . of good policy to balance these gains and losses. One man's politicization is another's democratic politics" (136).

9.6 Deficit Finance

During recessions, economists as well as political parties disagree on what to do about it. Some say do nothing, perhaps historically represented by President Hoover who did nothing. Others advocate cutting taxes especially on the rich so they will invest more. Still others suggest larger government deficits.

Pessimism does eventually run its course, but few want to wait that long. Making investment more profitable by cutting interest rates or taxation does little good if expectations are declining faster. The tax cuts just put more wealth in the hands of the wealthy. The Japanese economy was stagnant during the decade of the 1990s, even when interest rates were nearly zero. Referring to monetary policy, Galbraith (1975: 369) offers the judgment, "Only the enemies of capitalism will hope that, in the future, this small, perverse and unpredictable lever will be a major instrument in economic management." The conservatives are afraid that expanded government spending will not be temporary and counter-cyclical, but permanent and inflationary.

The psychology of optimism and pessimism is not immune to talk and symbolic events. Roosevelt said, "We have nothing to fear except fear itself" and companies advertised, "Business is Good." But talk is seldom sufficient to break the cycle. The essential Keynesian idea was that if consumers and business do not want to borrow to put available resources to work, government must do it.

People are suspicious of governments that make money to acquire goods with. In a full employment economy, more fiat money is equivalent to taxation. But, with less than full employment, it is a different story. Galbraith (1975) observed that the surest way for an economist to ruin his reputation was to have unconventional view of money. Since we are so desperate for new ideas, this author and a few others are willing to run the risk (Schmid 1984; Solo 1994). Any plans must recognize the following points, implicit in table 9.1.

A less than fully employed economy:

- does not have to save to increase output;
- does not have to tax (reduce the consumption of those employed) to put the unemployed to work.

Table 9.1 Banking as property rights creation

Situation	Structure	Performance
Good = unused resources, especially labor during the business cycle. IUG	Who can use? Who is entrepreneur? "Factor ownership" 1. *Stick*. Administration. Command. State owned firms. Former USSR. 2. *Totem*. Status. 3. *Dollars*. Market via bank loan.	All structures select who gets to be the entrepreneur.
	a. Loan to private party.	a. Limited during recession.
	b. Loan to government.	b. Interest liability. Tax transfer, poor to rich.
	c. Treasury checks.	c. No borrowing required.

When the private sector refuses to borrow enough to put all resources to work, government spending can increase aggregate demand with no opportunity cost. Coin and currency are non-interest paying government debt, as is a check issued by the Treasury drawn on the Federal Reserve Banks. Balance sheet logic indicates "the government need not borrow from the private sector by issuing bonds in order to enable it to spend in excess of current taxation" (Bell 2000: 613). There is no technical reason to limit public spending short of achieving full employment goals. Lerner (1943: 40) argued, "taxing is never to be undertaken merely because the government needs to make money payments." Wray (1998) turns the usual picture of government collecting taxes or borrowing in order to spend on its head. He reasons that government spending is fiat money that is valued because it is the means to pay taxes. Fiat money comes first – coin, currency – and is the basis of bank reserves that make possible the creation of private loans. Treasury checks deposited in a commercial bank increase bank reserves. When taxes are paid, reserves decline. Net deficit spending increases reserves that could drive the interest rates on Federal overnight funds (and thus short-term interest rates) to zero. This would defeat Federal Reserve interest rate targets. To mitigate this, the Treasury sells bonds. "Bonds, then, are used to coordinate deficit spending, draining what would otherwise become excess reserves" (Bell 2000: 613).[2]

The government injects reserves into the banking system by purchase of goods held by the public, including Treasury bills purchased by the Federal Reserve Open Market Committee. Government could purchase labor instead. Wray (1998) proposes that the government be the employer of last resort in recessions. The Treasury could write checks (non-interest bearing debt) to the unemployed (often of low skill) to perform public services. As the economy picks up, workers are released and made available to private employers. Low-skill workers then comprise a buffer stock. By setting the price of low-skill workers, government dampens the variation of all prices, and the buffer stock reduces business cycles by maintaining aggregate demand. Wray argues that the amount of bank reserves and private borrowing necessary to eventually increase the demand for low-skill workers is inflationary, while directly increasing the demand for these "off the bottom" workers is less so.

"Poverty occurs, not because of resource constraints or a lack of technical knowledge, but because institutions (distributional) arrangements have not been adjusted to the productive potential of the modern economy" (Peach 1994: 170). Some argue that even during nominal full employment, the potential capacity of capital goods is seldom achieved (Bazelon 1963). This is clear in the case of agriculture. Worldwide capacity in autos is only partially used. And, we could surely build more plant. In agriculture, governments try to restrict output to support prices. The auto companies do the same thing privately. Scarcity is now more contrived than built into nature and technology. Bazelon argues that there is no real scarcity and we should not make money scarce. He observes that expansions are often fueled by consumer credit. The security of consumer credit is a secure job. But, firms do not want to commit to jobs because it is individually profitable to cut employment if aggregate demand falls. The overall effect is to insure a fall in aggregate demand. Writing in 1963, Bazelon argued, "So instead of getting the best out of the system, the purpose of the Rearguarders is simply the minimal one of keeping it from going utterly to pot. Five million cars a year would mean a federally expensive recession, so they shoot for six-and-a-half to sustain a dismal prosperity, instead of for the nine or ten that the existing plant could turn out. And meanwhile they suggest that everybody should 'save' – money, that is – so next year they can get a new car. No! The real reason is so that money will retain its value as a symbol of scarcity for the benefit of their power and pelf" (1963: 137).

The modern economy needs people as consumers even if they are not earning a great deal. But, we hesitate to empower consumers. Bazelon purposes the following radical idea: "The Federal debt could, for instance, be converted into non-interest bearing money any time the political decision to do so were effected" (142). The money could be given to the foodless in the form of food stamps or the carless in the form of car stamps or public transportation. The money could be used to finance income supplements in place of the present financing by taxes.

9.7 The Fed and Cumulative Causation

The Fed is always guarding against chain reactions where default by one big player could cause cash flow problems of others. The big player might be a domestic bank or a foreign nation. In November, 1997, the Korean economy was on the verge of collapse from capital flight. Banks around the world were pulling out. Woodward (2000: 190) observed "A vicious cycle of growing and self-reinforcing fear could destroy the underpinning of any financial market – confidence." If most banks remained the crisis might be worked out, but the dominant choice for each creditor was non-cooperation unless they could be coordinated by some collective authority. Treasury Secretary "Rubin found that the main New York banks were sophisticated enough to know the benefits of collective action. Those calls were not difficult. One Chicago bank was reluctant. The CEO asked, Why should we do it? Rubin spent some time in conversation, and the CEO agreed to go along" (191).

The 1997–8 Asian Financial Crisis hit Thailand first. It had a large percentage of its total debt liabilities in short-term, unhedged, foreign currency denominated borrowing. Many loans to business were guaranteed by the government, creating a moral hazard. When growth faltered and projects failed, lenders called their loans, businesses failed, and the region was plunged into recession. The IMF conditions for aid were controversial (Stiglitz 2000).

The Mexican fiscal crisis of 1994 also caused a capital flight. The US government put together an aid package of loans and guarantees. Secretary of the Treasury, Robert "Rubin noted that markets were psychological animals, and if the world financial markets came to believe the package was sufficient to have a meaningful impact on Mexico, then international investment money would start to flow back into the country. The country had to regain the credibility of its people and the world investment community" (Woodward 2000: 141).

The Russian default in 1998 provides perhaps the most dramatic example of a cumulative causation problem. The default caused wild fluctuations in securities all around the world. The inherent interdependence (situation) in modern capital markets is explained by "Big bets by sophisticated investors, many made with borrowed dollars and many having nothing to do with Russia, suddenly went bad. In a scramble to shore up their crumbling finances and meet lenders' demands for more collateral, those investors were forced to sell out of other, safer investments. And as these investments in turn tumbled under the selling pressure, the urge to flee became contagious, spreading quickly until it hammered just about every financial instrument except supersafe US Treasury securities and German government bonds – which soared" (Siconolfi et al. 1998: A1).

Long-Term Capital Management, a hedge fund, suffered extreme cash flow problems (Lowenstein 2000). LTCM had implemented a leveraged strategy, betting that fluctuations in the spread between certain derivatives would return to historical patterns. LTCM "is holding something like $90 billion worth of positions on a capital base of just $2.3 billion" (Surowiecki 1998). The strategy was created by Nobel prize winning economists Merton Miller and Myron Scholes. All their past experience suggested it was a sure thing and LTCM's trading profits attracted huge investments by many of the worlds largest banks. But history has a way of destroying sure things, and it came in the form of a Russian default. If LTCM could not cover its trading losses, many banks and Wall Street houses that had invested and loaned money would be bankrupted. The New York Federal Reserve Bank brokered a meeting of the largest creditors urging them to make further loans instead of calling the present ones. The good offices of the Fed avoided the disastrous Nash equilibrium. So much for the automaticity of markets. The $3.5 billion bailout stopped further LTCM liquidations.

9.8 Financial Capital

Managers of large corporations have incentives to enlarge their firm. Some of this may be related to economies of scale, savings of transaction costs, and a sense that they can be more efficient than the previous managers. But, some is due to wanting to be known as the manager of a *Fortune* 500 company or one of its largest. Managers' salaries may be related to the size of the firm. Still, a large part of their remuneration comes from their ability to profit from changes in stock values. Top managers are increasingly being rewarded with stock options. If they can do something to affect market valuation of their firm, they stand to profit. Financiers also are motivated to rearrange ownership of firms in the hope of changing their market valuation (Burrough and Helyar 1990; Lewis 1989; Zey 1993; Stewart 1991).

The market capitalization of a firm is a matter of expectations and speculation. The essence of capitalism is the capitalization of expected future income flows. As Veblen put it, "Capital in the enlightened modern business usage means 'capitalized presumptive earning-capacity'" (Veblen 1958: 65). He added, "The magnitude and fluctuations of business capital, – 'capital' in the sense in which that term is used in business affairs, – of course, stand in no hard and fast relation to the material magnitude of the industrial equipment" (67). He notes, "The market fluctuations in the amount of capital proceed on variations of confidence on the part of investors" (74). So he concludes that, "under modern conditions the magnitude of business capital and its mutations from day to day are in great measure a question of folk psychology rather than material fact" (74). But material fact is not so easy to establish.

The evolution of financial institutions is driven not only by industrial firms, but also by financial firms seeking profits. Key questions are "What is being financed? What is the pivotal source of external financing? And what is the balance of economic power between those in business and banking." (Paraphrase of Hyman Minsky by Whalen (2001: 809).) The first stage up to 1813 was "merchant capitalism" wherein owner merchants vouched for the legitimacy of distant trade partners and financed goods in process, stock and transit. Private economic power was "fragmented and dispersed" (Minsky 1990: 67). The next stage (1813–90) was "industrial capitalism" featuring financial organizations such as J. P. Morgan that could mobilize resources needed for capital-intensive manufacturing. This was a period of classic competition wherein price-cutting threatened the security of investments.

A response to this insecurity was the rise of "banker capitalism" (1890–1933) wherein investment bankers aided the formation of cartels, trusts and mergers. This was the period in which John D. Rockefeller formed Standard Oil to aggressively consolidate the many small oil producers (Chernow 1998). Private economic power became concentrated. Investment bankers secured major shares of stock and seats on corporate boards. Morgan was able to stop the financial panic of 1907–08, but could not do it in 1929 (Chernow 1990). Minsky refers to the next period 1933–82 as "managerial capitalism." Federal Reserve policy, deposit insurance, securities regulation, and compartmentalization of financial organizations (Glass-Steagall) set the stage for stability and prosperity after WW II. Oligopolistic markets gave industrial managers some independence from bankers and stockholders. Minsky judged that this evolved to a more fragile system encouraging reductions in margins of safety and greater reliance on short-term debt (Whalen 2001: 813). The reliance on short-term debt for long-term enterprises is a perennial problem exemplified by the US Savings and Loan debacle in the1980s and the 1990s financial crises in Korea, Indonesia and other East Asian economies. Government regulators reduced regulation of the Savings and Loan Associations who were allowed to take on more risky investments, but deposits were still government guaranteed. The result was taxpayers bailing out a host of bankrupt organizations for something like $140 billion, which Mayer termed the "greatest-ever bank robbery" (Mayer 1990: 2).

During economic expansions, firms increase the proportion of short-term borrowing, reduce liquidity, and in general become more speculative. When the Federal Reserve increases interest rates to control inflation, it creates cash flow problems for firms (Minsky 1982). When these firms die or greatly reduce their output, it contributes to reduced expectations by other firms.

Managed money funds (pension funds, mutual funds, etc.) were a major institutional innovation in the 1980s. They control vast sums of money to buy securitized loans, commercial paper and stocks. On the plus side, money managers and venture capitalists contributed to the investment-led boom of the 1990s, much of it in computers and telecommunications (Whalen 2002). These large investors recognized a common long-term interest in developing technology. At the same time, "money manager capitalism" was more sensitive to short-term profits and stock prices. In the 1980s it fueled mergers, acquisitions, leveraged buyouts, stock buybacks, etc., all contributing to system fragility.

Some of the earlier financial system safeguards are being repealed. The probable impact of repeal of the Glass-Steagall Act in 1999 provides a case that can illustrate the application of the SSP framework developed in this book (Benston 1990). SSP theory suggests that we identify the source of the interdependence and the parties who are interdependent. This will let us understand the opportunities for cooperative gains and for conflict. Most attention has been given to possible gains to all players from reduction of transaction cost. These seem to be largely in the cost of assembling information rather than securing of synchronization of separable steps and operations. For example, an integrated financial services firm might more cheaply assemble a useful telemarketing program from common consumer records (mortgage, bank accounts, stock ownership, etc.). But there are two sides to every source of interdependence. The saving to the financial firm is a cost to consumer privacy – some don't want to be exposed to these tailored marketing schemes.

Another example of cost saving is in the cost of assessing stock underwriting projects if the bank already has the information from a loan application. This could be a Pareto-better cost saving if shared with customers. But, the saving is linked to larger sized firms who then have market power. Bank mergers have not resulted in lower fees to customers so one wonders about who pockets the cost savings. There is a conflict of interest when a financial services firm has equity interests, loan customers, underwriting interests, and stock buying customers.

The advocates of repeal have less to say about the original purpose of Glass-Steagall; that was to reduce the possibility of financial system meltdown in the face of radical uncertainty. There is an interdependence created by uncertainty or at least some tradeoffs between reducing information costs and increasing the possibility of banking system failure. The reduction of information costs to conglomerate financial firms may be at the cost of increased exposure to uncertainty. This latter cost is not fully borne by the conglomerate's own bankruptcy, but also by the general public who has a stake in avoiding circular and cumulative causation domino effects that could destroy the ability of the financial system to accommodate cash flow crises. Many of the institutions that reduce the transaction cost of agreements to protect specific assets are worthless in the face of radical uncertainty. Williamson's "hostages" protect against a trading partner's opportunism, but not against their bankruptcy.

In the case of radical uncertainty, there is often no way to avoid it – the question then is sharing it or isolating it. If insurance companies are also banks, a catastrophic insurance loss would be difficult to contain.

"Too Big to Fail" is a cost of transaction cost reduction. Super-mergers create firms whose bankruptcy can affect the whole financial system (see section above on "The Fed and Cumulative Causation"). The American taxpayer bailed out the Savings & Loan industry for their folly (Eichler 1989). It also provided loan guarantees for Chrysler because it was too big to allow to fail. Some economists are always objecting to unprofitable large state-owned firms such as those in China or as the mines once were in UK because the government can't afford to alienate large numbers of workers in these firms. But Wall Street is united in pronouncing the creation of super financial firms that will be too large to let fail as an unmitigated blessing. Metaphor and selective perception run wild.

The decade of the 1990s saw investors fixated on growth of corporate earnings to the exclusion of other measures of success (Collingwood 2002). Bounded rationality often means that simple measures are used to represent complex phenomena. In this culture, managers learned that share prices increased with increase in earnings, whatever their source. Many corporations gave large stock options to executives on the theory that it would be an incentive for good performance. In practice it created incentives for cooking the books. Executives surely knew that continuous double digit earnings growth was impossible, but did not care if they could cash out before it became obvious.

The bankruptcy of Enron in 2001 and Global Crossing Ltd in 2002 illustrate the extremes of managers trying to increase earnings to meet stockholder expectations and for their personal gain. It also illustrates the use of stock as money that contributes to financial instability. Enron created off-balance-sheet partnerships (special purpose entities) to make investments in physical assets (such as Enron owned power plants in India) while still allowing Enron some control over them (Forest, Zeller, and Timmons 2001). Sales show as income for Enron. Enron contributed its stock to the partnership to entice investment by institutional investors. One such partnership owned a combination of physical assets, Enron notes, and convertible stock. Enron promised to pay interest on the notes and to add more equity if asset sales could not cover debt. This was fine when stock prices were high, but unsupportable when prices fell. Enron's strategy was to "commoditize" and monetize anything. But, its trading margins did not provide enough cash flow to support its obligations, leading it to assume ever more risky deals.

The essence of capitalism is the capitalization of future income into present income. Structured finance has a long history such as when a company sells its accounts receivable to a bank. But, as the asset becomes more risky, public investors demanded credit enhancements such as stock and notes (Henriques 2002).

Corporate paper becomes money if it is accepted as payment by another entity. The establishment of confidence is easy when the original company creates the other entity and outside investors are drawn in by promises of better than average earnings. Kuttner (2001: 24) refers to the Enron partnerships as "complex variations of old-fashioned pyramid schemes, watering stock and soaking investors." These arrangements blur the definition of what constitutes a firm. They may reduce transaction costs but there are other consequences. The interconnection of different entities is the basis for circular and cumulative causation. If one link goes bad it can drag others down. The US Department of Treasury considered the effect of Enron's bankruptcy on the financial system and decided it would not intervene. The fact that it asked the question illustrates how we are no longer in the competitive situation where one firm has no effect on price and other firms. The fact that Enron's chief financial officer "earned" $30 million from these partnerships and Enron tried to influence government by contributing campaign funds to two-thirds of the Senate's members illustrates the consequences of concentrated power. But, the contribution of continually new financial institutions to financial instability may be the greater consequence.

Global Crossing Ltd. presents a similar picture of extreme measures to show earning to support stock prices. Global built extensive fiber optic networks. It sold space on these networks to companies such as AT&T and reported it as current income, and then bought back the space in a commitment covering 20 years. These newly invented Indefeasible Rights of Use are in reality a swap. But "Accounting rules allow the money from the sale of IRUs to be booked immediately. The money paid to buy IRUs can be depreciated over the life of the lease" (Maney 2002). Deals such as this made it look like Global had fast growing earnings, which was reflected in its stock price, making borrowing easy. But, Global earnings fell as a worldwide glut of network capacity caused prices to fall leading to bankruptcy. A firm cannot be sure of the capacity and eventual prices created by the aggregate behavior of all. New technologies are the context for human invention of new financial instruments. Costs and profits are not simply natural categories, they are social constructs, in this case depending on rules of the Internal Revenue Service.

9.9 International Dimensions

9.9.1 Money creation in developing countries

The negotiability of debt worked out in the seventeenth century was one of the greatest institutional inventions of all time (Commons 1924: 392). Still, many countries cannot make it work. Part of the problem may be that the creation of money in countries colonized by the West was kept in the hands of the colonizers and did not devolve to local initiative. The banking system imposed on poor countries by the IMF is not the banking system that was in place in the United States during its western migration. Local banks that saw local opportunities gave loans to local entrepreneurs. People accepted bank notes if they had confidence in the bank. People were not sitting around waiting for a World Bank or foreign private investment. They overcame the problem characterized above as that of the "missing hoe." Some of their experiments worked and some failed. Wildcat banking earned its reputation for excess, but in the process the west was settled. There were regional conflicts over power as eastern banks supported the gold standard and the west wanted to create more money based on silver that it had plenty of. Eventually the Federal Reserve System centralized decisions on the money supply.

The world economy is much different than in the wildcat days of the latter half of the nineteenth century US. Money created locally to use unused local resources may be spent to buy a TV from Taiwan. There are coordination problems connecting supply and demand over time and space. We are in need of some institutional innovations. We shall not find them if we are self-satisfied and assume that if the rest of the world had the modern institutions of the West they would be as rich as the West or that market equilibrium is automatic and instantaneous. There are no conclusive social experiments. It is always possible to argue that with time and rectitude that the present formula of open markets, centralized banking, etc. will eliminate world poverty. Still, institutional economists may be of service by putting some new ideas on the agenda.

9.9.2 Capital markets and international exchange rate policy

Institutional innovation in international trade and banking has not kept pace with the growing interdependencies. Davidson (1998) argues, "Persistent swings in exchange rates between groups of OECD nations has been a major contributor to the drastic decline in global economic growth rates and the creation of more than 130 million unemployed in OECD nations." Tobin argues that some form of government constraint on international financial flows is required.

Stiglitz (2002) is critical of IMF policy in response to the 1997–8 fiscal crisis in several poor countries. He argues that more loans have just put many countries deeper in debt, mostly to benefit rich country creditors. He would prefer bankruptcy. He is also critical of IMF insistence on higher interest rates, which it rationalizes as necessary to restore foreign confidence. Stiglitz (2000) is less concerned about investor psychology than the immediate effect on small business and unemployment due to inadequate aggregate demand. He emphasizes the moral dimensions of economic policy.

Davidson (1998) rejects changing the income tax to a value added tax or to drastic reductions of public spending and the social welfare net because "these policies imply that increased employment requires that workers be first forced to accept a lower real wage than that which prevails in the marketplace before the policy change."

9.9.3 Macro effects of low wages and globalization

Reference has already been made to the circular and cumulative process that accompanies attempts by individual firms to combat the effects of recessions. A similar process accompanies globalization, deindustrialization via movement of manufacturing to low-wage nations, and fighting unions and minimum wage laws (Melman 1983). Lowering wages in the aggregate can lower aggregate demand. Supply (cost) and demand are interdependent. Further, Keynes "pointed out that when money-wage rates are cut, prices fall more or less commensurately, so that costs in real terms are not reduced. All the strife and bitterness and relative injustices of trying to push wages down are incurred in vain; furthermore, if they did succeed, it would actually do harm by increasing the burden of liabilities fixed in terms of money and embarrassing the banking system" (Robinson 1979: 44).

Technological change is a good thing, but depending on institutions it can create structural problems. Leontief (1982: 188) argued, "When workers are displaced by machines, the economy can suffer from the loss of their purchasing power." The usual model of the effect of technological change on labor and income is that workers no longer needed in industry A are available for the expansion of industry B. But where is the demand for these new products of B? If many workers are now unemployed in A, they can't buy anything. Leontief argued that income must be transferred from profit owners to workers to retain aggregate demand and full employment. Capital owners are not going to agree to that even if it was in their long-term best interest. Leontief suggests transfers rather than minimum wages so that employers do not have further incentive to replace workers with machines. An alternative to transfers would be a shorter workweek at the same yearly income as before. Many European countries have gone this route as have some powerful unions in the US.

What do the capital owners do with their profits? The standard theory is trickle down. They buy more things and keep the workers busy. In part, true, but the rich can only consume so much. Instead they buy financial assets so they can be even richer in the next period (or their heirs). So stocks, etc. are bid up. The rich are buying stock from each other, but the aggregate demand for cars can't keep the car factories going because there are not enough workers making sufficient incomes. But, stock prices can only be sustained so long from increased buying by the rich, because profits will eventually fall if aggregate demand declines. Is this where we are today?

Individual firms are motivated to seek locations for factories in low-wage countries and sell the product into high-income countries. They assume that aggregate demand does not change as a result. For example, Japan now invests more in other Asian countries than it does in Japan, which contributed to the depression in Japan during the 1990s. Japan lowered interest rates almost to zero, but investments remained anemic and Japan did not employ all of its people (Callen and Ostry 2003). It is almost a sacrilege to question so-called free trade. But the theory only claims that total wealth would be raised if everyone produces at its comparative advantage. It does not claim that everyone will in fact be better off. If you have a job that is not threatened by cheap goods from other nations (such as that of professors, lawyers, and politicians), you enjoy low-cost imported goods made by people that earn a few dollars per day. But, if you lose your manufacturing job, you have no income to buy these imported or any other goods. Just as when workers displaced by machines cannot buy, neither can workers displaced by foreign workers.

Why is it necessary to take a job from one place to create a job in another. Why is it not possible for a poor country to use its labor to produce for its own people as well as export? Surely they need houses, clothing and food that they could produce for each other. Is this a problem of rights to credit – the creation of money? Why can't a domestic entrepreneur borrow to produce houses and clothing for domestic consumers? Because those domestic consumers don't have effective demand because they are unemployed or underemployed. This is a vicious circle! Can it be broken?

Could a poor country government buy more things from domestic producers? Note the question is buying from the private sector, not production by public firms. Could it print money (or distribute vouchers) and give it to the poor to buy from these same local producers? No, says conventional wisdom – this would not be sound public finance. Is the rejection of this approach just a ceremonial reinforcement of the *status quo* property rights? Are we caught in an ideology that says only the relatively wealthy have access to bank loans and it is the savings of the wealthy that make investment and economic development possible? In section 9.6 above, it was argued that a country does not have to save in order to invest when its resources are not fully employed.

9.10 Observations in Conclusion

The economy is, in part, coordinated through credit creation. It is not enough to know who owns the physical resources. We must ask who owns credit. Ownership is contained in the rules for borrowing from savers and for getting access to resources without dealing with savers. These rules govern the relationship of money to physical assets and the relationship among financial markets, including stocks, and new investment and distribution of income. Money matters. The creation and distribution of money is an essential component of the necessary exercise of power directing interdependence and its outcome. Performance variables include the business cycle, development, inflation, and income distribution. One of the key sources of interdependence in the macro economy comes from systems of circular and cumulative causation. Individual maximization at the margin may produce an aggregate performance that few want.

The banking system can be usefully thought of in property right terms. The problem of the economy is to organize its resources and capacities. Historically, the symbols used were the stick and the totem, and now its is money (debt). Just as there are many kinds of markets with different rules, there are many ways to capitalize the future. Macro institutions did not spring automatically from nature, and while some continuity is essential, we must not forget that they are variable human artifacts. Among the structures influencing coordination and performance are ownership of the right to create money, the right to influence its amount, and the rights contained in the rules of financial markets. Income can be gained by manipulation of capital assets as well as efficient production.

Modesty with respect to the impacts of macro policy is in order. These words of Samuels (1994: 663) are apt:

> Macroeconomic policy is a function not only of purely intellectual/scientific ideas (nor is it clear that it should be). The real world, and policy changes . . . are a function of power play, selective perception, complex individual and mass psychology, attitudes toward uncertainty, the quest for wealth, and so on. Thus, fiscal policy (and monetary policy) is dominated by attitudes toward the size and general role of government and by power play over the shifting of taxes, income, wealth, and opportunity, as well as over the power structure dominating and determining policy itself.

NOTES

1. "The process by which banks create money is so simple that the mind is repelled. Where something so important is involved, a deeper mystery seems only decent" (Galbraith 1975: 24).
2. Fewer bonds would be needed if reserve requirements were raised.

Chapter 10
Technology, Growth, and Institutions

Science and technology processes and products have several characteristics that create human interdependence. These include high exclusion costs, non-rivalry, economies of scale, networks, and fundamental uncertainty. This chapter first analyzes the role of institutions in technological change, then the impact of technological change on the evolution of institutions, and finally the difficulty of devising a science and technology policy to satisfy everyone.

10.1 Technological Change with Alternative Institutions

Why do technologies change? Which technologies change? What affects research and development investment? The literature has been summarized by Dosi (1988). Some of the explanatory factors include: relative prices, appropriability, firm and industry specific routines and standard operating procedures, transaction costs, market structure, irreversibility of technological paths, and lock-in. Institutions affect the contest to control technological change.

10.1.1 Markets and relative prices

The easiest way to explain technological change is to conceptualize it as the result of choice among known technologies according to their marginal cost and benefit as in any optimal resource combination problem. Sometimes these explanations are referred to as demand driven (Schmookler 1966) or induced technological change (Hayami and Ruttan 1985). Profit opportunities are certainly a factor. More research is done on major food crops than minor specialty crops for example. But opportunities are a matter of perception. The possibility of a new invention, its costs and eventual returns is problematic. Dosi (1988: 1142) says, "it appears misleading to consider innovation simply as a reactive process (to relative prices and demand, in one case, to new exogenous opportunities, in the other)." "Whether market signals change or not, firms try to perfect their products and processes, by trial-and-error mechanisms of search and imitations of the results already achieved by other firms, motivated by the competitive edge that innovations are expected to offer."

If all is a matter of straightforward profit calculations, then the results are inevitable. If there is no technological change in the area of your interest, that is the will of market participants and there is little to do about it. The only variable that suggests itself is the degree of market competition. Indeed, this has been a line of research summarized by Scherer (1992). Schumpeter (1983) originally argued that the entrepreneur was driven by profitability to innovate and this was to be found disproportionately in small firms. But this was later changed to feature large firms who could use monopoly profits to hire the best brains.

Scherer's review of the literature questions the advantages of large-scale firms as engines of technological change. Still he shows that the picture is mixed and different countries have successfully used different strategies. Japan has had good results with large integrated firms and a national industrial policy that favored selected industries. This raises the question of the role of cultural differences as well as different strategies for different technologies, such as major product advances vs. yield increasing, cost-reducing innovations.

10.1.2 Expectations, uncertainty, search, and selection

Whether formal or informal, for profit or not, research and development faces fundamental uncertainties. Costs and benefits are guesses. As found in earlier chapters, in the face of uncertainty, firms adopt routines and standard operating procedures. They may thus spend unproductively on some things and miss big opportunities in others, but they satisfice and avoid catastrophe; though competitive survival is known only after the fact and may have little impact on the strategies employed. Constancy is easier for established firms such as Philips, General Electric, 3-M, Dupont, and the former Bell Labs of AT&T, who can use retained earnings to finance research, than for small start-up firms who must seek outside finance (Hall 2002b).

In the face of fundamental uncertainty, firms often follow SOPs and routines, such as "spend X% of sales on R&D." Griliches and Pakes (1986) found that "the pattern of R&D investment within a firm is essentially a random walk with a relatively low error variance." Dosi (1988: 1134) observes that "companies tend to adopt steady policies (rules), because they face complex and unpredictable environments where they cannot forecast future states of the world. . . ." Knowledge is "embedded in the human capital of the firm's employees and is therefore lost if they leave or are fired" (Hall 2002b: 36). (See table 10.1.)

Research planning and investment faces a competence–difficulty gap identified by Heiner. Nelson and Winter (1974: 891) hypothesize that "a firm at any time operates largely according to a set of decision rules that link a domain of environmental stimuli to a range of responses on the part of firms." They observe, "Firms pursue profits (and perhaps other goals), but their choice sets are not sufficiently static and well defined to make profit maximization descriptively plausible" (903).

Risk-averse private firms may make fewer research investments than consumers in the aggregate would desire. This is often used to justify public subsidies and tax benefits to private research as well as public research. Examples of the latter are the in-house experiment stations of the US Department of Agriculture and state

Table 10.1 Uncertainty

Situation	Structure	Performance
Uncertain payoffs	1. Public grants and subsidies via taxes.	1. Some research done that otherwise would not.
	2. Private capital markets.	2. Less research.
	3. Standard operating procedures in large firms.	3. Stable R&D budgets over the business cycle.

universities, the Department of Defense, National Aeronautics and Space Administration, and grants by the National Science Foundation, Institutes of Health, and in Europe by the European Union and such labs as the Centre Européean Recherche Nucléaire (Peterson and Sharp 1998).

New start-up research firms have difficulty in raising capital. Investors demand extraordinary expected returns because they can't know as much about the prospect for new discoveries as the researchers. Asymmetric information creates the possibility of moral hazard. Firms may hesitate to fully reveal their good ideas to public investors for fear of losing them to competitors. For these reasons, Hall (2002b: 37) argues "it may be socially beneficial to offer tax incentives to companies in order to reduce the cost of capital they face for R&D investment, especially to small and new firms."

Nelson and Winter (2002) point to a "competence puzzle" wherein firms can perform a complicated production task with great competence and at the same time make huge mistakes in developing new products for market. They explain, "High competence is often achievable where skills and routines can be learned and perfected through practice" (29). But, similar learning is not available for new technologies. Firms do adopt technology strategies, but with no assurance that what worked in the past will work in the future. Informal "habits of management thought channel strategic choices" (33). For example, Polaroid developed a successful business model based on cheap cameras and expensive film. When they tried to apply it to digital cameras, it failed (Tripsas and Gavetti 2000). The role of alternative informal institutions in technological change is hard to research. Informal SOPs and routines do change, even if no one calculates the expected payoffs to alternatives.

10.1.3 Appropriability and exclusion costs

Many analysts have observed that if the benefits of a prospective technology cannot be appropriated by its creator, the research is not forthcoming from private firms (Dosi 1988). Knowledge, if used, is hard to physically contain, but rights to knowledge can be made exclusive at a cost. Patents can give exclusive use to a described invention. The exclusion cost is in proving that a copy has been made. The legal rule of equivalents controls how much different a thing must be to avoid being labeled a copy. Obviously changing the color of paint on a steam engine does not qualify as a separate invention. But, how different is different is not an easy question. To provide an incentive for innovation, the scope of the patent must allow for recovery of research costs, but if the scope is too wide, it stifles competition and further innovation. From chapter 6, we know that with high exclusion cost goods there is a tradeoff between the interests of wannabe riders (those who want the good created) and unwilling riders who with certain rules must pay for something they do not want. Knowledge is not like national defense or air quality whose use is inadvertent by all. Anyone incorporating knowledge does so deliberately. The user can't claim to be an inadvertent user and claim to be an unwilling rider if charged by its owner. Nevertheless, there is something akin to an unwilling rider if, because of a wide scope of equivalents, an innovator is required to pay royalties when they independently created a somewhat similar good without copying.

Consider exclusion costs and how the rule of equivalents works in the case of plants. The seed of an open-pollinated plant contains the genetic directions for its reproduction. The same seed sold for human or animal food also can be saved by the farmer and planted again without coming back to the breeder and paying for its creation. An open-pollinated seed is both product and factory, and if the farmer has the seed, he has the factory as well. For this reason, for many years in the US and many countries, agricultural research was performed in public organizations financed by taxes.

Public organizations released a new variety only if it was clearly superior to existing varieties. Varieties were multiplied by farmers specializing in seed production and seed prices were low and only covered the reproduction costs. Farmers returned to this source only when saving their own seed resulted in lower performance.

Congress passed the Plant Variety Protection Act (PVPA) in 1970, joining the Union pour la Protection des Obtentions Vegetales in Europe. It gave exclusive rights to sell a variety that was described morphologically by such traits as color and flower characteristics. This encouraged competing seed companies to do cosmetic breeding adding some distinguishing visible characteristic to a variety developed by someone else (Schmid 1985a). This created confusion among seed buyers now faced with many similar varieties. The law was modified to eliminate cosmetic breeding in 1991.

The cost of distinguishing one variety from another, which is necessary if exclusion is to be made effective, is a function of technology. As genetic structure became understood it became possible to describe a variety in terms of gene sequence. *Diamond v. Chakrabarty*, (447 US 303 [1980]) extended the general utility patent act to life forms and gave protection to the creators of a particular mix of gene sequences. The problem of how different some sequence must be to be a new invention remains. Organisms have the capacity for mutation and the sequence changes in nature. The original description may not fit the organism in the future and the courts are faced with deciding which variations are equivalent to the original. If the product space is drawn narrowly, some copies will be seen as different and patentable in their own right. If the product space is drawn widely, it will exclude independent inventions that are not copies, but have some similarities.

The argument over equivalents was illustrated when the University of California sued Genentech for allegedly infringing the university's rights in some genetic materials developed by university scientists who later went to work for Genentech. Genentech claimed that they did not use the university's patented materials in developing their own growth hormones, Nutropin and Protropin. Nevertheless, Genentech agreed to pay the university $200 million (Feder 1999). The transaction costs of these suits are often so great (the suit was in its ninth year) that the contending companies often agree to a cross-license figuring that it is better to share the benefits and concentrate on protecting their rights from still other competitors.

Returning to agriculture, whatever the protection patents can give one company vs. another, farmers saving their own seed are a major threat to breeders recovering their costs. In principle, a seed company could sue a farmer for not buying new seed every year, but in practice it is difficult. Remember that exclusion cost is a matter of technology. Change the technology and you may change exclusion costs. So private breeders have increasingly turned to hybrids that do not breed true in farmers' fields to provide the exclusivity that patents cannot. More recently they researched adding terminator genes to open-pollinated plants. The work was abandoned upon public protest. The research costs in developing terminator genes would have added nothing to the performance of the variety, but would increase its cost over what a public organization could have done because the latter would not worry about exclusivity if financed by taxes. This is just one example of how technology and institutions interact to affect the research agenda and scientific methods involved (Schmid 1985a).

The hybridization path has had profound impact on world agriculture favoring large-scale agribusiness on an industrial model rather than small, independent farmers. There is some evidence that the open-pollinated approach could have built on past crop improvements obtained by public research and farmer selection and over time produced the same yield improvements, but a different agricultural structure (Lewontin and Berlan 1990; Marglin 1996). The new science of biotechnology is writing the final chapter of the complete industrialization of agriculture where farmers are contractees and little more than piecework labor. Processors provide proprietary genetic material (seeds and baby animals). To be sure, industrialization has produced cheap and attractive food, but at the cost of higher risk monoculture and perhaps unsustainable dependence on chemicals.

There are several alternative institutions that can be applied to plant development: private or publicly financed research, two kinds of patent protection, and the detailed alternatives (definition of equivalents and product space). Each has its own performance consequences favored by different interest groups. (See table 10.2.)

10.1.4 Increasing returns (economies of scale) and standards

Once a particular technology is in place, it may be characterized by path dependency because of increasing returns to its wide and continued use even if an alternative was or becomes superior (Arthur 1994). For example, whether or not the VCR or Beta Max format was the best for video recording, once one system is in place and there are more titles available in one format, consumers will prefer it and unit costs

Table 10.2 Biotechnology

Situation	Structure	Performance

Living organisms: inherent variability and complexity of open-pollinated species. HIC to determine if copied. Costly to achieve stability. Parties: competing breeders, breeder and farmer.	1. Patent (PVPA)
	  a. Narrow product space defined morphologically.
	  b. Broad product space; many years of protection.
	  c. General patent, defined genetically.
		1. a. Cosmetic breeding avoids patent and leads to low returns to research. Many varieties confuse farmers. Rules out
		  b & c. Prevents cheap, slightly different copies. Possible monopoly independent creation as well. Large investment to achieve otherwise returns. No composite varieties. Protection useless stability. against other breeders, but not against farmers who save own seed.

	2. Public research	2. No incentive for cosmetic breeding. Fewer varieties.
Hybrids	3. No effective patent	3. Farmers can't save own seed. Breeders get high profit.
Industrial processes (e.g. aspartime made with a particular bacteria in a fermentation tank).	4. Trade secrets	4. Lots of investment. Farmers replaced by industry.
Low EC		

Based on (Schmid 1985a)

Table 10.3 Increasing returns

Situation	Structure	Performance
Increasing Returns	1. Industry standard emerges from competition. (E.g. Video format, Windows.)	1. Path dependence – hard to move to new standard.
	2. Collective action: Trade association. Government rule.	2. Move to new standard such as HDTV.

decline. The same is true of computer operating systems. Once one system is dominant and many applications are written for it, consumers will prefer it even if in terms of the basic technology, an entirely different operating system might be superior (Schmid 1985b). This is the source of Microsoft's near monopoly. Anticipating low returns, research on alternative systems may be absent. If an alternative technology is desired, it may require a conscious collective decision to get off one path and on to another.

The attractiveness of some technologies depends on the existence of compatibility among components in a system. An example is high-definition television and digital radio (table 10.3). Broadcasters will not make HDTV programming unless there are consumers who have the appropriate receivers. And, vice versa. Again, a switch from low- to high-definition TV depends on a collective decision to require the use of HDTV by a certain date. This is, in fact, the present policy in the US. In Europe, where publicly owned stations dominate, the move to HDTV preceded that in the US, but a Europe-wide policy has been difficult (Peterson and Sharp 1998).

The internet depends on a common set of standards that among other things allow different browsers to use it. The backbone of the internet was developed by the US Department of Defense and universities. What if it had been a private firm? Microsoft used its operating system dominance to bundle with it their own proprietary browser. Manufacturers of computers using Windows could only get it with Microsoft's browser included. This gave them a competitive advantage over other firms' browsers that would require extra steps to implement. After considering breaking up the company, a US District Court (231 F. Supp. 2d 144; 2002) ruled that this bundling was a restraint of trade. The ruling did not address Microsoft's aggressive acquisitions of small challenger firms that might eventually compete with it (Fligstein 2001: 227). The balance between stabilization and stifling of competition is difficult to achieve.

The tradeoff between achieving lowest unit cost and variety in non-rival or economies of scale goods was identified in chapter 6. In the case of new technologies there is a tradeoff between getting more research if returns are higher as a result of anticipated increasing returns to greater and longer use and benefits to consumers of moving to a new standard. Theory suggests that there is a tradeoff between the costs of duplication and variety. Parallel research by different firms with only one winner seems like a waste. Public grants to a limited number of firms reduce duplication. But given uncertainty, if one firm were assigned a line of research, there is no guarantee of their success.

10.1.5 Network relationships

The private returns to a given technology often depend on complementary public and private investments. Firm A may be working on a certain line of investigation whose product will be valuable if some complementary product is created by other firms. As these paths become known, the pieces fall into place. Like any complements, it is impossible to determine the marginal product of each. A firm may claim that it would invest more if it could capture all the benefits it creates, but such attribution is arbitrary. Do the railroads get credit for the economies of scale made possible in steel production, manufactures, and retailing? Or do the latter get credit for more demand and economies of scale in railroading? Each can argue that without their contribution, the product would be less. Should inventors of television get the rents from professional sports teams? "The extent of the rewards and penalties, and the rates of introduction and diffusion of new techniques, depends on a complex of environmental and institutional considerations that differs sharply from sector to sector, country to country, and period to period" (Nelson and Winter 1974: 903). Some technologies which stand alone are adopted quickly. Others that depend on complementary technologies and organizational and institutional accommodation take longer. For example Oliver Evans invented the steam wagon in 1785, but it was useless without roads and tracks. Clarence Birdseye invented flash freezing of foods in 1924, which greatly improved the quality, but it was many years before the rest of the system of refrigerated transport, in-store and home freezers could be built (Fucini 1985). The industry was instrumental in getting Congress to revise the Pure Food and Drug Act in 1938 to assure consumers of food safety.

Technological change in various industries seems to follow a particular trajectory with cumulative results (Freeman and Soete 1997). Once something is understood, it opens up other possibilities.

10.1.6 Dynamic sequence

Research often builds on previous research. For example, in the bio-medical field, cell lines, cloning tools, and reagents can become inputs into additional innovations. When knowledge is cumulative, who can say that invention number one in a sequence should capture all the rents that were created when number ten was made? What if the basic gene splicing process technology invented by Herbert Boyer and Stanley Cohen at the University of California and Stanford (and financed by the National Institutes of Health) had been invented by a profit-maximizing firm? The

scientists communicated their results widely and shared materials with other laboratories (Hughes 2001). Later the universities made the technology available for a
nominal fee as a strategy to avoid contesting the patent. The combination of public
funding and the pleasure of doing science seemed incentive enough, though Boyer
later helped found Genentech.

The transistor was created by Bell Telephone Labs in 1947. Subsequent "Commercial exploitation of Bell Laboratories' discovery was influenced by US antitrust
policy . . ." (Mowery and Rosenberg 1998: 124). A 1956 consent decree limited
AT&T to telecommunications and made its transistor technology available to others.
Texas Instruments added improvements in fabrication and purification of silicon,
and with demand for its products from the US military, the industry took off. Development of computers was heavily subsidized by the military. The military wanted
the widest possible growth in the industry and did not want to be dependent on a
single supplier. Its plans were widely circulated among government agencies and
universities. "Like the semiconductor industry, but for different reasons, intellectual
property rights were relatively weak in the early years of the computer industry"
(136n). One can only speculate what the industry might have looked like if some
firm had exclusive rights to the basic patents and had tried to maximize its profits
from royalties.

Alliances and joint ventures without fear of anti-trust regulation are another way
to account for spill-overs from one invention and function to another. Patents can
facilitate trade and accumulation of the pieces. But, transaction costs and uncertainty
may prevent such mutually beneficial combinations (Heller and Eisenberg 1998).
An integrator of various patents needed for a new application who assembles some
of the pieces has fixed costs that are subject to hold-up by the remaining patent
holders.

Length of patent protection and scope affect returns to the original work in a
sequence of innovation. Depending on the anticipated research cost, some promising lines may be left unexplored if the patent period is too short on the anticipated
original product (affecting product profit plus royalties from subsequent innovators)
(Koo and Wright 2002). On the other hand some promising add-ons may not be
explored because the anticipated returns less anticipated royalties to the original patent
seem inadequate. Quarrels over distribution can affect realization of the product.

10.1.7 Technological change and conflict

Technological change is not some benign process where everyone gains. Even if the
change has the potential to be Pareto-better, it may not be so in practice. Thus,
change is a function of which competing interests can control the process and this is
affected by institutions that influence whose preferences count.

Some technological paths are deliberately chosen by firms to achieve labor dominance. See David Noble (1979) on deliberate choice of computer directed vs.
computer-assisted machine tools and Sahal (1981) on the development of the tractor.

As the western US was settled, it became the source of beef for the cities of the
eastern seaboard. Cattle were driven overland to whatever were the railheads at the

time and then shipped to the big cities. Many local butchers in the cities received the live animals and prepared them for retail sale. But, Gustavus Swift had a better idea in the 1880s. He conceived of building refrigerated cars, slaughtering the animals in the Midwest and shipping dressed meat to eastern cities. This was opposed by both the railroads and the city butchers. The railroads already had investments in cattle cars and made money shipping live animals and refused to build refrigerated cars or to haul them if built by others (Chandler 1977: 299–302). The city butchers would lose their business if the animals were slaughtered elsewhere. Swift built his own cars and found one rail line that would carry them. Williamson (1985: 236) uses this example to argue that integration forward is due to efficiency and not an attempt to build market power. He finds generally that power is a poor explanation of economic events. But, the case can be used to illustrate the role of institutions that affect the distribution of power in technological change.

The railroads had immobile specific assets whose value would be destroyed if Swift were successful. Likewise, the eastern butchers had immobile assets subject to loss. If property rights protected these assets, Swift would have had to buy them out. Williamson argues that the gains in efficiency from shipping dressed beef could have been used to pay for any losses to others. In retrospect this was true, but at the time, if Swift had been required to borrow money up-front to reimburse the railroads and butchers, the project may have failed or have been delayed. This story is repeated over and over.

Another example was the change from direct to alternating current. Edison had investments in direct current generation when Tesla conceived of alternating current that was superior in driving electric motors. Edison spread rumors that users of alternating current would die in six months (Cheney 1981: 43). Again, one can say that the new technology was so superior, its entrepreneurs could have bought out the losers such as Edison (who in turn could have bought out the candle makers and the whale oil industry before him). But the point is that this process of creative destruction seldom compensates the would-be losers, and their attempts to avoid losses affect the path of change. Technological change has winners and losers, and institutions affect the outcome of the struggle and the content and timing of that change. It is simply not true that all entrepreneurs either use general-purpose technology or make contracts to protect immobile assets against opportunistic consumers or inventors, and many institutions help prevent it in some cases and aid it in others. For a general history of electric technology see Hughes (1982) and Soete and Dosi (1983).

Can science settle policy disputes? For some, the market promises a natural order. For others it is science. Veblen can be read as arguing that there is a natural instinct of workmanship and science which if left alone (absent ceremonial institutions), all will be well. Society-changing-technologies are launched whenever individual firms expect them to be profitable. The argument goes that if people buy it, it must be good. Still, the aggregative impact of these technologies is often not anticipated, or even if anticipated, there appears to be no process for deciding as a society whether to embrace the change. The automobile brought us mobility, but also a change in human settlement patterns as well as a cause of accidents and death.[1] (See Marcus (1974).) Modern farming brought us cheap food, but also changes in ownership and control and questions about sustainability. This is another case of change at the margin vs. choice of kind and direction.

Some argue for a wider participation in the adoption (if not also the research and development) of path-setting technologies. Busch (1999) proposes an extension of democracy to all institutions. "By so doing we neither put moral responsibility on the shoulders of individuals where it becomes crushingly heavy, nor on the shoulders of society where it becomes unbearably light." But, democratic participation runs into the limited information processing capacity of the human brain. Taking moral responsibility for choice of the path of technological change is hard work and many would rather watch TV, though some make it the defining activity of their lives – witness protestors against abortion clinics and genetically modified organisms. We shall have to pick and choose where to apply our scarce mental resources.

10.1.8 Organizing the research enterprise

The path of technological change is partly a matter of informal institutions within the research organization and between the research and production activities. The dominant fact of private corporate research in the US is that it is in-house rather than being contracted for. The make-or-buy decision favors making your own, including buying a firm with technological knowledge. This can be explained by transaction cost economics (Teece et al. 1988; Williamson 1985) and by the existence of organizational routines (Dosi 1988: 1132–3) noted above.

The transaction between producer users and researchers is complex and hard to specify in a contract. Proprietary information may be difficult to protect if outsourced. It is difficult to monitor costs whether inside or contracted out, but the balance may favor in-house work. Knowledge accumulates and business organizations learn and store it internally, something that specialized for-hire research firms are less able to do if they move from application to application. Firms build on their core competencies. When products require the integration of different competencies, some firms turn to joint ventures by loose agreement or by acquisitions.

The public sector has similar options. The US has government labs that do in-house research oriented to specific users in government (for example, The Waterways Experiment Station for the Army Corps of Engineers), or the clients of specific departments (The USDA Experiment Station at Beltsville), or are contracted out, such as is the Oak Ridge National Laboratory for the Atomic Energy Commission. On the other hand, major grants are made by the National Science Foundation and the National Institutes of Health. These grants are made to both universities and private research organizations. There are great variations in the rules such as the method of peer review, disciplinary requirements, and matching funds.

In agriculture, the bulk of the research is done by experiment stations in state universities. The Land Grant system financed by both Federal and state funds integrates research and delivery of technology by the Extension Service in each state university. This parallels the integration of research and production in private industrial firms. It might be argued that this is economic in reducing transaction costs between users and researchers. Still, each institution has its particular outputs, so it is hard to hold output constant and just minimize costs. For example, the state-by-state agricultural research sometimes results in discoveries that favor a particular state at the expense of producers in other states (Texas was working on a rice variety that would only do well in a particular area of the state and not in Louisiana.) The USDA researchers are less likely to engage in that sort of zero-sum research, but at the cost perhaps of accommodating local peculiarities. While the US Land Grant system is convinced it has the most efficient model, many countries in the world separate research and extension in different organizations. Sometimes extension is done on a fee-for-service basis, as in the UK, rather than paid for with public funds. The simultaneous existence of contrasting organization is testimony to the political economy of technology rather than technology dictating one efficient institution to fit it.

A major institutional change occurred in 1982 when the US Congress gave universities the right to patent discoveries financed by government grants. Supporters argued that unless exclusive rights were granted, many innovations would not be commercialized. This implies that normal profits in competitive markets were not sufficient even if the basic research was free to firms. Patent royalties to universities greatly increased and universities were increasingly sought as partners by private firms. The landmark example was the Berkeley/Novartis Research Alliance in which the University of California received $25 million. Because of its preeminence, Berkeley could obtain a contract that gave it control of the research agenda with Novartis only receiving "the right to negotiate to acquire at fair market value a percentage of discoveries that may result from research that it helps fund" (Rausser 1999).

10.2 Technology and Institutional Change

Changes in technology produce changes in institutions, as well as the other way around explored above. Parallel to the argument that relative prices determine technological change, it can be argued that relative prices determine institutional change to accommodate the technological potential. Both contain an element of truth, but the causality is complex. The Green Revolution of new plant varieties is much heralded in the developing world. For example, in the 1960s new rice varieties and irrigation works increased yields in the Philippines. Prior to this technology, the traditional institution allowed landless laborers to receive one-sixth of the harvest for harvesting and threshing. After the new technology, laborers had to contribute weeding as well as harvesting to qualify for one-sixth of the yield. Hayami and Ruttan (1985: 94–114) argued that the new technology increased the marginal return to agricultural labor above its opportunity cost in the city. Institutions had to change to equilibrate marginal returns in all comparable occupations. Further, any attempt to legislate better treatment of agricultural labor would result in inefficiency (Ruttan and Hayami 1984).

Why could not the increased returns to technology benefit labor as well as landlords? There was a struggle for the technological rents. The harvester's share of the harvest is not necessarily the same as the marginal cost of labor (Schmid 2000: 218). If the harvester had stock or some other part-ownership of the land, these dividends would not be a marginal cost. Rather it is simply a division of added earning among the several rights holders. Alternatively, if the government had sold water rights from its investment in dams and distribution systems or had sold the new seeds above the costs of production, it could give the revenues to any party without affecting the marginal cost of labor. There is nothing inherent in a technology that dictates the institutions that determine who benefits from it. The change in the institution of harvest distribution was not some automatic dictate of markets. The ability of the landlord class to control the local police and other authorities may have had something to do with the change in the traditional system. People don't just volunteer to contribute more labor for the same return just to satisfy someone's notion of equilibrium pricing.

Tenant solidarity to oppose the institutional change favored by the landlords would be harder to organize because the result is a high exclusion cost good, and the benefits to any one person are small given the large sized group. Theory suggests the importance of rules for making formal rules as an alternative to the evolution of informal rules. Veblen (1908) was correct in arguing that returns to factors are institutionally grounded in the social power of owners that enables them to capture the benefits of technological change. Distribution is not inherent in the nature of preferences, endowments, and technology.

The creation of a sugar cane industry in Kenya provides another example of technological demands on institutions that can be met in different ways. The economies of scale in processing could have been met by the factory owning sufficient land and hiring labor (hierarchy). Instead, the government retained small-scale farms by creating zones within which "the factory could legally function as a monopsonist" (Bates 1989: 78). Local entrepreneurs who brewed intoxicants were excluded. The farmers had to sign contracts specifying planting times and cultural practices to specifically meet the factory's needs.

While technologies affect institutions, institutions surely affect the adoption of technology and accompanying organizational changes. When the World Trade Organization agreements allowed direct foreign investments in formerly closed economies, multinational food chains moved into Latin America and other countries. In a few years, supermarkets replaced many small stores and market places (Reardon and Berdegue 2002). The chains wanted a constant supply of high-quality fruit, vegetables and milk products not available from traditional producers. Chains are developing contracts with their own specifications unrelated to any government grades and standards. Large numbers of small producers will be eliminated as was the case of dairy farms in the US when higher sanitary and refrigeration laws were introduced, favoring larger, more capital intensive farms. There is a degree of inevitability in these stories and those left behind seem powerless to change it. Still, there are cases discussed above where different responses to technological change were possible. The benefit of new rice varieties in the Philippines did not have to accrue only to landlords, and economies of scale in sugar processing did not dictate plantations with hired labor.

Technologies do not spring immaculate upon the world, but reflect detailed design decisions that affect adoption by users and the evolution of complementary firms. The adoption of a new technology is a balance of newness, technological and cost superiority on the one hand and links to existing and familiar products that make the consumer comfortable on the other. "While people make sense of the new only in terms of the old, the design of the new shapes which sense they make by determining which aspects of the old are invoked" (Hargadon and Douglas 2001: 479). For example, Edison purposely introduced electric lighting that in appearance was little distinguished from gas lighting, and was produced in central plants and delivered underground as was gas. He was opposed by vested interests of both private firms and government officials comfortable with their old relationships. Edison was initially denied an operating license and permission to dig up streets by New York City. Opponents emphasized the danger of electricity. Edison's contribution was more to develop a network of generation, input suppliers, investors, trained electricians, and customers than in technological invention that had largely preceded him. The same design decisions can be seen today in the introduction of genetically modified organisms. US consumers have been mostly convinced that the GMO foods are safe and advantageous while Europeans tend to see them as Frankenstein food. Institutional rules of labeling and world trade will affect the path of adoption and evolution of the technology. The impact of technology on institutional change will be further explored in chapter 13.

10.3 Technology Policy and Growth

It would be convenient if the various technology policies explored above could be combined in some optimum way to maximize welfare. But, the various sources of interdependence explored in chapter 6 and applied to technology above suggest that aggregate welfare analysis covers over conflicts of interest. Each policy favors some and harms others, and even defines what is meant by economic growth.

10.3.1 Capital goods and growth

If we are to relate alternative technology policies to growth, it is necessary to relate capital goods embodying technology to growth. This is not straightforward. Some history of thought is useful to understand where we are. Harrod-Domar models dominated economic thinking for years. Partly because of the intractability of measurement, it was convenient to assume a constant capital:labor ratio, even if counterfactual. This mind-set focused policy attention on the savings rate. Poor countries were urged to save more and rich countries focused on interest rates and tax policies. When econometric models (Abramovitz 1956; Denison 1985) relating changes in output to conventional measures of land, labor, and financial capital inputs left a large proportion of output unexplained, interest in technology and changes in the capital:output ratio increased. Calling the residual technological change put a name on it, but explained little. Measurement of the variables in a regression was problematic. How do you add up a hoe and a tractor, or put a number on a year 2000 tractor replacing a 1950s tractor? It is easy to count financial capital (savings and investment), but difficult to aggregate the quality and quantity of physical capital through time. Solow had trouble accepting that the savings rate was the only way toward growth. So he replaced the constant capital:output ratio of earlier growth models by a richer representation of technology (Prescott 1988). He suggested a "vintage approach" that better technology is embodied in more recent financial investment, and thus should be weighted more heavily. "The effectiveness of innovation in increasing output would be paced by the rate of gross investment" (Solow 1988: 315). While this seems plausible, Denison found it had little explanatory value. Solow acknowledged that "it could be the case that some countries are better able to exploit the common pool of technological progress than others, for reasons that have nothing to do with the rate of capital formation; but in exactly those technologically progressive countries investments are most profitable, so naturally the rate of investment is higher. Or else rapid technical progress [and] high investment could both be the result of some third factor, like the presence of conditions that encourage entrepreneurial activity" (315). Conditions like institutions?

Capital goods might be measured in terms of the present value of the flow of their services. But, to measure capital in terms of the value of services produced is circular (Solo 1967: 93). This was an element in the so-called "Cambridge Capital Theory Controversy" (Cohen and Harcourt 2003; Keen 2001: ch. 6). It also runs into the problem of business cycles that would cause a fluctuation in the value of capital assets and the equilibrium growth path (Mankiw 1995: 307n). Solow (1988) notes that contemporary macro theory evades the problem by assuming a single immortal consumer who can solve an infinite time utility-maximization problem. "This strikes me as farfetched" (310). "What we used to call business cycles – or a least booms and recessions – are now to be interpreted as optimal blips in optimal paths in response to random fluctuations in productivity and the desire for leisure" (310). "I find none of this convincing" (311). "The markets for goods and labor look to me like imperfect pieces of social machinery with important institutional peculiarities. They do not seem to behave at all like transparent and frictionless mechanisms for converting the consumption and leisure desires of households into production and employment decision. I cannot imagine shocks to taste and technology large enough on a quarterly or annual time scale to be responsible for the ups and downs of the business cycle" (311). "Historical time-series do not provide a critical experiment." "To believe . . . that empirical economics begins and ends with time-series analysis, is to ignore a lot of valuable information that cannot be put into so convenient a form. I include the sort of information that is encapsulated in the qualitative inferences made by expert observers, as well as direct knowledge of the functioning of economic institutions" (311). Many econometric models use the number of patents as the dependent variable, but while suggestive, this has obvious difficulties in accounting for the significance of different patents. Cross-sectional regressions of country growth rates on a number of variables run into problems of simultaneity, multicollinearity, and limited degrees of freedom, leading Mankiw (1995: 308) to conclude, "Basic theory, shrewd observation, and common sense are surely more reliable guides to policy."

Solow's and Mankiw's points make a case for pluralism in methods used to study technology and institutions. There is something to be learned from logical mathematical models, econometrics, and case studies.

10.4 Concluding Observations

There is much more to technological change, improved capital goods, and economic growth than interest, profit, and savings rates. When better understood, our heroes may switch from passive savers, The World Bank, and the central bank chair to inventive organizations, the Office of Technology Assessment, and the science advisor to the President. William Baumol (2002) celebrates product innovation resulting from competition among firms struggling for market share. But, there is more to technological change than private competition. There is also public investment in basic and applied research and its extension and dissemination. The technology that counts is that which is adopted and not just in laboratory notebooks. There are also strategic public decisions on how the cost and benefits of technological change are distributed.

Technology is not a variable in a production function in addition to capital goods. Rather, technological change results in different capital goods. Similarly, formal and informal institutions that facilitate technological change and the coordinated use of capital goods are not a separate argument in a production function, but condition what the production function contains. Patent policy is not a simple matter of rights stimulating research. The details impact the research agenda and distribution of its benefits. Creative destruction, yes, but it is institutions that influence what gets created and who gets the benefits and bears the costs. Exclusion cost (appropriability), economies of scale, transaction costs, and uncertainty are among the inherent situation variables relevant to understanding the impact of alternative institutions and both technological and institutional change.

There is nothing in a technology that dictates institutions or who benefits from a given technology. There are alternative paths of institutional response. No technology dictates that it must be adopted or that its benefits and costs must fall in a particular manner. With respect to patent policy, it is impossible to set years of protection and scope to achieve an optimum rate of research and development investment in all kinds of innovations with different costs. If some people care about one industry or another, there is a conflict over policy that sorts out the various interdependencies.

NOTE

1. Once a threshold of adoption is crossed, the effects are unavoidable even by those who abstain from adoption.

Chapter 11
Labor Institutions

I want to make the case that the labor market is really different.

Robert Solow

Low wages are by no means identical with cheap labour.

Joseph Stiglitz

Work is part of the creation of persons.

Folbre and Nelson

Labor is not a commodity like a sack of potatoes or a machine tool. It comes with an attitude. This and other characteristics of labor (situation) will be enumerated. Then alternative structures for relating labor to owners of other factors of production and alternative methods of compensation will be explored. These include the putting out system, cooperative, and capitalist among others. The performance impacts of alternative institutions of collective bargaining are compared. This is followed by how institutions affect the business cycle and unemployment (see also chapter 9 on institutions of the macroeconomy). Finally, issues of discrimination and gender are analyzed.

11.1 Characteristics of Labor

11.1.1 Information cost and moral hazard

In some kinds of work, it is easy to relate output to an individual laborer. For example, it is easy to measure the bushels of apples picked by an individual. In other cases, it is costly or impossible to determine the separate contribution of each worker in a team. It is difficult to measure the contribution to firm profits of another person in advertising, marketing, research and development. The standard theory suggestion that another worker of a given quality be added until the marginal value product (MVP) equals the wage rate is not so easy to implement.

Labor and capital are substitutes only to a degree. A machine can replace the work formerly done by many workers. But, for a given technology, the labor:machine ratio is given in the technology. One tractor needs one tractor driver. One workstation needs one worker. Labor is often a complement in production rather than a substitute. A complement has no identifiable marginal physical product. The employee who services the furnace is necessary for the other employees to work in a cold climate, but the whole output of the factory is not due to the furnace worker. This means that some other decision rules must prevail where MVP = wage cannot be implemented.

Human capital theory has called attention to how potential output is affected by the skills of labor. An educated person is a different input to production than a person who cannot read. But achieving that potential is a different matter still. It is not enough to assume that the threat of being fired is sufficient to motivate the potential existing in a person. The employer must be able to fire for performance below that contracted, assuming that the task can be workably described in advance. The employer must be able to cheaply monitor output and attribute it to individuals. Agreements tying wages to productivity "have the limitation that the individual's productivity is not easily isolated and measured in the context of modern industry, including many service industries" (Solow 1990). Moral hazard is defined as post-contract opportunism that arises when the actions desired of the employee by the employer are not freely observable.

Incentive or rational choice theory provides some guidelines as to design of contracts to combat moral hazard in an economizing framework (Macho-Stadler and Pérez-Castrillo 1997). The theory assumes that the employer knows exactly what is wanted of the employee and knows the workers' preferences for leisure. Thus, the employer can put herself in the worker's place. One example of problems that arise is if there are variables that affect output other than worker effort. If remuneration is tied to output, a risk-averse worker will not accept the contract. On the other hand, a fixed wage provides no motivation for best effort. "To solve this 'incentive vs. insurance' dilemma, the optimal payment scheme combines a fixed base pay and a variable bonus indexed on the observed result; yielding a nonlinear payment scheme" (Brousseau and Glachant 2002). Also see Laffont and Martimort (2002).

A field experiment found that while some workers opportunism responded to the level of monitoring, others did not (Nagin et al. 2002). The authors "suggest that management's perceived empathy and fairness in dealing with employees may play an important role in reducing workplace opportunism" (870). Rational choice models must be supplemented by those containing variables for social capital (empathy) and the learning of cultural norms.

Efficiency wage theory was developed to describe the phenomenon of some workers being paid more in some firms than the average for that occupation (more than the market clearing wage) (Yellen 1984; Milgrom and Roberts 1992: 252). Micro theory expects workers to be paid no more than their marginal value product, but this is a multiple equilibrium if the wage affects productivity. The efficiency wage is an incentive to work to the fullest of the worker's capacity. While the worker cannot be monitored continuously, if the occasional measure shows a shortfall and the worker is discharged, she could only earn the going wage for average work. The efficiency wage theory assumes people are always calculating and does not depend on learned norms.

The problem of determining if a borrower will make every effort to repay a loan is another case of moral hazard. The lower cost of information to local moneylenders in poor countries creates local monopolies and high interest rates.

11.1.2 Information cost and adverse selection

Adverse selection occurs when there is pre-contract opportunism that arises when the employee knows her competence (private information), but the employer only knows the average competence of members of some characteristic pool. Predicting the quality of a worker at the time of hiring is often costly to determine (see table 11.2 below, lines 3 and 7). Incentive theory deduces "The solution to adverse selection problems relies on the design of a 'menu of contracts' that will induce self-revelation by the agent of her private information" (Brousseau and Glachant 2002). The employer infers the employee's private information by her choice of contract.

The initiative may be taken by highly motivated prospective workers who don't want to be paid the average wage by signaling their greater than average competence by attaining some costly characteristic that lower competence workers are unwilling to attain (Spence 1973). Higher levels of education may signal general competence even if the specific skills learned are irrelevant to the job.

11.1.3 Fairness

The marginal value product of labor is often dependent on whether the worker feels that wages and other work conditions are fair. "Each individual has not just one marginal product, but many potential marginal products, depending on his motivation" (Thurow 1983: 202). If the potential in a particular human capital is not automatically forthcoming and not easily motivated by threat of dismissal or pay reduction, it means that decisions of workers affect their output. Solow (1990: 3) argues that the labor market "cannot be understood without taking account of the fact that the participants, on both sides, have well-developed notions of what is fair and what is not." People who think they are being fairly treated are more likely to work to their potential when they have a choice. "Wage rates may affect the intensity and thus the productivity of labor" (212–13). When notions of fairness are violated, there is more turnover and low morale. Labor economists have observed that workers come to regard the relative wages in different occupations as normal and expected. When these "wage contours" are violated, it is often the cause of labor unrest.

The role of fairness is also suggested by Stiglitz (1987: 22). "A worker who believes he is being treated more than fairly may not only get more job satisfaction from his job, but also may put out more for his employer." He adds further, "we can postulate that an individual's efforts depend not only on his own wage, but on the wage of others in his reference group. . . ." (See table 11.2 below, line 5.)

Fairness is related to the phenomenon that workers often differ in terms of productivity, but nevertheless are paid the same. One such case involved workers who posted accounts paid (Homans 1954). This is a task where it would be possible to pay by the piece, but this was not done. There was a standard of 300 postings per hour. Some workers greatly exceeded it. Why would they continue to perform over the standard for the same pay as their slower colleagues barely meeting the standard? Akerlof (1986: 145) reasoned, "workers acquire sentiment for each other and also for the firm." This sentiment is social capital benefiting slower workers. Akerof argued that the fast workers made a gift of their extra capacity in return for seeing that their colleagues are not dismissed and are paid perhaps more than their productivity would warrant. He cites reasons given for performance above standards in the army. Soldiers would report that one cannot work alongside others who are doing their best and see them penalized. Thus if the firm treats all workers fairly, the highcapacity workers are content. The firm is content because if it raised the standard and fired the slow workers, it would no longer receive a gift from the fast workers. The labor market may not clear.

Consumers also make judgments on the fair treatment of labor. A survey reveals that people do not think employers should take advantage of labor surpluses by lowering prevailing wages (Kahneman, Knetsch, and Thaler 1986). Market clearing is not acceptable to many who are willing to punish firms that do it.

11.2 Capital–Labor Relationships

11.2.1 Ownership of means of production

Who owns the machines and raw materials, labor or capitalists? What are the consequences of alternative degrees of hierarchy between workers and owners of capital goods? Out of many institutional alternatives, only three will be contrasted here to illustrate useful conceptual tools. These include putting-out federated, collective, and capitalist.

In the *putting-out system*, a merchant coordinator owns the materials and the work in progress. The coordinator contracts with workers each of who may produce a final product using their own tools or tools provided by the coordinator. An example was the assembly of sewing machines by farmers in Japan. It took advantage of the availability of seasonal labor. A modern example is the putting out of software writing jobs. The work may be done in India for American computer firms and returned to the American firm electronically. These examples both involve finished products that can be paid for on a piecework basis. One involves raw materials (or parts) furnished by the coordinator and the other does not. Williamson argues that if each worker station is physically separated, there is a problem of excess inventory if each worker chooses his/her own pace (Williamson 1985: 223–32). Marglin (1974) on the other hand, points out the importance of the ability of each worker to choose their own pace and the ability to do other tasks such as care of children. People are produced by an economy as well as widgets (Lane 1991; Sturgeon 1992; Folbre and Nelson 2000; Frey 1997). Efficiency, as always, depends on the definition of the relevant input and output categories. Marshall (1873: 115) insisted, "Work, in its best sense, the healthy exercise of faculties, is the aim of life, is life itself." Since people are both consumers and producers, why do we always speak of consumer sovereignty as a performance goal and seldom of worker sovereignty?

Williamson hypothesizes that there will be a problem with theft since monitoring will be costly at dispersed sites. Less so if federated workstations are at one site. Williamson assumes opportunism with gall and expects quality to be shaded if supervision and measurement are costly. But, this depends on internalized attitudes and cultural norms. We should remember that employees at one site can still steal. US stores suffer more losses from theft by employees than from customers.

Collectives or *worker cooperatives* are another alternative way to relate workers and capital goods. Workers may own the capital goods and hire managers. An example is the plywood cooperatives of the Pacific Northwest. Most workers are members and virtually all members are workers. Workers are semi-skilled and all are paid the same wage. Stock is owned mostly by active workers who can sell to the cooperative when they retire. Profits are returned in wages and seldom in dividends. A comparison of eight co-ops and 27 conventional corporations was made by Pencavel and Craig (1994). The first worker cooperative was established in 1921 and the study covered the late 1960s to mid 1980s. Following the suggestion of this book, the authors did not include institutions in their regression equation. Rather, they estimated separate equations for each ownership form and reasoned that the difference was due to the different institutions. The impact of alternative ownership forms interacting with different sources of interdependence is summarized in table 11.1.

Key performance indicators (and dependent variables) were employment and wages. Hourly earnings = f (output prices, input prices). They found that a 1 percent increase in the price of output induces a 1 percent change in real hourly wages in the co-op mills. But there was little correlation between wages and product prices for conventional firms. When the dependent variable is employment it was found that there was no association between movements in output prices and employment and annual hours per worker for co-ops. But for conventional firms, a 1 percent increase in output prices is associated with a 1 percent increase in man-hours (some in hours per worker and some in the number of workers).

Cooperative firms adjust to changes in prices by adjusting pay while conventional firms adjust employment. Worker-owned firms share the costs and benefits of demand fluctuations rather than let workers find other or no jobs elsewhere. In addition to the interdependence created by the incompatible use good of new income, there is an interdependence created by high information costs. Some hypothesize that worker-owners will not discipline themselves, treating the net profit as a high exclusion cost good. Workers have the opportunity to slack and still get the product of others' work. But in fact, Pencavel and Craig observed that MVP, output per hour, was higher for co-ops in the 1950s and 60s, but lower from 1972–80. The co-ops also spent less on supervision.

The literature notes that different forms of ownership change the maximand for the firm. It may also simply change the distribution of whatever is maximized. One theory has it that labor (any factor) is paid its MVP. If MVP is falling as more labor is hired (even of similar quality), this means that the product of the intra-marginal

Table 11.1 Worker cooperatives and conventional corporations

	Who hires whom? Factor Ownership. Who owns residual profit?	Over the business cycle –
Good = labor = labor's product. Business cycles. IUG	1. Worker owned co-op 2. Conventional corp.	1. Adjust wages. Spread available returns. Maximize net revenues per person hour. Capture employer surplus. 2. Adjust employment. Max. profits. (Both structures adjust inputs and outputs to demand and both survive.)
HIC. Hard to monitor output in some cases, especially for knowledge workers	Who makes decisions on adoption of technology, response to business cycle, and day-to-day routines. 1. Worker owned co-op 2. Conventional corp.	1. Workers feel in control of their environment. Quarrels among workers? Less opportunism, higher MVP and output per hour 1950s and 60s, but lower 1972–80. 2. High supervision costs.
Asset *specificity* in human capital and houses.	1. Worker owned co-op 2. Conventional corp.	1. Protection of housing asset values. 2. Asset losses if have to sell and move because of layoffs.

Based on Pencavel and Craig (1994)

workers accrues to the capital owners as a kind of employer surplus (Schmid 1987: 136). A worker cooperative would share the average product among the workers. If MVP is increasing, then the marginal worker cannot be paid its MVP because total costs would be greater than total returns. The relative wages (wage contours) are a matter of firm and industry custom. (See table 11.2, line 6.) Where economies of scale prevent equilibrium, standard operating procedures and norms emerge from evolutionary processes.

Efficiency is always a matter of whose costs count. The capitalist firm can save labor costs by dismissing workers during recessions. But the workers still have to live and their sustenance is a cost to the society. It is easy for capitalists to fire workers and then complain about paying taxes to provide welfare for the unemployed. The plywood cooperatives seem to share the available wealth among members during recessions rather sending the redundant out to fend for themselves and depend on others. Note that employees of a small city in Michigan agreed to all take a pay cut during a recession rather than have some laid off with no prospect for income.

Milgrom and Roberts (1992) argue that the representatives of physical capital owners should boss labor because (1) capital is more at risk than human capital and (2) capital has the longer planning horizon and therefore can invest in reputation to facilitate future dealings. "Both the decision power and the ownership of the rents should attach to those who can most easily and effectively transfer their claims at full value. In most contexts, this would seem to be the investors in the firm, whose claims take the form of marketable securities, rather than, say, laborers who would need to sell their jobs to transfer their claims. This is another reason why the boss as the person with the power to make decisions in unforeseen eventualities should very often be the representative of the providers of physical capital, rather than the providers of labor" (332).

Is it true that physical capital is less mobile and more at risk? Some machines can be moved. The semi-skilled workers may or not be able to find comparable jobs somewhere, and less likely in their locality. If they work for a major employer in an area and have to move, they may have to sell their houses at a loss, and in any case their family activities are disrupted. In Europe, workers are not very geographically mobile. Who has the longer planning horizon? Capital owners seem able and willing to move quickly in response to changes in demand and costs, often leaving less mobile workers behind. In practice, the stock values do appreciate, but not as much as if the profits were paid as dividends rather than wages. The co-ops do not apparently have any great trouble buying the stock of a departing worker and eventually reselling to new employees after they have proven themselves. Why should bosses make the decisions in unforeseen circumstances that may affect workers a great deal? Other performance variables might have been compared. Being in control of one's destiny may contribute to workers physical and mental health, family stability, training costs, and theft and down time.

The plywood study shows the complementarity between theory of the firm and institutional theory. The equations control for the usual items expected to affect wages and employment, namely, prices of inputs and outputs. Any remaining difference is arguably due to institutional differences. Would a co-op produce the same impact in another plywood firm? That depends on whether the analysts have fully

Table 11.2 Summary of interdependencies in labor markets

Situation	Structure	Performance
1. Keynes – rigid wages assumed as inherent fact over the business cycle.	a. Market. b. Market plus government control of aggregate demand.	a. Unemployment equilibrium. No self-correction. b. Full employment.
2. Assume labor is ordinary separable *incompatible use good* with productivity known and fixed.	a. Market competition. Auction market. b. Market with unions	a. Rigid wage (but usual theory predicts flexible wage, so situation poorly specified). b. Rigid wage.
3. The production function – Different kinds of labor are complements with no individual MP. *HIC.* Individual MVP unknown and variable.	a. Market with norm and SOP_1. Wage contours b. Market with SOP_2. Team incentives. c. Worker owned, SOP_3. d. Sex discrimination allowed or not. e. Comparable worth. f. Contract incentives.	a. Distribution X among team members. Relative wages across job classifications. b. Distribution Y. c. Distribution Z. d. Ratio of female to male wages. e. Nurses paid as much as janitors. f. Degree of adverse selection.
4. Skills endogenously learned. $MC = 0$ when skill transference is joint with product manufacture.	a. Market with seniority rights. Combined with flexible wages (bonus) over the business cycle *à la* Japan. Loyalty b. Market competition with flexible wages.	a. Learning occurs. Training costs low. Productivity. b. Less learning, higher training costs.

5. Interdependent preferences. Productivity variable and embedded in human mind. Fairness affects productivity. People care about relative wages. Quality of labor is *HIC*.	a. Wage flexibility. b. Rigid wage. Social capital – workers sympathetic to other workers.	a. Lowers marginal product of existing workers. Less on-job training. b. Productivity enhanced. New hires are of average quality.
6. *Economies of scale.* How relate to production function above? Can't pay a wage to all = MVP.	What rights (standard operating procedures) control this interdependence? Customary wage contours evolve.	Allocation of surplus among workers in different job classifications.
7. Inherently lazy or instinct of workmanship? Labor as a consumption good.	a. Status *vs.* incentives, piece-work, etc. b. Worker co-op. Industrial democracy	Supervision and training cost. Degree of alienation.
8. MVP of different workers is *HIC*. Business cycle: unemployed offers to work for less but employer not sure MVP = offered wage.	a. Employer accepts offer of unemployed worker. b. Employer rejects.	a. Flexible wage, but employer makes mistake. b. Sticky wages.

described the institution. There are always details to be worried about such as informal institutions embedded in the workers. This external validity problem is present whether one does a case study or an econometric analysis. The same questions also arise if one were to project this experience into another industry.

African traditional land tenure is marked by communal land ownership, individual capital goods ownership, and individual claim to harvest on land that the individual farms, even when some tasks are done by a group. To a limited extent, the rights of an individual family to work a particular area of land can be redistributed to accommodate new families, in practice the families farm the same land year after year and pass these rights on to family members. African traditional tenures have been widely criticized because land cannot be pledged by individuals as security for loans even in cases where the expected returns could support loan repayment. Still, in the context of frequent drought, loan terms that cannot accommodate years of non-performance are a recipe for loss of land ownership by the traditional workers.

Where farmers own their own land, they tend to hire capital and are owner-operators. This is the dominant form of farm structure around the world (Hayami and Otsuka 1993). Where they do not own land, farmers sometimes lease land and own capital goods, or are hired by a landowner who provides the machines. Land reform is a basic power struggle over who owns land, an IUG.

Corporate ownership of the means of production puts the representatives of the capital owners as the central contractor with labor and other inputs. Depending on the production process, the contract is necessarily incomplete and the details are continuously worked out within the specified "zone of acceptance." Williamson argues that over all considerations the corporate centralized authority is most efficient. "There may more or less preferred types of hierarchy; but hierarchy itself is unavoidable unless efficiency sacrifices are made" (Williamson 1985: 231). With more hierarchy, he expects to find employees "less given to aggressive subgoal pursuit and do not resist adaptations because they do not possess the requisite property rights" (228). They may not possess them, but they would like to, as witness unions' struggles to control adaptations that threaten jobs. Labor is agreeable to technological change if they can gain from the innovations and all does not go to stockholders. Distribution is not separable from economic growth. And, the problem with defining all labor and capital disputes as sub-goal pursuit (principally leisure) is that in complex production, the center can't know fully what goal to pursue without input from employees. Different employees and departments have different perspectives on how the firm's profits might be maximized. The problem is not necessarily shirking, but in knowing how to implement the agreed-upon goal.

Williamson asks if changes in the organization of work are best explained by seeking efficiency or power. He uses as a case study the organization of steel making in the late nineteenth century. Workers were represented by the Amalgamated Association of Iron, Steel, and Tin Workers. The union achieved practices that discouraged labor saving innovations (Stone 1974). After Carnegie and Frick broke a strike with the help of the state, there were many labor saving innovations. Williamson says this is evidence that efficiency was at work, not the use of raw power (1985: 236).

And besides, steel consumers gained cheaper steel, even if Carnegie and Frick became rich. But, where is the evidence that workers oppose innovation when they are given a share of the resulting cost saving rather than being tossed out to fend for themselves. Does labor oppose innovations in Germany where they are by law equally represented on corporate boards?[1] Does labor oppose innovations in Japan where it traditionally was assured of lifetime employment? Are workers just irrational Luddites? The contest for control of the surpluses of innovation is a matter of power distribution that affects the path of technological implementation.

Technological and organizational change reduces the value of specific human capital. Neoclassical theory largely ignores this on the assumption of zero transaction costs – the assets will automatically be reallocated with only a marginal loss of income. Even casual observation indicates that many workers get left behind. It is easier for large firms to innovate to find new products that their redundant workers might make than for individuals to do so. Because of laws of codetermination, the managers of large German firms have the incentive to find ways to use existing employees rather than casting them out to be a cost of society at large. The cost of labor reallocation can either be included as part of the cost of labor or in taxes.

The US corporation is a kind of collective, though it excludes workers. Following Max Weber, the modern corporation is a bureaucracy in which the "official works entirely separated from ownership of the means of administration" and is "selected on the basis of technical qualifications," as quoted in Pena (2001: xii). The stockholders are owners in common and have a contingent claim on profits depending on the choices of self-perpetuating boards of directors. Ownership is separated from management (Berle 1959).

11.2.2 Ownership of borrowing leverage of the firm

Who owns the returns to the capital leverage of a firm? Only the present stockholders or also the general employees? This question was raised by Kelso and Hetter (1967) who suggested a "Binary Stock Purchase" by workers. Also see Ashford and Shakespeare (1999). The ability of the corporation to repay a loan depends in part on the contribution of labor, though they are not now given any rights in the returns to the resulting investments. Instead of the banks loaning all the money for a new project directly to the corporation, some portion of it could be loaned to a workers trust that in turn passes it on to the corporation in return for stock. Dividends paid on this stock could repay the loan.[2] If the Federal Reserve can require a bank to have quality collateral for a loan, it can surely allow loans to individual workers based on corporate collateral. Ownership of the borrowing capacity of a corporation is made effective when banks respond to loan requests and assertions of collateral. A bank need not honor the assertion that the repayment capacity of a going concern is wholly owned by existing stockholders (Schmid 1984). (A bank would not make a loan on a house without asking who are all the owners.) Reform of ownership of the borrowing leverage of the corporation is an incompatible use power issue equivalent to those involved in land reform.

11.2.3 Labor institutions under capitalism

Given that some of the power issues have been settled when capitalists own the means of production, there are still many institutions affecting the rights of workers. These include: private choices of how labor is paid, and public policy on the structure of industry.

As a matter of firm policy, some employers have profit sharing plans while others do not. Is this a matter of informal or formal institutions or just maximizing calculation? Profit sharing creates an incentive for workers to act consistent with firm goals, but where the work of individuals can't be distinguished, a worker may gain the most by shirking and still claiming a share of others' contribution to firm profits. This is constrained by social pressure inside the group. Note that profit sharing may be as little as 1 percent of total employee compensation in the US and averages 25 percent in Japan (Milgrom and Roberts 1992: 413). This seems more a matter of informal institutions (custom) than any fundamental differences in kinds of industry or human capital specificity. Profit sharing seems more common in executive compensation than workers'. This also seems to be an informal institution and custom. (If it is impossible to attribute profitability (MVP) to specific individuals and functions in the firm, then assume that it is the product of a few people at the top!) See table 11.2, line 3.

Thousands of US corporations have instituted Employee Stock Ownership Plans (ESOPs) as part of the pensions offered employees (Scholes and Wolfson 1991). This makes employees part owners and provides some incentive for good performance, though with the commons problem noted above. ESOP popularity may also be due to favorable tax treatment written into law by the populist Senator Russell Long with the ideas of Louis Kelso.

Hodgson (1999b) argues that an alternative non-capitalist economy is possible. While retaining market processes and private ownership, it would de-emphasize the employment contract and put trust and commitment in its place. His vision of the knowledge economy places reliance on "the corporate culture and on the socialization process within the workplace. By and large, the workers manage the production processes themselves" (212). A part of this is what some refer to as self-directed teams (Leholm and Vlasin 2004).

Quite different systems of labor institutions can be seen in different wealthy countries. The US, Germany, France, and Japan differ in their relative emphasis on industrial vs. enterprise unions, where training is received and the degree of certification, role of credentials (role of educational organizations) in controlling labor supply, job security, and the flexibility given management to control work content. This results in different performance such as the annual days of labor lost from strikes in Japan is a fraction of that in the US (Gibney 1991). Worker loyalty and identity with the firm is greater in Japan and Germany than the US. Fligstein (2001: 103) observes strong path dependence in national labor systems that started different and remain different. He argues that only a crisis can cause substantial change. The German and Japanese systems, as well as many with strong job security, today are under considerable pressure from global competition.

11.3 Collective Bargaining

The right to bargain collectively was a major struggle in the US often marked by violence. In the 1880s courts regarded collective action as injurious to the employer's property and issued injunctions. Early union organizers were subject to dismissal and many workers were only offered "Yellow Dog" contracts that made them subject to dismissal if they joined. When these practices were outlawed by the 1935 Wagner Act, it was a power issue. Performance measured as change in union membership increased dramatically (Reynolds, Masters, and Moser 1998). Some analysts, however, argue that unions are just the result of negotiation and mutual gains from trade. Williamson (1985) says power is an ambiguous concept and instead offers the hypothesis that "the incentive to organize production workers within a collective governance structure increases with the degree of human asset specificity" (256). Williamson argues that in some cases unions are created by mutual agreement for efficiency reasons. If workers will not invest in firm specific human capital without job security, it is in the interests of both employer and employees to have a union or other means of security. So for example, he predicts that unions will be found in railroads where skills are specific and not in migrant farm labor where skills are less specific. Skilled or not, people want job security and decent pay and working conditions. Skilled or not, there are unambiguous costs to finding new jobs that may be greater than employers' cost of finding new workers. Migrant workers have higher cost of organizing workers in open fields as opposed to picketing a plant gate. The human capital of Pullman porters is not specific to railroads, but they were organized long before farm workers who are not covered by the National Labor Relations Act.

It is tempting to move from prediction to prescription. An example is the following: if non-firm specific workers organize it must be for power and monopoly reasons and not for efficiency. Industrial unions typically represent low-skill workers. Williamson (1985) opines that their existence depended primarily on the political process (The Wagner Act) because "they evidently lacked natural advantages of either contrived scarcity or efficiency kinds" (254). This reference to what is natural is an argument that nature (the character of specific assets) contains its own policy conclusions and any political contradiction is perilous for the public good. (Is there anything in nature that says that some portion of the plentiful supply of low-skilled workers can't receive more than subsistence wages just because there is a never ending supply of workers with poor alternatives?)

Part of labor's opportunity to get more than what the marginal worker will accept (part of the employer surplus, for example) depends on exclusionary power. The picket line is a substitute controller. Picketing is disagreeable activity. Many would like to benefit from higher wages without the cost of picket participation. It would be physically possible to give only union members and participants the negotiated wage, but it would violate most people's sense of fairness. So, in practice, the negotiated wage is a high exclusion cost good. If union members could not prevent free riders, they would have to rely wholly on social pressure for union contributions. If unions are allowed by law to negotiate for a union shop, then all employees must pay dues whether they are members or not. The union shop gives opportunity to those who want higher wages and are willing to bear picket and other costs. This opportunity is necessarily at the cost of unwilling riders who don't agree with union goals and tactics (or at least that is what they say if they deny being strategic free-riders). States that ban the union shop are often called "right to work" states. The "right to work" and not pay union dues is other workers' no-right to higher wages (right to work for poor wages). Employers and workers willing to work for marginal wages are allies. Unions would prefer to have closed shops where workers must belong to the union to work. This is prohibited by the Taft-Hartley Act.

What rights do workers have in their jobs? The National Labor Relations Act as interpreted by the Supreme Court allows an employer to hire permanent strike-breakers, which is attractive if costs of recruitment and training are reasonable (or the employer wants to strategically teach labor a lesson). The court has also ruled that strikers are entitled to preferential hiring if new vacancies become available. The Taft-Hartley Act of 1947 provides for temporary suspension of the right to strike if the President declares a national emergency. In some industries such as dockworkers and nursing, the effect of strikes on third parties is substantial. The fact that long-shoremen earn much more than nurses is related to differential willingness to exploit third party effects. All of these rights affect what the parties have to bargain with and the resulting performance. The starting place details determine what opportunities each party has at its disposal to get the agreement of the other party to a market transaction.

11.4 Worker Safety, Health, and Hours

Institutions affecting worker safety take many forms. Can a worker's body be exposed to danger? Use of that body to produce goods in a dangerous environment may mean that the worker does not fully own their incompatible-use body. If workers have no rights to a safe workplace, they can bargain individually. If enough refuse to work in a particular environment, employers will have to alter the environment or pay higher wages. The workers may also have the right to bargain collectively for workplace conditions. The shop steward may negotiate with the foreman on a daily basis. Workers in the US once turned to the common law courts and claimed negligence if harmed, but with little satisfaction. The court selected some standard of common practice and assessed damages or issued an injunction accordingly. The basis for the damages provides an incentive for the employer to maintain or alter workplace conditions. Compensation for injury was removed from the adversarial proceedings of courts by Worker Compensation laws. Medical costs and lost wages due to accidents were covered by a required insurance fund. John R. Commons invented the idea that if the insurance premium were proportional to the accident rate of a firm, it would have an economizing incentive to provide a safe workplace (balancing premium and accident prevention costs) (Harter 1962). The US Occupational Safety and Health Administration (OSHA) has the power to require specific workplace conditions (whether or not the workers have the bargaining power to negotiate them). Its rulings are subject to judicial review and influence through Congressional funding.

Safety in the workplace is sometimes a high information cost good. Workers cannot bargain intelligently when the extent of hazards are unknown. The Occupational Safety and Health Act of 1970 requires employers to inform employees of chemical hazards. This addresses the information asymmetry.

The workweek and extra pay for extra hours could be the subject of firm-by-firm collective bargaining. The Fair Labor Standards Act established a normal 40-hour workweek and requires a time-and-a-half payment for overtime. This is the result of collective action in securing national legislation. One performance consequence of a national standard is that no firm is at a competitive disadvantage if they offer a more generous compensation.

Employer-provided health insurance is common in union contracts, but many non-union workers are not covered. In Europe, with state health care, this is not a concern. The US is debating requiring all employers to provide some minimal health insurance, even if the worker cannot bargain effectively for it.

The outcome of the wage bargain for a particular work setting is a function of the rights of worker and employer. The right made effective by collective bargaining, court proceeding, statute, or regulatory commission is no more or less coercive. After the starting place rights are set, the parties can bargain to Pareto-better outcomes.

11.5 Wages, Unemployment, and the Business Cycle

It is an empirical fact that high levels of unemployment persist for considerable periods of time without self-correction (table 11.2, line 1). This fact is not compatible with the theory of market equilibrium (line 2). That story has it that firms would find that the MVP of labor drops in a recession and the derived demand curve for labor shifts to the left making intersection with the supply curve at a lower wage. Why do firms not generally offer lower wages and why do even out of work laborers not offer to work for less than recently observed wage standards? Do workers go through cycles of changing preference for leisure and thus are not really unemployed but voluntarily idle? Solow (1990: 29) says, "I do not find this account believable." Rather, he observes that both employers and workers have learned ideas of what constitutes fair wages. Employers hesitate to offer less and unemployed workers hesitate to offer to work for what is considered an unfair wage. "Wage rates and jobs are not exactly like other prices and quantities. They are much more deeply involved in the way people see themselves, think about their social status, and evaluate whether they are getting a fair shake out of society" (22). Solow suggests that workers may have rational reasons for rejecting lower wages if they understand that they are caught in a Prisoner's Dilemma and choose to play tit-for-tat (don't defect if others do not defect from the wage standard) because while you might be better off today, tomorrow all are subject to a low reservation wage. While he provides a calculated answer to the disequilibrium puzzle, he believes that norms play a pivotal role. "We do things because they are the right thing to do, not because we have reckoned all the consequences" (43). He further says, "I do not know how such norms get established, historically speaking, but once established they draw their force from shared values and social approbation and disapprobation, not from calculation" (49). (See table 11.2, line 3.)

There are high information costs to determine worker productivity at the time of hiring. In many cases, this means that the employer will only obtain the average productivity of labor when hiring. Stiglitz (1987: 3) then reasons that the price that a worker will accept is a quality signal. The employer has to ask why this person will accept less than the going wage. So if an unemployed worker offers to work for less, the suspicious employer may ignore it. Thurow offers an additional reason why low offers may be rejected. Much human capital is acquired on the job. If present workers regard the new worker as a threat to their job and present wage, they will not volunteer to give any on-the-job training to others. For these reasons, Thurow (1983: 212) argues that "long run fixed wages are more efficient than flexible wages." In summary, cheap labor is not a good bargain. And, "When quality depends on price, market equilibrium *may* be characterized by demand not equaling supply" (Stiglitz 1987: 4). Neither the employer nor the unemployed are interested in its equalization. These variables are summarized in table 11.2, lines 4, 5, and 8. Thurow (1983: 212) emphasizes the following situation variables:

1. Human capital is endogenous (learned in part on the job).
2. Predicting productivity of potential workers is high information cost.
3. Job satisfaction and marginal value product are conditioned by interdependent preferences and sense of fairness.

When these situations are combined with the privately chosen structures of rigid wages, a different performance is forthcoming than if combined with flexible wages. The custom of relatively rigid wages prevails without formal institutions or union power. Interviews with 336 employers revealed that "Asking directly about the choice between layoffs and pay cuts risked alienating managers, for most did not think of the two as alternatives. A common reaction to the question was puzzlement. Pay cuts would create little or no extra work and so would barely reduce the number of excess workers" (Bewley 1999: 181).

The US has a system of unemployment insurance financed by payroll taxes. Benefit amounts and duration vary from state to state as long as Federal guidelines are followed. This is in contrast to many European countries that have uniform nationally financed unemployment benefits.

If there is anyplace where economists are confident of their market equilibrium model, it is with respect to price controls that raise prices above equilibrium levels. A case in point is the minimum wage. Many are so confident of their deductive logic that no empirical investigation is thought necessary to show that a minimum wage would cause a decrease in employment. Nevertheless, Card and Krueger (1995) examined the experience of employment response to increases in the minimum wage in New Jersey and California. They found no evidence of job loss. No evaluation is perfect and those who are committed to equilibrium theory found much to object to. Probably, if it had confirmed the theory, the data would have been found acceptable even if not perfect. Is it possible that higher wages in large labor markets provide the effective demand for some products of labor? This is possible if workers as consumers are not homogeneous. Some economists are beginning to argue that low wages are a brake on economic development because the earners have no income to buy new output. Many cities in the US have not heeded mainstream economists' advice and have passed minimum wage laws for firms supplying city government.

The United States has been following a low wage policy in contrast to countries like Germany, Ireland, Japan, and Sweden (Commission on the Skills of the American Workforce 1990). The US has no national labor market system and its Federal training programs are fragmented. There is a poor transition from school to work and little training for front-line workers to develop thinking skills as opposed to being machine servers. Reliance has been placed on individual choices by workers rather than more collective and participatory labor policies that would increase the amount spent on continuous training and certification. Marshall (1996) is persuaded that "high performance systems work best when workers have an independent source of power" to participate in decisions that affect them. Industrial democracy can contribute to material and human growth (Melman 2001). (See table 11.2, line 7.)

11.6 Discrimination

Discrimination is a fundamental characteristic of the way the brain works. We use selected features from many possible features to distinguish one thing from another and categorize. Boulding (1976) observes that, "Our impressions and judgments about the world are inevitably derived from cues, all of which are more or less misleading." Humans generalize complex situations into simple categories to which action is attached. This ability to leap to action from a cue is both our strength and weakness. As Boulding puts it, "in the case of highly complex realities, where ignorance, if not bliss, is at least kept cheap." When applied to the assessment of persons who are indeed complex, this saving of scarce information processing capacity results in some serious errors that we call prejudice, whether based on race, gender, or funny looks. It takes some very conscious learning and collective action to counteract.

Discrimination against workers on the basis of gender or race is theoretically impossible in competitive markets. The theory of market equilibrium deduces that any employer that discriminated would have higher costs and lower profits and would thus fail (Becker 1957). But the deduction does not track with empirical observation. Bergmann (1989) finds that there are substantial and persistent differences in pay by gender holding other factors constant. Widely held cultural norms and perceptions must be accounted for (Bergmann 1995). If most employers and their employees believe female labor as inferior, discrimination can persist.

A major increase in labor force participation by women occurred during World War II when labor for defense work was scarce. Many of these women wanted to continue after the war, but most were dismissed. Ideology of women's roles continued to change and a feminist movement exerted political pressure for legislation. The Civil Rights Act of 1964 prohibited earmarking of jobs for one sex or the other. The Equal Pay Act of 1963 required equal pay for the same job. This resulted in a narrowing of the US gender pay gap. This narrowing decelerated in the 1990s (Blau and Kuhn 2000).

While the gender gap for the same kinds of jobs has narrowed, many women are stuck in traditionally female occupations that are low paid even when the work is skilled and seems of great value. For example, a college graduate nurse may receive the same income as a janitor with only a high school degree. This has led some to demand "comparable worth." Work with the same value and responsibility should receive the same wage. The concept goes beyond the legislated equal pay for the same job, to equal pay for the same value of work even if in different jobs (Gold 1991; Treiman and Hartmann 1981). Canada passed a Human Rights Act that resulted in the Canadian government paying $2.3 billion to women working as secretaries, clerks, librarians, etc., jobs which required as much education and responsibility as comparable traditionally male jobs paying much more (Brooke 1999). (See table 11.2, line 3.)

The belief that women or racial groups are inferior can become a self-fulfilling prophecy. It took the collective action of the civil rights movement and Federal legislation to begin to break the chain of circular and cumulative causation (recall section 6.6).

Where there are no laws prohibiting it, US workers are subject to being fired without reason if they are not members of unions that have negotiated protection. Stieber (1991) estimates that "60 million private-sector employees are not covered by collective bargaining, and statutorily protected employees who cannot demonstrate prohibited discrimination are subject to the Employment-at-Will doctrine." This doctrine is entrenched in the common law and is an example of a resolution of a basic interdependence in favor of employers.

Discrimination against women can be found around the world (United Nations 2000). In some countries, girl babies are smothered and if allowed to live receive less food, medical care, and education than boys. This has led Sen (1990) to declare, "More Than 100 Million Women Are Missing." These practices are the result of informal institutions. In 1996, Afghanistan declared that women could no longer hold jobs or attend school or college. Females constituted 70 percent of the country's teachers, but were dismissed. Wasting half of the creative energy of a country's population is a recipe for poverty.

11.7 Conclusion

Labor is not an ordinary commodity. It comes with a head, a cognitive element that makes perception and learning affect labor performance. Interdependence is created by the situational characteristics of labor including high information cost to determine quality at hiring and during work. Ideology, history, fairness, and relative status matter. Various institutional structures direct the interdependence and affect whose preferences count. Power is involved in establishing who has what to sell, including who owns the means of production and access to the borrowing power of the firm. After the basic rights are established, the parties can bargain to the particular efficient result associated with the starting place rights. Discrimination can persist from custom alone even in competitive markets.

NOTES

1. The Codetermination Act of 1976 gave workers an equal representation with the stock-holders having an extra vote in case of ties. See Backhaus (1999), Teubner (1986), and Hopt (1998).
2. Kelso argued that his universal capitalist plan could increase aggregate demand if workers captured in their incomes some of the productivity of capital goods, rather than having to bargain for it in their wages.

Chapter 12
Political Institutions

12.1 Constitutional Economics

When the sources of interdependence change, interest groups may press for formal institutional change in the everyday working rules. Which interests count is a function of the political rules for making these working rules and the ability to utilize them. If groups are to choose their political rules with intelligence, they need to predict how alternative political rules affect whose preferences count with respect to property rights. These political rules might be called constitutional level institutions and include not only literal constitutions but also the rules of legislative, judicial, and administrative bodies. This book has proposed an institutional and behavioral theory to guide research into the impact of alternative institutions. This theory is now aimed at political institutions or rules for making everyday economic rules of the economy. Since our purpose is to develop and illustrate a theory useful in application, examples will be chosen. For an overview of theoretical and empirical work, see Mueller (2003), Stevens (1993), Sugden (1981), and Shughart and Razzolini (2001). Among the political institutions examined here are who holds the voting franchise, rules for aggregating votes (electoral rules), separation and balance of powers, and boundaries.

There is probably more theoretical deductive literature than empirical literature. Some construct a deductive chain and draw implications for policy without any empirical grounding. The preferred practice in this book is to use theory to identify possibly relevant variables to include in empirical tests. The focus will be on how alternative political institutions affect substantive outcomes (who gets what), rather than on their equilibrium characteristics or welfare properties. However, the philosophic aspects cannot be avoided and are discussed in the final section below.

12.2 Axiomatic Theory

An argument has been presented here as to the limitations of rational choice theory and axiomatic reasoning. See also Green and Shapiro (1994). In rational choice theory, institutions structure choices of the self-interested maximizer. This ignores how the brain works and how self-interest is learned. Nevertheless, axiomatic theory does frame certain fundamental problems in the construction of political rules. It identifies the importance of the degree of unanimity for collective action, role of agenda setting, other voting rules, boundaries, and the impact of the median voter.

12.2.1 Political externality and transaction costs

Only unanimity can protect an individual from an action that decreased that person's welfare (a political externality). Question: when would an individual agree to a constitutional rule of public decision made by less than a unanimity rule? Answer: when the transaction cost of getting all others to agree to something the person wants is greater than the cost of getting something the person does not want (Buchanan and Tullock 1962). This type of abstract reasoning is suggestive even if it does not lend itself to empirical analysis and founders on uncertainty. It fits the fact that many people are comfortable with simple majority rules. It also fits the fact that some decisions require greater majorities. But it also suggests that not everyone will prefer the same decision rule and it says nothing about a host of other political rules. Can we find a set of rules that could command universal consent? See section 12.5 below.

12.2.2 Agenda power

Under some conditions (including multiple peaked preferences), the formation of winning coalitions is affected by the agenda (Arrow 1963). Suppose the preference ordering as shown in figure 12.1. If the agenda-maker puts up a choice between Y

Figure 12.1 Control of the agenda affects content of winning coalition

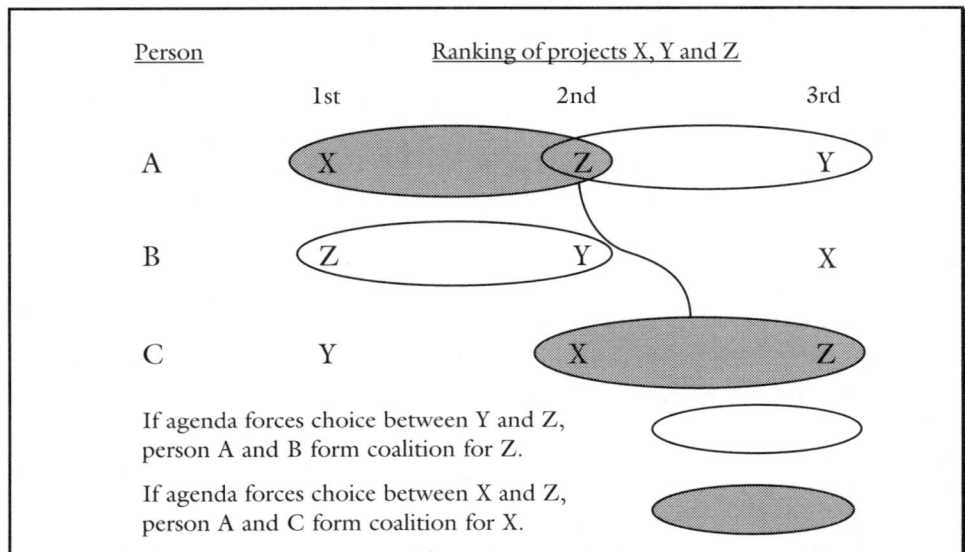

and Z, person A and B form the winning coalition for project Z. But if the choice were between X and Z, person A and C form the winning coalition for project X. Members of the rules committee of the US Senate understand this and committee membership is prized and its members are powerful. Potentially, the passage of working rules can cycle with first one coalition winning and then another. In practice, this is rare. Political leaders often can control amendments to proposals and there are costs to quickly bringing up the same issue.

The grouping of issues affects coalition formation. For example, Michigan allows citizens to petition to place an issue on the ballot. A group put together a transportation bond proposal that had a mix of funding for different types of roads and non-auto transport in cities and rural areas. Voters are faced with a "blue plate menu" problem. Some might prefer to support only parts of the package, but are forced to vote for or against the whole package. Similar issues arise in legislative proposals and whether the president can exercise a line-item veto.

12.2.3 Why vote?

It is hard to explain voting with a model of the calculated maximization of narrowly selfish preferences (Green and Shapiro 1994, ch. 4). It is hard to imagine that your vote can make a difference even when the perceived benefit exceeds your tax cost. Mueller (1989: 350) puts it this way:

> Several people have noted that the probability of being run over by a car going to or retuning from the polls is similar to the probability of casting the decisive vote. If being run over is worse that having one's preferred candidate lose, then this potential cost of voting alone would exceed the potential gain, and no rational self-interested individual would ever vote. But millions do, and thus the paradox.

Further, the results of voting are often high exclusion cost goods and free-riding is possible. Some have postulated a taste for voting or for performing a civic duty independent of its results. This saves the theory of rationality but this only puts a name on our ignorance. "Without a theory explaining the origin, strength, and extent of an individual's sense of civic duty, merely postulating a sense of civic duty 'saves' rational egoism by destroying its predictive power" (Mueller 1989: 351).

Empirical explanations of voting have included variables for personal characteristics, cost, strategic value of voting, interest, and obligation. Ashenfelter and Kelley conclude, "The theory of voting that is best supported by our results is that which posits a sense of duty or obligation as the primary motivation for voting" (Ashenfelter and Kelley 1975: 724). Individuals are conditioned to vote for the good of the community. This fits what we know about the human brain. Humans are both at times narrowly self-seeking and acting according to a learned norm or caring for others (Etzioni 1988). Bounded rationality suggests that it is impossible to trace all of the connections between a candidate's positions and one's future welfare. To save scarce information processing capacity, people fall back on labels like party and symbols. Sears, Lau, Tyler, and Allen's (1980: 679) assessment of survey data led to the conclusion that "in general symbolic attitudes (liberalism–conservatism, party identification, and racial prejudice) had strong effects, while self-interest had almost none." Models of voting behavior must be consistent with human cognition and include not only forward-looking benefit–cost variables, but also the history of learning. That learning includes norms, attitudes of caring for others, and responses to symbolic cues. It is possible to formulate a testable hypothesis without using the standard rational choice model. These broader models allow the discovery of variables other than strictly costs and benefits of voting.

Behavioral economics suggests that framing of decisions makes a difference. This is relevant to why people vote. Brennan and Lomasky (1993) argue that individuals vote not just to further narrow self-interest, but also to engage in "expressions of support" and to make "expressive demands." People often indicate they are of two minds. Their meta-preference is for some moral principle even if some of their behavior is contradictory. People can use the ballot as an opportunity to express commitment to a worthy principle that implies a concern for others. Politicians often frame issues as matters of principle. Thus, the endogeneity of preferences is inherent in the political process (Cullis and Jones 1998).

The same rational choice theory that posits that the rational individual would not vote also posits that individuals will not invest in becoming informed about political candidates (rational ignorance) (Downs 1957). The fact is that some do and some do not, and we must leave deductive theory for more empirical work on variables other than those reducible to simple costs and benefits.

Axiomatic theory does suggest some lines for research. What rules affecting costs affect the voting rate (or investment in information)? For example, what is the effect of sending absentee ballots to all eligible voters, making polling places more convenient, and mailing voter registration forms to unregistered voters?

12.2.4 Voting rules and boundaries

Just as there are many varieties of markets and capitalism, there are many varieties of democracies. One person, one vote is fundamental, but electoral details matter. Voting rules affect transaction costs and different groups react differently to these costs (for empirical studies see section 12.4.6 below). Voting rules affect coalition formation as shown above on agenda power. Some US states allow citizen referenda and others do not. Of 66 state initiatives in 1998, 39 became law (Broder 2000). Citizens of Swiss local governments vote directly on many public expenditures that would be decided by elected officials in the US.

A constitutional amendment to allow direct democracy has been proposed by former Senator Mike Gravel (Broder 2000). If 50 percent of the people in a national poll want to vote on an issue, it goes on the next general election ballot after Congress has held hearings and approved the language. Only individuals could contribute funds to the campaign.

Boundaries affect who is in the majority and who in the minority. The drawing of boundaries of state and national legislatures is a case in point. The US Supreme Court has ruled that boundaries cannot be drawn to maximize the votes of a particular racial group, but it is OK for any other purpose such as to maximize votes for a particular party. The present majority party gets to choose the boundaries for future elections. There is no escape from the path dependence of the rules for making political rules such as boundaries.

It is easy to show the effect of bullet voting vs. the requirement that one's vote does not count unless one votes for as many positions as are available in a multiple-seat jurisdiction. The city of Ann Arbor, Michigan, allows a voter to put all of the votes for open city council positions on one person. So, for example, if there are three councilpersons to be elected, a voter can vote for three or give all three votes to a single candidate, thus giving more weight to minority interests. Ireland and Australia have a Parliamentary voting system in multiple-seat districts that requires a person to vote for a candidate of first choice and another of second choice (sometimes referred to as the Borda count). The winner usually must have a certain number of second place votes to win. This was designed to make candidates appeal to both majority and minority interests. Logrolling is another institution that gives more power to a single interest minority. If a minority will give its support to laws it cares little about, it can obtain the support of other groups for laws dear to the minority. Different rules facilitate or hinder logrolling agreements.

The dates of US presidential primaries are selected by each state. The state that goes first influences the outcome of later primaries by establishing trends. A candidate may take positions to fit a particular state, win that primary, and then modify the position to fit later elections. The result might be different if the primaries were all on the same day. The president is the only national office that is elected by all the people. What if a certain number of Senators were elected at-large?

Some local governments elect city councilpersons at-large and some from districts (wards). If minorities are concentrated in one ward, election by ward is sure to give that minority a seat on the council. However, that representative may be outvoted, though if other members are split on an issue, the minority representative may be able to decide the winning coalition. Some nations elect each legislator separately (US) with the successful candidate in each district being the one with the most votes. Other countries use a proportional representation system (Italy). Some governments are unitary and centralized (France) while others are a federal system (Germany and US).

Which of the above alternative rules is more democratic? The question is empty. All are votes of the people, but people grouped in different ways. A better question is how do the rules affect whose preferences count. Some empirical evidence will be examined in section 12.4 below.

12.2.5 Median voter theory

What is the impact of majority rule in making public decisions on the amount of some publicly provided HEC good, and thus whose preferences count? A variant of the median voter theory assumes voters maximize utility subject to a budget constraint that includes their tax price. The winning coalition of voters is formed around the preferences of the median voter. The coalition is made up of the median voter and all those who prefer more of the good than the median voter. Those who prefer less lose. Government expenditure is a function of tax and income of the median voter plus a vector of taste parameters such as number of children and age. The theory has been tested using cross-sectional data from different communities and the studies generally show median income to be significant (Mueller 1989: 191). But, predictions from these studies are not significantly different from studies using more traditional theories that use mean income. Unfortunately, most of these studies are for communities with representative government rather than from direct votes. Some research suggests that mean income is significant with direct voting but not with representative government (Pommerehne 1978).

The role of income in predicting expenditures is questioned by studies showing a large variation in income elasticities and one showing no difference in taste for HEC goods between low- and high-income individuals (Gramlich and Rubenfeld 1982). While the theory is elegant, Mueller (1989: 193) judges, "As in all areas of economics, the sophistication and elegance of the theoretical models of public choice far exceed the limits placed by the data on the empirical models that can be estimated."

12.3 Institutional and Behavioral Theory

A literature has arisen in political science known as "historical institutionalism." It tends to see political actors as rule-following "satisficers" (DiMaggio and Powell 1991). Further, "while rational choice deals with preferences at the level of assumptions, historical institutionalists take the question of how individuals and groups define their self-interest as problematical" (Thelen and Steinmo 1992: 8). Both of these ideas are included in the approach of this book. The attention to where preferences come from explains the choice of the term "historical institutionalism." The approach tends to focus on intermediate-level institutions such as political parties and lobby groups rather than macro institutions such as class structures. "Historically evolved structures channel political battles in distinctive ways . . ." (28). The theory is generally inductive. The approach features three sources of dynamics: policy change within stable institutions as new actors and issues arise, which is included in this chapter; institutions as objects of change, and ideational innovation, which are included in the next chapter.

Institutional theory suggests that preferences are not fixed and may be formed in the way the proposition is framed. All of the money spent on campaign advertising is not some minor footnote to majority rule. For example, environmentalists proposed a tax to finance the purchase of farmland open space in a community in Michigan. The association of homebuilders hypothesized that much of the support came from urban people who not only enjoyed the landscape, but also wanted to do something good for farmers. When the builders found and dramatized that some farmers opposed the program, some urban supporters withdrew and the vote failed.

Behavioral economics suggests that citizens' perception of goods do not have some fixed name with preferences attached. Politicians' ability to shape perception may vary across jurisdictions. A Michigan legislator opposed legislation to require sales tax on e-commerce even though by law citizens were obligated to report e-commerce purchases and pay an equivalent tax even if the seller did not collect it. He framed this as a new tax (even though it only changed the point of collection) and he was categorically opposed to new taxes.

Other variables suggested by SSP include not just income level, but income distribution and social capital. There are possibilities for opportunistic free-rider behavior with respect to schools. The older generation may reason that since their children are out of the school, they can vote against school taxes without any loss of benefit. But a person who holds social capital for all children and has a sense of doing what is right will not take this opportunity. Communities may differ with respect to this informal institution. Majority rule is not the only relevant institution in the equation.

Interdependence related to transaction costs is also relevant. School elections in Michigan for example are special elections separate from general elections. Supporters of this rule for making rules hypothesize that only those with intense preferences will bother to vote in the special election and these will most likely be those who favor the tax increase. Is there data to test this? In general the point is that there are variables that affect the rate at which different groups bother to vote. There is nothing that says that those above or below the median voter come out to vote at the same percentage rate.

12.4 Empirical[1]

This section will survey some of the empirical evidence on the impact of alternative rules for making rules on whose interests count – whose preferences get expressed in the everyday property rights.

12.4.1 Representative government

One of the major institutional changes in the rules for making rules in the West was the development of representational government in England in the seventeenth century. Curtailment of the power of the king radically changed whose preferences counted in the making of everyday economic rules. In this chapter we are not asking how the constitution changed (only to note that it was the result of the revolution of 1688). Rather the question for empirical study is the impact of new political rules on the creation of everyday rules of the economy. North and Weingast (N&W) (1989) argue that a key everyday rule of great importance for economic development ment was the security of rights to property and person, which included the predictability of taxes and repayment of loans to the crown.

The barons had wrested some power from the king at the 1215 Battle of Runnymede codified in the Magna Carta. As a result of the revolution of 1688, the dominance of Parliament was established. Parliament had demonstrated that it could dethrone a king and it now established the principle that taxes could only be levied with Parliamentary consent. The king remained and retained the power to propose

Table 12.1 Political institutions in seventeenth century England and France

Situation	Structure	Performance

Land and commercial facilities are IUGs.	*Rules for making rules –*
	1. England
	  a. Parliament can remove king.
	  b. Only crown can propose taxes and expenditure.
	  c. No tax w/o consent of Parliament.
		1. Less insecurity of rights to property and person. Tax rates more predictable.

	2. France
	  a. King not limited until revolution of 1789.
	  b. King has standing army.
		2. Less secure rights. State commitments not reliable.

Adapted from North and Weingast (1989)

taxes and expenditures, but Parliament must approve and could audit the spending. N&W describe this as multiple veto points. The royal courts were removed and the common law courts that favored law supporting commercial interests were made dominant. The crown could not rule by decree. Further, the crown did not command a standing army to enforce its wishes.

What kind of everyday right emerged from these constitutional changes? N&W present evidence that there was less insecurity of rights to property and person and taxes were more predictable. They go on to do an impact analysis of these everyday rights, presenting evidence of a rapid expansion of loans to the crown since the crown's commitment to contract could be expected. There was also an expansion of private debt and the stock market.

In contrast, France retained the divine right of kings until its revolution in 1789. And, the French king had a standing army. N&W do not provide detailed analysis of whose interests royal decrees favored, but note that in 1690, France was the preeminent country is Europe, but then stagnated while England laid the groundwork for the industrial revolution. N&W do not claim that representative government favoring commercial growth was the only cause of England's development since religious and other economic institutions also played a role.

People are often interdependent because of the incompatibility of their claims on resources. Political rules influence whose claims count in this case by determining the power of a body representing the aristocracy versus a hereditary king. The situation, structure, and performance of this case study is represented in table 12.1. Recall that these SSP frameworks are nested and that analysis of the impact of the rules for making rules can be extended to the impact of the everyday rules chosen in the political process, which N&W went on to do in terms of impact on capital markets. The analysis may also be extended backwards to inquire into what institutions (probably informal) created the change in the constitutional rules. What led to the revolution of 1688?

12.4.2 Interest group power

Interest groups who wish to influence public policy must overcome the free-rider problem inherent in high exclusion cost goods. If the policy benefits a class of persons, no one can be excluded. Olson predicted that small groups with concentrated interests would have more success than large groups with diffuse interests (individually small, but large in the aggregate) (Olson 1965). He thought that the only way to avoid this result involved the use of coercion or the provision of low exclusion cost goods to finance the high exclusion cost goods. Empirically, he documented how farmers joined the American Farm Bureau to obtain marketable services and incidentally received lobbying services. SSP, however, suggests more ways to unseat the free-rider.

A case study of the American Soybean Association (ASA) illustrates the wide variety of opportunities utilized to mobilize an interest group (Schmid and Soroko 1997). In the early 1900s soybeans were a new crop and its spread could be speeded by a tariff on competing oilseeds. But a tariff benefits all farmers whether or not they contribute to the lobbying effort. Nevertheless, a handful of leaders led a successful lobbying effort. One historian notes, "Much of the committee work has been accomplished by men who were willing to give freely of their time and money so that soybean growers everywhere might profit thereby" (quoted in Schmid and Soroko (1997: 269–70). For a study of how different groups affected tariff policy, see Pincus (1977).

The ASA never provided selective benefits to members, but it did sell advertising space in its magazine. The leadership also took advantage of a period when the emotions of soybean farmers were aroused by government financing of technical assistance to farmers in poor, but competing countries. It was a time of depressed soybean prices and the farmers had an angry sense of relative deprivation. In that framework the leaders enlisted many new dues-paying members to help finance lobbying. "Groups and individuals are not merely spectators as conditions change to favor or penalize them in the political balance of power, but rather strategic actors capable of acting on 'openings'" (Thelen and Steinmo 1992: 17).

"A simple cross-sectional comparison of the characteristics of successful and latent interest groups is not sufficient to understand how they overcome the free-rider problem. It doesn't reveal how organizations get started and get in a position to provide selective services or to find substitutes and complements for them. An evolutionary methodology reveals a more complex picture" (Schmid and Soroko 1997: 282). Such an evolutionary study reveals that "History, negotiation, political entrepreneurship and cleverness, the state of countervailing power, political-representative institutions, dedication, and emotion count in determining interest group success, as well as selective incentives" (284). Interest groups also can use different institutions to differential advantage. Some groups pressure Congress, some the President and administrative agencies, some the courts.

The ability of labor to achieve the right to collective bargaining and other labor laws is another case of interest groups trying to change the rules. Comparison of the divergence in labor strategies in England and the US indicate the role of constitutional rules for making rules (Hattam 1992). Labor in both countries won legislative approval for collective bargaining in the last half of the nineteenth century. But, in the US, with its balance of powers, the courts overturned these laws. Albeit dangerous and at the margin of legality, the labor movement turned to strikes and agitation in individual firms rather than general legislation. In contrast, the more centralized government of England, where the courts are subordinate to the legislature, gave the workers rights by legislation. Unions identified with the Labor Party to achieve its goals while US unions did not form a political party.

12.4.3 Growth of government

There is a popular impression that the size of government has grown dramatically since the Great Depression. Measured in terms of budget and number of employees this is true. But, the meaning of size of government is more complicated and there are alternative explanations of its growth (Breton 1989). First, regulation and public spending are in part substitutes. Government can affect economic activity by producing goods and services paid for by taxes or by changing regulations, the market rules, and private property rights interpreted by the courts. Countries differ in the mix of each.

Second, the argument has been made above that where there is interdependence, there is government (or there is no order). So as the economy has become more complex in the ways that one person's action can affect the welfare of others, there will be more government – in the form of more spending, regulation, or changes in private rights. For example, the institutions needed to direct the interdependence of an economy of isolated fur traders are quite different from that of a global high tech economy independent of power hungry bureaucrats. Regulation and property rights of any kind allocate opportunities among conflicting parties, and it is obfuscation to label this a choice of the size of government. Less government could only mean less order unless it is provided by informal institutions.

Niskanen (1971) developed one of the early formal theories that fit the popular impression of growth in government. He said that utility-maximizing bureaucrats with a monopoly of a particular service proposed budgets to Congress that increased agency size beyond that needed to provide the promised level of service. They could get away with inflated budgets including higher salaries for themselves because of high information costs on the part of Congress to independently estimate costs per unit of service. Various political scientists, however, pointed out that Congress has some institutions to counteract this such as monitoring by Congress and constituency groups, and establishing competing agencies (Wintrobe 1997: 433–7).

While Niskanen's story fits many peoples' impressions, there is little systematic evidence. One empirical study found that there was no significant relationship between agency size and salaries holding other relevant variables constant (Johnson and Libecap 1989). A better theory would account for changes in interdependence and the competing multiple objectives of bureaucrats. There is competition among agencies (Carroll 1989). There is no significant relationship between bureau market share and budget growth (Carroll 1990).

To a degree, public and private agents compete to provide high exclusion cost (HEC) goods. Breton (1989) argues that the growth of government then depends on the relative efficiency of government and private organizations to control free-riders. Government controls this by compulsory taxes and private organizations by norms and social sanctions. So over time as the scope of the family narrows with mobility and urbanization, government becomes the cheaper producer of HEC goods that had once been (or could be) provided by intra-family transfers and charity.

Breton reduces the question of private or public provision of HEC goods to the standard model of comparative advantage. To do so, he must assume that free-riding is bad and the only question is the cheapest way to avoid it. But, how about genuine unwilling riders who are not strategically hiding their demand, but don't want the good at any price? Chapter 6 suggested that there is an inevitable tradeoff between the interests of want-to-be and unwilling riders. The growth of government then is not a matter of changing efficiency of alternative sources of supply, but a change in whose preferences count. Tax enforcement or social sanctions place a burden on unwilling riders and its absence places a burden on want-to-be riders who are willing to pay, but are denied the good (quantity or quality). Efficiency cannot be a guide to who coerces whom.

There is an ebb and flow of whose interests count as a function of ideology (history and symbolization count) and the evolving and contested rules for making rules. Political institutional detail matters and can't be collapsed in a black box of market-like competition. There is a competition in ideology and for the use of government as much as among costs of alternative sources of supply.

The big problem with deciding the size of budgets is how legislators and voters see opportunity cost. Some assume that a consumer or voter always has in mind all alternative uses of their money. But, institutional economics is aware of bounded rationality. Frames that remind people of particular tradeoffs affect decisions. It is easy for the individual to reason that his/her tax bill is fixed and the more spending projects that benefit that individual, the better. The total effect is perhaps total spending that few desire. Congress has tried to change that thinking by passing a budget resolution before individual appropriation committees go to work. The Assistant Secretary of the Army for Civil Works once tried to allocate the Corps of Engineers' budget to regions on a multiple year basis (Dola 1971). It was hoped that this would motivate local people to at least ask which project they preferred to spend their allotment on rather than reasoning that any project that comes along, however inefficient, added to their net benefit. A congressional committee objected to the scheme and eliminated staff support from the budget.

The question of size of government cannot be researched independently of the process of preference formation. There is not just a set of public preferences and a set of production functions with prices attached which can be reduced to a calculation of efficiency and a measure of waste and excessive size. Both public and private firms have the option of searching for ways to reduce the cost of supplying a given set of goods meeting the preferences of the moment or of devoting energy to altering those preferences. Lobbying groups, bureaucrats, and others not only try to influence legislatures and agencies, but also voter preferences and the framing of issues. Both the power to decide an agenda item and to shape its content (some issues never get formulated) are important (Bachrach and Baratz 1962). Also see Bartlett (1989: ch. 9, "Value Power").

"The American public wants government to do more than it is doing to solve public problems. And it wants government to be smaller, spend less, and be less intrusive" (Erikson, MacKuen, and Stimson 2002: 205). This inconsistency fits the facts of bounded rationality and the modular brain. Voters necessarily simplify. One simplification is to categorize specific political proposals into two boxes, labeled more or less government (more or less freedom). At the same time, citizens experience problems and want government to fix them.

The case has been made in this book for getting out of the armchair to ask people what they want rather than making assumptions about rationality. The problems with this are the well-known fact that questions are not perceived the same way by different people or over time. Erikson, MacKuen, and Stimson (2002: 194–5) offer an explanation consistent with bounded rationality: "Presented with a question on which no programmed response is available, where the real state of mind is ambivalence, the respondent does a brief search of his or her views that might be relevant, chooses one that comes to mind, and applies it to the issue at hand. In this context framing will make a difference."

Just as survey questions help voters frame issues, so do politicians. Different politicians have different skills in framing the issue that will trigger the "anti-government" response vs. "there is a solution to perceived ills" response. Some issues thrown up by events are easier to frame than others. Most people are loyal to a party over time. Still, there are enough people that switch between Republicans and Democrats to make a difference. Erikson, MacKuen, and Stimson (2002) interpret the empirical relationships between survey responses and elections as indicating that some voters change in response to performance of the parties. One of the strongest empirical regularities is that incumbent parties lose as actual and anticipated unemployment rises. A hypothesis from institutional economics is that significant unemployment gets categorized as something that government should fix and it is hard to convince people to suffer unemployment in the name of small government. Economic performance is relatively easy to measure even if the means to improvement are not easy to understand. Other issues are more subject to framing and can account for changes in party support without assuming people can evaluate government performance. Events and political cleverness can change enough to affect some voters' categorization of candidate platforms.

If the analysis of chapter 9 is correct, there is little a President can do to reverse recessions. Monetary policy is in the hands of the Federal Reserve. The budget grows regardless of the party in power. As President Nixon said, "We are all Keynesians now." The parties just spend for different things. For example, the Democrats spend more on direct aid to the unemployed. Taxes can be cut, but have little effect if business is pessimistic. The effects of these policies are sufficiently contestable that voters can be excused for using a simple decision rule of voting against the incumbent when they fear recession.

12.4.4 Bureaucracy

Competing interests use government to give them opportunities necessarily at the expense of conflicting groups. Groups that lose might better blame other interest groups rather than bureaucrats. The interests and ideology of bureaucrats are only part of the process determining who wins. How the influence plays out is in part a function of political institutions. For example, the Administrative Procedures Act can open up agency decision-making and reduce insulation. These rules necessarily favor certain interest groups over others. Sometimes they are used to establish *ex ante* control over agencies rather than using *ex post* monitoring (McCubbins, Noll, and Weingast 1987).

It cannot be assumed that Congress has singular objectives and is certain of the means to obtain them, thus reducing the problem to one of getting agencies to carry them out. In the face of conflicting interest groups, Congress often seeks credit for addressing an important issue, but ducks the hard choices by delegating details to an agency.

Do transaction costs prevent effective contracts between Congress and agencies and between managers and subordinates? If so, what institutions direct this interdependence? There is much literature on possible rearrangement of incentives. What does the SSP perspective have to add? Work is valued in itself and not just a means to income. Many workers like to get up in the morning and feel like what they will do is worth while. They respond to criticism of clients, fellow workers, academics, new media, and elected officials. They care for their regard and care for the welfare of selected clients. Like members of a private firm, the workers may have different ideas of how best to meet the organization's objectives and client needs. Their action is more complicated than a preference for leisure and perquisites.

The principal-agent problem between voters and bureaucrats is further complicated by the relationship between higher-level managers and lower-level workers. Managers may not be able to reward effort with salary. They can reward it with regard. But, caring (social capital) among network members can have different results. It may result in managers showing favoritism to their friends. Or, it may result in subordinates working to achieve the manager's and the organization's objectives even if high information cost interdependence allows for opportunism. Sometimes attempts to increase monitoring and pressure only increase efforts to get around them (Galeotti 1988; Frey 1993; Leibenstein 1979). Social capital among voters can also be a factor in monitoring public agencies. A comparative study of northern and southern Italy found that local governments were more productive in the north where there were strong horizontal ties within citizen networks (rather than patron–client relationships) (Putnam 1993).

Do different institutions affect the behavior of bureaucrats? A comparative study of civil servants in seven countries showed that those in parliamentary systems saw themselves as much less involved in active policy making than those in the US "Uncertain lines of authority encourage American bureaucrats to play political roles – to cut deals with congressmen who can protect their agencies from central executive control, to pursue the interests of clienteles who can help to protect their programs and to act as advocates for interests inadequately represented through the ostensible channels of political representation" (Aberbach, Putnam, and Rockman 1981: 99).

Much attention has been given to how to structure incentives so that the agent does what the principal wants. Sometimes we worry about the agent being too subservient in carrying out the wishes of those in authority. Those who carried out orders for the death of Jews in Nazi Germany constitute the polar case. The case is modeled by Milgram's (1974) famous experiment wherein people administered what they thought were marginally increasing electric shocks to subjects that were giving wrong answers to questions. Akerlof (1991) explains this behavior as a series of marginal choices each of which appears rational, but in the aggregate produce results that the actor does not want. (It has similarities to the Weber-Fechner Law described in chapter 3.)

What are the effects of organizational structure? There is reason to believe that control of the agenda makes a difference. Extending that idea, Hammond (1986) argues that a particular organizational structure is the organization's agenda. Structures affect outcomes, strategic behavior, and beliefs. Hammond shows, for example, that organizations that are organized on a geographical basis perform differently than those based on professional structures. Hammond and Miller (1985) in a formal model show that some of the slogans of public administration, such as decisions should be made on the basis of a clear assignment of authority, are inconsistent with other slogans.

The same organizational issues that face public agencies also face business. In business, a large firm can be organized in terms of functions such as marketing and finance, or multi-division (M-Form) by products, regions, or technology (Milgrom and Roberts 1992: ch. 16). While the organizational structure affects outcomes, no one form is best for all purposes. Cycles in structures can be observed with one form popular for awhile and then replaced. Organization is an easy and visible option available to a chief executive. A new executive can display her initiative by changing the organization chart. US presidents are often tempted to reorganize departments. A perennial candidate is the organization of Federal water agencies. Responsibility for water resources is scattered in several departments that are often champions for different interests. It is tempting to try to reduce conflict among interests and departments via consolidation. But powerful interests have to be compromised whether the bargaining is between departments or within a department (Schmid 1971). The detailed bargaining rules shaping the negotiations between interest groups are as important in determining whose interests count as the formal organizational structure. These include budgetary practices, personnel policies, access to courts, and public information procedures.

12.4.5 Elected or appointed

Whose preferences count when office holders are directly elected or appointed by other elected officials? Direct election appears to give the voter the most control, but in the face of bounded rationality, the information involved is difficult to process. If one elected official appoints another, the voter only has to obtain information on one candidate and can expect that the philosophy of the first will extend to those

Table 12.2 Political institutions

Situation	Structure (rules for making rules)	Performance
Model 1: Case 1, Judges and decisions Traffic fines IUG (model ignores transaction cost)	*Boundary rules similar to factor ownership:* a. Right to elect locally (reflecting local majority preferences). b. Right to appoint by state governor (reflecting state preferences).	*Hypothesized and observed:* a. Judge favors group A who prefers high fines. b. Judge favors group B who prefers low fines.
Case 2, Drunk driving fines IUG	a. Right to elect locally. b. Right to appoint by state governor.	*Observed:* a. Judge favors group A. b. Judge favors group A.
Model 2: *IUG with high transaction costs* HIC Public doesn't know what they do or will do. Problem of measurement as in some consumer products	Local election plus, a. Candidates can advertise. b. Advertising prohibited by law and culture.	*Hypothesize:* a. Judge favors group A. b. Judge (not significant)

Regresssion equation and coefficients:

Average traffic fine = f of

Judge selection	Religion	Political party	Income	Court expenditures/Case	Crime Rate
−3.47	−8.39	−13.5	−0.0012	+0.19	+17.32
(0.037)	(0.043)	(0.178)	(0.001)	(0.07)	(0.068)

Adapted from Broder (1977)

appointed. But, different voters have different information processing capacity and want to spend it on different offices. Thus, alternative rules for making rules can be expected to affect whose preferences count.

An opportunity for empirical research on the impact of alternative institutional structures was presented by the fact that local judges in Michigan are directly elected. However, if a judgeship becomes open in mid-term, the governor may appoint. Do elected judges rule differently than appointed judges? This was tested with the dependent performance variable being the amount of fine assessed for traffic offenses and for drunk driving. A regression equation was estimated with a dummy variable for the method of judge selection (rule for making working rules) (Broder 1977). Other community variables held constant included the dominant religion, political party, and income in the cross-section of jurisdictions. The results were mixed with the selection method significant for traffic fines, but not for drunk driving (see table 12.2).

If the availability of information on judges' values is considered, the mixed results are not surprising. In Michigan, as in most states, judges do not advertise their positions on issues (as is done for legislators). A private organization, the State Bar Association rules prohibit it. A judge's values are HIC to voters. The impact of allowing judges to advertise their attitude toward drunk drivers, etc. remains a hypothesis waiting the opportunity to be tested. A 2002 US Supreme Court decision declared state prohibitions of substantive judicial advertising unconstitutional.

12.4.6 Voting rules

History records the extension of the voting franchise to more and more people such as non-property holders, women, and African-Americans. But this is only half the battle. The details of voting affect which voter really counts. Ballot format matters. The "Massachusetts" ballot is organized by office under which the candidate of each party is listed. (Even the order of listing matters.) The voter must check off each office. The "Indiana" ballot allows a voter to vote for the candidates of one party with a single check (straight ticket). (See table 12.3.) The straight ticket saves information costs as the voter need only have an understanding of the philosophy of a party rather than the position of each office seeker. When voters of different parties differ in willingness to bear transaction costs, ballot format will affect which party wins (Zauderer 1972). It also affects who votes for minor offices if voters differ in suffering the fatigue associated with a long ballot. The dependent variable is the rate of fall-off in the number voting for the most prominent national office to the most obscure local office.

Legal requirements for registration might be expected to affect the number of registrants and voter turnout. Some states allow motor voters, that is registration when getting a drivers license. There is considerable variation in how far in advance of an election one must register. Cross sectional analysis shows that states with more liberal electoral laws have greater participation. But Uslaner (1998: 115–17) argues that correlation is not causation. When states change their laws, participation does not necessarily change. He argues that underlying cultural values dominate transaction

Table 12.3 Alternative ballot formats

Massachusetts Ballot	Indiana Ballot (Place X below to vote straight ticket)	
	Republican	Democrat
President	☐	☐
Bush (R) ☐		
Gore (D) ☐	*President*	
Debs (S) ☐	Bush ☐	Gore ☐
Governor	*Governor*	
Engler (R) ☐	Engler ☐	Who ☐
Who (D) ☐		
Dog catcher	*Dog Catcher*	
Wolf (R)	Wolf ☐	Schmo ☐
Schmo (D)		
Trotsky (S)		

cost changes. He is impressed with "how little registration and turnout respond to legal changes, with the notable exception of black turnout and the Voting Rights Act of 1965" (118).[2]

12.4.7 Majority and plurality systems vs. proportional representation

Some countries elect the members of their legislatures individually with either a majority or plurality vote. In two-party states, conceptually the legislature may be made up of members of one party who each won by a narrow margin while the minority party has no seats. In contrast, proportional systems would give a substantial number of seats to the minority party, which has the effect of requiring more compromise and consensus.[3] The United Kingdom and the United States are representative of the plurality system and Italy, Sweden, and Switzerland are representative of proportional representation. Lijphart (1999) used factor analysis to suggest two dimensions of majority vs. consensus systems. The "executives–parties dimension" is composed of features such as concentration of executive power in single-party majority cabinets vs. executive power-sharing in multiparty coalitions, two-party vs. multiparty systems, and pluralist interest groups vs. large coordinated "corporatist" interests groups. The second dimension is the "federal–unitary dimension" composed of a federalist constitution, bicameralism, constitutional rigidity, judicial review and central bank independence. What difference do these rules for making rules make in whose preferences count? A study of 36 democracies developed an index placing a country on the "executives–parties dimension." Lijphart (1999: 296) finds evidence that as this consensus index increased, countries had more features of a

welfare state, more social expenditures as a percentage of GDP, were more supportive of environmental improvement and energy efficiency, incarcerated a lower percentage of its population, had a more equal income distribution, and were more
generous in foreign aid among other things. The "federal–unitary dimension" was
only weakly correlated with various performance measures. The exception was the
degree of inflation, which is not surprising since one of the ingredients was central
bank independence.

Voters in proportional systems with many parties tend to repeat their support for
a party over time (Galeotti 1999). A continuum of increasing proportionality from
the US, Germany, to Italy shows decreasing volatility in party support from election
to election. Environmentalist voters swing back and forth between Republicans and
Democrats in the US depending on their relative performance on what is a minor
part of their platforms, but stay with the Green party in more proportional systems.

There are huge differences in land use rights and urban planning in the US,
Canada, and the United Kingdom. The US is marked by urban sprawl while Canada
and the UK have more compact cities. Is this due to differences in rules for making
rules or in preferences? It probably has more to do with the wide-ranging power of
local governments (little federal legislative or judicial review) than with voting rules
in general. Also in the US, there is a cultural reaction to planning, which engenders
an SOP of disapproval even if the actual result were favorable to many. A few studies
try to compare public opinion to political outcomes (Broder 1983).

12.4.8 Redistribution

Middle-income people are in the majority in the US and on a strictly selfish motivation might be expected to vote for taxes that redistribute income from the minority
of high-income people and low-income people. The top 20 percent of families
received half of household income in 2001. The hypothesis that redistribution in
a democracy is from the tails of the income distribution to the center is known as
Director's Law. The opposite has occurred in the US. Redistribution is from the
middle to the two ends (Aaron and McGuire 1970). What can institutional theory
suggest? Cognition is more complicated than simple current income maximization.
Perhaps middle-income people expect to be rich someday. Perhaps they regard the
income of the rich as deserved. Perhaps they have sympathy (social capital) for the
poor. Better models will include measures of perception rather than the easy to
observe income variables. A US survey indicates that the more firmly poor people
believe in the chance of bettering their income, the less likely is their support of
wealth redistribution (Alesina and La Ferrara 2001).

Specific redistribution programs may be targeted to those whose voting behavior
is most elastic (Persson and Tabellini 2000: ch. 3), or to groups that may be decisive
in a particular Congressional election when party majority is at stake. That may
explain the huge payments to agriculture in the 2002 Farm Bill. The preponderance
of benefits to large wealthy farmers is more related to their lobbying influence and
campaign contributions that are disproportionate to their numbers (Schweikhardt
and Browne 2001).

12.4.9 Research perspective

Much of the literature has sought to use abstract logic to show whether or not government is too large, too inefficient, or bureaucracy or a particular interest group too powerful. The perspective of institutional theory rather asks empirically how do different rules affect whose preferences count recognizing that there are many groups and that issues have multiple dimensions. It acknowledges that power lies not only in making actors behavior consistent with the preferences of those who can use government, but also in shaping preferences (learning). The institutional perspective searches for complementarity and substitutability among institutions. Actors, whether presidents, courts, interest groups, legislators, etc., choose from a menu of institutions. The way one works depends on who is using other institutions; and when one fails, others may be substitutes. For example, environmental groups switch from trying to influence presidents, key legislators, or courts depending on who occupies each position.

It is easy to list the formal rules for making rules that are available to different actors. In the US, presidents have veto power, congress can create agencies, and fund them, the bureaucracy often has delegated discretion, interest groups provide campaign finance and shape public values, courts rule on constitutionality and consistency of agency action with the law (as interpreted by the judges), and voters have the franchise as influenced by voting rules and boundaries. Each, of course, is not a single actor.

Good theory will build on the themes described in this section, such as selective utility maximization (sometimes referred to as the new economics of politics), moral rules and striving for regard and self-respect, problems of collective action respecting exclusion and transaction cost, organization and control, and political exchange. If all of this is made too complicated, it collapses and becomes unmanageable. If made too simple, the theory ignores important variables and actors. There is no easy answer. One can sympathize with Terry Moe who says, "As far as complexity is concerned, the task for the future is not to avoid simplification, and certainly not to disavow the new economics. The task is to make the right kinds of simplifications . . ." (Moe 1997: 478).

12.5 End of the "God Trick"

12.5.1 Impossibility theory

Arrow (1963) examined the possibility that some widely held ethical axioms could be the basis for a constitution. He considered the following:

1. Unanimity (Pareto-better outcome).
2. Non dictatorship.
3. Transitivity.
4. Unrestricted domain (any possible ordering of alternatives).
5. Independence of irrelevant alternatives.

He formally demonstrated that these could not be simultaneously achieved and thus the exercise became known as the "impossibility theorem." No social welfare function satisfies all of these propositions. One does not need formal logic to see the inconsistencies. The political process must choose alternatives where interests are conflicting. It is always better to be an owner (seller) than a buyer. These starting places are what politics must choose. As Barry (1965: 313) puts it, "a political situation is precisely one that arises when the parties are arguing not about mutually useful trades but about the legitimacy of one another's initial position." Further, "in the context of an evolving institutional system, terms such as 'economic efficiency' or 'social benefit' become uncomfortably difficult to define" (Rutherford 1994: 6).

12.5.2 Process vs. substance: Buchanan and Rawls

The problem of order is central. The only thing worse than living with rules you don't like is living in unpredictable chaos. But how shall that order be established? Seeing the great conflicting preferences among people, many despair in finding consensus on what kind of substantive world to live in. This despair has driven many such as James Buchanan to focus on process. He concentrates on finding good decision rules independent of their substantive outcomes. Are there some rules for making rules that could command consent? Buchanan argues that politics is not a process of fact finding, but rather the resolution of conflict. He abhors a welfare analysis that could tell the political process which laws to pass. He wants it tested by actual approval.

Choice among one's options given by the constraint of working rules and the choice of these options (opportunity sets) are two different things. If the starting place rights are accepted by all parties then it is possible to insist on Pareto-better changes, a kind of test of the degree of voluntary participation or freedom. But Buchanan notes, "Any allocation of resources that is to be classified as 'efficient' depends necessarily on the institutional structure within which resource utilization-valuation decisions are made."[4] Buchanan recognizes the distinction of freedom to choose one's opportunity set and freedom to choose within it (Buchanan and Brennan 1977). How can we know that people have consented to their opportunity set (who is seller and who is buyer)? Again, Buchanan pins his hopes on agreement on process. He has no use for welfare economics. For Buchanan it is the job of analysts to suggest policies for public approval. The people must decide. But *which* people under *what* rules? We have seen above how different rules for making rules favor different people. Arrow's impossibility theorem says you can't build up a social welfare function by aggregating individual preferences under the most simple of constitutional principles.

Can people agree on a process independent of expected substantive outcomes? Buchanan following Rawls expects wide consent if people choose behind a veil of ignorance, not knowing where they will be in life's future games. A metaphor might be people deciding on the rules of basketball and the height of the baskets before they knew how tall they were. Rawls expected people to choose rules so that everyone is guaranteed survival. But, one can observe that some people are gamblers and will go for broke and enjoy that game, while others might opt for a safe game. In any case, no realistic veil can be drawn and voters do have ideas of their present and future interests as the game unfolds. There is no way to make a constitutional choice once and forever. The constitution has to be interpreted along the way, which is why we have courts. No Supreme Court decision is made without reference to the constitution, but the substantive outcomes differ over time as different interpretations are made. For example, consider the rights of Blacks to vote in the face of language in the Declaration of Independence that "all men are created equal." The Court's early answer was that Blacks were not men, and of course women were not men so they could not vote either. If words spoke for themselves for all times, we would not have this history. What appears to one person as the natural meaning seems unnatural to another. Supreme Court judges pledge to uphold the constitution, but which meaning?

Buchanan argued that the southern states should have been free to secede from the union to protect their freedom to own slaves. Freedom? Freedom for the slave owners, but what about freedom for the slaves? Buchanan urges us to value liberty above all else. Milton Friedman says, "Freedom is my god." But a transactional view reveals that freedom for one person is a lost opportunity for another person. Freedom can't be a guide to choosing either constitutional or working rules. Its use always involves selective perception. It is quite honest to say that my freedom is more important than yours, but people hesitate to admit this is all they are saying when they speak of freedom is my god.

Tiebout (1956) argued that "voting with your feet" in choosing which local government jurisdiction to live in maximizes voter utility and thus is a justification for decentralized government. This theory fails to take a transactional perspective and ignores the people left behind. For example, many whites have left central cities such as Detroit. This increased their welfare but left a decaying center with few fiscal resources for renewal. The history of racial discrimination in the South is one of fulfilling the preferences of some southern voters at the expense of Blacks. The local sheriff (such as Bull Connor in Alabama) helped preserve discrimination and it was the National Guard under the control of President Eisenhower that supported Black rights to attend integrated schools. One cannot advocate a structure of government without taking sides.

A study of Indianapolis found that the citizens of a neighborhood within the city had similar preferences as Speedway, a contiguous independent city (Ostrom et al. 1973). The peripheral areas preferred more visible police patrols rather than the on-call deployment of officers practiced in Indianapolis. In terms of the effective use of available resources for the entire city of Indianapolis, the on-call system was thought efficient. But the peripheral areas would have used (and did use) the tax money differently and had less interest in crime in the central city (assuming it would stay there). Again, it is an issue of who is responsible for controlling central city crime and who owns the tax base. Which citizens' preferences count?

12.5.3 Necessity for moral choice

Alternative political institutions for making working rules influence whose preferences count. Power to the people is meaningless if people disagree. The question is always, which people, which part of the public? Judging political institutions on the basis of whether it is more effective, representative, even democratic is no less a chimera than judging working rules on the basis of efficiency. Both beg the question, who counts? Extending the franchise is no small achievement, but as has been seen above, the electoral details matter as do subsequent rules for making legislative, executive and court decisions.

Bromley (forthcoming) takes the pragmatist view that we learn what we want as we see what is possible in interacting with others. Without including others in our identity (social capital), we consign ourselves to a Hobbesian world. Neither human wills nor the political rules affecting what is learned and who counts are fixed. The reality is a never-ending evolutionary process with no givens except memory and hope.

When issues of substance threaten the peace, it is tempting to argue that our position is not just for our own benefit, but rather meets some criteria that enjoy wide consent. But these criteria command consent largely because they are empty, hide conflict and contradictions, and involve selective perception. Arrow's impossibility theorem and the transaction perspective of institutional economics have swept illusion aside. We are left to persuade others that our demand for rights is morally defensible, not just efficient or the result of something vaguely called democracy.[5] As Joan Robinson (1962) put it in a slightly different context, "The Keynesian revolution has destroyed the old soporific doctrines, and its own metaphysics is thin and easy to see through. We are left in the uncomfortable situation of having to think for ourselves." Just who is my brother or sister? Neither logic nor process can save us from the agony of balancing the interests of self and others.

12.5.4 War and peace

War can destroy wealth faster than economic development can create it. War and peace have been a topic of inquiry by institutional economists from Veblen (1964) to Keynes (1920). War and violence is the breakdown of the political process and threats thereof are part of many political negotiations. Space and the author's knowledge do not permit further exploration here, except to note that peoples' attitude toward each other is a product of the economy as much as are the usual goods and services. Fishman (2002: 35) observes that "With few exceptions, wars have become conflicts over property rights to natural resources that attract global capital." See also Elbadawi and Sambani (2000) and Collier and Hoeffler (1998).

12.6 Concluding Observations

The theory developed to hypothesize the impact of alternative everyday institutions on the interests of different groups in the previous chapters has also proven useful to hypothesize the impact of political rules for making the everyday rules. Situational characteristics of incompatible use, high exclusion cost, and transaction costs including information costs are relevant to understanding interest group formation, the political principal-agent problem, and the impact of alternative voting rules. The behavioral implications of bounded rationality and learning are also important. Politicians as well as business people do not take preferences as given. Moral issues surrounding the use and claim of power can't be avoided.

NOTES

1. For a review of empirical studies, see Saint-Paul (2000).
2. Uslaner (1998: 102–3) argues that informal rules (culture) are central and not on a causal par with legal institutions. While culture supports formal law, law also can change culture, albeit slowly. Evolving ideology and political contest contributed to new civil rights law, but the law also contributed to further evolution of ideology. There is much debate in the literature over the relative importance of formal and informal institutions. For example, the so-called "behavioral school" of political science dominant in the 1950s and 60s emphasized informal institutions related to class, ethnicity, language, culture, ideology, and religion and downplayed formal political structure. This led March and Olsen (1989) to write *Rediscovering Institutions*. "Bureaucratic agencies, legislative committees, and appellate courts are arenas for contending social forces, but they are also collections of standard operating procedures and structures that define and defend values, norms, interests, identities and beliefs" (17).
3. For a review of theories of proportional representation, see Mueller (1989: ch. 12). For an earlier exploration, see Commons (1907). Commons showed who won and lost under different rules and did not try to justify any rule with a general welfare argument. By his own values he preferred more power in the legislature and less in the executive if the former could directly represent all interests. "Proportional representation is not advocated only to give the minority a hearing, but mainly to give all the people confidence in their rulers and in one another" (225).
4. Many economists object. "The alternative of defining efficiency in terms of any result of voluntary transactions relative to the institutional structure seems to me a much less powerful and precise tool for analyzing market outcomes" (Sandmo 1990: 59).
5. A similar point is made by Mueller (1989: 110) when he says, "Wicksell did not elaborate on how the majority rules would be used to settle distribution issues, and the entire normative argument for the use of the unanimity rule to decide allocation decision is left to rest on the *assumption* that a just distribution has been determined prior to the start of collective decision making on allocation issues." "At some point, the issue of how fairness is introduced into the decision process and how it is agreed upon, must be faced" (111).

Chapter 13
Institutional Change Analysis

Institutions change as people interact with each other in the context of changes in population, resources, technology, and people's subjective perception and imagination. These changes cause people to change their behavior which when aggregated and regularized become new informal institutions. Those behaviors, which become conscious, may result in pressure for formal institutional change as well. The result of "demands" for new formal institutions depends on the rules for making rules (constitutions) that sort out whose demands count when there is conflict. To understand institutional change is not an easy task. More than one response is possible to a change in population, technology, and resources. And there can be no response at all, at least for some time. One of the prevalent facts to be explained is that of path dependence – the path of change is heavily influenced by past changes.

The first section of this chapter presents some theories of institutional change. The second section contains a discussion of how informal institutions evolve in the context of changes in population, technology, resources, and ideas. It also includes how these become widespread and regularized or not. The third major section is focused on the impact of alternative rules for making formal rules. Finally, since corporate law and organization are so central to the economy, a fourth section explores its evolution. While this chapter focuses on institutional change, keep in mind previous chapters that discussed change such as some of the case studies of section 7.3.1 and 7.3.3, the role of technology in 10.3, and political institutions in chapter 12.

13.1 Theories of Institutional Change

A pluralistic methodology of inquiry will be employed here. It employs three principles that Toboso (2001: 773–4) calls "institutional individualism." (1) "Only persons can pursue aims and promote interests." Depending on the period and context, preferences and ideology may be stable or changing, and people may be acting alone or consciously with others. It will be useful to speak of individuals participating in organizations and of competition among groups. (2) "Formal and informal sets of institutional rules affecting interactions among persons must be part of the explanatory variables." The institutional structure such as the political rules for making rules may be exogenous for the period of analysis or people may aim to change them (or the rules may change unintentionally). The formal and informal institutional structure may shape the opportunity set of actors as they pursue their preferences, or the structure may influence the evolution of preferences. (3) "Marginal institutional changes always result from the independent or collective actions of some persons and always take place within wider institutional frameworks." The degree of calculation, habit, cued or strategic behavior, foresight, imagination, etc. are empirical matters in the case investigated and not to be assumed.

Theories of institutional change can be grouped into functional, power, isomorphic, and learning–evolutionary models. Functional theories conceive of a rational actor who acts to change institutions so that they better serve the actor's interests. One version visualizes the process as one of Pareto-better transactions wherein institutions change only if the winners can compensate the losers. Power theories visualize a dominant group that has the power to make changes in its interests without the consent of others. Isomorphic theories conceptualize a process wherein institutions can be stable or change even if the actors do not know the connection between alternative institutions and performance. Learning–evolutionary theories emphasize that human objectives and preferences change without any necessary change in environment. Each of these theories has persisted for some time. When this is the case there is usually some utility and truth in each in specific contexts, even if at first they may appear contradictory.

13.1.1 Functional

The Nobel Prize citation for Douglass North reads, "As one of the pioneers in the 'new institutional economics,' North has demonstrated the role of institutions, including property rights . . ." (Myhrman and Weingast 1994: 158). According to North, new institutions arise when groups in society perceive a possibility of availing themselves of profits that cannot be realized under prevailing institutional conditions. If external factors permit an increase in income, but it is prevented by institutional factors, then new institutional arrangements are likely to develop. "Changes in relative prices and fluctuations in population growth led to institutional changes" (158). This is a functional theory in which rational utility-maximizing individuals shape formal institutions. North qualifies functionality with bounded rationality which limits the ability of people to process functional information even if it were available, which it often is not. He also notes the role of ideology and cultural norms that are the basis for other theories outlined below.

The external factor leading to a functional change in private governance may be provided by change in transaction costs. Williamson (1985) argues that transacting firms will seek governance arrangements to minimize transaction costs. Thus, firms using a general-purpose technology are predicted to be related by markets. If the technology changes and firms see an advantage to using specific assets, Williamson predicts a functional change to hierarchy or at least the creation of hostages to provide incentive to maintain the transaction.

Complex systems, however, generate their own endogenous change. Olmstead and Goldberg (1975) point out that a group finding a new opportunity can do more than obtain a right to exploit it. They can try to change public attitudes or change the rules for making rules. In doing so they will be in conflict with other groups and thus any theory of change must examine power issues (Schmid 1977).

Equilibrium is a feature of functional theories. An example discussed in chapter 10 is that of Ruttan and Hayami (1984) who argue that new plant varieties in the Philippines upset the equality between marginal returns to labor in rural and urban areas. The traditional institution for sharing the harvest among tenants, landless labor, and landowners then had to change to restore the rural and urban wage equilibrium. This ignores possible power explanations of why landlords captured the gains from the Green Revolution (Schmid 2000; Bromley 1989: 18–27). Bardhan (1989: 1391) notes that "changes in relative prices can't predetermine the balance of class forces or the outcome of social conflicts." He asks if the institutional changes favoring landlords "come about because the disequilibriium between labor productivity and wage 'demanded' such a change, or because population pressure on land made collective action on the part of employers easier (or that on the part of laborers weaker) . . ." (1393).

The reproduction of institutions involves a tension between continuity and change (Samuels 1992b: 24–8). Certainty is valued when making plans and invest-ments. But at the same time, complete certainty and stability produces boredom and stagnation. US common law celebrates continuity with reference to precedent. But this is often selectively perceived when several precedents are possible. When we approve of change we call it judicial creativity and when we prefer continuity, we call change judicial trespass on natural law or legislative authority (Samuels 1984: 52–5).

A functional theory of institutional change assumes some given opportunity to increase total wealth, whether its source is a change in population, a new techno-logy, discovery of a natural resource, or a change in consumer preferences. It ignores power questions of whose interests are served and the distribution of that wealth. Asymmetry in alternative opportunities among the parties affect bargaining power (Knight 1995: 117). Further, it assumes an obvious exogenous opportunity for gains from trade, not affected by cognitive structures. People will put their creative skills to work to find institutional ways of achieving this gain if the *perceived* benefits exceed the costs. And, perceptions are affected by institutions.

Sjostrand (1993) sees the above functional conception as circular because institu-tions shape individuals. "The institutional setting at a certain moment represents the individual's (organization's) incentives to act. At the same time the institutions represent the standards for eliminating 'failing' attempts, either individual or organ-izational (or organizing). What then explains the possible motive for an individual to do something new, something that is not part of the incentives built into the existing institutions? Success based on such efforts is impossible, since the existing institutions define the criteria." "How, then, is it possible to change institutions, to develop new paths, when the institutions themselves (as constraints) define both incentives and outcomes?" (34). Sjostrand is speaking of informal institutions that "refer to norms for organizing rather than to any a priori defined organizational norms. Institutions do not 'provide' structures for exchange or interaction; they constitute generalized regularities in the organizing activities themselves" (35). The concept of transaction or interaction is preferred to exchange in this context.

The functionalism of an institution is in the eye of the beholder. Mantzavinos (2001: 93n) says, "What function an institution has depends on the point of view that one adopts. Therefore, it is better to abandon altogether the notion of function and focus on the effects that certain institutions have for the individuals of the social group under examination." He emphasizes that what is seen as functional is based on subjective experience, imagination, and mental models. This makes institutional change hard to predict from only observing price or technological changes.

13.1.2 Power theories and the power elite

The problem with functional theories is that they often beg the question of functional for whom. The focus on facilitation of exchange (realization of Pareto-improvements) begs the question of who has what to trade. This question leads to power theories. If people are interdependent, as enumerated in chapter 6, not everyone gets their first choice, and exercise of power is inevitable. Institutional change is ongoing and at any given time embedded in rules for making rules and informal ideology favoring one party over another. The power of force and bargaining are path dependent. The more you have in time 1, the more you get in time 2.

In practice, groups do not accept the status quo as the basis for negotiations over institutional change. The focus on facilitation of exchange (realization of Pareto-improvement) begs the question of who has what to trade. Kuznets (1972) pointed out that growth leads to shifts in the relative positions of different groups in a society and that a key determinant of long-term growth is the flexibility of the society to moderate such conflicts through the sovereign state. A powerful technology may bring surprises. Emphasis on labor saving devices "may not be suited to the more traditional life patterns of the agricultural communities that dominate in many less developed countries." Kuznets observed that new technology requires "numerous and varied adjustments by individual participants in the economic process represented by individual participants . . ." (Kuznets 1972: 442). These are "so far-reaching that it may not be possible to establish an adequate calculus of costs and returns for comparison with the pre-existing patterns of life and work." Kuznets observed the dislocations and "costs and difficulty of moving from established uses, that have become obsolete, to new uses. The specific characteristics of material capital, whether natural resources or existing reproducible capital, may limit mobility to alternative uses" (445). (He anticipated Williamson and specific assets.) "The problem of obsolescent and unemployed productive resources is a constant accompaniment of the continuous sequence of technological innovations in modern economic growth" (445). When Kuznets is speaking of the "specific characteristics of capital," he is speaking of what here has been called "situation."

Institutions are central for Kuznets. He begins with a functional theory. "The difficulty of making the institutional and ideological transformations needed to convert the new large potential of modern technology into economic growth in the relatively short period since the late eighteenth century limited the spread of the system" (Kuznets 1973: 250). He adds some power elements. "Moreover, obstacles to such transformations were, and still are being, imposed on the less developed countries by the policies of the developed countries" (250). "In that modern economic growth has to contend with the resolution of incipient conflicts continuously generated by rapid changes in economic and social structure, it may be described as a process of controlled revolution" (252). Schumpeter called this "creative destruction" (Schumpeter and Swedberg 1991).

While North's emphasis has been on institutions to capture gains from trade, he does not ignore power. "Institutions are not necessarily or even usually created to be socially efficient; rather they, or at least the formal rules, are created to serve the interests of those with bargaining power to create new rules" (1994: 360-1). This power is influenced by the rules for making rules (see chapter 12). The formal constitutional rules that emerge are the result of a mixture of functional, power, and isomorphic processes. The sustainability of power is always problematic. Use of raw power begets resistance. The evolution of the use of power by others affects institutional change and its impact. The learning and reinforcement of legitimacy has a lot to do with institutional change or stability.

Many political scientists acknowledge the role of power in determining winners and losers. For example, Steinmo (1993) explains cross-national differences in tax policy by differences in political institutions that structure which groups are represented.

Are issues of power avoided with informal institutional change? New objectives, ideologies, and norms are learned without anyone consciously trying to change them. Still, some people are more influential in this process than others, whether they lead by charisma, strength, or intelligence. For example, women's preferences for home and work changed dramatically in the last 30 years. Part of this was the result of an organized movement, but part was an informal process of learning. Whether laws were passed prohibiting gender discrimination or social norms changed which made it unthinkable, the power relationships changed.

Perhaps one of the more subtle expressions of power is in control of the agenda (Bartlett 1989; Lukes 1974). (Recall section 12.2.2.) Whether conscious or not, we learn what institutions are variable and subject to change and what never come up. Because of bounded rationality, we never examine all options, and the options considered are shaped by informal institutions. The formal political rules for making rules can affect the formation of winning coalitions (Weir 1992).

Regulation theory: The distinctive features of "*regulation* theory" developed by Boyer (2001) and others are consistent with power theories. (1) It "considers that institutional forms emerge through resolution of social conflict . . . which in turn calls for political intervention and recognition by decree, law or even constitutional change." (2) "Major capitalist institutions do not emerge out of the aggregation of purely local and isolated compromises: they derive from systemic processes." (3) "Social contradictions, political conflicts and economic unbalances are always present and eventually manifest themselves through crises during which the acceptance and viability of past institutional compromises are challenged" (115–6).[2]

13.1.3 Isomorphic theories (path dependence)

To the extent that functional and power theories explain institutional change, a change in environment and opportunities should lead to changes in institutions. However, institutions often display stability in the face of great environmental change and exhibit considerable dysfunction, even to the detriment of the elite.[1] DiMaggio and Powell (1983: 157) offer a theory of isomorphism to explain "the irrationality, the frustration of power, and the lack of innovation that are so commonplace in organizational life." Bounded rationality is central to the theory. Part of the environment of an organization is the behavior of other organizations (Schelling 1978: 4). To reduce uncertainty, it is better to be like others even if that form of organization is not entirely functional for the organization in question. A firm can change its internal rules or it can lobby government to require others to be more like it.

Organizational goals and methods to achieve them are often ambiguous, and the connections uncertain. While specific performance outcomes may be hard to measure, organization charts and internal rules are easily observable to outside stakeholders. Thus a firm may adopt the organizational form of other prestigious firms to bask in their glory and achieve legitimization. "Similarity can make it easier for organizations to transact with other organizations, to attract career-minded staff, to be acknowledged as legitimate and reputable, and to fit into administrative categories that define eligibility for public and private grants and contracts. None of this, however, insures that conformist organizations do what they do more efficiently than do their more deviant peers" (DiMaggio and Powell 1983: 153–4).

Institutional change often involves a mixture of functional, power, and isomorphic processes. An illustrative case is provided by the institutions surrounding medical education. At one time in the US, there were several theories of medicine and medical education. With the publication of the Flexner Report by a prestigious foundation in 1910, one dominant version emerged and almost all the other schools disappeared. If you wanted to be licensed you had to graduate from a certain kind of school. This can be interpreted as functional survival of the fittest. Or, it can be interpreted as a power grab or as an isomorphic process in which any of the schools might have emerged victorious as long as the public would not be confused by competing claims and lose confidence in the service provided. Alternative homeopathic and other approaches are only now reappearing.

13.1.4 Social learning, evolution, and emergence

An economy can be conceptualized as a system of systems (Potts 2000). A system is composed of elements and connections that define each other. Any complex system can be disaggregated into subsystems and in turn be part of higher-order systems. The connections (including institutions) of the elements and subsystems are not given, but endogenously created via learning, human imagination, and other processes. A system is marked by emergence – self-organization, non-linearity, and feedback. Connections are necessarily incomplete, and those existing are continually evolving.

New objectives, ideologies, and values are learned without anyone necessarily consciously trying to shape them. A social force is defined by Field as a force that cannot be attributed to any individual or group and cannot be explained by an aggregation of the decisions of many maximizing individuals (Field 1979: 54). Some argue that this is an empty set and all behavior including that which exhibits caring, trust, and willingness to play by the rules is really calculated to serve narrow utility maximization. To the contrary, these behaviors are generally learned and internalized without any specific promise of *quid pro quo*. Rules and habits may be followed which shape behavior independent of the payoff and the probability of sanctions. Institutions supply a cue of social appropriateness rather than a logic of instrumentality (March and Olsen 1989: ch. 2).

Interests to be functionally implemented with institutional change or imposed by the use of power come from learning that is subject to change. North recognizes that it is perception of opportunities that drives actors to change behavior and institutions. He sees both unintended and unanticipated results. Our cultural heritage is a kind of "beyond rationality" beliefs and their role "may be a superior survival trait to possess some explanation rather than no explanation for phenomena beyond our scientific reach" (North 1998).

North (1997: 13) argues, "The process of change results from a continuous change in that reality which results in changing the perceptions which in turn induce the players to modify or alter the structure which in turn leads to changes in that reality – an ongoing process." He sees this in evolutionary terms. "This institutional framework has evolved over many generations, reflecting, as Hayek reminds us, the trial and error process which has sorted out those behavioral patterns that have worked from those that have failed." But of course, failure depends in part on who decides where the economy or firm should go. Trial and error as a selection story is clouded by the fact that the particular behavior and environment undergoing trial (and henceforth referred to) is a matter of perception and salience. The interpretation of what constitutes error (and what of many ongoing behaviors caused it) is also subjective and influenced by institutions (feedback from others). What provides the dynamics? North says, "The perceptions of political and economic entrepreneurs change reflecting ubiquitous competition amongst organizations with changes in relative prices, other new information leading such entrepreneurs, given their beliefs and the constraints imposed by the existing scaffold (not to mention the standard economic constraints) to modify or alter institutions to improve their competitive positions. The result is to alter the 'REALITY' of the economic system which in turn will lead to altered perceptions and BELIEFS of the system which in turn will lead to further INSTITUTIONAL change in an endless process of societal change" (13). The point is well taken even if the analyst has a problem in distinguishing belief and reality. Profit may be a test for an entrepreneur, but its attribution to particular behaviors is sometimes problematic.

Among other things, people learn to see things as variables that they once took as part of nature. People learn to change their discount rates and planning horizons and the period over which their limited maximization is calculated. People learn malevolence and benevolence that affect who they will trade with and treat as object or subject. They change their expectations and imaginations of the future and the possible.

Evolutionary theory borrowed and expanded from biology provides a useful framework to organize observations of institutional change. Its key processes are variation, selection, and reproduction. In biology, *variation* is caused by random mutation. In societies, it is a function of selective perception, human imagination, creativity, and selective perception. Foster and Metcalfe (2001: 10) suggest, "The rate of economic progress that we observe, reflects guided variation within conceptual schemes that are non-random aspects of development processes." While creativity may in part be purposeful, the environment is complex and its comprehension always uncertain.

Then there is some process of selection or *sorting*. Competition is one such process, but not the only one. Key adjustment processes include "public opinion, learning and selective perception, expectations and discounting, legitimation, control of government (that is, of the uses to which government is to be put), administrative agencies, the legislature, and the courts" (Samuels, Schmid, and Shaffer 1994). One of the critical processes is that of increasing returns and cumulative and circular causation described in previous chapters. In both biology and society, the sorting may be at the individual or population level. It must be emphasized that the selection is not done to maximize fit to some given environment, but that environment is also changing and, most importantly, the environment is not simply an independent fact, but also subject to cognition and interpretation. "Fitness is not an attribute of any particular selective unit, it is a derived consequence of interaction within a given environmental context" (Foster and Metcalfe 2001: 7). The selective unit coevolves with its social, technological, and natural environment (Gowdy 1994; Norgaard 1994). Just as individuals affect institutions and institutions affect the preferences and cognitions of individuals, human behavior changes to fit the environment and alters the environment. "Selection does not optimize, but is irreducibly a historical contingent process" (Potts 2000: 33).

Imagining and deciding what system elements to connect, and how, and to what purposes is an ongoing interacting process of emergence. Some of the knowledge used to form new connections (institutions) among the elements of a social system is supplied (created) by the participants. The system is self-organizing and not the result of inevitable givens. The emergence of new order engenders a situation where the whole can be greater than the sum of the parts (or less).

The evolving choices of others are part of the environment of an individual. Person A is trying to develop her best strategy based on the anticipated action of B who is trying to do the same anticipating A. The aggregate result of this sorting under uncertainty may be nothing that either party fully anticipated. "Emergence and perpetual novelty are ever present in games where the opponents are adapting to each other" (Holland 1998: 42). "Emergence is above all a product of coupled, context-dependent interactions. Technically these interactions, and the resulting system, are *nonlinear*. The behavior of the overall system *cannot* be obtained by summing the behaviors of its constituent parts" (121–2).

Then the selected characteristic must be *replicated* and passed from one generation to the next. In biology, genes are the carrier, while in society this is done by routines and learned habits (Nelson 2001: 22). Routines that survive are part of systems of routines. This means that methodologically, observation at the population level is appropriate. Change can be gradual or punctuated. The mode of coordination is "social technologies" or institutions. Nelson argues, "This formulation naturally induces one to see prevailing institutions not so much as do some analysts as 'constraints' on behavior, but rather as defining the effective way to get things done when human cooperation is needed" (24). "The learning of new routines by actors is a time consuming, costly and risky thing" (25). In the empirical cases to be noted below we shall be alert to how the creation of new technologies is in part shaped by institutions and how technology and perceptions thereof in turn shape institutions.

There has been a long and continuing debate over the direction of causality between individuals and institutions. Do individuals create institutions or do institutions shape individuals? Both can be true. Recalling the point of chapter 4, neither individuals nor institutions are a starting place for analysis. Both are an outcome of a process and constitute a complex system. "Institutions and human actions, complements and antitheses, are forever remaking each other in the endless drama of the social process" (Hamilton 1932: 89). Even when norms shape the individual, "the individual can 'chose' among several simultaneously existing but often unrelated or sometimes even conflicting norms. One important source of this (partial) individual freedom of action, the capacity to 'choose', rests on the ability of people to discriminate between 'what is' and 'what should be'. It rests on the human capacity of imagination" (Sjostrand 1993: 39). Also, individuals "face the problem of how to select and fit a norm to a situation" (40). So while institutions shape individuals, they leave plenty of room for the causality to run the other way. A similar point is made by Hodgson when he says, "Individuals both constitute, and are constituted by, society. Unidirectional modes of explanation, such as from parts to wholes – and vice versa – or from one level to another are thus thwarted. There is both 'upward' and 'downward' causation" (Hodgson 1999b: 139).

Individuals experience institutions piecemeal in real time and particular environments with limited scope. Systems are incomplete; everything is not connected. Communication can result in common understanding, a social construction of reality. However, Sjostrand (1993: 39) says, "An activity could also have multiple meanings to different individuals, thus becoming the focus of conflicting institutional definitions and demands." Working out these conflicts may not be containable informally and there may be a demand for formal institutional change via government.

A formal institution is enforced by the state or an organization, but its effectiveness is affected by the degree of calculated self-enforcement. Its longevity depends on reinforcement. Institutions are self-enforcing when "each individual's behavior is the best he or she can do given the behavior and expected behavior of others" (Greif forthcoming). See also Aoki (2001).[3] In other words, there is no advantage to act apart from the institution. In Greif's terms, institutions are "self-reinforced" if the engendered behaviors do not set in motion variables that would change the calculation of advantage. Greif provides the thirteenth century example of German medieval merchant guilds that needed assurance that their goods would not be confiscated by the local rulers in Bruges. When merchants were scarce, the local rulers did not want to lose their trade. But as trade grew and there were many merchants to replace any lost ones, the rulers harassed the German merchants. The very growth of trade undermined the institution of property and the calculating ruler could gain by breaking his commitment. Merchants from other countries had strong associations, and if one of their number was harassed, they all withdrew. This non-marginal threat of exit was "self-enforcing" because the ruler could not gain outside of the agreement. On the other hand, if the changes in other parameters (such as number of merchants) work against the status quo, the institution has sown the seeds of its own destruction. The circular and cumulative effect makes it harder for the commitment to sustain itself. The conditions enabling self-enforcement are not reinforced. German merchants saw the advantage of group action and later acted in concert.

Individuals and organizations often fit behaviors to environment "not because it advances the means–ends efficiency of the organization but because it enhances the social legitimacy of the organization or its participants" (Hall and Taylor 1998). Managers who participate in professional forums and read the business press unconsciously learn to follow current themes of diversification, downsizing, greenness, or whatever (Fligstein 1990). Feedback of approval and regard may subconsciously reinforce a behavior as the term was used in section 3.5.

All of the above theories of institutional change must be built upon the same behavioral foundations as the impact theories of the previous chapter. For example, these theories must accommodate learning and reinforcement, bounded rationality, and circular and cumulative causation. Institutional change can result from groups identifying the sources of their interdependence (incompatibility, exclusion cost, etc.). These factors are at work even with unconscious learning. With this conceptual background, let us now turn to several examples of informal institutional change to be followed by a section on formal institutions. These two sets differ by their mode of origin and enforcement but both apply to general everyday operational rules, rules of a given organization, and rules (foundations) for making rules (Vanberg 1989).

13.2 Informal Institutional Change

The making of informal rules and custom is shaped by informal institutional structures and mental processes as surely as the formal rules for making rules shape formal rules. Learning is structured by concepts that influence images of how the world works and what is possible. Mental health requires some degree of order and predictability (Mantzavinos 2001). We like to think we have reasons for our behavior. Schlicht (1998: 2) portrays custom "as emerging from the individual's desire to align behavior, conviction and emotion tightly with one another." A person who accepts an obligation toward another provides an entitlement to them. Obligations "that are subjectively accepted, and go along with a motivational disposition to respect these claims" function the same as formal legal rights and often provide the rationale for them.

People make inferences from settled categories fitting behavior (own and expected of others) to new areas. They imitate those who are successful (Boyd and Richerson 2001). If these mental models are widely shared, a custom emerges and is reinforced by the approval of others. Given bounded rationality, these images necessarily simplify and categorize a complex world. These images shape the evolution of informal rules just as constitutions and political rules affect whose preferences count in the making of formal rules (discussed in a following section). Language and concepts ultimately influence whose interests count and are thus part of the power structure. The fact that they are shared, implicit, subconscious, and appear natural gives them great stability. Nevertheless, they change. General attitudes toward free speech and deviants affect informal institutional change.

Inadvertent defenders of the status quo informal rules achieve isomorphic stability if the rules appear universal, objective, and natural. This can be achieved through various pedagogic processes that reinforce and reproduce the cultural system of meaning and symbolism. Bourdieu (1986) refers to this "cultural capital" as symbolic violence when the subject class does not recognize their own self-interest. Some examples of dominant symbolism are slogans of "lower taxes" without identifying the public services that are to be cut; of "free markets" which ignore the effect of existing rights; and of seeing "externalities as a special case" requiring removal when they are ubiquitous and the only choice is who bears them.

Informal institutions are learned and reinforced without necessarily thinking about the aggregate performance. They may arise and die without conscious thought of their passing. They are part of the woodwork. They seem spontaneous and part of nature. Their change is also accomplished without people being aware of the process or predicting the aggregate result. This makes them very hard to study. Nevertheless, it is the selective bringing to light of what we must necessarily be largely unaware that is the utility of research on informal institutions (Foucault 1970).

Informal foundational institutions shape the evolution of everyday informal institutions. Informal foundational institutions are equivalent to formal constitutions and other political rules for making formal rules to be discussed below. To the extent that formal institutions are part of the environment for learning, they also can change the informal foundational institutions and ideologies. What are the foundational institutions that give order to the making of new everyday informal institutions? One is language and conceptual frameworks such as those in this book. We see what we have a language to see (Samuels 2001; Nooteboom 2001). Habits of thought frame issues and what can be seen as variable. Bounded rationality means that not everything is seen as variable. Not everything is seen as salient, even if in some sense functional. There are increasing returns to continued use of informal institutions just as in physical capital. See table 13.1, contrasting performance resulting from two cultures. North (1990) contrasts the higher order mental models of English and Spanish cultures. Macfarlane (1978) documents how the English structure of the village community, family, and organization of work created an individualistic attitude since the thirteenth century that was not found in Spain. It is difficult to disentangle an evolutionary process when structure shapes performance that feeds back again on structure.

An evolutionary model is used by scholars working in the Austrian tradition. According to Kasper and Streit (1999), "The process by which internal rules change has the characteristics of all decentralized order: there is decentralized experimentation with breaches of existing rules (institutional innovation); there are decentralized, spontaneous selection processes in which innovations are accepted until they gain critical mass to become new standards or are rejected" (393). "Such evolution

Table 13.1 Informal institutional change

Situation	Structure	Performance
Status quo informal everyday habits, institutions, SOPs and routines in $time_1$; e.g. arbitrary land rents. Path dependency. Circular and cumulative causation. Increasing returns.	1. Culture A, e.g. England. Language and concepts. Mental models, imagination and saliency. Ideology for making ideologies. Informal institutions within which new informal institutions evolve, are reinforced or die. Attitude toward free speech and deviants.	1. Everyday ideology, informal habits, and customs in $time_2$ that allocate opportunities and obligations; e.g. customary land rents became established.
	2. Culture B, e.g. Spain. Different language and concepts. Ideology, e.g. collective.	2. A contrasting everyday custom allocating economic opportunities; e.g. arbitrary land rents continue.

captures the wisdom and judgment of the many . . ." (393). This interpretation is a functional theory as shown by the statement, "Only if experience shows repeatedly that the old customs and conventions yield poor results and cause people to miss opportunities will the pressure of expediency induce an adaptation of internal institutions" (390).

Note above that "people" is undifferentiated. When people are interdependent, someone's missed opportunity is often the realization of the opportunity of others. There are some informal innovations that are widely embraced. Others are hotly contested. Reference was made above to a change in the customary share of rice harvest in the Philippines between landless labor and landowners when technological change enhanced yields. The landlords who asserted an increased share could be regarded as innovating deviants. Poor performance (benefit of technology to harvesters) from the landlords' view was good performance for the harvesters. It is presumptive to glorify the result as the collective wisdom of a "million little mutinies" (391). This is power play, not natural collective wisdom.

If people differ in their learning, imagination, ideas of saliency, and interests, does this mean that informal institutional change is impossible? Not necessarily. The saliency that occurs to a powerful or persuasive individual or group makes one informal rule emerge rather than another. And once in place, people may forget its origin.

Attitudes toward people of different races, gender, and national origin are reflected in a host of behaviors many of which are customary. Long before civil rights were legislated, racial attitudes evolved. Many did not perceive any conflict between slavery and the equal rights to all men declared in the US Constitution because they did not see Blacks as men. Words do not speak for themselves, and meaning is always a matter of human structures. "Only the human animal uses words, but he does so in an endless flow and for a variety of purposes. Words not only communicate factual information. They also impel, repel, encourage, rebuke – and deceive" (Breimyer 1991: 3). Other informal mental models evolved as a product of communication, literature, and religion. Slavery persisted in the US for decades. There was some kind of equilibrium among the actors. The feedback from the environment convinced the slave owners that it was a good idea. The white southern working class gave tacit approval since the system allowed them to feel superior to a major group of people even if they shared their poverty. The poor whites and the poor Blacks did not see themselves as a political group (class).

Myrdal conceived of the concept of circular and cumulative causation to describe the *American Dilemma* (recall chapter 6 above). Many people rationalized discrimination against Blacks by regarding them as inferior. They received feedback from the environment by observation of low incomes earned by Blacks. This feedback is the circular part of the process. This perception of inferiority justified the discrimination and denial of education and other opportunities to the Blacks. This amplified the original state of low income that further supported even more discrimination. This is the cumulative part of the process. Greif (forthcoming) refers to this amplification as a process of endogenous "self-reinforcement." The informal institution contains within itself a process that affects the kind and rate of its own change.

While Blacks mounted small-scale revolts, change came as northerners increasingly learned to regard slavery as immoral. War changed the property rights in a power struggle. The informal learning process evolved into war and change in the formal rules with a constitutional amendment and implementing legislation that continued to evolve through the 1950s' civil rights movement. Blacks like Rosa Parks refused to sit at the back of the bus. Leaders like Martin Luther King confronted the nation's professed ideals in the Constitution with reality. He asked if it really meant that all were created equal under the law. Protests (power) and ideological challenge eventually led to the 1964 Civil Rights Act. And passage of the Act again affected informal attitudes. Widely held informal ideologies and practice are always in evolution. Sometimes the status quo is reinforced and sometimes the clash produces cognitive dissonance and something gives.

Black protests were joined by whites who thought discrimination was wrong. Changes in ideology lead to changes in overt protest and political movements. As the laws changed, ideology changed as some tacitly supporting discrimination were subject to social pressure and held in low regard. Some eventually changed their mind. The removal of apartheid in South Africa in 1994 came from a combination of change of heart by the whites in power represented by DeClerk, international withdrawal of regard, and the protests of the Blacks represented by Mandela.

What are some informal institutions in the sense of habits of thought and perception that are important for economic life? One is our attitude toward debt. One of the early changes was the separation of debt from the person. In Roman times, debt was seen as a personal obligation, and failure to repay resulted in prison. A debt could not be sold to a third person. This has evolved into modern formal institutions of bankruptcy and trade in mortgages, but behind it is an informal attitude that make these things seems natural. For many years debt was regarded as undesirable, and only something for the desperate. Consumer debt was not widespread until the invention of the credit card in the 1950s. Some of this negative attitude has carried over in the attitude toward public debt. Most people see private and public debt as similar and regard public debt as one of the major public policy problems of our time.

People learn basic attitudes toward honesty. These are largely followed without thinking about whether the behavior can be monitored and sanctions applied. If formal policing were required for all transactions, most of the GNP would be in police. We return lost money and mistakes in change. We tip even in places we will never return to. We tend to split pots 50:50. We honor queues. These things do change over time and differ somewhat from society to society, but are nevertheless remarkably stable.

We learn to regard a particular structure of relative wages as being fair. Firemen make more than police, and college teachers make more than grade school teachers. We won't accept less than what is considered the going wage for a job even if we are unemployed.

Many business practices are the equivalent of cultural rules of thumb. In fact we speak of business culture in general and the culture of particular firms. The new employee with a new suggestion is often met with "That's not the way we do things around here." Much pricing is done in terms of traditional markups. For example, for long periods of time there was no thought of change in retailing. Then along came some entrepreneur with imagination, and the discount store is born with lower margins and higher volume. There are many areas of business inputs where the connection between input and output is difficult to ascertain. In this context certain rules of thumb such as the desired ratio of R&D or advertising to total sales emerges. There are fads in business organization as there are in consumer preferences. They go by the name of TQM, M-form, and perhaps even waves of downsizing. The firms in an industry tacitly cooperate and agree to compete on things other than price. Then along comes a new kid on the block and cut-rate no-frills airlines are born; and, then sometimes disappear, as the old order is re-established. An isomorphic process is replaced by functional or power demands.

Everyone searches for the meaning of life and their identity. In the broad sweep of human history our identity and loyalty have shifted a bit from family, tribe, and religion to occupation and avocation. There are still major parts of the world where political parties are largely tribal, ethnic, or religious based rather than differentiated by broad political philosophy and which party promises to provide more help for farmers or small business. The concepts of the nation state and the unit of patriotism are continually evolving. Some people get their sense of identity from a fundamental religious belief. Non-believers are seen as the evil enemy and a challenge to one's salvation and self-respect. The evil must be eliminated. Its tolerance makes you evil. This can lead to violent terrorism, whether bombing of the World Trade Center, the other party's shrines, or an abortion clinic.

Our fundamental attitudes to others are continuously changing. Our informal sense of equity evolves and affects the evolution of formal rules such as those that relate to gender and racial differentiation. "In a 1977 poll about two-thirds of the Americans surveyed agreed that 'It is much better for everyone if the man is the achiever and the woman takes care of the home and family.' By 1998, only one-third agreed: the proportions had reversed" (Folbre 2001: 4). It is a change in informal habits that slowly during the feminist movement made formal gender discrimination undefendable. Fundamental religious societies such as that which once dominated Afghanistan removed women from the workplace, even as schoolteachers. What seems natural to them seems monstrous to those in the West and vice versa. But, those in the West must remember that it was not so many years ago that women were not allowed to vote or be full members of the University of Cambridge. The effect of education and communication on the imagination may eventually catch up with the economic argument against discrimination.

The concepts of the "free market," "free trade," and "government intervention" enable many people to selectively and often tacitly support habitual ways of acting in given situations (and support codification into formal laws as well). Neither markets in general nor international trade in particular are a free for all. All markets have rules to govern the interdependencies that arise, not least of which is who is buyer and who is seller. In the case of trade, we have only to remember the West sending gunboats to China and Japan to force them to open their markets to imports. Or, more recently, we can recall the protests at the 2001 meeting of WTO in Seattle and trade ministers in Genoa. The neoclassical theory of trade only promises that trade will increase wealth in general, not that everyone automatically gains. The free market concept allows people to regard gunboats as a legitimate means of forcing free trade. Dugger and Sherman (2000) regard these as enabling myths.

Government is necessarily involved in giving order to interdependencies, but which actions get labeled as "intervention" and therefore undesirable is a matter of learned cognition formed by the language buried in the media and courses in economics (Breimyer 1991). It is these concepts that allow people to regard a law giving apple owners the right to destroy ornamental cedars that harbor an apple disease as an intervention, while an implicit law giving ornamental cedar owners the right to harm apple growers is seen as a natural thing (Samuels 1971). The same internalized way of thinking accounts for the ability of some to regard regulation of polluters as an intervention while the right to pollute is not. Whether these ways of thinking are part of daily practice that gets implemented by way of common law court decisions or rationalizes legislation, language and concepts shape whose interests count.

Metaphors are important in both informal and formal institutional change and maintenance. One of the powerful metaphors in economics is that of the market or institutions as "mechanisms." This conjures up something like a set of interlocking gears with fixed ratios. After it runs forward, if you crank it backward to its starting place, the original values hold. Mechanisms have no memory, learn only in a very limited way, don't get mad or emotional, or try to get even. It is difficult to incorporate cognition into a mechanistic metaphor. Gears just fit together and don't vary in their recognition of each other. Mechanisms are *ahistorical*. "Organism" would be an alternative metaphor for human relationships (institutions) and would shape inquiry in a different way.

13.2.1 Population, technology, resources, and imagination

The theory developed here can be applied for illustrative purposes to a series of examples ranging from land tenancy to consumer behavior. Changes in population, technology, resources, and imagination will be seen to play a role in informal institutional change as well as being interdependent with it.

FEUDAL LAND TENANCY IN ENGLAND

Customary land tenure is an example of an informal institution, albeit often abetted by formal legal institutions. It is always arbitrary to cut into a historical process at a particular time, but it is necessary if we are to have a manageable case study. Let us begin with several formative sources of medieval seigniorial proprietorship as distinct from previous clanship systems according to Max Weber (1961: ch. 3). (1) "Internal differentiation developed through the appearance of a professional military class." People who could provide specialized skills or military equipment (knights) were given privileged holdings. (2) "Conquest and subjugation of some enemy people." Slaves could clear land that became controlled by the overlords. (3) "Voluntary submission of the defenseless man to the overlordship of a military leader." (4) "Land settlement under feudal terms," including exploitation of a superior economic position such as leasing to foreign craftsmen. (5) "Profession of magic." A medicine man or rainmaker can convert taboos into personal possessions. (6) "Regulation of trade with other communities." All of these are a mixture of function and power and what seems right and natural at the time, including path dependencies therefrom. The evolution of land tenure is in part a continuous process of turning arbitrary decisions into customary practices with more predictability.

Oversimplified, the prevailing feudal institution of serfdom consisted of peasants having a private plot for their own working and also providing labor services upon the lord's land. This labor and other dues became regularized over time. Some pastureland was held in common. The very success of the military protection produced feedback leading to the downfall of the seigniorial system and the great manors (Pirenne 1937). From the middle of the tenth century, the population of Western Europe increased as a result of security from marauders. The excess population had to create new cultivable land or migrate to the towns. Pirenne called them "colonists" and they were attracted by the possibility of freedom, the avoidance of personal serfdom that largely disappeared by the end of the thirteenth century.

The growth of population and towns increased the price of foodstuffs, but the lords could not benefit. The customary rents were so firmly established that the landowner could not get a share of the rising value of production by unilaterally increasing rents. The lords' response was to offer their serfs personal freedom in exchange for cash. The peasant could then remain on the land at a renegotiated rent more favorable to the lord.

Rising agricultural productivity made possible evolutionary change from self-subsistence to trade or what might be called the mercantilization of agriculture. As towns become significant, they needed food. The lords encouraged the peasants to take their surplus produce to market (Gerschenkron 1971: 180). The lords then instituted cash rents that functioned to give them higher incomes than could be obtained from selling produce from their own lands using obligated labor. Here both function and power are involved in institutional change. Gershenkron (1971: 180) observes that if markets had been larger, it might have paid the lords to sell surplus from their own lands rather than collect rents from small sales by peasants from the peasants' land.

The new towns were making their own institutional changes. By collective action they acted as monopsonists. "The density of urbanization was thus one of the important elements entering the lord's decision, as was the provision policy of the towns, which again depended on their power to establish monopsonistic positions and to force the peasantry within a certain radius from the city to deliver the produce to the city markets that were regulated by artisans organized in craft guilds" (Gerschenkron 1971: 180). When the terms of trade turned toward the towns, the lords tried to recommute the money dues back into labor services so that the lords could countervail by controlling larger lots. This became even more attractive to the lords as long distance trade expanded. Nevertheless, they were largely unsuccessful as other changes reinforced the status quo. Gershenkron (1971: 180) observed, "To the extent that the commuted payments were lastingly fixed in money terms, the debasements of currencies and the inflation of the sixteenth century considerably reduced their real values. Accordingly, it became possible for peasants to buy freedom from servile status." Inflation is not bad for everyone.

New profit opportunities played a role in institutional change. But this is not the whole story as different interests conflict to control the gains. The feudal lords were both legislature and judiciary and used their power to inflict uncompensated losses on the peasants. Both functional and power theories are relevant (Brenner 1976). The line of causality between profit opportunities and institutional change is not unidirectional. Profit opportunities are not independent of institutions. For example, at any given time profits in land and sheep are influenced by other institutions relating to international trade in wool. It is also relevant that non-property owners could not vote in Britain until 1867. Profit opportunities would be of little interest to the lords if they had not learned to differentiate themselves by the consumption of luxury goods. Learning and preference evolution must be added to the function and power explanation.

Agricultural prices and incomes have always been influenced by cycles of weather and technology affecting supply and population affecting demand. For example, in the 1640s, rising population in England and the needs of the Parliamentary army contributed to rising prices (Thirsk 1997: 25). It had long been the policy of government to restrict export of grain to favor domestic consumers during periods of relative shortages. Still, just a few years later in 1656, shortages turned to surpluses and farmer ruin. In response, Parliament removed the export ban and subsidized exports and encouraged domestic use of spirits that required large quantities of grain to produce.

This evolutionary process continues. Today, western countries are trying to export their way out of grain surpluses and subsidize industrial use of grain such as ethanol. Price change surely drives some groups to seek relief in institutional change, but that does not answer the question of why they were successful and why the losers lost. This is ultimately a power question framed by the rules for making rules as well as a matter of learning new ideologies.

Technology creates new opportunities for profit, fame, power, and prestige and a demand for institutional change to realize them. But at the same time, institutions and ideology are also affecting technology. In the 1400s landowners spent little time managing their farms. But after the printing press was invented and made practicable, the classical writers on agriculture became available to wealthy landowners (Thirsk 1997: 27). These writers contributed to the idea that agricultural experimentation was an intellectual activity worthy of the upper class. Changes in attitudes and ideology are just as observable as technological changes. While we are never sure of people's attitudes, there is evidence in the record of what people say.

OPEN FIELDS AND ENCLOSURE

In addition to the institution of serfdom there was the institution of open fields. The essential features of English medieval agricultural organization were these: a lord who owned all of the land; peasants who were required to work on the lord's fields, but had fields of their own which they managed and were entitled to the harvest thereof, but when their arable land was fallowed it was subject to communal grazing; permanent pasture lands that were communally grazed (each peasant owned their own livestock, but they were herded all together). The individually managed plots were arranged in large open fields (no fence between individual holdings) and the plots of an individual were scattered. How did this come about? What is illuminated by functional, power, isomorphic, and social learning theories? Let's begin with William the Conqueror in 1066. Land ownership was a spoil of war, most certainly a result of power. Dahlman (1980: 49–55) argues that the lords could not exploit the peasants since peasants' labor on the lord's holdings was little more than a rental payment reflecting differentially productive land. However, he presents no data to show that no labor was owed to lords on marginal land, which would have made the wage equal on all lands in equilibrium.

Dahlman argues that fallow was necessary to maintain soil fertility. If the fallowed land were to be grazed, this meant that peasants must follow similar rotations in large enough blocks to make herding efficient. At a minimum, a peasant needed two plots, one in the large open field that is cropped and another lying fallow. But why large herds? The answer is economies of scale. It was efficient to hire a herdsman to watch all of the village animals because cattle naturally graze over a large area better than individually and intensively on a small plot. This was true for both the permanent pastures and the temporarily fallowed areas. Fencing was expensive relative to the value of livestock. See also White (1963).

Given economies of scale in livestock production, how could a large acreage be assembled if the pastures were individually owned? The transaction costs in negotiating with many individual small plot owners would have been prohibitive. Communal ownership and management with rules formed by the village council or court was the answer according to Dalhman. But why several scattered arable plots that are costly for the peasant to access? Some historians said it was to achieve equity in holdings, for an individual could have a mixture of soil types that have different yields in various years depending on the weather. Dahlman rejects this kind of explanation as ad hoc and incapable of being tested. While the historical record of what motivated people is foggy, it is not empty. What is the alternative to knowing ancient minds? Assume narrow short-run individual utility maximization? This assumption by the analyst hardly solves the problem.

What story then fits this very functional individual calculation? Dahlman (1980: 130) explains the scattered holding thusly, "It is the cost of enforcing and reaching the agreements of using the privately owned open fields that determines the scattering." If a peasant exchanged land to consolidate his holdings and fenced them, he would gain relative to others if they did not follow. The consolidator could put cattle on his own fenced fallow and still run his share of cattle on the common pastures. This has elements of the classical Prisoner's Dilemma problem with the potential for an unproductive equilibrium. Still Dahlman asserts, "Both joint and individual wealth maximization dictates that no individual be allowed to consolidate his strips. The infringements upon the economic activities of the rest of the community cannot be tolerated" (128). "The side effects of scattering are, as it were, imposed on the tenant in order to strengthen the viability of the collective decision making organization" (126). Imposed? This surely involves power.

It is well known in Prisoner's Dilemma situations that mere knowledge of the possibility of a low-level equilibrium is not enough to avoid it. If individuals are short-run utility-maximizers, they will follow the lead of the first consolidator-enclosure. Some writers such as Olson (1965) argue that narrow self-interest will result in defection and attempts to free ride, while Dahlman argues that self-interest results in cooperation without any use of power, though he recognizes a free-rider problem. But, narrow individual rationality can't be used to explain both cooperation and defection. As Field (1979: 57) puts it, "this conflict between the fact that cooperative solutions are often Pareto efficient and the fact that the free rider problem creates incentives for rule violation and coalition disintegration will not disappear." Analysts must know what is people's heads including what it is that they are maximizing, over what length of run, and strength of norms and learning.

Field argues that the length of run for utility maximization, if that is relevant at all, is a matter of institutions affecting people's world-view. This gets dangerously close to observation that Dahlman avoids, namely what is in people's heads. Dahlman (1980: 127) himself speaks of "communal ties" when explaining how village courts effectively enforced open fields and might have also been the forum for choosing to scatter holdings. Consolidation would give an individual more holdout power to bargain for more access to the commons in return for not enclosing. Scattered holdings decrease the returns to going it alone. But if people are to forego short run advantage and agree to open fields and scattered holdings, their short run calculations must be checked. And if everyone does not have the same length of run in their minds, the differences are resolved by power. Further, if some of the initial cooperators get mad at the defectors, they will not be willing to bargain with the defectors even if doing so would be Pareto-better. Some exogenous variable is needed that cannot be derived from rational choice models.

The use of power is demonstrated in the record (Tawney 1912). Some individuals did enclose and the village courts held them in check with fines for violating custom. Not everyone agreed to the system of open fields and scattered holdings. Where did the communal ties come from that supported the village courts? Dahlman (1980: 142) notes that prior to the English feudal system, the Germanic tribes practiced a kind of communal agriculture in open fields. It is always easier to extend the function of an existing collective organization than to create one from scratch. There is a path dependence for good or evil. Further, a collective body that could police the common pastures could also enforce open fields and scattered holdings. Land could be exchanged, but was subject to fines by the village court.

The role of technology and transaction costs are not to be ignored, but neither can be the institutions and ideologies that people hold in their minds. The desire for equity, sense of community, or lack of malevolence are no more or less ephemeral than communal ties and taking the long view when calculating advantage. All of these variables must be documented and interpreted. Thirsk's (1997) finding that the aristocracy ignored their holdings for a time and then found it worthy of their social standing to engage in farm management and experimentation is just as much a part of explaining institutional change as the changing price of wool. The French revolution was more a matter of the change of ideology questioning the divine right of kings than a change of technology and transaction costs. A theory which has no place for habit and ideology affecting what is seen as a variable and the length of the planning horizon is a crippled theory.

Dahlman (1980: 100) assumes that the lord and large- and small-holders can all be lumped together and the actual process of decision-making (rules for making rules) can be ignored. All that counts is total net output because the parties will find a Pareto-better solution if present. But, the claim of a particular group on production is often institutionally tied to a particular right and cultural practice. Change the nature of the right and practice and you change the legitimacy of the claim on output. It is hard to imagine that the village court is first calculating how to maximize total product and then easily recognizes a status quo point from which bargaining over the potential gain can occur among the lord and various sized serfs and free holders. There are many constraints on realization of Pareto-better gains even if seen by all. For example, over time, the labor obligation was commuted to rental rates that were fixed by custom. This meant that any increase in productivity or prices were claimed by the peasants. The mentality and world-view of a free man is different from that of a serf. But this will not be investigated if these institutions are considered soft and ad hoc.

Dahlman (1980: 100) does not find it necessary to examine the lord's interest different from the peasants. He rejects any possibility of exploitation. He reasons that if enclosures had been efficient earlier, the lords would have agreed to it for they could always bargain for a change in distribution to get more of the larger pie if there were one. A disequilibrium of unrealized Pareto-better changes is by definition not possible unless government interfered. This leads to an easy conclusion that all institutions are functional and efficient because if they were not, people would change them. (For a critique, see Bromley (1989: 14–18).) This circular reasoning is further buttressed by dismissing a "dumb peasant" explanation of institutional stability. The open field system persisted for hundreds of years. But one does not have to assert that people were dumb to note the effect of bounded rationality and the effect of world-view on such things as what is seen as a variable and the length of one's planning horizon. There may also be a place for isomorphic theories of change. In an uncertain world where the existence of Pareto-better opportunities is a matter of image and expectation, there is room for following the leader. Do what others are doing unless the system has entirely broken down. Further, the persistence of rules does not prove their functionality at each period. Useful rules require some stability. "Effectiveness of rules rests on the expectation that they will persist" (Field 1979: 59). So on the one hand it may be quite rational to attempt to modify institutions so that they fit some function of a dominant group and on the other to resist changing them to maintain predictability and fulfill expectations. Assuming that people are rational does not tell us much about which way it goes.

Differential communal ties, enmity among lords and peasants, and planning horizons can be expected to vary among villages and regions and is consistent with the facts of differential rates of change in the open field system. But consistency is not enough, one has to actually find evidence of these states of mind. But, they will never be found if theory ignores them. World-view affects what can be seen by analysts as well as by English peasants.

While open fields persisted for over 300 years, they did evolve and eventually disappear. Dahlman (1980: 131) rejects any theory of enclosure depending solely on technological change because that would have caused rational actors to change the institution right away. His explanation is the expansion of markets and specialization. A village specializing in grain does not need large communal pastures, and transaction costs associated with achieving them are irrelevant (156–7). Likewise it does not need scattering to support the communal system. Similarly, a village specializing in livestock would evolve to a single herdsman using the entire acreage with no need for communal rules or scattered plots (158). (And incidentally, no need for all of the previous peasants!)

While the enclosure movement proceeded for hundreds of years, there was a 100 year outburst beginning in the mid 1400s referred to as the Tudor enclosures. Rising population and export demand resulted in increased demand for wool and mutton. Large areas of tillable land were converted to pasture. "As a consequence, the amount of employment available in the agricultural sector diminished sharply, and some of the country became depopulated" (163). There is much literature describing the human misery. Who benefited from this wealth increasing enclosure? The unemployed peasants did not get severance pay.

The right of the lord to enclosure seems to have been established early. The 1235 Statute of Merton gave the lords the right to enclosure of part of the waste (permanent pastures) that the freeholders' peasants were not using. The peasants may not have kept animals beyond their subsistence needs if there was no market. While there were some early enclosures, the right remained largely dormant until the value of sheep made it possible for the lord to use the waste without needing much labor.

When sheep became more profitable in Tudor times (1450–1550), they were even more profitable if the number sharing in the revenue decreases as peasants are pushed out. The lord had earlier been content to collect rent on arable land when there was nothing he could do with it without intensive labor. But when he could get great revenue with only a few herdsmen, he grabbed it – not only the permanent pastures but also the arable lands now to be planted to grass.

Dahlman says that from 1550 to 1650 the enclosures proceeded more slowly and only with unanimity. Was this due to a political backlash to slow the human misery of the previous hundred years? He surmises, "the forces working for enclosure were so strong that no legislation could ever hope to halt it, much less reverse it" (163–4). The functional drive to take advantage of new profitable opportunities may be strong, but the distribution of the gains is subject to institutional direction influenced by learning and power play.

AFRICAN LAND TENURE

Communal land tenure evolved informally in sub-Saharan Africa and facilitated the survival of agriculturists often under harsh conditions. Households were assigned plots for their use. The plots were heritable, but not exchangeable. There was some flexibility to accommodate new households. In times of drought, harvests were shared to some extent so that some did not have a lot while others starved. It is a mistake to make only a functional interpretation of an institution. Just because communal African land tenure seems to fit its environment, one should not assume that some other institutions would not also fit or that it is in any sense optimal or beneficial to all.

The colonial powers often displaced the native peoples from their best lands and gave western style private ownership to colonists (Seidman 1973). The colonial owners via such things as land expropriation, missionaries, and partial replacement of tribal law also destroyed the self-respect of indigenous people, which made them more subservient. When new independent states were created, many declared the land to be owned by the state, but in practice the traditional tenures continued for indigenous people on the land they still controlled. The process of making land into a commodity with no social meaning is still going on as western organizations urge that individual exchangeable land titles be given.

There are currently communal lands in Africa where fences are absent (and often too costly relative to their benefits), which require all crops to be harvested at the same time so cattle may be allowed onto the stubble. No individual can grow a later maturing crop. As noted above, the same kind of constraint existed in the medieval open field system of England wherein a peasant farmed several scattered strips within the large open field. Open fields required a collective decision on what and when to plant and harvest and restricted individual initiative. On the other hand, open fields facilitated some cultural improvements such as flowing water over large pastures that would have been difficult to organize on an individual basis. The enclosure movement had a parallel in Japan where rice fields were once irregular in shape, undrained and shallow plowed (Iinuma 1995). The government passed a Re-Adjustment Act in 1899 wherein approval by two-thirds of the landowners allowed the fields to be rearranged and drained allowing a more productive deep plowing by a newly designed plow.

In both England and Japan it can be argued that the institutional change associated with enclosures and re-adjusted fields was functional and potentially Pareto-better. Since the rights to individual holdings and claims on the common pastures were entrenched in custom, the lord could not unilaterally change them. Some persuasion and compensation of all rights holders would have been required to enclose and reassemble the strips. However, it may not have been so clear at the time and compensation of the losers was not always made. Some English peasants were not offered a choice under the Parliamentary Commissions and the minority of Japanese farms did not count as a result of the rules for making rules. Again, we see a combination of function and power at work in institutional evolution.

PRIMITIVE AND ANCIENT ECONOMIES

We can't know much abut the institutions of early people, but that has not kept many from speculating that the propensity to truck and barter and form markets is innate. What clues we have from anthropologists' observations of primitive people question the timelessness of theoretical constructs. The work of Boas, Thurnwald, Mauss, and Malinowski suggest that "the acquisitive motivations characteristic of economic life in modern society were generally not to be found among primitive peoples, and that the market institutions of modern society were definitely not the rule in primitive society" (Fusfeld 1957: 345). Goods movements were primarily organized by gift-giving (reciprocity) and ceremonial distribution. Buying and selling was absent. "Economic activities became entwined with motives of maintaining and promoting kinship and friendship ties" (349). There was little formal choice as assumed in economic theory.

Polanyi (1957) in *Trade and Market in the Early Empires* emphasizes that redistributive administrative transactions were the mode for much of human history. The few exchange transactions were heavily circumscribed. Traveling merchants were scorned and kept outside the city. In Babylon at the time of Hammurabi (1795–50 BC) there was widespread use of money and foreign goods moved over large distance, but little evidence of markets and economizing. Equivalencies (prices) were established by authority and custom, often involving treaties, gifts and reciprocity. Local economies were organized into a redistribution system with priests and kings at the center.

INDUSTRIALIZATION

Economic history can be seen as a chronicle of the making of land and human beings into commodities (Polanyi 1944). In chapter 11, we saw that this has still not been entirely completed in the case of labor. In many respects the commodification of life is still proceeding as many functions that were organized by families such as social security become organized by markets (buying annuities) and government. Feudalism was a personal relationship between the lord and peasant who was tied to a specific location. There was no labor market. As trade developed, English landlords were happy to have their peasants engage in cottage industry as long as they were available for peak planting and harvesting periods. They were concerned that the peasants would migrate to towns for higher wages. Formal legal change became increasingly important alongside the traditional tenures. The 1662 Act of Settlement tied the peasants to the parish where they were born. This parish serfdom was relaxed in 1795 in the interest of employers in towns. But, incomes of both rural and town people were increasingly variable as the economy became subject to drastic changes in supply and demand from abroad. This created great economic distress unknown to the self-sufficient peasantry. The justices of Berkshire met in Speenhamland in 1795 and recommended that every person be given a subsidy equal to the cost of bread to maintain life. This soon became law. Two laws in the same year created the basis for a labor market and then destroyed it by removing all incentive to migrate and work (Polanyi 1944). Speenhamland may have been designed to help the poor, but it enabled the landlords to pay next to nothing for labor as it kept a reserve of labor available for their beck and call. Note that the law provided a minimum income and not a minimum wage. A fully competitive labor market was not firmly established until 1834 (Polanyi 1944: 83).

Hicks (1969) and other writers have conceived of history as a series of transformations of the mercantile or market economy beginning with the custom–command (administrative transactions) or revenue economy from which it emerged until the present (Bauer 1971). Gershenkron (1971) describes the transition from the textile age to the iron and steel age as follows. Initially "the relations between factory owners and the labour force assumed many aspects of the relations between the lord and the enserfed peasant. The policies of the state and the value system of the society worked in the same direction and added the elements of administrative and judicial discrimination and of social discrimination and segregation to the inferior position of labour in the market. The labour movement helped to transform the market into a socially beneficial institution, introducing into it and strengthening within it the 'principle of all-round advantage'." But there is more at work than functionality. Gershenkron argued that "this improvement in the functioning of the market was not the result of the activities of the merchants, however glorious their contribution may have been in other respects, but of a movement whose ideology paradoxically was so often radically opposed to the principles of the market and the system of private enterprise" (184). Note that the institutions and attitudes developed for agricultural labor were carried into industrial labor illustrating what Sjostrand (1993) calls "flows of norms between contexts." Industrial workers sought to avoid arbitrary dismissal and improve their incomes by collective action. But this was forestalled by the 1799–1800 Anti-Combination Laws that regarded such action as conspiracies.

SACRED COWS AND DIRTY PIGS

Veblen is known as an institutional economist though he seldom found an institution that he liked. His biting satires exposed many a ceremony that seemed opposed to the obvious progress of technology. The adjective "imbecile" often got attached to habits of thought and "ceremonialism" became a dirty word. He could have had great fun with the belief in sacred cows in India. Why let old cows wander through the streets when they have no economic value? Anthropologist Harris (1974) thinks he has a functional answer rooted in long-term human survival and environmental protection. He argues that during droughts there is great temptation to kill cows and use the little grain available for human consumption. But, if this is done, there is no breeding stock to begin again after the drought in the provision of draft power, etc. Thus Harris argues that more people survive over a longer period of time if cows are protected.

Did cows have to be made sacred to accomplish this? Under cruel conditions, the sacred may be the only way to prevent a short-run benefit–cost analysis. Note again the role of institutions in determining the length of run for rational calculation. The sacred and the emotional remove some things from the agenda of rational calculus. Further, one can imagine that different people would have different ideas of the tradeoff between short- and long-run food supply. Institutions as always represent the resolution of whose interests count. There is no technological or biological fact that dictates institutional change.

Harris finds many other examples of informal institutions that apparently serve functional environmental needs. Periodic pig feasts in New Guinea are seen not as quaint parties, but as unconscious management of the hog to land ratio. Taboos against pork consumption in desert societies can be seen as a way to protect the quality of scarce oasis sites. Again, one must be careful not to confuse a particular functional relationship with necessary institutional choice or optimality. There may have been other institutions which would have accomplished the same performance or done it better (depending on whose conception of better counts). To say that an institution survives is not to say it was best – only that it did survive. When something is learned to be natural or sacred, it can survive even in the face of what appears to us as a great dysfunction because the dysfunction is not so labeled or is not seen as related to the institution. Everything is not connected to everything.

EVOLUTION OF THE COMMON LAW

The courts in common law countries such as the US and United Kingdom provide an intermediate example somewhere between informal and formal institutional change. These courts consider the precedent of what is often referred to as best practice as a standard for determining tort liability when one person's acts are asserted to unlawfully damage another. This process necessarily involves selective perception of what constitutes best practice and what new cases are to be classified and guided by which precedent. When customs conflict, the parties often turn to formal processes for resolution.

CONTEMPORARY BUSINESS CUSTOMS

Contemporary economic customs are hard to see because they are followed without much reflection. Economic theory of markets concludes that price will be adjusted until markets clear. But we can observe major exceptions where consumers object to firm market clearing behavior. Kahneman, Knetsch, and Thaler (1986) presented consumers with a number of hypothetical situations such as a dramatic change in supply which makes existing stocks more valuable. Consumers objected to firms raising the price on existing stock and were willing to sanction firms who did so. This is an expression of informal custom.

Chief executive officers of large corporations are in a position to name their own compensation as a result of appointing boards of directors. Krugman (2002) notes that the 13,000 richest US families have almost as much annual income as the 20 million poorest. Part of the explanation is the fact that the average real pay of the top 100 CEOs went from $1.3 million in 1970 to $37.5 million in 1999. Since the incestuous control of executive salaries has long been there, why the big change in the last 30 years? Krugman argues that it is a matter of corporate culture. "For a generation after World War II, fear of outrage kept executive salaries in check. Now the outrage is gone" (66). There was only admiration and positive reinforcement from the broader environment.

WHAT'S COOL TO CONSUME?

If institutions include any widely practiced behavior, we shall have to say something about consumption habits. Veblen (1953: 98–9) poked fun at people with lush lawns, but no cows to eat it. He created the theory of conspicuous consumption to explain it. See also Leibenstein (1950); Frank (1985). Much consumption had no function other than to impress one's neighbors and gain presumed regard. He could certainly have great fun with some of today's fads such as body piercing. How do consumer habits change? There is a huge advertising industry devoted to it. One ingredient is the balance of being different and the same as everyone else. We copy others to a degree so that we will not be embarrassed by being different. This may be related to human survival. Conform and eat what other living people are eating and you can survive like them.

In the never-ending search for identity, we also want to be different, at least different from those you want to be superior to and the same as those whose regard you desire. The consumption of celebrities has always been copied. If the king ate white bread, then everyone who could afford it ate white bread even if nutritionally inferior. If western mothers feed their children formula, then mothers in poor countries who want to be perceived as modern will use formula even if their own milk is superior. For more examples over time, see Appadurai (1986).

Status emulation drives people to work long hours to earn more money even when the things it can buy provide little added pleasure (Frank 1999). If only being Number 1 satisfies, then most people are doomed to unhappiness. The team that loses the Super Bowl or the World Cup final is labeled a failure no matter how good its prior season. This led Frank to suggest that collective limits to consumption might enhance the welfare of many.

Human imagination never ceases and as soon as one high-status good becomes widely available, a new cool good is created for the few. Major industries and related media are continually creating new goods and demands. Did we always have a demand for cell phones so we could call while driving or annoy others in restaurants? Neoclassical economics may maintain its assumption of constant preferences by saying we have a demand for talk and means are substituted as availability and prices change (Stigler and Becker 1977). But, this is of little help to marketing managers, or little welfare justification to devoting huge resources to advertising.

If a commodity is a prior single thing (a point), then the only connection consumers can have with it (and to each other) is price. But, if a commodity is a system of characteristics, then consumers may connect with some characteristics and not others. Earl's lexicographic decision making and Thaler's mental accounts, described in chapter 3, are recognition of complex commodities with which consumers make selective connections to product characteristics. So, one can't describe choice simply as a function of price. Rather it requires deep understanding of which of the multiple characteristics will be perceived. Business people understand this and give attention not only to price, but also to how they might affect consumers' perceptions. Coke and Pepsi don't compete on price, but rather on image. Consumers are not connected to brown sweetened carbonated water only by price. The shifts in market shares of competing soft drink manufactures and their share *vis-à-vis* other drinks are more a function of imagination than change in relative prices. What is cool to consume is continually evolving and affected by approving feedback from others.

Change in smoking habits is an example of a major change (not gradual) in what is cool to consume and in associated institutions. Few would have predicted it 40 years ago. Movies showed high status people smoking. The US military distributed cigarettes to its personnel in World War II. Cigarette companies gave free samples. Advertising was everywhere. Cigarette breaks were customary. Then came growing information on health risks (including that from second-hand smoke). Congress ordered health warnings on cigarette packages in 1956 and the number of smokers declined. The informal right to smoke anywhere also changed (Schaler and Schaler

1998). Before, non-smokers in a restaurant might send a signal of condemnation that smokers ignored or returned. The feedback tended to extinguish the challenge to the incumbent informal right. Institutions are in part out there in the minds of others (mental model) that affect the collective feedback to individual behavior. And, they are in part in the mind of the individual when interpreting that feedback.

As the number of ex-smokers grew, non-smokers challenged the incumbent right to smoke and the challenger became the new incumbent and resulted in reinforcers being sent to smokers making them timid to assert their rights. Righteousness can lead to strong assertions of informal rights. Airlines and restaurants responded with no-smoking areas. This change in informal right to smoke in public grew into formal laws requiring non-smoking areas and even smoking bans in government buildings.

The process of informal institutional change has its higher order rules as formal rules change has its constitutional rules. The ability of individuals to send effective reinforcers to others depends on such things as the ability to make the *status quo* or its change appear to be natural, practiced by people worthy of emulation, and fits what is perceived to be the salient facts. The speed of change depends on the convergent contingencies. What is selected (eliminated) survives and is reproduced until the process is repeated. There is a power struggle involved in informal rule change as in formal political change. Conflicting options means "The more the rules conflict, the more contingencies can determine the result of process, and the less the past (embodied in informal rules) is able to condition the direction of change" (Fiori 2002: 1039).

SPONTANEOUS OVERTHROW OF COMMUNISM AND OTHER MAJOR CHANGES

The overthrow of communism in the USSR and Eastern Europe was not predicted by many. It was akin to a punctuated equilibrium. People's preferences were hidden from each other and not revealed by behavior. But when some dramatic event showed that overthrow was possible, suddenly, communism had few supporters (Kuran 1995). Institutions affect what is seen as variable. Why did the divine right of kings last so long? This is a case of the role of imagination more than any cause from population, technology, or prices. The presence and perception of alternatives is also critical. The American Revolution and the writings of political philosophers made a difference, both those for and against.

What have been the arguments against some of the major institutional changes in modern history? Hirschman (1991: 7) considers the movements asserting equality before the law and of civil rights in general, the expansion of suffrage, and the Welfare State. He observes three kinds of reactions: "According to the *perversity* thesis, any purposive action to improve some feature of the political, social, or economic order only serves to exacerbate the condition one wishes to remedy. The *futility* thesis holds that attempts at social transformation will be unavailing, that they will simply fail to 'make a dent.' Finally, the *jeopardy* thesis argues that the cost of the proposed change or reform is too high as it endangers some previous, precious accomplishment."

If preferences and ideologies do not change there can only be a war among conflicting parties. Hirschman observes, "Modern pluralistic regimes have typically come into being . . . not because of some preexisting wide consensus on 'basic values,' but rather because various groups that had been at each other's throats for a prolonged period had to recognize their mutual inability to achieve dominance" (1991: 168). Hopeful that preferences do evolve, Hirschman suggests dialog and deliberation. "Deliberation is here conceived as an opinion-forming process" (169). He is not unmindful of the difficulty. "A people that only yesterday was engaged in fratricidal struggles is not likely to settle down overnight to those constructive give-and-take deliberations" (169).

13.2.2 Conventions

Conventions refer to those institutions that are self-reinforcing, because once in place, no one can gain by contrary behavior. Any of a number of rules is acceptable as long as everyone follows. The common example given is driving on the right or left. No one unilaterally departs from the convention if others are observing it. A convenient functional historical explanation of left-hand driving was to favor predominantly right-handed swordsmen who wanted to pass each other on their right. If there is to be change, it requires collective action. The French Revolution and Napoleon brought right-hand driving to much of Europe. Swedish drivers drove on the left, but some saw an advantage to switching to the right to match the predominant rules in Europe. So a law was passed implementing the switch in 1967. Still, not all agreed that the benefits exceeded the costs. The fact that left-hand driving was the product of emergence does not privilege the old convention or the formal change.

Behavior related to time is often customary, but increasingly formal. Local sun dials coordinated behavior for centuries. When public clocks became available, they were a convenient local reference. This was not good enough for railroad coordination. British railroads established a common time zone in the 1840s, a kind of private central planning. Standard time zones in the US and Canada were established privately by the railroads in 1883. An international conference in 1884 established Greenwich as the Prime Meridian. However, standard time zones in the US were not made law until 1918.

Today, business hours are predominately an eight to five convention within each zone. It is useful in coordinating with other firms to know that they will be in the office at the same time as you. It is convenient for everyone to have the same time of day. Daylight savings time was temporarily implemented during World War I to save fuel generating electricity. If business wants to change time in the summer so that consumers have more daylight at the end of their workday to spend on outdoor leisure, it takes formal legal change to daylight savings time. The wisdom of individuals and towns acting alone is hotly contested. Indoor leisure firms and farmers tend to prefer sun time. Once the common time is established, it is costly for an individual to depart from it, although not all agree on its establishment.

13.2.3 Why study informal and unconscious institutional change?

If informal change is not the result of calculation, what is the role of knowledge? There are several answers. (1) We are continuously debating the merits of un-planned, spontaneous change vs. planned, calculated change and the relative scope of each. Knowledge of informal institutional change and its capacity for multiple equilibria raise questions about what is natural and functional. (2) Because of bounded rationality, much change must remain unconscious. There is no other game than to make our collective leaps of intuition. Nevertheless, we have some choice as to what to bring to the fore for greater explicit group choice. Just as a legislator has a choice of which of the hundreds of bills on the agenda to study in detail, all of us have some choice of what to think deeply about. Social critics and modern day Veblenians are competing for our attention when they ask us to consider selected instances of what we have backed ourselves into. Maybe it is the national debt, or land tenure, volunteerism, or body piercing. We can't do them all, but we can do one rather than another.

13.3 Formal Institutional Change

In discussing informal institutional change, the interaction of informal and formal institutions was noted. People learn not to accept the informal rules and turn to explicit rule-making by collective organizations that can deliver sanctions for viola-tion including physical force. Here, various factors contributing to formal institu-tional change will be introduced. Formal institutional change refers to changes in public law and privately made rules that are usually written and consciously adopted. It includes statute law, court decisions, administrative rules, as well as the by-laws and internal rules of corporations, unions, clubs, churches, and other private organ-izations. While formal sanctions usually apply, some kind of self-enforcement is also relevant. After examining how organizations form, changes in the several major examples of formal institutions will be analyzed – business corporations, labor un-ions, and water use. This is followed by a discussion of changes in the rules for making rules.

13.3.1 Formation of interest group organizations

The formation of an interest group is a link between informal and formal institu-tional change. In the cases above, people with common interests may have made individual decisions that in the aggregate resulted in institutional change. They may have been unconscious of how their choices might aggregate. But formal institu-tional change is often the result of people joining organizations to accomplish the change. North (1990: 5) has insisted that organizations be distinguished from institu-tions. It is organizations that pressure for formal institutional change defined as either the everyday institutions governing economic transactions or constitutional institutions constituting the rules for making the everyday rules.

Why do organizations for conscious action form? While they may work consciously for change, their formation is often informal and the result of cultural institutions contained in people's habits and world-view. By definition, the beneficiaries of organized activity are all members of the category whether they are members of the organization or not. It is the classic free-rider problem. People must suspend their narrow individual calculation and operate from some sense of community, solidarity, and commitment. Particularly at the inception of an organization there must be some leader(s) who probably will put in more than they can get out. (Recall section 12.4.2.) The formation of interest group organizations will be particularly noted below and in section 13.4 concerning the rules for making rules.

In developing countries, foreign country donors and non-governmental organizations are a factor in institutional change. The path of change is different if the donors have their own agenda or seek participatory learning and action from local people (Chambers 1997). It is a matter of who is empowered and whose reality counts.

13.3.2 Constitutions, courts, and legislatures

Magna Carta of 1215 was one of the earliest of constitutions that set out the rules for making rules. It also contained some everyday rules such as removal of fish-weirs from the Thames and creation of standard weights and measures. Kings had ruled by might and customary divine right. Enough barons overcame the free-rider problem to challenge King John and force him to sign Magna Carta giving the barons the right to be tried before a jury of their peers and establishment of a baronial council to oversee the king's adherence to the Charter. The threat to remove the king was made real in 1327 when Edward II was deposed by Parliament. The serfs were left out and could only appeal for better conditions to the manorial courts that were run by the feudal lords that oppressed them. Still, once the idea that authority should originate from the ruled was established, it evolved further. The sharing of power was an incompatible use good and the king's loss was the barons' gain and eventually the gain of peasants and an emerging business class. See table 13.2. Evolving custom of peasant rights became codified into a right to traditional rents. By the end of the Middle Ages, everybody was entitled to trial by a jury of their equals and everybody's property was protected by law.

The challenge to the king's rule-making right was achieved by power play. Further functional change can be seen in the new profit making opportunities that the feudal lords wanted to take advantage of. They asserted the right to establish towns and merchant fairs. They enclosed the land (see above on the enclosure movement). The extension of aristocratic rights to peasants and merchants exhibits elements of isomorphic path dependence.

Both the English and the Spanish kings needed money for wars in the sixteenth century. But the functional need resulted in different institutions (North 1990: 113–6). In Spain, the property of the nobility was often confiscated to finance the king, which put potential business entrepreneurs at risk. Spain remained a centralized monarchy and bureaucracy. The barons in England on the other hand, through

Table 13.2 Formal institutional change

Situation	Structure	Performance
Everyday rules, period 1: *Transaction costs* of change or maintaining status quo. Rule is HEC among beneficiaries. Path dependence – cumulative causation. *Increasing returns* to existing institutions. *Uncertainty* – shared visions of the future. Change in relative prices. Change in tastes, ideology, and what seems natural. Perception (subjective models) of unrealizable opportunities so individuals and organizations try to change institutions.	War at Runneymede → *Constitutional rules* in period 2 for making everyday rules. 1. England: Parliament. Judiciary. Cost of organizing to lobby. Ideology: learning 2. Spain: Centralized bureaucracy. New business class not represented.	Magna Carta. 1215. Becomes constitutional structure in next period. ← *Everyday rules, period 2:* 1. Merchant fairs; enclosures; freemen in cities; peasants got right to traditional rents; court enforcement of contract; predictable taxes. Eventually, joint-stock co. and capital mobility and debt; patent law; insurance to spread risk. 2. Feudal aristocrats maintained status quo rights *vis-à-vis* peasants and business. King confiscated nobles' property.

evolving parliamentary power, participated in setting taxes, which became more predictable.

North (1990: 130) observes, "Stories of stability and change go to the heart of the puzzle about the human economic condition." North is modest about what he can predict because of randomness in human perception of possibilities.

13.3.3 Corporate law and organization

Modern business is marked by specialization requiring complex relationships among people for production. What are the ways that people can be related to each other to produce goods and services and how have these changed? Before this question can be addressed some theoretical concepts and variables must be identified.

The structural variables include the following.

1. Employment or sales contract.
   An employment contract means that the employer owns and controls the product.
2. Command vs. negotiation.
   Degree to which the good/service at issue is specified initially or subsequently. This specifies some range of initial agreement of services to be performed and leaves some range of discretion for one party, such as the employer/foreman.
3. Degree of competition, custom, and substitutability among transacting parties.
4. Degree to which the product is a commodity that can be sold, gifted, leased, and otherwise conveyed separate from its producers.
5. Degree to which the collective decision rule requires unanimity.
   Degree of hierarchy. Degree to which participants are bound by collective decisions. (For example, those made by a corporate board of directors. Another example is how many owners must approve the sale of a corporation.)
6. Separation of ownership and control. Role of professional management.
7. Relation to the state.
   Degree to which any organization can influence law, and the degree to which any initial grant of rights can be changed by law.

Institutions ranging from the auction market to the modern corporation can be described with various mixes of the above institutional variables.

COLLECTIVITIES AS PERSONS

Over millennia, people understood collective action in customary families, clans, and administrative kingdoms. The relation between the patriarch, chief, pharaoh, or prince and others active in production was not as employee and employer. When the employment relationship developed, it seemed natural to structure it as a personal one such as master and apprentice or master and servant. It was quite paternalistic with a good deal of discretion allowed the master within a frame of rules given by the medieval and renaissance guilds organized on a commodity basis.

As the production groupings became larger, the formal concept of the partnership arose to regularize the relation of equals active in an organization. As tasks grew, larger groupings of resources were necessary for internal improvements and foreign trade. Joint stock companies were organized to build canals and for foreign trade such as the East India Companies. These were authorized by royal charters since the king could not ignore a collective alternative to his governance.

In the United States, state governments granted corporate charters that specifically outlined the powers and purpose of the corporation, implying what was in the public interest. These grants were subject to favoritism and fraud, which led to passage of general rules for incorporation (Hurst 1956: 15–17). Further pressures in this direction came because people who broke contracts with corporations were escaping performance by claiming that the corporation had acted outside of its grant. Consolidation of corporations would have been difficult if each had a special charter. New Jersey was among the first states to allow corporations to own shares in other corporations in 1889. In this context, law evolved to define general corporate rights such as the power to make contracts, sue and be sued, have protection against self-incrimination, etc. "Up through the 1880s, there was a strong tendency to analyze corporation law not very differently from the law of partnership" (Horwitz 1987: 20). For example, shareholder unanimity was required for changes in corporate purpose and sale.

For purposes of legitimation, it was necessary to create the conception that power flowed from the shareholders to directors to management. This was eventually achieved (after 1900) by conceiving of the board and its officers as the corporation itself. The corporation was conceived of as a legal person with all rights of a person and then some (Samuels 1987). Limited liability was not a right of individuals or partnerships. And, it was not the norm in America until after 1900. Until then, industrial securities except in coal and textiles were almost unknown, as was the stock market. "Only after 1879, in the midst of the merger movement, did companies publicly offer shares of stock, replacing the system of 'private' subscriptions that had prevailed throughout the nineteenth century" (Horwitz 1987: 43). The evolution of corporate law represents the essence of the institutional structure of business. Its path is in part functional and part power and part the learning of new ideologies via the creative use of metaphor for legitimation of changes in the conception of the shareholder from active owner to passive investor. This change was as important as any changes in markets vs. hierarchy, the make or buy decision, or internal structure of the firm. The personification of the corporation is a good example of the learning process that North regards as a function of "the way in which a given belief structure filters the information derived from experiences . . ." (North 1994: 364).

Legal treatment of a corporation as a person gives them great power *vis-à-vis* real persons. Lindblom (2001: ch. 17) worries that corporations are a threat to democracy. Corporations have sued individuals for civic activities opposing corporate interests. Even if the suits are not successful, the threat of legal costs affects citizen behavior. Corporate spending on elections gives them great advantage over citizen groups.

PRIVATE GOVERNANCE

The same kind of issues noted in chapter 12 with respect to governments occur in private organizations. Some of the rules for making rules within private organizations are left to them to decide and others are deemed to be of enough general consequence that the rule making rules are decided by public government. Just two instances will be detailed. In the efforts of stockholders to oust boards of directors or change corporate policy, the availability of stockholder names and address is critical. The Securities Exchange Act of 1934 required corporations to provide lists. Without the corporation's cooperation, there would be great transaction costs to solicit votes.

Labor unions are private bodies, but elections held to determine whether workers want a union and which unions are legally circumscribed. Likewise the election of union officers is framed by the 1935 National Labor Relations Act. (See chapter 11 on Labor.) The Wagner Act and other major changes in labor law changes came during the Great Depression with leadership from Franklin Delano Roosevelt. See Burawoy (1985) on the rise of the corporation as state. The private governance subsystem is conditioned by the system of public rules within which it is embedded.

INTERNAL ORGANIZATION OF COLLECTIVE BODIES (ORGANIZATIONS)

Any collective body (organization) whether public or private has some rules for binding its members (subjects) to decisions. This applies to legislatures, unions, religious organizations, philanthropic organizations, or other corporate bodies. Sanctions include expulsion, dismissal, altering wages, and fines. Over time, the kind of sanction and incentives used evolves.

FUNCTIONS OR SECTORS?

The work of any large, complex organization must be subdivided. The US Congress has subject matter committees such as agriculture and national defense. Is the school lunch program under agriculture or under social welfare? Are the committees parallel to agencies or to functions that cut across agencies? These organizational decisions affect information flows, what alternatives are seen as options, and the formation of coalitions and compromises. Different organization charts may interact with inherent transaction costs to affect performance. (See chapter 12 above.)

The same point can be made about how business charts and organizational structure affects the working rules of corporations. Shall the corporation be organized by functional divisions such as production, design, and marketing or by geography or product lines? Early in the twentieth century most big corporations had a single dominant product. This evolved to multi-division firms such as DuPont, General Motors, Standard Oil, and Sears (Chandler 1962; Chandler and Hikino 1990). Much of the explanation of this evolution is in functional terms such as the ability to achieve economies of scale and scope and to save on coordination costs. Activities were combined if the profit created by doing both is greater than the sum of the individual profits. As Milgrom and Roberts (1992: 546) observe, "No matter how the cuts are made to divide up the company's business, there will inevitably be mismatches between the way problems present themselves and the way the company is structured." Uncertainty leaves room for business ideology, fads, and isomorphic behavior.

13.3.4 Industrial stages, classes, and organizations

AMERICAN SHOEMAKERS

The pressure on wages from technological, global, and market change is not new. Several stages in the evolution of shoe making over the period 1648–1895 illustrate a process that is still going on (Commons 1909). The settled shoemakers of Boston were granted a charter in 1648 that effectively protected them from competition from itinerant shoemakers. Because of high information costs to determine quality by the buyer, the price of well-made shoes was the same as those of inferior quality. "The itinerant was likely to be poorly trained and he could escape supervision by his fellow craftsmen" (42). Commons writing in 1909 understood the interdependence created by transaction costs even if he did not coin the term. "The bargaining power of the merchant is menaced by the incapacity of customers accurately to judge the quality of goods as against their capacity clearly to distinguish prices" (44). The charter allowed the settled shoemakers to in effect license producers much as we do today for physicians, undertakers, and beauticians. The shoemaker combined the functions of merchant, master (control of the workplace), and journeyman with his own tools whose income depended on the skill, speed, and quality of work. The owner-merchant-worker could differentiate the market and sell shoes to lower income buyers without affecting the price of custom work (capture consumer surplus).

The separation of functions (classes) appeared in the case of the cordwainers of Philadelphia 150 years later. The individual shoemakers had been displaced by workshops with masters (who also became merchants) employing workers willing to work for very little. As merchants, the masters began to stock standardized shoes rather than only doing custom work. This required capital. The wage was determined by the willingness to accept by the marginal worker. The intra-marginal worker objected. The worker was paid by the shoe regardless of the buyer of the shoes (consumer surplus to the master). The form of private governance (to use Williamson's term) changed because of the extent of the market. Contrary to Williamson, "It was the widening out of these markets with their lower levels of competition and quality, but without any changes in the instruments of production, that destroyed the primitive identity of master and journeyman cordwainers and split their community of interest into the modern alignment of employers' association and trade union" (Commons 1909: 50). The widening of the market due to improvements in transportation had led to a separation of functions. The capital needed for custom work was much less than for retail stock and less still than that needed to sell to wholesalers as the time between manufacture and final sale increased. The capital and risk had to be compensated and as regional competition grew, it could not be passed on in the price of the finished goods, but only by reducing wages. The struggle over wages and prices is intertwined with financial markets.

The cordwainers staged a strike in 1805 trying to obtain their previous wages and were brought to court charged with conspiracy. It is not clear how the workers overcame the free-rider problem and presented a more or less united front controlling scabs that had destroyed earlier worker organizations by selling home production at reduced prices in public markets. This was against society (union) rules and undermined the ability of masters to pay union demands.

Space does not permit discussion of all of the stages of organization identified by Commons in the evolution of the shoe industry as representative of the whole modern economy. At each stage there is a "competitive menace" that the various interests (classes) attempt to control. And the success of each group to use government to control its menace affects income distribution. The sewing machine in 1852, the factory, and further widening of the market and new financial institutions created further separation of interests who each had a different view of what was an unfair menace including immigrants, child labor, and eventually production in other countries. Commons emphasized the role of the merchant-capitalist who controlled capital and labor. "If the merchant has a market he can secure capital" (1909: 78). Commons does not here relate the strategic role played by capital to macro performance and the accompanying fragility of the financial system. He emphasizes that the consumer favors institutions giving power to the marginal producer to control (menace) other producers and labor – consumers with a well-paying job that is.

AGRICULTURE AND FOOD

Agriculture has always been given as the archetype of perfect competition. While it may have been at one time, it too has become industrialized. The story can begin with the local butcher in American cities in colonial times. The butcher combined slaughter, cutting, and retailing. Growing the animals was a separate function and ownership. But, as cities grew, economies of scale were achieved by large specialized slaughterhouses. The Louisiana legislature granted a monopoly to a New Orleans slaughterhouse to be used by the butchers. The butchers objected and in 1872, the Supreme Court of the United States ruled that the monopoly was not a deprivation of property or liberty as defined in the Constitution (16 Wall. 36, 1872). The law had reduced the exchange value of the butchers' assets, but had not physically taken them. The prevailing cognition of property only applied to trespass and destruction of use-value (Commons 1924: 11–21). One of the dissenting justices later cited Adam Smith's *Wealth of Nations* as his justification for protecting exchange value (111 US 746, 757).

New marketing systems were developing, including giant warehouses for the storage of goods. The Illinois legislature was concerned with the economic power of these warehouses and began to regulate their rates. In *Munn v. Illinois* (94 US 113, 1876) the court kept to its concept of physical assets and upheld the regulation. The concentration of power in the railroads provided another contest over the law. In the Minnesota Rate Case (*Chicago, M. and St. P. Ry. Co. v. Minnesota*, 134 US

418, 1890), the court changed its mind and held that regulation that reduced the exchange-value of assets was a taking of property. Words do not speak for themselves and always involve a cognitive and creative element. *Allgeyer v. Louisiana* (165 US 578, 589, 1897) extended the meaning of protected property rights to access to markets.

Government is not the only actor affecting exchange values. Private firms destroy each other's asset values all the time. Case in point was Augustus Swift's innovation of refrigerated rail cars bringing dressed beef to eastern cities in the 1880s (Chandler 1977: 300). This destroyed the asset value of the old rail cars for live animals as well as the butcher shops in the receiving cities. If Swift had taken a sledgehammer to the rail cars or butcher shops, he certainly would have been prosecuted for destroying property, but the courts in their selective perception did not extend the meaning of property to exchange value destruction by private competition. Economists defend creative destruction in the name of greater total wealth, but those caught with losses to fixed assets are not impressed with potential Pareto-improvements – they want the real thing.

It is easy to see the historical evolutionary process as inevitable. Could it have been different? If it gave consumers cheap shoes (and labor saving technology), who can complain? Marx complained that the workers were exploited (and alienated) and believed that common ownership was the answer. Commons avoided that language and emphasized that what constituted an "unfair menace" necessarily had to be worked out in the specifics of laws ranging from child labor to tariffs. The historical path was the result of political contests in legislatures and courts as groups struggled for income and to avoid wipeouts of immobile assets, including the human. Present groups objecting to NAFTA and the WTO, as well as those raising questions about financial trading, accounting rules, or the repeal of Glass-Steagall banking act, are all part of the ongoing evolution. Whether states offer subsidies to firms to locate within their boundaries, or bail out firms, banks, pay unemployment and other welfare benefits, distributive issues are always tied together with investment and what is called economic growth and progress. There is no way for the analyst to view it from on high and pronounce some abstraction called the free market as the best of all possible worlds.

Take another example. The quality of milk is a high information cost good, and unscrupulous sellers have taken advantage of this with adulterated product. The common law of nuisance was not very effective as damage was hard to prove by an individual consumer. "In practice, the interest of private litigants proved insufficient to provide a pattern of regulation out of suits in contract or tort. Statutes gave form to the substance of public interest in this field" (Hurst 1960: 95). Milwaukee passed a milk inspection ordinance in 1887. "The Wisconsin legislature first adopted a butterfat criterion against adulterated milk in 1889, hard on the publication of the first workable butterfat content tests, and regulatory effort against adulteration gained real momentum after the devising of the Babcock test in 1890" (1960: 99). Changing technology alters the situation and impacts the law. This can be seen when regulation was extended to bacteria after the work of Pasteur and others in the late nineteenth century. The requirements for cleanliness eventually had the perhaps unintended effect of driving small hand-work producers out of business to be replaced by larger producers with milking machines and parlors sending the milk by pipe to refrigerated tanks.

Hurst emphasizes that the evolving law and technology were more than regulatory (1960: 99–101). For example, milk farmer associations overcame their free-rider problem and lobbied the Wisconsin legislature to provide funds for university research and extension education of farmers in the use of new technology. Funds were also obtained to improve roads so the milk could be shipped to cities and markets expanded.

New technologies and organizational innovations continue to affect the distribution of opportunities. The creation of large integrated firms in chickens and pork has meant that formerly independent feeders are now little more than contract employees of integrated processors and feed companies, paid on a piece-rate basis (Martin 1997). Industrial agriculture has shifted the transaction from a sales contract to an employment contract. A new innovation in beef fattening is contract feeding. An investor buys calves and contracts with a large feeder at a cost per day. Modern rations emphasize corn, antibiotics, and hormones. Bovines have rumens evolved to transform forage into meat, but the modern culture transforms corn into meat. Looking at the total system, this means that petroleum is necessary to make fertilizer used to grow corn (Pollan 2002). The heavy corn diet stresses the animals, which makes antibiotics necessary to maintain health. The rumen using forage is pH neutral, but with corn it becomes acidic. Medical researchers are now concerned that bacteria evolving to survive in the acidic rumen may carry over to humans and survive in the acidic human stomach where pH neutral bacteria were formerly killed. Nitrogen from fertilizers and hormones added to the feed get in the groundwater and raise human health questions there. But, this system produces cheap beef – cheaper than in Europe where some of the feed additives are prohibited.

Again, who can complain about cheap beef? Those concerned about human health, the environment, and the geopolitics of oil. Their interests are not costs to beef producers and consumers. Whether these costs are seen as costs by the animal industry depends on institutions that determine who has to buy out who. Rights make one group's interests a cost to other interdependent actors. Regulation is often condemned as raising cost, but it really only shifts costs. The interdependence and opportunity costs were already there, and regulations and other rights inevitably determine which effects are a cost to whom. Complex interacting systems of animal and plant ecology, hydrology, and geopolitics of oil all can be interconnected in various ways by institutions affecting human organization and behavior to produce different results. No institution can be privileged by reference to efficiency or survival of the fittest. It depends on whose vision of the future evolves and counts.

13.3.5 Labor unions

Collective or corporate action for labor was slower in coming than that for employers. Any collective action by labor was dealt with as a conspiracy, while the corporate form of business came to be regarded as natural. As employers grew larger, the labor bargain was between a large employer and many individual employees. The employer had more options than the employees. The wage was determined by the reservation price of the marginal worker. Only by acting collectively could the workers get more of the economic pie. One worker refusing to work has no bargaining power, but if all employees strike, there is greater ability to bargain. But how can an effective participation in a strike be obtained if workers calculate that they can continue to earn while others strike and if successful in obtaining higher wages, all will get the benefit?

This is the classical free-rider problem. Just sharing common goals is not enough. Olson (1965) emphasized that the only answers lay in compulsion from above or to find some low exclusion cost good that could be tied to the high exclusion cost good. To obtain compulsion from government only pushes the free-rider problem back one step to organizing a lobby to obtain the compulsory law. The American labor movement did not attempt to find a tie-in good. Labor historians such as Perlman looked into the mind of the working person for the answer.

Perlman (1949: 162–3) understood the free-rider problem and believed that, "The overshadowing problem of the American labor movement has always been the problem of staying organized" and "the lack of class cohesiveness" and "lack of spontaneous class solidarity." Perlman found the best answer in human emotions. When people are emotional and are setting out to right a wrong, they do not make individual benefit–cost calculations. Perlman believed that the emotion came from workers' most threatening experience – namely the consequences of losing one's job to someone willing to work for less. He suggested that labor leaders should not stray far from the rationale for collective action that evokes the greatest emotional response. A portrayal of "us vs. them" gets the emotional juices working especially if the "them" is a recent migrant.

Olson (1965: 77–9) reasoned that if job security was the driving force, unions should grow during periods of unemployment. He correlated job availability with union growth and found little correlation. Periods of great labor demand were also periods of union growth. This need not disprove Perlman's point. When jobs are plentiful, a strike for union recognition and closed shops is more effective. To understand participation in unions and their effectiveness in changing the rules, we will have to inquire into workers' reasoning.

The labor movement like any other never reached unanimous solidarity. Its history is replete with violence against those that union members regarded as scabs. It achieved compulsory union dues by bargaining with employers and lobbied states to make the closed shop legal. Labor history is the co-evolution of ideology, cognition, legislative approval of collective action and closed shops and strikes to obtain them (Commons 1905). Landmark legislation was the 1935 National Labor Relations Act and the Taft-Hartley Law. Laws that prohibited employers from dismissing employees who tried to organize were particularly important.

13.3.6 Water law

The evolution of water law in the Great Lakes states illustrates the mix of functional, power, and learning variables (Schmid 1960; Schmid 1962). The Northwest Ordinance of 1787 gave primacy of rights to navigation that was essential to frontier development before roads were built. As isolated rural settlements were established, water power was essential to grind grain into flour. Settlements created demand for new law and law facilitated (reinforced) settlements. But, dams interfered with navigation and the reservoirs required land that its owners, realizing limited substitutability, asked high prices for. The milldam entrepreneurs won and the 1840 Wisconsin Mill Dam Act allowed a kind of eminent domain for private purpose (actually the dam and reservoir could be built without the flowage land owner's permission – they could only sue for damages after the fact).

When land transport for grain became cheaper, the local mills were less important. Lumber became an important commodity after the Civil War and again it had to move by water. River structures to facilitate log sorting and transport were allowed. This continued until 1900 when hydropower became attractive, even if it meant logs could not move freely. But, logs were not the issue in the twentieth century. Recreational interests objected to dams and in 1929 the legislature declared the enjoyment of natural scenic beauty and fishing had to be considered in granting a hydro-dam permit. Later, water diversion for irrigation became profitable, but trout streams were thereby damaged. Recreational interests in 1959 succeeded in prohibiting diversion from trout streams without approval of the Conservation Department.

From frontier days to present, the public interest in water courses in principle depended on its being navigable. But, words do not speak for themselves and law does not administer itself. So the definition of navigability that began with the literal test of being able to float a saw log (really a canoe) got bent to accommodate milldams, structures to facilitate sorting of logs, hydro-dams, irrigation, and finally back to saw logs to fit the coincidental interests of fishermen. This tortuous evolution can be interpreted strictly as functional accommodation to new technologies, products, and profit opportunities.

But, is this a simple functional story of the law responding to the most valuable use of water? Surely, influencing the legislature and courts is in part a function of economic assets. But, if this were the straightforward story, rights in waters could have been set and the new interests could have bought out the old rights in the market (Coase Rule). If relative prices and profits affect the path of available technology, and if water-powered gristmills and hydropower generation were made more costly by water laws favoring extensive uses, some other kinds of technologies might have been invented. Were rights given to hydro interests because it was efficient over some period of time, or was hydro low cost because it did not have to buy out the fishers? If Wisconsin and Michigan loggers had not been able to move logs cheaply, Chicago and its wooden houses would not have grown so rapidly. And, more old-growth timber would be left today which may well be justified by the recreational values now evident. We are talking about how law defines alternative growth content and paths as well as how economic growth places some demands on law. The process is far from automatic and inevitable.

Those who lost were not compensated so there was no actual test of it being Pareto-better. The courts and legislature did not so much secure efficiency, as define whose interests count when efficiency is calculated – whose interests are a cost to whom. The prevailing ideology that made possible different meanings of words was as much a part of the picture as functional accommodation to a given efficiency at each moment. Interests given an advantage at one time could use their gains to obtain more help from government. Different images of the future contested for bringing it to fruition.

13.4 Evolution of Rules for Making Rules

Some of the institutional change in constitutional rules noted in chapter 12 will be reframed here to investigate their source. Political change especially involves a mix of power and evolving ideas of what is right and fair. The central situational feature of rules for making rules is that they empower all members of the group that benefit from the change. This creates the classic free-rider problem. Why would a person bear the costs of achieving a change in the rules for making rules when if it is done by others, one can ride free? Just as people learn to be opportunistic they can learn not to feel right about themselves if they did not participate. The people working to change the rules for making rules have a functional objective in mind. But this begs two questions. Where did the objective come from and why did the group with objective one win out over the status quo group with another objective? In equation summary form we have:

Change in rules for making rules = f (ideas, power, function)

Change is a function of ideas and ideals, the power to overcome opposing groups, and the functionality of the rules. When a group no longer accepts the status quo and sees an opportunity to achieve their goals if the rules for making rules could be changed (functionality), it will work to change them if it can overcome the free-rider problem.

13.4.1 Women's suffrage

The voting franchise is one of the most central rules for making rules. Non-property owners were not allowed to vote in England until 1867. Black men were not allowed to vote in the US until after the Civil War. Women were not allowed to vote in the US until 1920 and 1928 in the UK. US Senators were not elected until 1913. Consider first the suffragette movement that was worldwide. The first US formal women's convention was in 1848. The two best-known names were Elizabeth Cady Stanton and Susan B. Anthony. They devoted their lives to organizing women to lobby for the vote. They bore huge personal costs and much abuse. They did it because they considered it the right thing to do and not from any calculation of personal benefits and costs. In the end, success required the consent of many men. The point can be illustrated by the vote of Henry Burn, a Tennessee state senator, at the moment when Tennessee was the last state that could provide a two-thirds majority to amend the Constitution (rules for making rules). Passage of the nineteenth amendment appeared doomed on the basis of known stands by the senate members. But at the vote, Burn changed his mind. He had received a letter from his mother who said she knew he would do the "right thing."

The evolution of civil rights for Blacks was discussed above in section 13.2.

13.5 A Welfare Economics of Change?

It will be noted above that the measures of performance are in terms of which group gets what everyday rules to their liking from political processes. There is no attempt to label one everyday working institution or rule for making rules as universally better than another. This follows from the discussion of social choice in chapter 5 and section 12.5.

13.6 Conclusion

The chapter demonstrates that much of the same theory developed in chapter 6 that illuminates the impact of alternative everyday institutions on performance can also be used to illuminate the evolution of alternative rules for making rules. Further, the same concepts can be used for understanding change in both formal and informal everyday institutions. These theories of institutional change are built upon the same behavioral foundations (such as bounded rationality) as were the theories of institutional impact. They use the same SSP framework and emphasize substantive performance rather than abstract labels of efficiency that hide the issue of efficiency for whom. Institutional structures respond to changes in the sources of human interdependence (situation) as well as cause change in that interdependence. Change in formal everyday institutions is a function of the impact of rules for making rules. Ultimately, the formal rules for making rules as well as the informal everyday institutions emerge from the interplay of function, power, isomorphic, and learning–evolutionary processes.

STEPS IN SSP INSTITUTIONAL CHANGE ANALYSIS

1. Begin with the status quo situation of interdependence and institution at a moment in history.
2. Note the situation of the interacting parties – for example, who are incompatible, who shares HEC benefits, the context of increasing returns to continual use of status quo, and degree of uncertainty.
3. For formal institutions (structure):
   Specify the prevailing rules for making rules as suggested by theory and the case. The impact of alternative rules for making rules can also be studied (see table 13.2 for model).
   For informal institutions (structure):
   Specify the higher order informal institutions that constrain and enable trans-actions and feedback between those comfortable with the status quo and the deviants. These include language, metaphors, communication, mental models,

ideology, including ideas of fairness and self-identity, attitude toward deviants, and other things that affect whether the incumbent and challenger behavior are seen to fit and be natural. Change can be understood with an evolutionary model of variation, selection, and reproduction (see table 13.1 for model).

4. The performance (dependent) variable is the prevalence of particular everyday institutions (that are the structural variables in impact analysis).

5. Formulate testable hypotheses relating situation, structure, and performance:

For formal institutions:

For example, contrast performance in two jurisdictions with similar starting place everyday formal institutions, but different rules for making rules.

For informal institutions:

Similar to that above except that the structure is contrasting mental models, etc., such as individualism and attitude toward deviants. Countries with different informal institutions can be contrasted.

6. Test hypotheses using methods of chapter 7. Look for historical patterns.

NOTES

1. What constitutes dysfunction is in the eye of the beholder.

2. Any economy is a complex of institutions that in the aggregate results in a particular kind of economic growth and its beneficiaries and its stability. Those in the Marxian tradition refer to this as the "social structure of accumulation" (Gordon, 1998; O'Hara, 2000). Various authors emphasize different institutions in the mix, such as the monetary system, dominant forms of ownership and business organization, international trade rules, labor law, or military power as well as the informal institutions affecting trust and culture. These can be mixed in so many different ways that the old categories of capitalism and socialism lose meaning. Certain newer collections of policies such as the Washington Consensus for economic development have degenerated into ideology that ignores the consequences of the implementing details. The promotion of these categories is part of the process of institutional change.

3. Aoki uses game theory to show that informal custom can arise and provide order without any conscious collective decision. Whether most want to live under that emerging order is another matter.

Chapter 14
Recapitulation

This book began with an immodest goal of finding and creating a theory (variables and relationships) that could provide insight into both the *impact* of alternative institutions and the process of institutional *change*. Further, it sought a theory common to both *formal* (legal) and *informal* institutions. It is to each reader to decide whether the goal has been approached, let alone reached. It has been argued that the SSP framework is useful for all of the above. Unless the characteristics of *situations* and goods that cause human interdependence are understood, the alternative institutional *structures* that control and shape *performance* cannot be identified. Just speaking of widgets will not do. Different goods create different interdependencies. All policy analysis implicitly or explicitly notes the character of goods such as incompatibility, exclusion cost, cost of another user, economies of scale, etc. The argument here is that analysis is improved by making these situational characteristics explicit and central. Many institutional economists use different terms for situational variables and thus appear to be talking of different things. It would be helpful if a common terminology could be adopted. The SSP framework helps us see that various writers are really talking about the same thing, which would allow our work to be more cumulative.

A clear understanding of how the brain works is fundamental for both impact and change analysis, and for both formal and informal institutions. Just speaking of utility or profit maximization will not do. Bounded rationality and the limited information processing capacity of the human brain are fundamental. Learning is fundamental to impact and change analysis. Preferences are variable.

Substantive performance has been emphasized that identifies *whose preferences count*, rather than some presumptive total welfare maximization that presumes the outcome of conflict of interests. The value circularity problem must be avoided. If you have read thus far (or are beginning here) and conclude (or desire) that this book is an argument for or against markets, planning, capitalism, privatization, regulation, *laissez faire*, or whatever, please reconsider.

Alternative institutions differ in benefits and costs, and in their distribution. Substantive impact analysis illuminates the fact that institutional choice involves a moral choice of whose interests count. The contest over gains and losses is part of the process of institutional change.

Impact and change theories are embedded in each other. The independent variable in one equation becomes the dependent variable in another. The impact of political rules for making working rules is the adoption of a working rule whose impact on the economy can be studied. The links between different levels of analysis and theories are outlined below in the *situation, structure, performance* framework.

1. Impact theory (everyday institutions). (From chapter 6)

Situation	Structure	Performance
Sources of interdependence. HEC IUG, etc.	1. Institution A, both formal and informal as relevant. 2. Institution B	Performance 1 Who gets what. Performance 2

Which alternative formal and informal structure prevails depends on processes 2 and 3 below.

2. Institutional change (everyday *formal* institutions). Which structure above will be chosen and prevail? (From chapter 13)

HEC IUG, etc.	1. Rule 1 for making rules. 2. Rule 2 for making rules.	1. Institution A is chosen. 2. Institution B is chosen.

Which alternative rule for making rules prevails depends on process 4 below.

3. Institutional change (in everyday *informal* institutions). Which informal structure emerges? (From chapter 13)

HEC within a group. IUG between groups. Cumulative causation. Increasing returns.	Function, power, isomorphic, and learning. Language. Higher order informal rules.	Informal institution A_i emerges.

4. Change in the rules for making rules. Which constitutional rule emerges? (From chapter 12)

HEC IUG, etc.	Function, power, isomorphic, and learning.	Rule 1 for making rules emerges.

References

Aaron, H., and McGuire, M. C. 1970: Public Goods and Income Distribution. *Econometrica*, 38 (November), 907–20.

Aberbach, J. D., Putnam, R. D., and Rockman, B. A. 1981: *Bureaucrats and Politicians in Western Democracies*. Cambridge, MA: Harvard University Press.

Abramovitz, M. 1956: Resource and Output Trends in the United States since 1870. *American Economic Review*, 46 (2), 5–23.

Agrawal, A. 2001: Common Property Institutions and Sustainable Governance of Resources. *World Development*, 29 (10), 1623–48.

Ahlbrandt, R. 1973: *Municipal Fire Protection Services: Comparison of Alternative Organizational Forms*. Beverly Hills: Sage.

Akerlof, G. A. 1970: The Market for Lemons. *Quarterly Journal of Economics*, 84, 488–500.

——. 1982: Labor Contracts as Partial Gift Exchange. *Quarterly Journal of Economics*, 97 (November), 543–69.

——. 1986: *An Economic Theorist's Book of Tales*. Cambridge: Cambridge University Press.

——. 1991: Procrastination and Obedience. *American Economic Review*, 81, 1–19.

Alesina, A., and La Ferrara, E. 2001: *Preferences for Redistribution in the Land of Opportunities*. Cambridge: National Bureau of Economic Research.

Allais, M. 1979: The Foundations of a Positive Theory of Choice Involving Risk and a Criticism of the Postulates and Axioms of the American School. In M. Allais and O. Hagen (eds), *Expected Utility Hypotheses and the Allais Paradox*. Dordrecht: D. Reidel Publishing.

Alston, L. J., Eggertsson, T., and North, D. C. 1996: *Empirical Studies in Institutional Change: Political Economy of Institutions and Decisions*. Cambridge: Cambridge University Press.

Anderson, J. R. 1987: Skill Acquisition: Compilation of Weak-Method Problem Solutions. *Psychological Review*, 94, 192–210.

Andreoni, J., and Miller, J. H. 1996: *Giving According to Garp: An Experimental Study of Rationality and Altruism*. Madison: University of Wisconsin, Social Systems Research Institute.

Aoki, M. 2000: *Information, Corporate Governance, and Institutional Diversity: Competitiveness in Japan, the USA, and the Transitional Economies*. Oxford: Oxford University Press.

——. 2001: *Towards a Comparative Institutional Analysis*. Cambridge: MIT Press.

Appadurai, A. 1986: *The Social Life of Things: Commodities in Cultural Perspective*. Cambridge: Cambridge University Press.

Argyle, M. 1999: Causes and Correlates of Happiness. In D. Kahneman (ed.), *Well-Being: The Foundations of Hedonic Psychology*. New York: Russell Sage.

Arrow, K. J. 1963: *Social Choice and Individual Values*. New Haven: Yale University Press.

——. 1986: Rationality of Self and Others in an Economic System. *Journal of Business*, 59 (4), S385–99.

Arthur, W. B. 1990: Positive Feedbacks in the Economy. *Scientific American*, February, 92–99.

——. 1994: Path Dependence, Self-Reinforcement, and Human Learning. In W. B. Arthur (ed.), *Increasing Returns and Path Dependence in the Economy*. Ann Arbor: University of Michigan Press, 133–58.

Ashenfelter, O., and Kelley, S. 1975: Determinants of Participation in Presidential Elections. *Journal of Law and Economics*, 18 (December), 695–733.

Ashford, R., and Shakespeare, R. 1999: *Binary Economics: The New Paradigm*. Lanham, MD: University Press of America.

Axelrod, R. M. 1984: *The Evolution of Cooperation*. New York: Basic Books.

Ayres, C. E. 1957: Discussion: Institutional Economics. *American Economic Review*, 47 (2), 26–7.

Ayres, I., and Siegelman, P. 1995: Race and Gender Discrimination in Bargaining for a New Car. *American Economic Review*, 85 (3), 304–21.

Bachrach, P., and Baratz, M. S. 1962: Two Faces of Power. *American Political Science Review*, 56 (4), 947–52.

Backhaus, J. G. 1999: The Codetermined Corporation as a Player in the Labour Market. In G. deGeest (ed.), *Law and Economics and the Labour Market*. Cheltenham: Edward Elgar.

Bardhan, P. 1989: The New Institutional Economics and Development Theory. *World Development*, 17 (9), 1389–95.

Barnard, C. I. 1948: *Organization and Management*. Cambridge: Harvard University Press.

Barry, B. M. 1965: *Political Argument: International Library of Philosophy and Scientific Method*. London: Routledge and K. Paul.

Bartlett, R. 1989: *Economics and Power: An Inquiry into Human Relations and Markets*. Cambridge: Cambridge University Press.

Bates, R. H. 1989: *Beyond the Miracle of the Market: The Political Economy of Agrarian Development in Kenya*. Cambridge: Cambridge University Press.

Batten, D. F. 2000: *Discovering Artificial Economics: How Agents Learn and Economies Evolve*. Boulder, CO: Westview Press.

Bauer, P. T. 1971: Economic History as Theory – a Review. *Economica*, 38 (150), 163–79.

Baumeister, R. F., and Sommer, K. L. 1997: Consciousness, Free Choice, and Automaticity. In R. S. Wyler (ed.), *The Automaticity of Everyday Life: Advances in Social Cognition*. Mahwah, NJ: Erlbaum.

Baumol, W. J. 2002: *The Free-Market Innovation Machine*. Princeton: Princeton University Press.

Bazelon, D. T. 1963: *The Paper Economy*. New York: Random House.

Becker, G. S. 1957: *The Economics of Discrimination*. Chicago: University of Chicago Press.

Bell, S. 2000: Do Taxes and Bonds Finance Government Spending? *Journal of Economic Issues*, 34 (3), 603–20.

Benston, G. J. 1990: *The Separation of Commercial and Investment Banking: The Glass-Steagall Act Revisited and Reconsidered*. New York: Oxford University Press.

Berger, H., Noorderahaven, N. G., and Nooteboom, B. 2002: Determinants of Supplier Dependence: An Empirical Study. In G. M. Hodgson (ed.), *A Modern Reader in Institutional and Evolutionary Economics*. Cheltenham, UK: Edward Elgar.

Bergmann, B. 1989: Does the Market for Women's Labor Need Fixing? *Journal of Economic Perspectives*, 3 (1), 43–60.

——. 1995: Becker's Theory of the Family: Preposterous Conclusions. *Feminist Economics,* 1 (1), 141–50.

Bergstrom, T. C. 2002: Evolution of Social Behavior: Individual and Group Selection. *Journal of Economic Perspectives,* 16 (2), 67–88.

Berle, A., Jr. 1959: *Power without Property: A New Development in American Political Economy.* New York: Harcourt, Brace, and World.

Bernatzi, S., and Thaler, R. H. 1995: Myopic Loss Aversion and the Equity Premium Puzzle. *Quarterly Journal of Economics,* 11 (1), 73–92.

Berscheid, E., Boye, D., and Walster, E. 1968: Retaliation as a Means of Restoring Equity. *Journal of Personality and Social Psychology,* 10 (4), 370–76.

Bewley, T. F. 1999: *Why Wages Don't Fall During a Recession.* Cambridge: Harvard University Press.

Binmore, K. G. 1994: *Game Theory and the Social Contract.* Cambridge: MIT Press.

——. 1999: Goat's Wool. In A. Heertje (ed.), *Makers of Modern Economics.* Cheltenham: Elgar, 119–39.

Binmore, K. G., and Vulkan, N. 1999: Applying Game Theory to Automated Negotiation. *Netmonics,* 1, 1–9.

Blau, F. D., and Kuhn, L. M. 2000: Gender Differences in Pay. *Journal of Economic Perspectives,* 14 (4), 75–99.

Blount, S. 1995: When Social Outcomes Are Not Fair. *Organizational Behavior and Human Decision Processes,* 63 (2), 131–44.

Boulding, K. E. 1961: *The Image: Knowledge in Life and Society.* Ann Arbor: University of Michigan Press.

——. 1973: *The Economy of Love and Fear.* Belmont, CA: Wadsworth.

——. 1976: Toward a Theory of Discrimination. In P. Wallace (ed.), *Equal Employment Opportunity and the AT&T Case.* Cambridge: MIT Press.

Bourdieu, P. 1986: The Forms of Capital. In J. G. Richardson (ed.), *Handbook of Theory and Research for the Sociology of Education.* Westport, CT: Greenwood, 241–58.

Bowles, S. 1998: Endogenous Preferences: The Cultural Consequences of Markets and Other Economic Institutions. *Journal of Economic Literature,* 36 (March), 75–111.

Boyd, R., and Richerson, P. J. 2001: Norms and Bounded Rationality. In G. Gigerenzer and R. Selten (eds), *Bounded Rationality: The Adaptive Toolbox.* Cambridge: MIT Press, 281–96.

Boyer, R. A. 2001: The Diversity and Future of Capitalisms: A Regulationist Analysis. In G. M. Hodgson, M. Itoh, and N. Yokakawa (eds), *Capitalism in Evolution.* Cheltenham, UK: Edward Elgar.

Braudel, F. 1981: *Civilization and Capitalism, 15th–18th Century.* London: Collins.

Breimyer, H. 1991: Government "Intervention": A Deceptive Label. *Choices* (2nd Quarter), 3.

Brennan, G., and Lomasky, L. 1993: *Democracy and Decision: The Pure Theory of Electoral Preference.* Cambridge: Cambridge University Press.

Brenner, R. 1976: Agrarian Class Structure and Economic Development in Preindustrial Europe. *Past and Present,* 70 (February), 30–70.

Breton, A. 1989: The Growth of Competitive Governments. *Canadian Journal of Economics,* 22 (4), 717–50.

Brickman, P., and Campbell, D. T. 1971: Hedonic Relativism and Planning the Good Society. In M. H. Apley (ed.), *Adaptation-Level Theory: A Symposium.* New York: Academic Press, 287–302.

Brickman, P., Coates, D., and Janoff-Bulman, R. 1978: Lottery Winners and Accident Victims: Is Happiness Relative? *Journal of Personality and Social Psychology,* 37, 917–27.

Broder, D. 2000: Laws without Government. *Detroit Free Press*, April 21.

Broder, J. 1977: The Provision of Court Services – an Inquiry into the Allocation of Opportunities to Rural Communities. Ph.D., Department of Agricultural Economics, Michigan State University, East Lansing.

——. 1983: Public Choice in Local Judicial Systems. *Public Choice*, 40 (1), 7–19.

Bromley, D. W. 1989: *Economic Interests and Institutions: The Conceptual Foundations of Public Policy*. New York: Basil Blackwell.

——. 1997: Rethinking Markets. *American Journal of Agricultural Economics*, 79, 1383–93.

——. Forthcoming: *Sufficient Reason: Volitional Pragmatism and the Meaning of Economic Institutions*. Princeton: Princeton University Press.

Bromley, D. W., and Cernea, M. M. 1989: *The Management of Common Property Natural Resources: Some Conceptual and Operational Fallacies*, World Bank Discussion Papers, 57. Washington, DC: World Bank.

Brooke, J. 1999: Equity Case in Canada as Redress for Women. *New York Times*. November 19.

Brousseau, E., and Glachant, J. M. 2002: Contract Economics and the Renewal of Economics. In E. Brousseau and J. M. Glachant (eds), *The Economics of Contracts: Theories and Applications*. Cambridge: Cambridge University Press.

Bruner, J. S., and Potter, M. C. 1964: Inference in Visual Recognition. *Science*, 144 (3617), 424–5.

Buchanan, J. 1991: *Constitutional Economics*. Oxford: Basil Blackwell.

Buchanan, J. M. 1968: *The Demand and Supply of Public Goods*. Chicago: Rand McNally.

——. 1992: *Better Than Plowing, and Other Personal Essays*. Chicago: University of Chicago Press.

——. 1996: Economics as a Public Science. In S. Medema and W. Samuels (eds), *Foundations of Research in Economics: How Do Economists Do Economics*. Cheltenham: Edward Elgar.

Buchanan, J. M., and Brennan, G. 1977: Towards a Tax Constitution for Leviathan. In R. D. Tollison and V. J. Vanberg (eds), *Economics: Between Predictive Science and Moral Philosophy*. College Station: Texas A&M University Press.

Buchanan, J. M., and Samuels, W. J. 1975: On Some Fundamental Issues in Political Economy: An Exchange of Correspondence. *Journal of Economic Issues*, 9, 15–38.

Buchanan, J. M., and Tullock, G. 1962: *The Calculus of Consent*. Ann Arbor: University of Michigan Press.

Burawoy, M. 1985: *The Politics of Production: Factory Regimes under Capitalism and Socialism*. London: Verso and Schocken Books.

Burrough, B., and Helyar, J. 1990: *Barbarians at the Gate: The Fall of RJR Nabisco*. New York: Harper and Row.

Busch, L. 1999: Beyond Politics: Rethinking the Future of Democracy. *Rural Sociology*, 64 (1), 2–17.

Calabresi, G. 1985: *Ideals, Beliefs, Attitudes, and the Law: Private Law Perspectives on a Public Law Problem*. Syracuse, NY: Syracuse University Press.

Callen, T., and Ostry, J. D. (eds) 2003: *Japan's Lost Decade: Policies for Economic Revival*. Washington: International Monetary Fund.

Callon, M. 1998: Introduction: The Embeddedness of Economic Markets in Economics. In M. Callon (ed.), *The Laws of the Markets*. Oxford: Blackwell, 1–57.

Camerer, C. 1995: Individual Decision Making. In J. Kagel and A. E. Roth (eds), *Handbook of Experimental Economics*. Princeton: Princeton University Press, 587–616.

——. 1997: Labor Supply of New York City Cabdrivers: One Day at a Time. *Quarterly Journal of Economics*, 112 (2), 407–41.

——. 2003: *Behavioral Game Theory: Experiments in Strategic Interaction*. Princeton: Princeton University Press.

Camerer, C., and Thaler, R. H. 1995: Anomalies: Ultimatums, Dictators and Manners. *Journal of Economic Perspectives*, 9 (2), 109–220.

Caplow, T., Hicks, L., and Wattenberg, B. J. 2001: *The First Measured Century: An Illustrated Guide to Trends in America, 1900–2000*. Washington, DC: AEI Press.

Card, D. E., and Krueger, A. B. 1995: *Myth and Measurement: The New Economics of the Minimum Wage*. Princeton, NJ: Princeton University Press.

Carroll, K. A. 1989: Industrial Structure and Monopoly Power in the Federal Bureaucracy: An Empirical Analysis. *Economic Inquiry*, 27, 683–703.

——. 1990: Bureaucratic Competition and Efficiency: A Review of the Literature. *Journal of Economic Behavior & Organization*, 13, 21–40.

Carter, R. 1998: *Mapping the Mind*. Berkeley: University of California Press.

Cassirer, E. 1953: *Substance and Function*. Translated by W. C. Swabey and M. C. Swabey. New York: Dover.

Chambers, R. 1997: *Whose Reality Counts? Putting the First Last*. London: Intermediate Technology Development Group.

Chandler, A. D. 1962: *Strategy and Structure: Chapters in the History of the Industrial Enterprise*. Cambridge: MIT Press.

——. 1977: *The Visible Hand: The Managerial Revolution in American Business*. Cambridge: Belknap Press.

Chandler, A. D., and Hikino, T. 1990: *Scale and Scope: The Dynamics of Industrial Capitalism*. Cambridge: Belknap Press.

Cheney, M. 1981: *Tesla, Man out of Time*. New York: Dorset Press.

Chernow, R. 1990: *The House of Morgan: An American Banking Dynasty and the Rise of Modern Finance*. New York: Grove Press.

——. 1998: *Titan: The Life of John D. Rockefeller, Sr*. Boston: Little, Brown.

Chick, V. 1983: *Macroeconomics after Keynes*. Deddington: Philip Allan.

Chwe, M. S.-Y. 2001: *Rational Ritual: Culture, Coordination and Common Knowledge*. Princeton: Princeton University Press.

Coase, R. H. 1946: The Marginal Cost Controversy. *Economica*, n.s., 14, 169–82.

——. 1960: The Problem of Social Cost. *Journal of Law and Economics*, 3, 1–44.

——. 1992: The Institutional Structure of Production. *American Economic Review*, 82 (4), 713–19.

Cochrane, W. W. 1958: *Farm Prices, Myth and Reality*. Minneapolis: University of Minnesota Press.

Cohen, A. J., and Harcourt, G. C. 2003: Whatever Happened to the Cambridge Capital Theory Controversies? *Journal of Economic Perspectives*, 17 (1), 199–214.

Colby, B. 2000: Cap-and-Trade Policy Challenge: A Tale of Three Markets. *Land Economics*, 76 (4), 638–58.

Collier, P., and Hoeffler, A. 1998: On the Economic Cause of Civil War. *Oxford Economic Papers*, 50, 563–73.

Collingwood, H. 2002: The Earnings Cult. *New York Times Magazine*, June 9, 68–72.

Collins, J. C. 2001: *Good to Great: Why Some Companies Make the Leap – and Others Don't*. New York, NY: Harper Business.

Commission on the Skills of the American Workforce. 1990: *America's Choice: High Skills or Low Wages*. Rochester, NY: National Center on Education and the Economy.

Commons, J. R. 1907: *Proportional Representation*. 2nd edn. New York: Macmillan.

——. 1909: American Shoemakers, 1648–1895: A Sketch of Industrial Evolution. *Quarterly Journal of Economics*, 24 (November), 39–84.

——. 1924: *Legal Foundations of Capitalism*. New York: Macmillan.

——. 1934: *Institutional Economics*. New York: Macmillan.

——. 1950: *The Economics of Collective Action*. New York: Macmillan.

——. (ed.) 1905: *Trade Unionism and Labor Problems*. Boston: Ginn & Company.

Cooter, R., and Ulen, T. 1988: *Law and Economics*. Glenview, IL: Scott, Foresman.

Cory, G. A. 1999: *The Reciprocal Modular Brain in Economics and Politics: Shaping the Rational and Moral Basis of Organization, Exchange, and Choice*. New York: Kluwer Academic/Plenum Publishers.

Cosmides, L., and Tooby, J. 1994a: Better Than Rational: Evolutionary Psychology and the Invisible Hand. *American Economic Review*, 84 (2), 327–32.

——. 1994b: Beyond Intuition and Instinct Blindness; Towards an Evolutionary Rigorous Cognitive Science. *Cognition*, 50 (1–3), 41–77.

——. 1997: *Evolutionary Psychology Primer*. Available from http://www.psych.ucsb.edu/research/cep/primer.html.

Crocker, T. D. 1971: Externalities, Property Rights, and Transaction Costs: An Empirical Study. *Journal of Law and Economics*, 14, 451–64.

Crosson, R. T. A. 1995: Expectations in Voluntary Contribution Mechanisms. Philadelphia: University of Pennsylvania, Wharton School.

Croyle, J. L. 1979: An Impact Analysis of Judge-Made Products Liability Policies. *Law and Society Review*, 13 (4), 949–67.

Cullis, J. C., and Jones, P. R. 1998: Towards a "New" Outrageous Public Choice. *Journal of Socio-Economics*, 27 (5), 623–40.

Cyert, R. M. 1988: *The Economic Theory of Organization and the Firm*. New York: Harvester-Wheatsheaf.

Dahlman, C. J. 1980: *The Open Field System and Beyond: A Property Rights Analysis of an Economic Institution*. Cambridge: Cambridge University Press.

Dallas, L. 1997: Proposals for Reform of Corporate Boards of Directors: The Dual Board and Board Ombudsperson. *Washington and Lee Law Review*, 54 (1), 105–8.

——. forthcoming: *Law and Behavioral Economics*.

Daly, H. E. 2002: Sustainable Development: Definitions, Principles, Policies. In *Invited Address, World Bank*. Washington, DC.

Damasio, A. R. 1994: *Descartes' Error: Emotion, Reason, and the Human Brain*. New York: Putnam.

Davidson, P. 1972: *Money and the Real World*. London: Macmillan.

——. 1982: *International Money and the Real World*. New York: Wiley.

——. 1982–83: Rational Expectations: A Fallacious Foundation for Studying Crucial Decision-Making Processes. *Journal of Post Keynesian Economics* (Winter), 182–98.

——. 1998: Post Keynesian Employment Analysis and OECD Unemployment. *Economic Journal*, 108 (448), 817–31.

Davis, John. 2003. *The Theory of the Individual in Economics*. London: Routledge.

Dawes, R. M. 1988: Anomalies: Cooperation. *Journal of Economic Perspectives*, 2 (3), 187–97.

——. 1990: Cooperation for the Benefit of Us – Not Me or My Conscience. In J. Mansbridge (ed.), *Beyond Self Interest*. Chicago: University of Chicago Press.

——. 1994: Experimental Demand, Clear Incentives, Both, or Neither? Unpublished paper, Carnegie Mellon University, Pittsburgh.

Dearborn, D. C., and Simon, H. A. 1958: Selective Perception: The Identifications of Executives. *Sociometry*, 21.

Denison, E. 1985: *Trends in American Economic Growth, 1929–1982*. Washington: Brookings.

Diamond, J. M. 1997: *Guns, Germs, and Steel: The Fates of Human Societies*. New York: W.W. Norton.

Dietrich, M. 1994: *Transaction Cost Economics and Beyond: Towards a New Economics of the Firm*. London; New York: Routledge.

DiMaggio, P., and Powell, W. W. 1983: The Iron Cage Revisited: Institutional Isomorphism and Collective Rationality in Organizational Fields. *American Sociological Review*, 48 (April), 147–60.

——. 1991: Introduction. In W. W. Powell and P. DiMaggio (eds), *The New Institutionalism in Organizational Analysis*. Chicago: University of Chicago Press.

Dola, S. 1971: The Evolution of a Funding Policy. *Water Spectrum (U.S. Army Corps of Engineers)* (Fall), 1–6.

Dosi, G. 1988: Sources, Procedures, and Microeconomic Effects of Innovation. *Journal of Economic Literature*, 26 (September), 1120–71.

Dosi, G., and Orsenigo, L. 1988: Coordination and Transformation. In G. Dosi (ed.), *Technical Change and Economic Theory*, London: Pinter Publishers, 13–37.

Dow, S. C. 2000: Prospects for the Progress of Heterodox Economics. *Journal of the History of Economic Thought*, 22 (2), 157–70.

Downs, A. 1957: *An Economic Theory of Democracy*. New York: Harper & Row.

Dugger, W. M., and Sherman, H. J. 2000: *Reclaiming Evolution*. London: Routledge.

Earl, P. E. 1983: *The Economic Imagination: Towards a Behavioural Analysis of Choice*. Brighton: Wheatsheaf Books.

Easterlin, R. A. 1995: Will Raising the Incomes of All Increase the Happiness of All? *Journal of Economic Behavior and Organization*, 27, 35–47.

Eggertsson, T. 1990: *Economic Behavior and Institutions*. Cambridge: Cambridge University Press.

Eichler, N. 1989: *The Thrift Debacle*. Berkeley: University of California Press.

Elbadawi, E., and Sambanis, N. 2000: Why Are There So Many Civil Wars in Africa: Understanding and Preventing Violent Conflict. *Journal of African Economies*, 9, 244–69.

Ellickson, R. C. 1991: *Order without Law: How Neighbors Settle Disputes*. Cambridge, MA: Harvard University Press.

Elster, J. 1984: *Ulysses and the Sirens*. Revised edn. Cambridge: Cambridge University Press.

——. 1998: Emotions and Economic Theory. *Journal of Economic Literature*, 36 (1), 47–74.

Emirbayer, M. 1997: Manifesto for a Relational Sociology. *American Journal of Sociology*, 103 (2), 281–317.

Ensminger, J. 2001: Reputations, Trust, and the Principal Agent Problem. In K. S. Cook (ed.), *Trust in Society*. New York: Russell Sage Foundation.

Erikson, R. S., MacKuen, M., and Stimson, J. A. 2002: *The Macro Polity: Cambridge Studies in Political Psychology and Public Opinion*. Cambridge: Cambridge University Press.

Etzioni, A. 1988: *The Moral Dimension: Toward a New Economics*. New York: Free Press.

Feder, B. J. 1999: Genentech Agrees to Settle Patent Dispute. *New York Times*, November 17, 1999.

Felton, E. 2001: Finders, Keepers? *Reader's Digest* (April), 103–7.

Fetherstonhaugh, D. 1997: Insensitivity to the Value of Human Life: A Study of Psychophysical Numbing. *Journal of Risk and Uncertainty*, 14 (3), 283–300.

Field, A. J. 1979: On the Explanation of Rules Using Rational Choice Models. *Journal of Economic Issues*, 13 (March), 49–72.

——. 1991: Do Legal Systems Matter? *Explorations in Economic History*, 28, 1–35.

——. 2001: *Altruistically Inclined?: The Behavioral Sciences, Evolutionary Theory, and the Origins of Reciprocity, Economics, Cognition, and Society*. Ann Arbor: University of Michigan Press.

Fiori, S. 2002: Alternative Visions of Change in Douglass North's New Institutionalism. *Journal of Economic Issues*, 36 (4), 1025–43.

Fischoff, B. 1975: Hindsight Is Not Equal to Foresight: The Effect of Outcome Knowledge on Judgment under Uncertainty. *Journal of Experimental Psychology: Human Perception and Performance*, 104 (1), 288–99.

Fisher, I. 1932: *Booms and Depressions, Some First Principles*. New York: Adelphi.

Fishman, T. C. 2002: Making a Killing: The Myth of Capital's Good Intentions. *Atlantic Monthly*, August, 33–41.

Fligstein, N. 1990: *Transformation of Corporate Control*. Cambridge: Harvard University Press.

——. 2001: *The Architecture of Markets: An Economic Sociology of Twenty-First-Century Capitalist Societies*. Princeton: Princeton University Press.

Fogel, R. W. 1975: The Limits of Quantitative Methods in History. *American Historical Review*, 8 (2), 329–50.

——. 1989: Afterword: Some Notes on the Scientific Methods of Simon Kuznets. In *Economic Development, the Family, and Income Distribution: Selected Essays*. New York: Cambridge University Press, 413–38.

——. 1997: Douglass C. North and Economic Theory. In J. N. Drobak and J. V. Nye (eds), *The Frontiers of the New Institutional Economics*. New York: Harcourt, Brace, 13–28.

Fogel, R. W., and Engerman, S. L. 1977: Explaining the Relative Efficiency of Slave Agriculture in the Antebellum South. *American Economic Review*, 67 (3), 275–96.

Folbre, N. 2001: *The Invisible Heart: Economics and Family Values*. New York: New Press.

Folbre, N., and Nelson, J. 2000: For Love or Money–or Both? *Journal of Economic Perspectives*, 14 (4), 123–40.

Forest, S., Zeller, W., and Timmons, H. 2001: The Enron Debacle. *Business Week*, November 12, 106.

Foss, N. J., and Knudsen, C. 1996: *Towards a Competence Theory of the Firm*. London: Routledge.

Foster, J., and Metcalfe, J. S. 2001: Modern Evolutionary Economic Perspectives: An Overview. In J. Foster and J. S. Metcalfe (eds), *Frontiers of Evolutionary Economics: Competition, Self-Organization, and Innovation Policy*. Cheltenham, UK: Edward Elgar, 1–18.

Foucault, M. 1970: *The Order of Things: An Archaeology of the Human Sciences*. New York: Pantheon Books.

Frank, R. H. 1985: *Choosing the Right Pond*. Oxford: Oxford University Press.

——. 1988: *Passions within Reason: The Strategic Role of Emotions*. New York: Norton.

——. 1997: *Microeconomics and Behavior*. 3rd edn. New York: McGraw-Hill.

——. 1999: *Luxury Fever: Why Money Fails to Satisfy in an Era of Excess*. New York: Free Press.

Franklin, J. 1987: *Molecules of the Mind: The Brave New Science of Molecular Psychology*. New York: Atheneum.

Freeman, C., and Soete, L. 1997: *The Economics of Industrial Innovation*. 3rd edn. London: Pinter.

Frey, B. S. 1993: Does Monitoring Increase Work Effort: The Rivalry with Trust and Loyalty. *Economic Inquiry*, 31, 663–70.

——. 1997: *Not Just for the Money: An Economic Theory of Personal Motivation*. Cheltenham: Edward Elgar.

——. 2001: *Inspiring Economics: Human Motivation in Political Economy.* Cheltenham: Edward Elgar.

Friedman, L. M. 1965: *Contract Law in America: A Social and Economic Case Study.* Madison: University of Wisconsin Press.

Frijda, N. H. 1986: *The Emotions.* Cambridge: Cambridge University Press.

Frijda, N. H. 1999: Emotions and Hedonic Experience. In D. Kahneman (ed.), *Well-Being: The Foundations of Hedonic Psychology.* New York: Russell Sage, 190–210.

Fromm, E. 1941: *Escape from Freedom.* New York: Avon Books.

Fucini, J. J. 1985: *Entrepreneurs.* Boston: G.K. Hall.

Fukuyama, F. 1995: *Trust.* New York: Free Press.

Fusfeld, D. R. 1957: Economic Theory Misplaced: Livelihood in Primitive Society. In K. Polanyi, C. Arensberg, and H. W. Pearson (eds), *Trade and Market in the Early Empires.* Glencoe, IL: Free Press.

Gaffney, M., and Harrison, F. 1994: *The Corruption of Economics.* London: Shepherd-Walwyn.

Galbraith, J. K. 1967: *The New Industrial State.* Boston: Houghton Mifflin Company.

——. 1975: *Money: Whence It Came, Where It Went.* New York: Bantam Books.

Galeotti, G. 1988: Rules and Behaviors in Markets and Bureaucracies. *European Journal of Political Economy,* 4 (extra issue), 213–28.

——. 1999: Political Parties and Representative Democracy. In S. Bowles, M. Franzini, and U. Pagano (eds), *The Politics and Economics of Power.* New York: Routledge, 129–40.

Garnett, R. F. J. 2002: Paradigms and Pluralism in Heterodox Economics. In *Paper presented to Conference on the History of Heterodox Economics in the 20th Century,* Kansas City, MO.

Gazzaniga, M. S. 1985: *The Social Brain: Discovering the Networks of the Mind.* New York: Basic Books.

Georgescu-Roegen, N. 1968: Utility. In *International Encyclopedia of the Social Sciences.* New York: MacMillan, 236–67.

Gerschenkron, A. 1971: Mercator Gloriosus: Review of Hicks, a Theory of Economic History. *Economic History Review,* 24 (4), 635–66.

Gibney, F. 1991: Japanese Unions. In L. G. Reynolds, S. H. Masters, and C. H. Moser (eds), *Readings in Labor Economics and Labor Relations.* Englewood Cliffs: Prentice-Hall.

Gigerenzer, G., and Selten, R. 2001: Rethinking Rationality. In G. Gigerenzer and R. Selten (eds), *Bounded Rationality: The Adaptive Toolbox.* Cambridge: MIT Press, 1–12.

Godley, W., and Izurieta, A. 2001: The Developing U.S. Recession and Guidelines for Policy. Annandale-on-Hudson, NY: Levy Economics Institute.

Goetz, C. J. 1984: *Cases and Materials on Law and Economics, American Casebook Series.* St. Paul, MN: West Publishing Co.

Gold, M. E. 1991: A Dialogue on Comparable Worth. In L. Reynolds, S. Masters, and C. Moser (eds), *Readings in Labor Economics and Labor Relations.* Englewood Cliffs, NJ: Prentice Hall.

Goranson, R. E., and Berkowitz, L. 1966: Reciprocity and Responsibility: Reactions to Prior Help. *Journal of Personality and Social Psychology,* 3 (2), 227–32.

Gordon, D. M. 1998: Putting Heterodox Macro to the Test: Comparing Post-Keynesian, Marxian and Social Structuralist Macroeconometric Models of the Post-War U.S. Economy. In S. Bowles and T. E. Weisskopf (eds), *Economics and Social Justice.* Cheltenham: Edward Elgar, 362–404.

Gourville, J., and Soman, D. 2002: Pricing and the Psychology of Consumption. *Harvard Business Review* (September), 91–6.

Gowdy, J. M. 1994: *Coevolutionary Economics: The Economy, Society, and the Environment; Natural Resource Management and Policy.* Boston: Kluwer.

Gramlich, E. M., and Rubenfeld, D. L. 1982: Micro Estimates of Public Spending Demand Functions and Tests of the Tiebout and Median-Voter Hypothesis. *Journal of Political Economy*, 90 (June), 536–60.

Granovetter, M. 2002: A Theoretical Agenda for Economic Sociology. In M. F. Guillen (ed.), *The New Economic Sociology: Development in an Emerging Field*. New York: Russell Sage.

Green, D. P., and Shapiro, I. 1994: *Pathologies of Rational Choice Theory: A Critique of Applications in Political Science*. New Haven: Yale University Press.

Greif, A. 1992: Institutions and International Trade: Lessons from the Commercial Revolution. *American Economic Review*, 82 (2), 128–33.

——. 1998: Historical and Comparative Institutional Analysis. *American Economic Review*, 88 (2), 80–84.

——. forthcoming: *Institutions: Theory and History*. Cambridge: Cambridge University Press.

Greif, A., Milgrom, P., and Weingast, B. 1994: Coordination, Commitment, and Enforcement: The Case of the Merchant Guild. *Journal of Political Economy*, 102 (4), 912–50.

Griliches, Z., and Pakes, A. 1986: The Value of Patents as Indicators of Inventive Activity. Paper read at Conference on the Economic Theory of Technology, at London.

Grossman, S. J., and Hart, O. 1986: The Costs and Benefits of Ownership: A Theory of Vertical Integration. *Journal of Political Economy*, 94 (4), 691–719.

Guth, W., and Tietz, R. 1990: Ultimatum Bargaining Behavior: A Survey and Comparison of Experimental Results. *Journal of Economic Psychology*, 11 (3), 417–49.

Hall, B. H. 2002a: The Assessment: Technology Policy. *Oxford Review of Economic Policy*, 18 (1), 1–9.

——. 2002b: The Financing of Research and Development. *Oxford Review of Economic Policy*, 18 (1), 35–52.

Hall, P. A., and Taylor, C. R. 1998: Political Science and the Three New Institutionalisms. In K. Soltan, E. M. Uslaner, and V. Haufler (eds), *Institutions and Social Order*. Ann Arbor: University of Michigan Press.

Hamilton, W. 1932: Institution. In E. R. A. Seligman and A. Johnson (eds), *Encyclopedia of the Social Sciences*. New York: Macmillan, 84–9.

Hammond, T. H. 1986: Agenda Control, Organizational Structure, and Bureaucratic Politics. *American Journal of Political Science*, 30, 379–420.

Hammond, T. H., and Miller, G. J. 1985: A Social Choice Perspective on Expertise and Authority in Bureaucracy. *American Journal of Political Science*, 29, 1–28.

Hardin, R. 2003: *Indeterminacy and Society*. Princeton: Princeton University Press.

Hargadon, A., and Douglas, Y. 2001: When Innovations Meet Institutions: Edison and the Design of the Electric Light. *Administrative Science Quarterly*, 46, 476–501.

Harris, M. 1971: *Culture, Man and Nature*. New York: Crowell.

——. 1974: *Cows, Pigs, Wars, and Witches: The Riddles of Culture*. New York: Vintage Books.

Harrison, J. L. 1995: *Law and Economics in a Nutshell*. St. Paul, MN: West Publishing.

Harter, L. G. 1962: *John R. Commons, His Assault on Laissez-Faire*. Corvallis: Oregon State University Press.

Hattam, V. C. 1992: Institutions and Political Change: Working-Class Formation in England and the United States, 1820–1896. In S. Steinmo, K. A. Thelen, and F. Longstreth (eds), *Structuring Politics: Historical Institutionalism in Comparative Analysis*. Cambridge: Cambridge University Press, 155–87.

Hayami, Y., and Otsuka, K. 1993: *The Economics of Contract Choice*. Oxford: Clarendon Press-Oxford.

Hayami, Y., and Ruttan, V. 1985: *Agricultural Development*. 2nd edn. Baltimore: Johns Hopkins Press.

Hayek, F. 1960: *The Constitution of Liberty*. London: Routledge & Kegan Paul.

——. 1975: The Pretence of Knowledge. *Swedish Journal of Economics*, 77 (4), 433–42.

Heimer, C. A. 2001: Cases and Bibliographies: An Essay on Routinization and the Nature of Comparison. *Annual Review of Sociology*, 27, 47–76.

Heiner, R. 1983: The Origins of Predictable Behavior. *American Economic Review*, 73 (September), 560–95.

Heller, M., and Eisenberg, R. 1998: Can Patents Deter Innovation? *Science*, 28 (May), 698–701.

Helson, H. 1964: *Adaptation Level Theory: An Experimental and Systematic Approach to Behavior*. New York: Harper and Row.

Henriques, D. B. 2002: The Brick Stood up Before. But Now? *New York Times*, March 10, 1.

Heyne, P. 1994: *The Economic Way of Thinking*. New York: Macmillan.

Hicks, J. R. 1969: *Theory of Economic History*. Oxford: Clarendon Press.

Hirschman, A. O. 1970: *Exit, Voice and Loyalty*. Cambridge: Harvard University Press.

——. 1977: *The Passions and the Interests: Political Arguments for Capitalism before Its Triumph*. Princeton: Princeton University Press.

——. 1984: *Getting Ahead Collectively: Grassroots Experiences in Latin America*. New York: Pergamon Press.

——. 1991: *The Rhetoric of Reaction: Perversity, Futility, Jeopardy*. Cambridge: Belknap Press of Harvard University Press.

Hodgson, G. M. 1993: *Economics and Evolution: Bringing Life Back into Economics*. Cambridge: Polity Press.

——. 1994: Cultural and Institutional Influences on Cognition. In G. M. Hodgson, W. J. Samuels, and M. Tool (eds), *Elgar Companion to Institutional and Evolutionary Economics*. Aldershot, UK: Edward Elgar.

——. 1998: The Approach of Institutional Economics. *Journal of Economic Literature*, 36 (March), 166–92.

——. 1999a: *Economics and Utopia: Why the Learning Economy Is Not the End of History*. London: Routledge.

——. 1999b: *Evolution and Institutions: On Evolutionary Economics and the Evolution of Economics*. Northampton, MA: E. Elgar Publishing.

——. 2001: *How Economics Forgot History: The Problem of Historical Specificity in Social Science, Economics as Social Theory*. London: Routledge.

Hoehn, J., and Randall, A. 1989: Too Many Proposals Pass the Benefit Cost Test. *American Economic Review*, 79 (3), 544–51.

Hoffman, E., and Spitzer, M. L. 1982: The Coase Theorem: Some Experimental Tests. *Journal of Law and Economics*, 25 (April), 73–98.

——. 1985: Entitlements, Rights, and Fairness: An Experimental Examination of Subjects' Concepts of Distributive Justice. *Journal of Legal Studies*, 14 (June), 259–97.

——. 1986: Experimental Tests of the Coase Theorem with Large Bargaining Groups. *Journal of Legal Studies*, 15 (January), 149–71.

Hofstadter, D. R. 2001: Analogy as the Core of Cognition. In D. Gentner, K. J. Holyoak, and B. N. Kokinov (eds), *The Analogical Mind: Perspectives from Cognitive Science*. Cambridge: MIT Press.

Hohfeld, W. N. 1913: Some Fundamental Legal Conception as Applied in Judicial Reasoning. *Yale Law Journal*, 23, 16–59.

Holland, J. H. 1998: *Emergence: From Chaos to Order*. Reading, MA: Helix Books.

Holland, J. H., Holyoak, K., Nisbett, R., and Thagard, P. 1986: *Induction: Process of Inference, Learning and Discovery*. Cambridge: MIT Press.

Homans, G. C. 1950: *The Human Group*. New York: Harcourt Brace Jovanovich.

——. 1954: The Cash Posters. *American Sociological Review*, 19 (December), 724–33.

Hopt, K. J. 1998: *Comparative Corporate Governance: The State of the Art and Emerging Research*. Oxford: Oxford University Press.

Horwitz, M. J. 1977: *The Transformation of American Law, 1780–1860. Studies in Legal History*. Cambridge: Harvard University Press.

——. 1987: Santa Clara Revisited: The Development of Corporate Theory. In W. J. Samuels and A. S. Miller (eds), *Corporations and Society: Power and Responsibility*. New York: Greenwood Press, 13–63.

——. 1992: *The Transformation of American Law, 1870–1960: The Crisis of Legal Orthodoxy*. New York: Oxford University Press.

Hotelling, H. 1938: The General Welfare in Relation to Problems of Taxation and of Railway and Utility Rates. *Econometrica* (July).

Hughes, S. S. 2001: *Interview with Herbert W. Boyer*. Oral History Office, Bancroft Library, University of California, Berkeley.

Hughes, T. P. 1982: *Networks of Power: Electrification in Western Society*. Baltimore: Johns Hopkins University Press.

Huigens, K. 2001: Review Essay: Law, Economics and the Skeleton Value Fallacy. *California Law Review*, 89, 537–.

Hurst, J. W. 1956: *Law and the Conditions of Freedom in the Nineteenth Century United States*. Madison: University of Wisconsin Press.

——. 1960: *Law and Social Process in the United States*. Ann Arbor: University of Michigan Law School.

Hutchins, E. 1995: *Cognition in the Wild*. Cambridge: MIT Press.

Iinuma, J. 1995: *Japanese Farming: Past and Present*. Tokyo: Nobunkyo.

Jaffee, S. 1995: Transaction Costs, Risk and the Organization of Private Sector Food Commodity Systems. In S. Jaffee (ed.), *Marketing Africa's High-Value Foods: Comparative Experiences of an Emergent Private Sector*. Dubuque, IA: Hunt.

Jennings, A. L., and Waller, W. 1994: Cultural Hermeneutics and Evolutionary Economics. In G. M. Hodgson, W. J. Samuels, and M. R. Tool (eds), *Elgar Companion to Institutional and Evolutionary Economics*. Aldershot UK: Edward Elgar, 108–15.

Jennings, D. L., Amabile, T. M., and Ross, L. 1982: Informal Covariation Assessment: Data-Based Versus Theory-Based Judgments. In D. Kahneman, P. Slovic and A. Tverskey (eds), *Judgment under Uncertainty*. Cambridge: Cambridge University Press.

Johnson, G. L. 1986: *Research Methodology for Economists: Philosophy and Practice*. New York: Macmillan.

——. 1997: Work on Asset Fixity or Investment/Disinvestment Theory. In A. A. Schmid (ed.), *Beyond Agriculture and Economics*. East Lansing, MI: Michigan State University Press, 91–120.

Johnson, G. L., and Quance, C. L. 1972: *The Overproduction Trap in U.S. Agriculture; a Study of Resource Allocation from World War I to the Late 1960s*. Baltimore: Published for Resources for the Future by the Johns Hopkins University Press.

Johnson, R. N., and Libecap, G. D. 1989: Agency Growth, Salaries, and the Protected Bureaucrat. *Economic Icquiry*, 27, 431–51.

Jolls, C., Sunstein, C. R., and Thaler, R. H. 1998: A Behavioral Approach to Law and Economics. *Stanford Law Review*, 50, 1471–550.

Jones-Lee, M. W., and Loomis, G. 1995: Scale and Context Effects in the Valuation of Transport Safety. *Journal of Risk and Uncertainty*, 11 (3), 183–203.

Just, R. E. 2001: Addressing the Changing Nature of Uncertainty in Agriculture. *American Journal of Agricultural Economics*, 38 (5), 1131–53.

Kahneman, D. 1999: Objective Happiness. In D. Kahneman, E. Deiner, and G. Schwartz (eds), *Well-Being: The Foundations of Hedonic Psychology*. New York: Russell Sage Foundation, 3–25.

Kahneman, D., Fredrickson, B. L., Schreiber, C. A., and Redelmeir, D. A. 1993: When More Pain Is Preferred to Less: Adding a Better End. *Psychological Science*, 4, 401–5.

Kahneman, D., Knetsch, J. L., and Thaler, R. H. 1986: Fairness as a Constraint on Profit Seeking: Entitlements in the Market. *American Economic Review*, 76 (4), 728–41.

Kahneman, D., and Tversky, A. 1979: Prospect Theory: An Analysis of Decision under Risk. *Econometrica*, 47 (2), 263–91.

——. 1982: Subjective Probability: A Judgment of Representativeness. In D. Kahneman, P. Slovic, and A. Tversky (eds), *Judgment under Uncertainty*. Cambridge: Cambridge University Press, 32–47.

Kaldor, N. 1972: The Irrelevance of Equilibrium Economics. *Economics Journal*, 82 (December), 1237–55.

——. 1985: *Economics without Equilibrium*. Armonk, NY: M.E. Sharpe.

Kasper, W., Streit, M. E., and Locke Institute. 1999: *Institutional Economics: Social Order and Public Policy*; John Locke Series in Classical Liberal Political Economy. Northampton, MA: Edward Elgar.

Kates, R. 1962: *Hazard and Choice Perception in Flood Plain Management*. Chicago: University of Chicago, Department of Geography.

Kay, N. M. 1982: *The Evolving Firm: Strategy and Structure in Industrial Organization*. New York: St. Martin's Press.

——. 1999: *The Boundaries of the Firm: Critiques, Strategies, and Policies*. New York: St. Martin's Press.

Keen, S. 2001: *Debunking Economics: The Naked Emperor of the Social Sciences*. Annandale: Pluto Press Australia, St. Martin's Press.

Kelso, L. O., and Hetter, P. 1967: *Two-Factor Theory: The Economics of Reality*. New York: Random House.

Kendall, D., and Dorman, C. 2001: Taking Community Rights by Initiative: Lessons from Oregon, Arizona and Washington. Washington DC: Community Rights Counsel.

Keynes, J. M. 1920: *The Economic Consequences of the Peace*. New York: Harcourt Brace and Howe.

——. 1926: *The End of Laissez-Faire*. London: L. & V. Woolf.

Kiser, L. L., and Ostrom, E. 1982: Three Worlds of Action: A Metatheoretical Synthesis of Institutional Approaches. In E. Ostrom (ed.), *Strategies of Political Inquiry*. New York: Russell Sage.

Knack, S., and Keefer, P. 1997: Does Social Capital Have an Economic Payoff? A Cross-Country Investigation. *Quarterly Journal of Economics*, 112, 1251–88.

Knetsch, J. 1989: The Endowment Effect and Evidence of Nonreversible Indifference Curves. *American Economic Review*, 79 (5), 1277–84.

Knight, F. H., and Bonner, H. 1947: *Freedom and Reform; Essays in Economics and Social Philosophy*. New York: Harper & Brothers.

Knight, J. 1995: Models, Interpretations and Theories: Constructing Explanations of Institutional Emergence and Change. In J. Knight and I. Sened (eds), *Explaining Social Institutions*. Ann Arbor: University of Michigan Press, 95–119.

Knight, J., and North, D. 1997: Explaining Economic Change: The Interplay between Cognition and Institutions. *Legal Theory*, 3, 211–26.

Koo, B., and Wright, B. D. 2002: Economics of Patenting a Research Tool. Washington: International Food Policy Research Institute Working Paper No. 88. http://www.ifpri.org/divs/eptd/dp/papers/eptdp88.pdf

Korobkin, R. B., and Ulen, T. S. 2000: Law and Behavioral Science: Removing the Rationality Assumption from Economics. *California Law Review*, 88, 1051–154.

Korsmeyer, C. 1999: *Making Sense of Taste: Food and Philosophy*. Ithaca: Cornell University Press.

Krasner, S. 1983: Structural Causes and Regime Consequences: Regimes as Intervening Variables. In S. Krasner (ed.), *International Regimes*. Ithaca: Cornell University Press.

Krugman, P. R. 1996: *The Self-Organizing Economy*. Cambridge, MA: Blackwell Publishers.

——. 2002: For Richer. *New York Times*, October 20, section 6, 62ff.

Kuran, T. 1995: *Private Truths, Public Lies: The Social Consequences of Preference Falsification*. Cambridge: Harvard University Press.

Kuttner, R. 2001: The Lesson of Enron: Regulation Isn't a Dirty Word. *Business Week*, December 24, 24.

Kuznets, S. 1972: Innovations and Adjustments in Economic Growth. *Swedish Journal of Economics*, 74 (4), 431–51.

——. 1973: Modern Economic Growth: Findings and Reflections. *American Economic Review*, 63, 3 (June), 247–58.

Laffont, J.-J., and Martimort, D. 2002: *The Theory of Incentives: The Principal-Agent Model*. Princeton, NJ: Princeton University Press.

Lane, R. E. 1991: *The Market Experience*. Cambridge: Cambridge University Press.

Langlois, R. R., and Cosgel, M. M. 1998: The Organization of Consumption. In M. Bianchi (ed.), *The Active Consumer*. London: Routledge, 107–21.

Lawson, T. 1997: *Economics and Reality*. London: Routledge.

Leamer, E. 1982: Let's Take the Con out of Econometrics. *American Economic Review*, 73, 31–43.

Ledeneva, A. V. 1998: *Russia's Economy of Favours: Blat, Networking, and Informal Exchange*. Cambridge *Russian, Soviet and Post-Soviet Studies 102*. Cambridge: Cambridge University Press.

LeDoux, J. E. 1998: *The Emotional Brain: The Mysterious Underpinnings of Emotional Life*. London: Weidenfeld & Nicolson.

Ledyard, J. 1992: *Public Goods: A Survey of Experimental Research*. Pasadena: California Institute of Technology.

Lee, F. S. 1984: The Marginalist Controversy and the Demise of Full Cost Pricing. *Journal of Economic Issues*, 18 (4), 1107–32.

Leholm, A., and Vlasin, R. D. 2004: *The Anatomy of Fifteen High Performance Teams: Energizing the Human Spirit*. East Lansing: Michigan State University Press.

Leibenstein, H. 1950: Bandwagon, Snob, and Veblen Effects in the Theory of Consumer Demand. *Quarterly Journal of Economics*, 64, 193–207.

——. 1979: A Branch of Economics Is Missing: Micro-Micro Theory. *Journal of Economic Literature* (June), 477–99.

Leontief, W. W. 1982: The Distribution of Work and Income. *Scientific American*, 247 (3), 188–204.

Lerner, A. 1943: Functional Finance and the Federal Debt. *Social Research*, 10 (February), 38–51.

Lewin, R. 1999: *Complexity: Life at the Edge of Chaos*, 2nd edn. Chicago: University of Chicago Press.

Lewis, M. 1989: *Liar's Poker: Rising through the Wreckage on Wall Street*. New York: Norton.

Lewontin, R. C., and Berlan, J. P. 1990: The Political Economy of Agricultural Research: The Case of Hybrid Corn. In C. R. Carroll, J. H. Vandermeer, and P. M. Rosset (eds), *Agroecology*. New York: McGraw-Hill, 613–28.

Liebhafsky, H. H. 1973: The Problem of Social Cost: An Alternative View. *Natural Resources Journal*, 13 (October), 615–76.

Lijphart, A. 1999: *Patterns of Democracy: Government Forms and Performance in Thirty-Six Countries*. New Haven: Yale University Press.

Lindahl, E. 1958: Just Taxation – a Positive Solution. In R. A. Musgrave and A. T. Peacock (eds), *Classics in the Theory of Public Finance*. New York: Macmillan, 168–76.

Lindblom, C. E. 2001: *The Market System: What It Is, How It Works, and What to Make of It*, The Yale Isps Series. New Haven: Yale University Press.

Littlechild, S. C. 1986: Three Types of Market Process. In R. N. Langlois (ed.), *Economics as a Process: Essays in the New Institutional Economics*. Cambridge: Cambridge University Press.

Loasby, B. J. 1999: *Knowledge, Institutions, and Evolution in Economics; The Graz Schumpeter Lectures*, 2. London: Routledge.

Loewenstein, G. 2000: Emotion in Economic Theory. *American Economic Review*, 90 (2), 426–33.

Loewenstein, G., and Adler, D. 1995: A Bias in the Prediction of Tastes. *Economic Journal*, 105, 929–37.

Loewenstein, G., and Schkade, D. 1999: Wouldn't It Be Nice? Predicting Future Feelings. In D. Kahneman (ed.), *Well-Being: The Foundations of Hedonic Psychology*. New York: Russell Sage Foundation.

Lord, C. G., Ross, L., and Lepper, M. R. 1979: Biased Assimilation and Attitude Polarization. *Journal of Personality and Social Psychology*, 37 (11), 2098–109.

Lowenstein, R. 2000: *When Genius Failed: The Rise and Fall of Long-Term Capital Management*. New York: Random House.

Lukes, S. 1974: *Power: A Radical View*; Studies in Sociology. London: Macmillan.

Luna, F., and Perrone, A. 2002: *Agent-Based Methods in Economics and Finance: Simulations in Swarm*; Advances in Computational Economics; V. 17. Boston: Kluwer Academic Publishers.

Luna, F., and Stefansson, B. 2000: *Economic Simulations in Swarm: Agent-Based Modeling and Object Oriented Programming*; Advances in Computational Economics; V. 14. Boston: Kluwer Academic.

Macfarlane, A. 1978: *The Origins of English Individualism: The Family, Property and Social Transition*. Oxford: Blackwell.

Macho-Stadler, I., and Pérez-Castrillo, J. D. 1997: *An Introduction to the Economics of Information: Incentives and Contracts*. Oxford: Oxford University Press.

Maney, K. 2002: A Word About Indecipherable, Er, Indefeasible Rights of Use. *USA Today*, February 27, 3B.

Mankiw, N. G. 1995: The Growth of Nations. *Brookings Papers on Economic Activity*, 1995 (1), 275–310.

——. 2004: *Principles of Economics*, 3rd edn. Mason, OH: Thomson South-Western.

Mantzavinos, C. 2001: *Individuals, Institutions, and Markets: Political Economy of Institutions and Decisions*. Cambridge: Cambridge University Press.

March, J. G., and Olsen, J. P. 1989: *Rediscovering Institutions: The Organizational Basis of Politics*. New York: Free Press.

March, J. G., and Simon, H. A. 1958: *Organizations*. New York: Wiley.

Marcus, S. 1974: *Engels, Manchester, and the Working Class*. New York: Random House.

Marglin, S. A. 1974: What Bosses Do: The Origins and Functions of Hierarchy in Capitalist Production. *Review of Radical Political Economics*, 6, 60–112.

——. 1996: Farmers, Seedsmen, and Scientists: Systems of Agriculture and Systems of Knowledge. In F. Apffel-Marglin and S. A. Marglin (eds), *Decolonizing Knowledge: From Development to Dialogue*. Oxford: Oxford University Press.

——. 1999: John Kenneth Galbraith and the Myths of Economics. In H. Sasson (ed.), *Between Friends: Perspectives on John Kenneth Galbraith*. Boston: Houghton Mifflin, 114–38.

Margolis, H. 1987: *Patterns, Thinking, and Cognition: A Theory of Judgment*. Chicago: University of Chicago Press.

Marshall, A. 1873: The Future of the Working Class. In A. C. Pigou (ed.), *Memorials of Alfred Marshall*. New York: Augustus Kelley, 101–18.

Marshall, R. 1996: Human Resources, Labor Markets, and Economic Performance. In C. J. Whalen (ed.), *Political Economy for the 21st Century*. Armonk, NY: M.E. Sharpe.

Martin, L. L. 1997: Production Contracts, Risk Shifting and Relative Performance Payments in the Pork Industry. *Journal of Agricultural and Applied Economics*, 29 (December), 267–78.

Marwell, G., and Ames, R. E. 1997: Economists Free Ride; Does Anyone Else? Experiments on the Provision of Public Goods. In *Culture, Social Norms and Economics*. Cheltenham: Edward Elgar.

Masten, S. E. 1996: *Case Studies in Contracting and Organization*. New York: Oxford University Press.

Mayer, M. 1990: *The Greatest-Ever Bank Robbery: The Collapse of the Savings and Loan Industry*. New York: C. Scribner's Sons.

——. 2001: *The Fed: The Inside Story of How the World's Most Powerful Financial Institution Drives the Market*. New York: Free Press.

Mayer, T. 1992: *Truth Versus Precision*. London: Edward Elgar.

Mayhew, A. 1994: Culture. In G. M. Hodgson, W. J. Samuels, and M. Tool (eds), *Elgar Companion to Institutional and Evolutionary Economics*. Aldershot, UK: Edward Elgar.

Mazzotta, M., and Opaluch, J. 1995: Decision Making When Choices Are Complex: A Test of Heiner's Hypothesis. *Land Economics*, 71 (4), 500–15.

McCloskey, D. N. 1985: *The Rhetoric of Economics*. Madison, WI: University of Wisconsin Press.

McCubbins, M. D., Noll, R. G., and Weingast, B. 1987: Administrative Procedures as Instruments of Political Control. *Journal of Law, Economics, and Organizations*, 3, 243–77.

McFadden, D., and Leonard, G. K. 1993: Issues in the Contingent Valuation of Environmental Goods: Methodologies for Data Collection and Analysis. In J. A. Hausman (ed.), *Contingent Valuation: A Critical Assessment*. Amsterdam: North-Holland.

Megginson, W. L., and Netter, J. M. 2001: From State to Market: A Survey of Empirical Studies on Privatization. *Journal of Economic Literature*, 39 (2), 321–89.

Melman, S. 1983: *Profits without Production*. New York: Alfred A. Knopf.

——. 2001: *After Capitalism: From Managerialism to Workplace Democracy*. New York: Alfred A. Knopf.

Milgram, S. 1974: *Obedience to Authority*. New York: Harper and Row.

Milgrom, P., and Roberts, J. 1992: *Economics, Organization and Management*. Englewood Cliffs: Prentice Hall.

Minsky, H. P. 1982: The Federal Reserve: Between a Rock and a Hard Place. In H. P. Minsky (ed.), *Can It Happen Again? Essays on Instability and Finance*. Armonk, NY: M.E. Sharpe, 192–202.

——. 1986: *Stabilizing an Unstable Economy, A Twentieth Century Fund Report*. New Haven: Yale University Press.

——. 1990: Schumpeter: Finance and Evolution. In A. Heertje and M. Perlman (eds), *Evolving Technology and Market Structure: Studies in Schumpeterian Economics*. Ann Arbor: University of Michigan Press.

Mirowski, P. 1996: Do You Know the Way to Santa Fe? In S. Pressman (ed.), *Interactions in Political Economy*. London: Routledge, 13–40.

——. 2001: What Economics Can and Cannot Tell Us About Historical Actors. In J. Biddle, J. B. Davis, and S. G. Medema (eds), *Economics Broadly Considered*. London: Routledge, 182–200.

——. 2002: *Machine Dreams: Economics Becomes a Cyborg Science*. Cambridge: Cambridge University Press.

Mittone, L., and Patelli, P. 2000: Imitative Behavior in Tax Evasion. In F. Luna and B. Stefansson (eds), *Economic Simulations in Swarm*. Boston: Kluwer.

Moe, T. M. 1997: The Positive Theory of Public Bureaucracy. In D. C. Mueller (ed.), *Perspectives on Public Choice*. Cambridge: Cambridge University Press, 455–80.

Mowery, D. C., and Rosenberg, N. 1998: *Paths of Innovation*. Cambridge: Cambridge University Press.

Mueller, D. C. 1988: The Corporate Life Cycle. In P. Allan (ed.), *Internal Organization, Efficiency and Profit*. Oxford: Oxford University Press, 38–64.

——. 1989: *Public Choice Ii*. Cambridge: Cambridge University Press.

——. 1997: Public Choice in Perspective. In D. C. Mueller (ed.), *Perspectives on Public Choice: A Handbook*. Cambridge: Cambridge University Press, 1–17.

——. 2003: *Public Choice Iii*. Cambridge: Cambridge University Press.

Murrell, P. 1991: Can Neoclassical Economics Underpin the Reform of Centrally Planned Economies? *Journal of Economic Perspectives*, 5 (4), 59–76.

Myers, D. G. 1999: Close Relationships and Quality of Life. In D. Kahneman (ed.), *Well-Being: The Foundations of Hedonic Psychology*. New York: Russell Sage.

Myhrman, J., and Barry Weingast. 1994: Douglass C. North's Contributions to Economics and Economic History. *Scandanavian Journal of Economics*, 96 (2), 185–93.

Myrdal, G. 1944: *An American Dilemma: The Negro Problem and Modern Democracy*. New York: Harper.

——. 1975: The Equality Issue in World Development. *Swedish Journal of Economics*, 77 (4), 413–32.

Nagin, D. S., Reibitzer, J. B., Sanders, S., and Taylor, L. J. 2002: Monitoring, Motivation, and Management: The Determinants of Opportunistic Behavior in a Field Experiment. *American Economic Review*, 92 (4), 850–73.

Nee, V., and Ingram, P. 1998: Embeddedness and Beyond: Institutions, Exchange, and Social Structure. In M. C. Brinton and V. Nee (eds), *The New Institutionalism in Sociology*. New York: Russell Sage Foundation.

Nelson, R. R. 1995: Recent Evolutionary Theorizing About Economic Change. *Journal of Economic Literature*, 33 (March), 48–90.

——. 2001: The Coevolution of Technology and Institutions as the Driver of Economic Growth. In J. Foster and J. S. Metcalfe (eds), *Frontiers of Evolutionary Economics*. Cheltenham, UK: Edward Elgar, 19–30.

Nelson, R. R., and Winter, Jr., S.G. 1974: Neoclassical Vs. Evolutionary Theories of Economic Growth: Critique and Prospectus. *Economic Journal*, 886–905.

——. 1982: *An Evolutionary Theory of Economic Change*. Cambridge: Belknap Press of Harvard University Press.

——. 2002: Evolutionary Theorizing in Economics. *Journal of Economic Perspectives*, 16 (2), 23–46.

Netting, R. 1981: *Balancing on an Alp*. Cambridge: Cambridge University Press.

Niskanen, W., Jr. 1971: *Bureaucracy and Representative Government*. Chicago: Aldine-Atherton.

Noble, D. F. 1979: Social Choice in Machine Design: The Case of Automatically Controlled Machine Tools. In A. S. Zimbalist (ed.), *Case Studies on the Labor Process*. New York: Monthly Review Press, 18–50.

Nooteboom, B. 2001: From Evolution to Language and Learning. In J. Foster and J. S. Metcalfe (eds), *Frontiers of Evolutionary Economics*. Cheltenham, UK: Edward Elgar.

Norgaard, R. B. 1994: *Development Betrayed: The End of Progress and a Coevolutionary Revisioning of the Future*. London: Routledge.

North, D. C. 1990: *Institutions, Institutional Change and Economic Performance*. Cambridge: Cambridge University Press.

——. 1994: Economic Performance through Time. *American Economic Review*, 84 (3), 359–68.

——. 1997: The Process of Economic Change. Unpublished paper distributed at the first conference on the International Society for the New Institutional Economics, St. Louis, MO.

North, D. C., and Wallis, J. 1994: Integrating Institutional Change and Technical Change in Economic History: A Transaction Cost Approach. *Journal of Institutional and Theoretical Economics*, 150 (4), 609–624.

North, D. C., and Weingast, B. 1989: Constitutions and Commitment: Evolution of Institutions Governing Public Choice. *Journal of Economic History*, 49 (2), 803–32.

Nussbaum, M. C. 2001: *Upheavals of Thought: The Intelligence of Emotions*. Cambridge: Cambridge University Press.

Nye, R. D. 1992: *The Legacy of B. F. Skinner: Concepts and Perspectives, Controversies and Misunderstandings*. Pacific Grove, CA: Brooks/Cole.

O'Hara, P. A. 2000: *Marx, Veblen, and Contemporary Institutional Political Economy: Principles and Unstable Dynamics of Capitalism*. New Horizons in Institutional and Evolutionary Economics. Cheltenham, UK: Edward Elgar.

Olmstead, A. L., and Goldberg, V. P. 1975: Institutional Change and American Economic Growth: A Critique of Davis and North. *Explorations in Economic History*, 12, 193–210.

Olson, M. 1965: *The Logic of Collective Action; Public Goods and the Theory of Groups*, Harvard Economic Studies, V. 124. Cambridge: Harvard University Press.

——. 1996: Why Some Nations Are Rich, and Others Poor. *Journal of Economic Perspectives*, 10 (2), 3–24.

Ostrom, E. 1986: A Method of Institutional Analysis. In F.-X. Kaufman, G. Majone, and V. Ostrom (eds), *Guidance, Control and Evaluation in the Public Sector*. New York: Walter de Gruyter.

——. 1990: *Governing the Commons: The Evolution of Institutions for Collective Action*. Cambridge: Cambridge University Press.

Ostrom, E. et al. 2002: *Aid, Incentives, and Sustainability*. Stockholm: Swedish International Development Cooperation Agency.

Ostrom, E., Baugh, W. H., Guarasci, R., Parks, R. B., and Whitaker, G. P. 1973: Community Organization and the Provision of Police Services. Beverly Hills, CA: A Sage Professional Paper.

Ostrom, E., Gardner, R., and Walker, J. 1994: *Rules, Games, and Common-Pool Resources*. Ann Arbor: University of Michigan Press.

Ostrom, E., Schroeder, L. D., and Wynne, S. G. 1993: *Institutional Incentives and Sustainable Development: Infrastructure Policies in Perspective*. Boulder: Westview Press.

Park, W. M., and Shabman, L. A. 1982: Distributional Constraints on Acceptance of Nonpoint Pollution Controls. *American Journal of Agricultural Economics*, 64, 455–62.

Peach, J. 1994: Distribution Theory. In G. M. Hodgson, W. J. Samuels, and M. Tool (eds), *Elgar Companion to Institutional and Evolutionary Economics*. Cheltenham: Edward Elgar.

Pena, D. S. 2001: *Economic Barbarism and Managerialism*. Westport, CN: Greenwood.

Pencavel, J., and Craig, B. 1994: The Empirical Performance of Orthodox Models of the Firm: Conventional Firms and Worker Cooperatives. *Journal of Political Economy*, 102 (4), 718–44.

Penrose, E. T. 1995: *The Theory of the Growth of the Firm*, 3rd edn. Oxford: Oxford University Press.

Perlman, M. 1984: Perlman on Shackle. In H. Speigel and W. J. Samuels (eds), *Contemporary Economists in Perspective*. London: JAI Press.

Perlman, S. 1949: *A Theory of the Labor Movement*. New York: New York Lithographing Corporation.

Persson, T., and Tabellini, G. E. 2000: *Political Economics: Explaining Economic Policy*, *Zeuthen Lecture Book Series*. Cambridge: MIT Press.

Pert, C. B. 1997: *Molecules of Emotion*. New York: Scribner.

Peterson, J., and Sharp, M. 1998: *Technology Policy in the European Union*. New York: St. Martin's Press, chapter 8, Decision-Making: Who Gets What and Why?

Peterson, W. C. 1996: Macroeconomics and the Theory of the Firm. In C. J. Whalen (ed.), *Political Economy for the 21st Century*. Armonk, NY: M.E. Sharpe, 151–70.

Pierre, K. *The Susceptibility of Property Rights Heuristics to Framing in Public Opinion Polls and Voting* 1999 [cited]. Available from www.msu.edu/user/schmid/pierre.htm.

Pincus, J. 1977: *Pressure Groups and Politics in Antebellum Tariffs*. New York: Columbia University Press.

Pinker, S. 1997: *How the Mind Works*. New York: Norton.

Pirenne, H. 1937: *Economic and Social History of Medieval Europe*, A Harvest Book; Hb-14. New York: Harcourt Brace.

Platt, J. 1973: Social Traps. *American Psychologist* (August), 641–51.

Plott, C. 1995: Dimensions of Parallelism: Some Policy Applications of Experimental Methods. In J. H. Kagel and A. E. Roth (eds), *Handbook of Experimental Economics*. Princeton: Princeton University Press.

Polanyi, K. 1944: *The Great Transformation: The Political and Economic Origins of Our Time*. New York: Rinehart.

——. 1957: *Trade and Market in the Early Empires; Economies in History and Theory*. Glencoe, IL: Free Press.

Polinsky, A. M. 1980: On the Choice between Property Rules and Liability Rules. *Economic Inquiry*, 18, 233–46.

Pollan, M. 2002: Power Steer. *New York Times Magazine*, March 31, 44ff.

Pommerehne, W. W. 1978: Institutional Approaches to Public Expenditures: Empirical Evidence from Swiss Municipalities. *Public Finance Quarterly* (April), 395–407.

Postrel, V. 2003: Looking Inside the Brains of the Stingy. *New York Times*, February 27.

Poteete, A., and Ostrom, E. 2003: *In Pursuit of Comparable Concepts and Data About Collective Action*. (CAPRi Working Paper No. 29). Washington: International Food Policy Research Institute. Available from http://www.capri.cgiar.org/pdf/capriwp29.pdf.

Potts, J. 2000: *The New Evolutionary Microeconomics*. Cheltenham, UK: Edward Elgar.

Poundstone, W. 1992: *Prisoner's Dilemma*. New York: Doubleday.

Praag, B. M. S. v., and Frijters, P. 1999: The Measurement of Welfare and Well-Being: The Leyden Approach. In D. Kahneman (ed.), *Well-Being: The Foundations of Hedonic Psychology*. New York: Russell Sage.

Prelec, D. 1991: Values and Principles: Some Limitations on Traditional Economic Analysis. In A. Etzioni and P. Lawrence (eds), *Socioeconomics: Toward a New Synthesis*. New York: M.E. Sharpe.

Prescott, E. D. 1988: Robert M. Solow's Neoclassical Growth Model: An Influential Contribution to Economics. *Scandinavian Journal of Economics*, 90 (1), 7–12.

Przeworski, A., and Teune, H. 1970: *The Logic of Comparative Social Inquiry.* New York: Wiley-Interscience.

Putnam, R. D. 1993: *Making Democracy Work: Civic Traditions in Modern Italy.* Princeton: Princeton University Press.

Qian, Y. 1999: Institutional Foundations of China's Market Transition. Paper read at World Bank Annual Bank Conference on Development Economics, at Washington, DC.

Rabin, M. 1998: Psychology and Economics. *Journal of Economic Literature,* 36 (1), 11–46.

Ramstad, Y. 1986: A Pragmatist's Quest for Holistic Knowledge: The Scientific Methodology of John R. Commons. *Journal of Economic Issues,* 20 (December), 1067–105.

——. 1996: Is a Transaction a Transaction? *Journal of Economic Issues,* 30 (2), 413–25.

——. 2001: John R. Commons' Reasonable Value and the Problem of Just Price. *Journal of Economic Issues,* 35 (2), 253–77.

Ramstad, Y. Rausser, G. 1999: Private/Public Research: Knowledge Assets and Future Scenarios. *American Journal of Agricultural Economics,* 81 (5), 1011–27.

Reardon, T., and Berdegue, J. A. 2002: The Rapid Rise of Supermarkets in Latin America. *Development Policy Review,* 20 (4), 371–88.

Reber, A. S. 1993: *Implicit Learning and Tacit Knowledge: An Essay on the Cognitive Unconscious.* Oxford: Oxford University Press.

Reisman, D. A. 2002: *The Institutional Economy: Demand and Supply.* Cheltenham, UK: Edward Elgar.

Reynolds, L. G., Masters, S., and Moser, C. 1998: *Labor Economics and Labor Relations.* 11th edn. Upper Saddle River, NJ: Prentice Hall.

Rizzello, S. 1999: *The Economics of the Mind.* English language edn. Cheltenham, UK; Northampton, MA: Edward Elgar.

Robinson, J. 1962: *Economic Philosophy, The New Thinker's Library.* London: C.A. Watts.

——. 1979: Solving the Stagflation Puzzle. *Challenge* (November–December), 40–6.

Robison, L. J., and Schmid, A. A. 1991: Interpersonal Relationships and Preferences. In R. Frantz (ed.), *Handbook of Behavioral Economics.* Greenwich: JAI Press.

——. 1994: Can Agriculture Prosper without Social Capital. *Choices* (Fourth Quarter).

Robison, L. J., Schmid, A. A., and Siles, M. E. 2002: Is Social Capital Really Capital? *Review of Social Economy,* 60 (1), 1–21.

Rodrik, D. 2002: Globalization for Whom? *Harvard Magazine,* 104 (6), 29–31.

Roe, M. J. 1994: *Strong Managers, Weak Owners: The Political Roots of American Corporate Finance.* Princeton: Princeton University Press.

Ronis, D. L., Yates, J. F., and Kirscht, J. P. 1989: Attitudes, Decisions, and Habits as Determinants of Repeated Behavior. In A. R. Pratkanis, S. J. Breckerler, and A. G. Greenwald (eds), *Attitudes, Structure, and Function.* Hillsdale, NJ: Erlbaum.

Roth, A. E. 1995: Bargaining Experiments. In J. H. Kagel and A. E. Roth (eds), *The Handbook of Experimental Economics.* Princeton: Princeton University Press.

Rotheim, R. J. 1996: Paul Davidson. In W. J. Samuels (ed.), *American Economists of the Late Twentieth Century.* Cheltenham: Edward Elgar.

Rutherford, M. 1994: *Institutions in Economics: The Old and the New Institutionalism, Historical Perspectives on Modern Economics.* Cambridge: Cambridge University Press.

Ruttan, V., and Hayami, Y. 1984: Toward a Theory of Induced Institutional Innovation. *Journal of Development Studies,* 203–23.

Sahal, D. 1981: The Farm Tractor and the Nature of Technological Innovation. *Research Policy,* 10, 368–402.

Saint-Paul, G. 2000: The New Political Economy: Recent Books. *Journal of Economic Literature,* 38 (December), 915–25.

Samuels, W. J. 1971: Interrelations between Legal and Economic Processes. *Journal of Law and Economics*, 14 (October).

——. 1984: Posnerian Law and Economics on the Bench. *International Review of Law and Economics*, 4 (December).

——. 1987: The Idea of the Corporation as a Person: On the Normative Significance of Judicial Language. In W. J. Samuels (ed.), *Corporations and Society*. New York: Greenwood Press, 113–29.

——. 1989: The Legal–Economic Nexus. *George Washington Law Review*, 57, 1556–78.

——. 1992a: An Economic Perspective on the Compensation Problem. In W. J. Samuels (ed.), *Essays on the Economic Role of Government*. New York: New York University Press, 247–66.

——. 1992b: The Nature and Scope of Economic Policy. In W. J. Samuels (ed.), *Essays on the Economic Role of Government*. New York: New York University Press, 3–55.

——. 1994: On Macroeconomic Politics. *Journal of Post Keynesian Economics*, 16 (4), 661–70.

——. 1997: The Case for Methodological Pluralism. In A. Salanti and E. Screpanti (eds), *Pluralism in Economics: New Perspectives in History of Economic Thought*. Cheltenham: Edward Elgar, 67–88.

——. 2001: Some Problems in the Use of Language in Economics. *Review of Political Economy*, 13 (1), 91–100.

Samuels, W. J., and Mercuro, N. 1992: A Critique of Rent-Seeking Theory. In W. J. Samuels (ed.), *Essays on the Economic Role of Government*. New York: New York University Press, 111–28.

Samuels, W. J., and Schmid, A. A. 1976: Polluter's Profit and Political Response: The Dynamics of Rights Creation. *Public Choice* (Winter), 99–105.

—— 1997: The Concept of Cost in Economics. In W. J. Samuels, S. G. Medema, and A. A. Schmid (eds), *The Economy as a Process of Valuation*. Cheltenham: Edward Elgar.

Samuels, W. J., Schmid, A. A., and Shaffer, J. D. 1994: An Evolutionary Approach to Law and Economics. In R. England (ed.), *Evolutionary Concepts in Contemporary Economics*. Ann Arbor: University of Michigan Press, 93–110.

Samuelson, P. A. 1969: Pure Theory of Public Expenditure and Taxation. In J. Margolis and H. Guitton (eds), *Public Economics: An Analysis of Public Production and Consumption and Their Relations to the Private Sector*. London: St. Martin's Press, 98–123.

Sandmo, A. 1990: Buchanan on Political Economy. *Journal of Economic Literature*, 28 (1), 50–65.

Schaler, J. A., and Schaler, M. E. 1998: *Smoking: Who Has the Right?*, Contemporary Issues. Amherst, NY: Prometheus Books.

Schap, D. 1986: Nonequivalence of Property Rules and Liability Rules. *International Review of Law and Economics*, 6, 125–32.

Schelling, T. C. 1978: *Micromotives and Macrobehavior*. Fels Lectures on Public Policy Analysis. New York: Norton.

Scherer, F. M. 1992: Schumpeter and Plausible Capitalism. *Journal of Economic Literature*, 30 (September), 1416–33.

Schlicht, E. 1998: *On Custom in the Economy*. Oxford: Clarendon Press.

Schmid, A. A. 1960: *Evolution of Michigan Water Laws; Response to Economic Development*. Circular Bulletin 227. East Lansing: Michigan Agricultural Experiment Station.

——. 1962: Water and the Law in Wisconsin. *Wisconsin Magazine of History*, XLV (Spring), 203–15.

——. 1971: Impact of Alternative Federal Decision-Making Structures for Water Resource Development. Washington: National Water Commission. Available from National Technical Information Service, PB 211 441.

——. 1972: Analytical Institutional Economics. *American Journal of Agricultural Economics*, 54 (5), 893–901.

——. 1973: The Role of Grants, Exchange, and Property Rights in Environmental Policy. In K. Boulding, M. Pfaff, and A. Pfaff (eds), *Transfers in an Urbanized Economy*. Belmont, CA: Wadsworth.

——. 1977: The Role of Private Property in the History of American Agriculture, 1776–1976. *American Journal of Agricultural Economics*, 59 (3), 587–9.

——. 1984: Broadening Capital Ownership: The Credit System as a Locus of Power. In G. Alperovitz and R. Skurski (eds), *American Economic Perspectives: Problems and Prospects*. Notre Dame: University of Notre Dame Press.

——. 1985a: Biotechnology, Plant Variety Protection, and Changing Property Institutions in Agriculture. *North Central Journal of Agricultural Economics*, 7 (2), 129–38.

——. 1985b: Intellectual Property Rights in Bio-Technology and Computer Technology. *Journal of Institutional and Theoretical Economics*, 141 (1), 127–41.

——. 1987: *Property, Power, and Public Choice: An Inquiry into Law and Economics*, 2nd edn. New York: Praeger.

——. 1992: Legal Foundations of the Market: Implications for Formerly Socialist Countries of Eastern Europe and Africa. *Journal of Economic Issues*, 26, 707–32.

——. 1994: State and Market When Command Goes Capitalist. In D. Reisman (ed.), *Economic Thought and Political Theory*. Dordrecht: Kluwer, 129–45.

——. 1999a: Circular and Cumulative Causation. In P. O'Hara (ed.), *Encyclopedia of Political Economy*. London: Routledge, 87–90.

——. 1999b: Government, Property, Markets . . . In That Order . . . Not Government Versus Markets. In N. Mercuro and W. Samuels (eds), *The Fundamental Interrelationships between Government and Property*. Stamford, CN: JAI Press.

——. 2000: An Institutional Perspective on Agricultural Systems. In J. P. Colin and E. W. Crawford (eds), *Research on Agricultural Systems: Accomplishments, Perspectives and Issues*. Huntington, NY: Nova Science, 205–21.

——. 2001: The Institutional Economics of Nobel Prize Winners. In J. Biddle, J. B. Davis, and S. G. Medema (eds), *Economics Broadly Considered: Essays in Honor of Warren J. Samuels*. London: Routledge.

——. 2002: Using Motive to Distinguish Social Capital from Its Outputs. *Journal of Economic Issues*, 36 (3), 747–68.

Schmid, A. A., and Soroko, D. 1997: Interest Groups, Selective Incentives, Cleverness, History and Emotion: The Case of the American Soybean Association. *Journal of Economic Behavior & Organization*, 32, 267–85.

Schmid, A. A., and Thompson, P. 1999: Against Mechanism: Methodology for an Evolutionary Economics. *American Journal of Agricultural Economics*, 81 (5), 1160–65.

Schmookler, J. 1966: *Invention and Economic Growth*. Cambridge: Harvard University Press.

Schneider, G., and Aspinwall, M. (eds) 2001: *The Rules of Integration: Institutionalist Approaches to the Study of Europe*. Manchester: Manchester University Press.

Scholes, M., and Wolfson, M. 1991: Employee Stock Ownership Plans and Corporate Restructuring: Myths and Realities. In A. W. Sametz (ed.), *The Battle for Corporate Control: Shareholder Rights, Stakeholder Interests, and Managerial Responsibilities*. Homewood, IL: Business One Irwin.

Schumpeter, J. A. 1950: *Capitalism, Socialism, and Democracy*. 3rd edn. New York: Harper.

——. 1983: *The Theory of Economic Development: An Inquiry into Profits, Capital, Credit, Interest, and the Business Cycle*, Social Science Classics Series. New Brunswick, NJ: Transaction Books.

Schumpeter, J. A., and Swedberg, R. 1991: *The Economics and Sociology of Capitalism.* Princeton: Princeton University Press.

Schwartz, H. H. 1998: *Rationality Gone Awry?: Decision Making Inconsistent with Economic and Financial Theory.* Westport, CN: Praeger.

Schweikhardt, D. B., and Browne, W. P. 2001: Politics by Other Means: The Emergence of a New Politics of Food in the United States. *Review of Agricultural Economics*, 23, 302–18.

Scitovsky, T. 1976: *The Joyless Economy: An Inquiry into Human Satisfaction and Consumer Dissatisfaction.* London: Oxford University Press.

——. 1998: The Need for Stimulating Action. In K. Dennis (ed.), *Rationality in Economics: Alternative Perspectives.* Boston: Kluwer.

Sclar, E. D. 2000: *You Don't Always Get What You Pay For: The Economics of Privatization.* Ithaca, NY: Cornell University Press.

Scott, R. E. 2001: The Limits of Behavioral Theories of Law and Social Norms. *Virginia Law Review*, 86, 1603–47.

Sears, D. O., Lau, R. R., Tyler, T. R., and Allen, H. M. 1980: Self-Interest Vs. Symbolic Politics in Policy Attitudes and Presidential Voting. *American Political Science Review*, 74 (September), 670–84.

Seidman, R. 1973: Contract Law, the Free Market, and Intervention: A Jurisprudential Perspective. *Journal of Economic Issues*, 8, 553–76.

Seligman, M. 1975: *Helplessness: On Depression, Development, and Death.* New York: W. H. Freeman.

Sen, A. 1977: Rational Fools: A Critique of the Behavioral Foundations of Economic Theory. *Philosophy and Public Affairs*, 6 (Summer), 317–44.

——. 1990: More Than 100 Million Women Are Missing. *New York Review of Books*, December 20.

Shackle, G. L. S. 1949: *Expectation in Economics.* Cambridge: Cambridge University Press.

——. 1955: *Uncertainty in Economics, and Other Reflections.* Cambridge: Cambridge University Press.

——. 1961: *Decision, Order, and Time in Human Affairs.* Cambridge: Cambridge University Press.

——. 1979: *Imagination and the Nature of Choice.* Edinburgh: Edinburgh University Press.

——. 1992: George L. S. Shackle. In P. Arestis and M. Sawyer (eds), *A Biographical Dictionary of Dissenting Economists.* Aldershot: Edward Elgar.

Shackle, G. L. S., and Ford, J. L. 1990: *Time, Expectations, and Uncertainty in Economics: Selected Essays of G. L. S. Shackle.* Aldershot: Edward Elgar.

Shafir, E., Simonson, I., and Tversky, A. 1993: Reason-Based Choice. *Cognition*, 49 (1–2), 11–36.

Shughart, W. F., and Razzolini, L. 2001: *The Elgar Companion to Public Choice.* Cheltenham, UK; Northampton, MA: Edward Elgar Pub.

Siconolfi, M., Raghavan, A., Pacelle, M., and Sesit, M. 1998: How Russia Set Off Wave That Swamped Markets World-Wide. *Wall Street Journal*, September 22, A1.

Simon, H. A. 1972: Theories of Bounded Rationality. In C. B. McGuire and R. Radner (eds), *Decision and Organization: A Volume in Honour of Jacob Marschak.* Minneapolis: University of Minnesota Press.

——. 1979: Rational Decision Making in Business Organizations. *American Economic Review*, 69 (4), 493–513.

——. 1982: *Models of Bounded Rationality*. Vol. 1, Economic Analysis and Public Policy. Cambridge: MIT Press.

——. 1991: Organizations and Markets. *Journal of Economic Perspectives*, 5 (2), 25–44.

——. 1992: Scientific Discovery as Problem Solving. In H. A. Simon (ed.), *Economics, Bounded Rationality and the Cognitive Revolution*. Aldershot: Edward Elgar.

Simonson, I., and Tversky, A. 1992: Choice in Context: Tradeoff Contrast and Extremeness Aversion. *Journal of Marketing Research*, 29 (3), 281–95.

Sippel, R. 1997: An Experiment on the Pure Theory of Consumer's Behavior. *Economic Journal*, 107, 1431–44.

Sjostrand, S.-E. (ed.) 1993: *Institutional Change: Theory and Empirical Findings*. New York: M.E. Sharpe.

Skinner, B. F. 1971: *Beyond Freedom and Dignity*. New York: Alfred A. Knopf.

Skott, P. 1994: Cumulative Causation. In G. Hodgson (ed.), *Elgar Companion to Institutional and Evolutionary Economics*. Aldershot: Edward Elgar, 119–22.

Smith, V. L. 1989: Theory, Experiment and Economics. *Journal of Economic Perspectives*, 3, 151–69.

——. 2000: *Bargaining and Market Behavior: Essays in Experimental Economics*. Cambridge: Cambridge University Press.

Soete, L., and Dosi, G. 1983: *Technology and Employment in the Electronics Industry*. London: Francis Pinter.

Solo, R. A. 1967: *Economic Organizations and Social Systems*. New York: Bobbs-Merrill.

——. 1994: A Modest Proposal for a New Technique of Non-Diversionary Public Spending. *Journal of Economic Issues* (September).

Solow, R. M. 1988: Growth Theory and After. *American Economic Review*, 78 (3), 307–17.

——. 1990: *The Labor Market as a Social Institution*. Cambridge: Basil Blackwell.

Soltan, K. 1998: Institutions as Products of Politics. In K. Soltan, E. M. Uslaner, and V. Haufler (eds), *Institutions and Social Order*. Ann Arbor: University of Michigan Press.

Soto, H. D. 1989: *The Other Path: The Invisible Revolution in the Third World*. New York: Harper & Row.

Spence, M. 1973: *Market Signaling: Information Transfer in Hiring and Related Processes*. Cambridge: Harvard University Press.

Sraffa, P. 1926: The Law of Returns under Competitive Conditions. *Economic Journal*, 40, 538–50.

Stanfield, J. R. 1979: *Economic Thought and Social Change*. Carbondale: Southern Illinois University Press.

Stefansson, B. 2002: *Swarm*. Santa Fe Institute. Available from www.swarm.org.

Steinmo, S. 1993: *Taxation and Democracy: Swedish, British, and American Approaches to Financing the Modern State*. New Haven: Yale University Press.

Stephenson, K. 2003: An Institutionalist Perspective on Environmental Goal Setting. In M. Tool and P. D. Bush (eds) *Institutional Analysis of Economic Policy*. Boston: Kluwer, 433–60.

Stevens, J. B. 1993: *The Economics of Collective Choice*. Boulder, CO: Westview Press.

Stewart, J. B. 1991: *Den of Thieves*. New York: Simon & Schuster.

Stieber, J. 1991: Employment at Will. In L. Reynolds, S. Masters, and C. Moser (eds), *Readings in Labor Economics and Labor Relations*. Englewood Cliffs, NJ: Prentice Hall, 76–83.

Stigler, G., and Becker, G. S. 1977: De Gustibus Non Est Disputandum. *American Economic Review*, 67 (2), 76–90.

Stiglitz, J. E. 1987: The Causes and Consequences of the Dependence of Quality on Price. *Journal of Economic Literature*, XXV (March), 1–48.

——. 1999: Whither Reform? Ten Years of the Transition. Paper read at World Bank Annual Bank Conference on Development Economics, at Washington, DC.

——. 2000: What I Learned at the World Economic Crisis. *The New Republic*, April 17.

——. 2002: *Globalization and Its Discontents*. New York: Norton.

Stinchcombe, A. L. 1995: *Sugar Island Slavery in the Age of Enlightenment: The Political Economy of the Caribbean World*. Princeton: Princeton University Press.

Stone, K. 1974: The Origins of Job Structures in the Steel Industry. *Review of Radical Political Economics*, 6 (Summer), 61–97.

Streeton, H. 2000: *Economics: A New Introduction*. London: Pluto Press.

Sturgeon, J. I. 1992: Nature, Hammers, and Picasso. *Journal of Economic Issues*, 26 (2), 351–64.

Sugden, R. 1981: *The Political Economy of Public Choice: An Introduction to Welfare Economics*. Oxford, UK: Martin Robertson.

Sunstein, C. R. 2000: *Behavioral Law and Economics*. Cambridge Series on Judgment and Decision Making. Cambridge: Cambridge University Press.

Surowiecki, J. 1998: *Long-Term Capital's Bad Bet*. Slate 1998. Available from www.slate.com/Code/Moneybox.asp?SHOW=9/28/98&.

Sutton, J. 2000: *Marshall's Tendencies: What Can Economists Know?* Cambridge: MIT Press.

Tawney, R. H. 1912: *The Agrarian Problem in the Sixteenth Century*. London: Longmans Green.

Taylor, J. F. A. 1966: *The Masks of Society*. New York: Appleton-Century-Crofts.

Teece, D. J., et al. 1988: The Nature and the Structure of Firms. In G. Dosi (ed.), *Technical Change and Economic Theory*. New York: Columbia University Press.

Teece, D. J., and Pisano, G. 1994: The Dynamic Capabilities of Firms: An Introduction. *Industrial and Corporate Change*, 3 (3), 537–56.

Tesfatsion, L. 2001: *Agent-Based Computational Economics*. Available from http://www.econ.iastate.edu/tesfatsi/ace.htm.

Teubner, G. 1986: Industrial Democracy through Law. In T. Daintith (ed.), *Contract and Organization*. Berlin: Walter de Gruyter.

Thaler, R. H. 1980: Toward a Positive Theory of Consumer Choice. *Journal of Economic Behavior and Organization*, 1 (1), 39–60.

——. 1985: Mental Accounting and Consumer Choice. *Marketing Science*, 4 (3), 199–214.

——. 1992: *The Winner's Curse: Paradoxes and Anomalies of Economic Life*. New York: The Free Press.

——. 1996: Doing Economics without Homo Economicus. In S. Medema and W. Samuels (eds), *Foundations of Research in Economics: How Do Economists Do Economics*. Cheltenham: Edward Elgar, 227–37.

Thelen, K. A., and Steinmo, S. 1992: Historical Institutionalism in Comparative Politics. In S. Steinmo, K. Thalen, and F. Longstreth (eds), *Structuring Politics: Historical Institutionalism in Comparative Analysis*. Cambridge: Cambridge University Press, 1–32.

Thirsk, J. 1997: *Alternative Agriculture: A History from the Black Death to the Present Day*. Oxford: Oxford University Press.

Thurow, L. C. 1983: *Dangerous Currents: The State of Economics*. New York: Random House.

Tiebout, C. M. 1956: A Pure Theory of Local Government Expenditures. *Journal of Political Economy*, 64, 416–24.

Titmuss, R. M. 1971: *The Gift Relationship: From Human Blood to Social Policy*. New York: Random House.

Toboso, F. 2001: Institutional Individualism and Institutional Change: The Search for a Middle Way Mode of Explanation. *Cambridge Journal of Economics*, 25 (6), 765–83.

Tomer, J. F. 1987: *Organizational Capital: The Path to Higher Productivity and Well-Being*. New York: Praeger.

Tool, M. R. 1979: *The Discretionary Economy: A Normative Theory of Political Economy*. Santa Monica, CA: Goodyear.

Train, K. E., McFadden, D. L., and Goett, A. A. 1987: Consumer Attitudes and Voluntary Rate Schedules for Public Utilities. *Review of Economic Statistics*, 69 (3), 383–91.

Trebing, H. M. 1995: Market Failure and Regulatory Reform. In C. M. A. Chark (ed.), *Institutional Economics and the Theory of Social Value*. Boston: Kluwer.

——. 2001: New Dimensions of Market Failure in Electricity and Natural Gas Supply. *Journal of Economic Issues*, 25 (2), 395–403.

Treiman, D., and Hartmann, H. (eds) 1981: *Women, Work, and Wages: Equal Pay for Jobs of Equal Value*. Washington: National Academy Press.

Tripsas, M., and Gavetti, G. 2000: Capabilities, Cognition and Inertia: Evidence from Digital Imaging. *Strategic Management Journal*, 21 (10–11), 1147–61.

Tversky, A., and Kahneman, D. 1982a: Belief in the Law of Small Numbers. In D. Kahneman, P. Slovic, and A. Tversky (eds), *Judgment under Uncertainty: Heuristics and Biases*. Cambridge: Cambridge University Press, 23–31.

——. 1982b: Judgment under Uncertainty: Heuristics and Biases. In D. Kahneman, P. Slovic, and A. Tversky (eds), *Judgment under Uncertainty: Heuristics and Biases*. Cambridge: Cambridge University Press, 3–20.

Tyler, T. R. 1990: Justice, Self-Interest, and the Legitimacy of Legal and Political Authority. In J. J. Mansbridge (ed.), *Beyond Self-Interest*. Chicago: University of Chicago Press.

——. 2001: Why Do People Rely on Others? Social Identity and the Social Aspects of Trust. In K. S. Cook (ed.), *Trust in Society*. New York: Russell Sage Foundation.

United Nations. 2000: *State of the World Population Report 2000*. New York: United Nations Population Fund.

Uslaner, E. M. 1998: Field of Dreams: The Weak Reeds of Institutional Design. In K. E. Soltan, E. M. Uslaner, and V. Haufler (eds), *Institutions and Social Order*. Ann Arbor: University of Michigan Press.

Vanberg, V. J. 1989: Carl Menger's Evolutionary and John R. Commons' Collective Action Approach to Institutions: A Comparison. *Review of Political Economy*, 1 (3), 334–60.

——. 1992: Innovation, Cultural Evolution and Economic Growth. In U. Witt (ed.), *Explaining Process and Change, Approaches to Evolutionary Economics*. Ann Arbor: University of Michigan Press.

Vatn, A. 2002: Efficient or Fair: Ethical Paradoxes in Environmental Policy. In D. W. Bromley and J. Paavola (eds), *Economics, Ethics, and Environmental Policy*. Oxford: Blackwell.

Veblen, T. 1908: Professor Clark's Economics. *Quarterly Journal of Economics*, 22 (2), 147–95.

——. 1919: *The Place of Science in Modern Civilization and Other Essays*. New York: B.W. Huebsch.

——. 1953: *The Theory of the Leisure Class: An Economic Study of Institutions*. New York: The New American Library.

——. 1958: *The Theory of Business Enterprise*. New York: The New American Library. Original edition, 1904.

——. 1964: *An Inquiry into the Nature of Peace and the Terms of Its Perpetuation*. New York: A.M. Kelley.

Vickrey, W. 1994: Some Objections to Marginal-Cost Pricing. In R. Arnott and et al. (eds), *Public Economics*. Cambridge: Cambridge University Press.

Waligorski, C. P. 1990: *The Political Theory of Conservative Economists*. Lawrence: University Press of Kansas.

Wallis, J., and North, D. 1987: Measuring the Transaction Sector in the American Economy. In S. L. Engerman and R. E. Gallman (eds), *Long-Term Factors in American Economic Growth*. Chicago: University of Chicago Press, 95–148.

Walton, M. 1986: *The Deming Management Method*. New York: Dodd Mead.

Warde, A. 1996: Afterword: The Future of the Sociology of Consumption. In S. Edgell, K. Hetherington, and A. Warde (eds), *Consumption Matters*. Oxford: Blackwell.

Warr, P. 1999: Well-Being and the Workplace. In D. Kahneman (ed.), *Well-Being: The Foundations of Hedonic Psychology*. New York: Russell Sage.

Weber, M. 1961: *General Economic History*. New York: Collier.

Weir, M. 1992: Ideas and the Politics of Bounded Innovation. In S. Steinmo (ed.), *Structuring Politics*. New York: Cambridge University Press.

Whalen, C. J. 2001: Hyman Minsky's Theory of Capitalist Development. *Journal of Economic Issues*, 35 (4), 805–23.

——. 2002: Money Manager Capitalism: Still Here, but Not Quite as Expected. *Journal of Economic Issues*, 36 (2), 401–6.

White, L. T. 1963: *Medieval Technology and Social Change*. Oxford: Clarendon Press.

Whitley, R. 1999: *Divergent Capitalisms: The Social Structuring and Change of Business Systems*. New York: Oxford University Press.

Wilbur, C. K., and Harrison, R. S. 1978: The Methodological Basis of Institutional Economics: Pattern Model, Storytelling, and Hollism. *Journal of Economic Issues*, 12 (March), 61–89.

Wilde, K. D., LeBaron, A. d., and Israelsen, L. D. 1985: Knowledge, Uncertainty, and Behavior. *American Economic Review*, 75 (2), 403–8.

Williamson, O. E. 1985: *The Economic Institutions of Capitalism: Firms, Markets, Relational Contracting*. New York: Free Press.

——. 2000: The New Institutional Economics: Taking Stock, Looking Ahead. *Journal of Economic Literature*, 38 (3), 595–613.

——. 2002: The Lens of Contract: Private Ordering. *American Economic Review*, 92 (2), 438–43.

Wilson, T. D., and LaFleur, S. J. 1995: Knowing What You'll Do: Effects of Analyzing Reasons on Self-Prediction. *Journal of Personality and Social Psychology*, 68 (1), 21–35.

Winter Jr., S. G. 1982: An Essay on the Theory of Production. In S. H. Hymans (ed.), *Economics and the World around It*. Ann Arbor: University of Michigan Press, 55–91.

Wintrobe, R. 1997: Modern Bureaucratic Theory. In D. C. Mueller (ed.), *Perspectives on Public Choice*. Cambridge: Cambridge University Press.

Wiseman, J. 1983: Beyond Positive Economics – Dream and Reality. In J. Wiseman (ed.), *Beyond Positive Economics*. London: Macmillan.

Woodward, B. 2000: *Maestro: Greenspan's Fed and the American Boom*. New York: Simon & Schuster.

Wray, L. R. 1996: Monetary Theory and Policy for the Twenty-First Century. In C. J. Whalen (ed.), *Political Economy for the 21st Century*. Armonk, NY: M.E. Sharpe.

——. 1998: *Understanding Modern Money: The Key to Full Employment and Price Stability*. Cheltenham: Edward Elgar.

Yates, J. 1989: *Control through Communication: The Rise of System in American Management, Studies in Industry and Society*. Baltimore: Johns Hopkins University Press.

Yellen, J. 1984: Efficiency Wage Models of Unemployment. *American Economic Review*, 74 (2), 526–38.

Yonay, Y. P. 1998: *The Struggle over the Soul of Economics: Institutionalist and Neoclassical Economists in America between the Wars*. Princeton, NJ: Princeton University Press.

Young, A. 1928: Increasing Returns and Economic Progress. *Economic Journal*, 38, 537–42.

Zajonc, R. B. 1997: Emotions. In D. T. Gilbert, S. T. Fiske, and G. Lindzey (eds), *Handbook of Social Psychology*. New York: Oxford University Press, 591–632.

Zauderer, D. G. 1972: Consequences of Ballot Reform: The Ohio Experience. *National Civic Review*, 61, 505–7.

Zey, M. 1993: *Banking on Fraud: Drexel, Junk Bonds, and Buyouts, Social Institutions and Social Change*. New York: Aldine de Gruyter.

Index